PROPAGANDA BY SHORT WAVE

PROPAGANDA
BY SHORT WAVE

EDITED BY

Harwood L. Childs and

John B. Whitton

Princeton

PRINCETON UNIVERSITY PRESS

LONDON: HUMPHREY MILFORD
OXFORD UNIVERSITY PRESS

1943

Second Printing, 1943

COPYRIGHT, 1942, BY PRINCETON UNIVERSITY PRESS
PRINTED IN THE UNITED STATES OF AMERICA BY PRINCETON
UNIVERSITY PRESS AT PRINCETON, NEW JERSEY

*The Publication of this book has been
aided by the Princeton University
Research Fund*

PREFACE

A LITTLE white frame house on a quiet side street in the town of Princeton, New Jersey, was the center for a period of twenty months—practically from the start of the second World War until the summer of 1941—of a remarkable activity that employed the talents of scholars, engineers, linguists, stenographers. This was the headquarters of the Princeton Listening Center, and it was America's eavesdropper on the radio propaganda of the world. For some time broadcasting companies had picked up certain foreign programs for rebroadcasting to American audiences or for the information of their news departments, but the Princeton Listening Center was the pioneer in systematic monitoring.

This book has been written by members of the staff of the Listening Center to report some of the important findings made through the months of monitoring, transcribing, translating, and analyzing short-wave propaganda. The reader may be interested in a brief statement of the history of the Princeton Listening Center in order that he may know something of the purposes and methods of that unique enterprise.

In February 1938, Professor Whitton was serving as director of the Geneva Research Center. As a result of talks with Edward R. Murrow, European representative of the Columbia Broadcasting System, he became deeply impressed by the increasing use of radio as a weapon of politics, particularly in the hands of Nazi propagandists. To study the matter more fully he engaged the services of a research worker, Mr. Thomas Grandin, who, after months of travel and investigation in the capitals of Europe, and much listening at a receiving post set up in a Montmartre hotel, produced a little book, *The Political Use of the Radio,* published by the Geneva Research Center in 1939.

Upon Mr. Whitton's return to Princeton late in 1938, the School of Public and International Affairs of Princeton University appointed a committee consisting of Professors John B. Whitton, Hadley Cantril, William S. Carpenter, and Harwood L. Childs of Princeton University; Professor O. W. Riegel of Washington and Lee University; and Mr. Brunson S. McCutchen, an engineer, to formulate plans for a continuing study of short-wave propaganda. The Rockefeller Foundation generously agreed to finance the project for an experimental period, and Harold N. Graves, Jr., was engaged to administer the enterprise.

Mr. Graves proceeded at once to recruit the necessary technical and research staff and quarters were established in a house at 69 Alexander Street, Princeton, graciously donated for the purposes of the experiment by the Institute for Advanced Study through its director, Dr. Frank Aydelotte. Operations actually commenced in November 1939. The Center did not attempt to receive and record all short-wave broadcasts from Europe audible in this country, contenting itself with a representative sample of newscasts and topical talks disseminated from Berlin, London, Rome, Paris, and to some extent Moscow. At the time reception was discontinued in June 1941 the Center had on file more than 100 volumes of short-wave typescripts of 250 or more pages each. This unusual collection of propaganda material is now housed in the Princeton University Library. For the period covered it is the only reasonably complete and representative file of war propaganda by short wave in this country.

The daily routine of the Center soon became well established. From three o'clock in the afternoon until eleven in the evening, six days a week, the receivers, recorders, and transcribers were in almost continuous operation. Incoming broadcasts were recorded on wax cylinders and then transcribed, translations being made into English when necessary. The quality of reception varied, of course, from country to country, and from time to time. On the whole it was quite satisfactory.

During the experimental period the Center devoted its attention primarily to perfecting the mechanical phases of its task and to preparing biweekly digests and summaries of the programs heard. These summaries, published in pamphlet form, were distributed without cost to all those interested, notably to certain officials of the federal government, newspaper editors, radio executives and commentators, professors, and other specialists in international relations, propaganda, public opinion, and radio research. In all, twenty such reports were issued between December 15, 1939, and July 15, 1941.

The experiment proved so successful and the material collected promised to be of such value, that before the trial period was over plans were made for enlarging the scope of the undertaking to provide for a more extensive program of research. To these plans the Rockefeller Foundation gave its approval and financial support, and in June 1940 the grant to the Center was renewed and enlarged for a year.

Professor Childs was asked by the executive committee to outline a plan of research and supervise its execution, and under his direction a number of projects were undertaken. Most of these studies were based primarily on the material collected and recorded by the Center. This was not the case, however, with the individual projects undertaken by Professor Childs, and by Professor Whitton in collaboration with Dr. John H. Herz. The former, financed by a special grant from the Rockefeller Foundation, was set up to ascertain the character, extent, and listening habits of the American short-wave listening audience, concerning which there was almost no reliable information. The latter, also financed by a special grant from the Rockefeller Foundation, was to provide a much needed statement of the historical development of this new medium of international communication. In studying the American listening audience Professor Childs enlisted the cooperation of Professor Harold F. Gosnell of the University of Chicago, Professor Herman C. Beyle of Syracuse University, Professor Edgar A. Schuler of Louisiana State University, Dr. Jerome S. Bruner of Harvard, the American Institute of Public Opinion, and the Office of Radio Research, Columbia University. The present volume is both an individual and collective product, for the conclusions reached by the individual investigator have usually been tempered by the criticism and comments of the staff as a whole.

During the early months of 1941 word came to the Center that the Federal Communications Commission contemplated setting up a special section to monitor short-wave broadcasts from abroad on a much more comprehensive scale than was possible at the Center. This action on the part of the federal government came as no surprise in view of similar action taken earlier by European countries. Nor was it altogether a surprise when the Commission requested the services of Mr. Graves and several other members of the Center's staff to assist it in launching this new service. But it soon became evident that as soon as the Commission's Monitoring Service was in full operation and an official record of short-wave broadcasts to supplement and continue the files of the Center was available, the mechanical side of the work in Princeton should be discontinued. This action was taken, and since June 1941 members of the staff have devoted themselves exclusively to the preparation of this book.

CONTENTS

RADIO IN INTERNATIONAL POLITICS

By John B. Whitton and John H. Herz

Dr. Whitton is Associate Professor of Politics at Princeton, and a specialist in the field of international law and relations. As Director of the Geneva Research Center, 1936-38, and a member of a League of Nations Committee on Radio and World Peace, he initiated an early study of radio propaganda with one of his research assistants, Thomas Grandin. Mr. Whitton was largely responsible for the establishment of the Princeton Listening Center in 1939, and served as chairman of its Executive Committee. After the resignation of Mr. Graves on April 1, 1941, he became the Center's administrative director.

Dr. Herz is a Lecturer in the Department of Politics at Howard University, Washington, D.C. He received his Ph.D. degree at the University of Cologne in 1931. In 1938 he received the diploma of the Graduate Institute of International Studies in Geneva, and came to the United States to become a member of the Institute for Advanced Study in Princeton. As Professor Whitton's special research assistant he devoted his time in 1940-41 exclusively to this historical study.

RADIO IN INTERNATIONAL POLITICS

THE story of radio in international affairs is part of the story of power politics. It is one of the most fascinating in modern history, an innovation of tremendous importance.

Radio in the first World War had many uses—it was used for espionage and intelligence when the Allies dropped Marconi senders on occupied territory; for communication with neutral countries across blockade, as in the case of the historic Zimmermann Message which was transmitted to the German Embassy in Washington, intercepted and decoded by British counterespionage, and then communicated to the American authorities; and even for communication between the enemies themselves when peace preliminaries were transmitted to Nauen on behalf of President Wilson.

But radio was used only falteringly in the war of 1914-1918 for the purposes of propaganda. That war was the first "total war" not only in its mobilization of industrial and manpower resources, but also in its systematic use of the psychological weapon of propaganda. Wireless telegraphy, though technically still in its infancy, played a part in this psychological warfare. The fact that this part was a minor one should not deceive us as to its historic importance. For upon the foundation of that first World War has been built a structure which in recent years has shaken the world.

The Germans turned to radio in the first World War for the natural reason that the Allies controlled the cables. And in spite of technical shortcomings, the organization of Germany's earliest radio propaganda shows some surprising similarities to more modern techniques.

As early as 1915 a regular service provided radio amateurs and agents in neutral countries with daily news reports. Relayed through local stations and offered as a free service to local newspaper editors, these messages found ready acceptance among many provincial editors and were extensively used from Persia to Mexico. There were daily news communiqués, commentaries in various languages, code messages to secret agents, and even messages by foreign correspondents.[1]

Although these efforts were mainly directed toward neutral countries, attempts to influence enemy opinion were not lacking. Since more

[1] Irwin: *Propaganda and the News*, New York, 1936, pp. 130f.; Huth, *La radiodiffusion: Puissance mondiale*, Paris, 1937, p. 32.

general dissemination of wireless propaganda was hampered by the lack of receiving facilities, the common device was to maintain radio contact with agents who then would spread propaganda throughout enemy territory. Thus a United States censor picked up a code transmission directed "To propagandists in North Africa: spread the following rumors among the tribes. . . ."[2] On the part of the Allies, the most conspicuous example of wireless propaganda was the sending out of Wilson's Fourteen Points all over the world.

Radio and World Revolution

Bolshevist propaganda for proletarian world revolution was the first instance of veritable revolutionary propaganda in the international field since the days of the French battle cry of *guerre aux châteaux, paix aux chaumières*. Convinced that the Russian Revolution constituted the first step in a movement which would soon engulf the world, the Bolsheviks, cut off from the West when they came to power, and still at war with the Central Powers, immediately turned to wireless telegraphy not only as a means of communicating with the world at large but also for purposes of propaganda proper. Their ambition in this respect is illustrated by the words, "To all, all, all!" which initiated every one of their flashes. These messages were directed to the proletarian masses everywhere and admonished them to rise against their "bourgeois and military oppressors" and to conclude a general peace without annexations, victors or vanquished; in this matter, the slogans of Wilson's Fourteen Points were invoked.[3] During the peace negotiations at Brest-Litovsk the Russians used the radio as a medium of propaganda and, at the same time, as a weapon of pressure on the German leaders. Trotsky insisted on the textual broadcasting of the negotiations by telegraph and wireless, so that the Bolsheviks could appeal to world opinion over the heads of the enemy delegates. Thus, while negotiating, they at the same time exposed the annexationist aims of the Central Powers and incited German workers, soldiers and marines to strikes and insubordination. In this maneuver they persisted, deaf to German protests.[4]

How much this kind of propaganda contributed to the revolutionary

[2] Irwin, *loc. cit.*

[3] S. N. Harper: *Civic Training in Soviet Russia*, Chicago, 1929, p. 323; K. F. Nowak (ed.): *Aufzeichnungen des Generalmajors Max Hoffmann*, Berlin, 1929, Vol. 2, pp. 208, 213.

[4] Nowak, *loc. cit.*, pp. 184ff.; Louis Fischer: *The Soviets in World Affairs*, New York, 1930, pp. 43ff.

movements and general unrest which prevailed in Central Europe in those years is a matter of conjecture, but certain measures taken by the "attacked" themselves would testify to its effectiveness. Prior to and during the short life of the Hungarian Soviet Republic, for instance, Bela Kun was able to keep up wireless communication with the Soviets.[5] Likewise, during the wars of intervention and also the Polish war of 1920, radio served to convey appeals to leftist elements in the "enemy" countries and to mobilize a strong body of public opinion against their policies.[6]

World revolutionary propaganda reached its peak in those early years of Bolshevist rule. The subsequent technical development of broadcasting in the 'twenties was not accompanied by a proportionate increase in its adaptation for propaganda abroad. While it was made into an all-penetrating instrument of "civil training" and propaganda within the Soviet Union itself, its role in foreign affairs reflects the ambiguity of a policy vacillating between Russian *Real-Politik* and Marxist revolutionary ideology. Thus, while the Soviet government concluded treaties with various countries solemnly promising to abstain from revolutionary propaganda, the Comintern time and again "intervened" in the domestic affairs of these same countries, using the radio to spread propaganda during such incidents as the English general strike or the sabotage trial of foreign engineers in 1930. In 1926, Moscow embarked upon a radio war with Rumania over Bessarabia which was characterized by the more traditional "irredentist" type of propaganda, while more revolutionary appeals were sent to the German workers in 1930 and the ensuing years of pre-Nazi crisis.[7] All this, however, was not part of a systematic and continuous revolutionary effort. Although Comintern congresses since 1928 had passed resolutions for the formation of listening groups abroad and had stressed the importance of radio in arousing the masses, they always became lost in theoretical debates and in practice achieved little.[8]

In the 'thirties, with the growing "nationalism" of Soviet policies, its radio propaganda evolved more and more toward the "traditional"

[5] A. Kaas and F. de Lazarovics: *Bolshevism in Hungary*, London, 1931, pp. 66f., 76, 171.

[6] Fischer, *op. cit.*, pp. 237, 265; Niessel, "La propagande par radio," *Revue des Deux Mondes*, Vol. 47, 1938, p. 831.

[7] Biro, "The International Aspects of Radio Control," *Journal of Radio Law*, Vol. 2, 1932, pp. 60, 61.

[8] Hadamovsky: *Dein Rundfunk*, Munich, 1934, pp. 82f.

type of nationalistic propaganda, dwelling upon descriptions of Russian life under the regime, its social and economic achievements, and even its amusing or picturesque features. When, upon the adoption of Stalin's "Constitution" in 1936, the Moscow radio announced to the world that "the dream of centuries has come true; the sun of Communism has risen in the world," it was satisfied with informing the world of these happy tidings from Russia without worrying very much whether the "sun" would in fact run its course toward the West. Radio now became entirely dependent on the vagaries of Russian foreign policy. From 1933 to 1939 it attacked Fascism, Nazism in particular, and in fact Moscow was almost the only station sending subversive propaganda to Germans in the German language. All this was changed with astounding suddenness when Stalin switched his policy from anti-Fascism and "collective security" to form his temporary quasi-partnership with Hitler. Moscow now denounced British and American imperialism, and the Russian propagandists collaborated with the Nazi propaganda machine in various ways. They even copied the Nazi method of launching a radio campaign as a psychological preparation for aggression. Thus, prior to the Finnish war, with a characteristic mixture of threats and promises peculiar to totalitarian "strategy of terror," Moscow called on the Finns to overthrow their government and "to escape the fate of Poland."[9] Radio, weapon of world revolution, had become the instrument of totalitarian "power politics."

Soviet short-wave propaganda played a great part internally throughout the wide spaces of the Union and its polyglot population, as programs were broadcast in many languages and dialects. But since its development came during the 'thirties, Soviet foreign short-wave broadcasts have been characterized by the same discrepancies and vacillations as those carried over long and medium waves. And even with respect to certain outlying regions, such as Latin America, short-wave propaganda is characterized by illusions and doctrinairism peculiar to Bolshevist ideology. Thus, programs in Spanish to Latin America are not different from programs destined for other parts of the world and do not take account of different national and cultural conditions and ways of life. Apparently Moscow presupposes the basic situation of proletarian class struggle to be identical all over the world. According to most observers, Russian short-wave propaganda in Latin America has been

9 *New York Times*, November 28, 1939; cf. also November 16 and 30.

unsuccessful,[10] and there is no reason to suppose that the result has been different in other parts of the world.

Early Cases of Hostile Radio Propaganda

Throughout the 'twenties most governments had not yet formulated "doctrines" and "ideologies," and the effort to mold public opinion abroad had not yet become a regular weapon of foreign policy. Governmental use of radio in international politics was limited to isolated issues, and came to the fore only on rare occasions. Then the radio would suddenly assume the menacing character of a dangerous and powerful weapon of political struggle, only to recede into the background as soon as the issue was settled or became less acute. Thus, an early case of "radio warfare" occurred between Berlin and the Eiffel Tower station during the Ruhr invasion.[11] Questions of "irredentas," minorities, and frontier disputes were those most likely to call forth the radio as a political weapon. It was thus used by Germany and Poland during their perennial dispute over the Upper Silesian question, ending in 1931 with the conclusion of a radio "non-aggression pact."[12] Radio was similarly used in the Danube region, where problems of Hungarian revisionism were entangled with questions of agrarian reform and feudal interests of landowners, and where Italian-Yugoslav antagonism increased the tension.[13] In that period Latin America, classic region of boundary controversy, also witnessed a number of radio "wars," as well as disputes arising over use of the radio by refugee members of defeated and expelled factions and regimes.[14]

Although such incidents were relatively rare and usually of short duration, they could not fail to create a vague feeling of uneasiness over the possibilities inherent in this novel instrument of mass propaganda. This gave birth to a twofold reaction, one directed toward the peaceful settlement of such issues, the other toward "protective" measures taking the form of a radio armament race. Formation of international organizations such as the International Broadcasting Union led to

---

[10] Beals: *The Coming Struggle for Latin America*, New York, 1938, pp. 133*ff*., 143, 158.

[11] *New York Times*, March 6, 1923 and March 9, 1923.

[12] Saerchinger: *Hello America!*, New York, 1938, p. 371; Tomlinson: *The International Control of Radiocommunications*, Geneva, 1938, p. 226.

[13] Hanighen, "Propaganda on the Air," *Current History*, Vol. 44, June 1936, pp. 48*f*.

[14] Berchtold, "The World Propaganda War," *North American Review*, Vol. 238, 1934, p. 425; Blankenhorn, "The Battle of Radio Armaments," *Harpers*, December 1931, p. 88.

attempts to bring "warring" parties together and even to prevent future incidents by the conclusion of bilateral or multi-party agreements of non-interference and abstention from hostile propaganda. On the other hand, countries were led, through fear of radio attacks, to strengthen their radio "weapons" by building new and ever stronger stations, especially near frontiers and at other "strategic" points.

Short-Wave Broadcasting and the Consolidation of Empires

The technical development of short-wave broadcasting in the late 'twenties coincided with the growing threat to colonial empires of the disintegrating forces of autonomy, native nationalism and race consciousness of colored populations, making it imperative that defensive measures be instituted. As a consequence, this period witnessed the establishment of short-wave radio services in all countries with important colonial interests.

Holland was the pioneer in short-wave broadcasting. An experimental service to the Netherlands Indies began in 1927, and by 1929 a regular service in the Dutch language was started over PHOHI, destined for Dutch settlers.[15] These services were not directed to natives but only to the ruling emissaries from the "homeland."

The BBC started experimental overseas transmission in 1927, but the project for a regular service met with financial difficulties, so that it was not before the end of 1932 that regular Empire broadcasting began. This was broadcast directionally and the schedule was later so arranged that listeners in each area had a choice between at least two programs. Broadcasts were in English. They concerned "Imperial affairs" and always stressed "Empire unity."

The French inaugurated a regular "Empire Service" over Paris-Colonial in May 1931, on the occasion of the Colonial Exhibition at Paris. Some of these government-controlled broadcasts, sent into five zones, were from the outset in those non-French languages frequently spoken in some parts of the French colonial Empire and thus testify to the French colonial principle of "assimilation." French Empire broadcasting maintained a high cultural level and tended to avoid political propaganda and polemics. Fan mail revealed that the programs were highly esteemed by groups of educated listeners even outside the Empire, such as in Latin America, where Paris-Colonial spread French

---

[15] Huth, *op. cit.*, p. 200.

cultural propaganda. As a whole, however, the service does not seem to have been very successful. From the beginning, it was said, the transmissions lacked power and in many regions reception was bad.[16]

Belgium erected a short-wave station at Ruysselede for transmission to the Congo, and after 1934 maintained a daily colonial service. Other countries with colonies, such as Portugal, followed suit.[17] Later, some countries without "Empires" but with numerous nationals or former nationals abroad began establishing overseas short-wave services for them in the homeland; Switzerland and Czechoslovakia are examples.[18] But this leads to an entirely different use of the short-wave by Fascists and Nazis in order to appeal to their "blood brothers" overseas, which will be discussed later on.

Collective Security and Its Failure: Radio Nations and Far Eastern Aggression

The same period which witnessed the rise of short-wave broadcasting for Empire services was also one during which the postwar system of collective security was being tested. The radio during this period reflected both internationalist and nationalist tendencies.

The concept of an international system of law and order, as incorporated in the League Covenant, would have been immensely strengthened by internationalist propaganda which, by means of the radio, penetrated into each country. As it happened, the League eventually set up its own radio machinery, but the use made of it was anything but "political" and bold; it remained formalistic and bureaucratic.[19] After long and arduous negotiations with Swiss authorities, facilities were put at the disposal of the League, and *Radio Nations* opened its doors in February 1932. But radio was considered a means of communication and information, not of propaganda. As such it served to keep up communication between the League and its members, among the members, and with League organs such as the Lytton Commission during the Manchurian conflict. It was used during the Chaco war,

[16] *World Radio*, May 18, 1934, p. 706.
[17] Schroeder: *Ein Sender erobert die Herzen der Welt*, Essen, 1940, p. 34.
[18] Saerchinger, "Radio as a Political Instrument," *Foreign Affairs*, Vol. 16, 1937-38, p. 257.
[19] For the following cf. Potter, "League Publicity: Cause or Effect of League Failure?", *Public Opinion Quarterly*, Vol. 2, 1938, p. 404; Van Dissel, "League of Nations Wireless Station," *Proceedings of the Institute of Radio Engineers*, Vol. 22, 1934, pp. 431ff.; Plagge, "Radio-Nations," *Rundfunk-Archiv*, Vol. 5, 1932, pp. 471ff.

and even helped to organize sanctions against Italy during the Ethiopian conflict. But the most vital function of radio was neglected, namely, the active propagation of the League idea during those crises when everything depended on mobilizing public opinion for the maintenance of world peace and order.

While the professed champions of international law neglected radio, the lawbreakers made it into an effective instrument of the "new order" with its own kind of "law." The first open defiance of the League was accompanied by the first use of radio for war propaganda. During the Manchurian conflict it helped to arouse and maintain the martial spirit in Japan, even bringing the din of battle into the homes of the individual citizens. After the conquest, broadcasting was organized in Manchukuo to instill new loyalties among the conquered and cut them off from Chinese influence. A strong station was erected at Hsinking to broadcast programs, partly originating in Japan, in Japanese and "native" tongues. Cheap or free receiving sets were distributed, an action not without danger, however, for many people preferred to tune in on the strong Chinese station at Nanking; Japan occasionally was forced to jam the Chinese broadcasts, thereby blotting out part of its own.[20] The years following the Manchurian conquest also meant radio penetration of newly conquered Chinese territory: new stations at Peiping and Tientsin, in Japanese, Chinese, and English, sang the praises of the "New Order" and blaring public loudspeakers urged peasants to cooperate with Japan. But wherever the occupying forces were spread thin, the loudspeakers were frequently found bringing "standfast" messages from the Chunking government, behind the backs of the conqueror.[21]

In order to consolidate her "Empire," Japan instituted short-wave broadcasting in 1935, first in Japanese and English from Tokyo to Hawaii and the West Coast of America, and then in 1936, to eastern North America and South America. Since 1937 programs have been beamed to all parts of the globe in four zones, and in many languages. Technically, these programs have suffered from faulty pronunciation of foreign languages; politically, besides insisting on Japan's right and

[20] International Broadcasting Union: *Broadcasting Abroad*, Chicago, 1934, pp. 89, 92; Schaefer, "Rundfunk in der Mandschurei," *Zeitschrift für Geopolitik*, 1937, pp. 491ff.
[21] Van Gelderland, "The War in the Ether," *Nation*, 1938, p. 300; Muller, "Waging War with Words," *Current History*, August 1939, p. 25.

China's wrong in "the current incident," they have been less openly aggressive than those of their Axis brethren and are more in the manner of trade and "culture" propaganda.[22]

Rather early the Japanese experienced also the other side of radio warfare, namely, hostile interference from abroad, mainly from Chinese and Russian stations. As countermeasures, sets with short-wave bands were altogether forbidden in Japan and standard sets for local reception only were distributed.[23]

Radio and the Second World Revolution

The 'thirties witnessed the second attempt, since the end of the World War, to revolutionize the world in the name of a new *Weltanschauung*. But while Bolshevist propaganda had been spread by convinced believers in a definite doctrine, Nazi "world revolution" is entirely opportunistic and its propaganda, therefore, is free from dogma and always adapted to the requirements of the moment. It changes according to time and region. Here, it appeals to "Germans abroad" but elsewhere betrays and sells them out; here it poses as "leftist" and there as "rightist," here as "proletarian" and elsewhere as anti-Bolshevist; here it appeals to the upper classes and there to the lower strata of society. It poses as proponent of peace and, again, threatens force, avows respect for alien nationalities and denies the right of existence to just such nationalities. It is consistent only with respect to its ultimate goal—power and domination. But it is revolutionary in so far as it destroys traditional values and disrupts existing loyalties.

Radio, the ideal vehicle for propaganda, was immediately exploited when Germany was turned over to Hitler in 1933. It did yeoman service for the Nazis at home and very shortly appeared on the international scene as a very potent supporter of the cause. It was not by short wave, however, but rather by means of the channels devised for internal broadcasting that the Nazis set out to gain ideological control over European countries. The first great test of the system came when the Saar was psychologically prepared by German propaganda for reentry into the Reich. Radio's role in that campaign is strikingly instructive as to the subsequent policies of Nazi broadcasting.

---

[22] Harris, *Radio Propaganda in Latin America*, Princeton Senior Thesis, 1939, pp. 106ff.; Grandin, "The Political Use of the Radio," *Geneva Studies*, Vol. X, no. 3, August 1939, pp. 61f.
[23] Kranz, "War on the Short Wave," *Nation*, 1940, p. 127.

Nazis and the Saar: The First Hitler Victory by Ether Waves

The Saar plebiscite of January 13, 1935, when an overwhelming proportion of the Saar population voted for its return to Germany, is often cited to show how under international supervision and with proper guarantees a fair solution of a burning territorial question can be achieved. Actually the Saar plebiscite demonstrates how, with the aid of radio, an unscrupulous party can attain a *de facto* monopoly of opinion. Similar phenomena are familiar to any student of ward politics and "gang rule" in certain well known American cities.

The Germans had one cardinal objective in exerting their influence on the Saar—to prove that Nazism had become *the* political philosophy of Germany, and this presupposed that the plebiscite vote would yield at least as overwhelming a result in favor of return to Nazi Germany as pre-Hitler Germany could have expected. Hitler's advent to power, however, had alienated a considerable portion of those who would otherwise have voted for return. Realizing this, the German propagandists faced the disturbing prospect that the vote might follow one of the other two alternatives provided by the Treaty of Versailles. The first of these—union with France—caused them no worry, but the second—maintenance of the *status quo,* or League administration—had a disquieting element of possibility. Consequently Nazi propaganda aimed above all at eliminating this alternative. Besides using propaganda proper, Nazism resorted to methods of terror and intimidation calculated to create the "totalitarian atmosphere" which inside totalitarian frontiers had produced the famous majorities of 90-100 per cent. Here the Nazis were greatly aided by the simple fact that the Saar's return to Germany was a practical possibility, because fear of what might happen to open opponents "afterwards" was itself a potent weapon of psychological compulsion capable of turning anticipation into practical certainty.

The single issue of the Saar was built up as the center of political interest in Germany throughout the campaign period, and German broadcasting, too, was specially organized for the campaign.[24] Certain

[24] The following contains but a very condensed extract from a larger study which the author hopes to publish separately and for which mainly the following newspapers of the period in question have been consulted: (Nazified) *Frankfurter Zeitung,* (anti-Nazi Saar) *Deutsche Freiheit, Le Temps.* The *Official Journal* of the League of Nations also contains much Saar material. Important secondary sources concerning the Saar struggle, and the Nazi campaign in particular,

stations became "radio capitals" for the Saar. Daily "Saar news" was carried over all stations, and there were radio plays (frequently giving gruesome atrocity stories), "Saar song" transmissions, political interviews with Saar workers, broadcasts on Saar landscape, Saar economy, Saar youth, and, above all, the broadcasting of huge mass meetings outside Saar territory in which thousands of Saarlanders participated, Hitler and other Nazi leaders delivering impassioned speeches. Reception of these broadcasts in the Saar was thoroughly organized with the help of the camouflaged Saar Nazi organization, the "German Front." Factory owners and others arranged for group listening. Since there was no station in the Saar territory itself which could offer the opposition a channel for expressing its opinion over the air, and foreign stations, in particular those of neighboring countries, had little opportunity to speak out for fear of irritating Germany's rulers, the Nazis gained a "monopoly of sound" which in itself had a symbol value of overwhelming power.

It would require a more detailed study to go into the contents of these programs and to show how everything French was attacked while simultaneously France and the League were successfully appeased through promises and assurances. The Church was appeased and thus made an ally in a propaganda struggle against those Saar Catholics who had joined the anti-Nazi front. The workers were lured away by promises, while all their antipathy and wrath were turned against their Marxist leaders and "seducers" and the status-quo leaders, who were vilified as paid "traitors" and "separatists." Every measure of the League Governing Commission, which was vainly trying to assure the opposition a minimum of fair dealing, was branded as brutal oppression of the "German will" of Saarlanders by an alien regime under the influence of "Jewish émigrés." Finally the main emphasis was always on "return to Germany whatever her present regime"— Germany being represented as the "eternal fatherland," while after the victory was won it was immediately interpreted as an overwhelming choice for *Nazi* Germany.

But even with the monopoly of the air, the Nazis could never silence the opposition so long as it possessed other means of expressing opinion,

are: Bartz: *Weltgeschichte an der Saar*, Heidelberg, 1935 (official Nazi presentation); Wambaugh: *The Saar Plebiscite*, Cambridge, 1940; Iwo: *Goebbels erobert die Welt*, Paris, 1936; Chakotin: *The Rape of the Masses*, London, 1940.

such as press, mass meetings, etc. So the Nazi radio, in close collaboration with Saar groups and organizations such as the German Front,
industrial leaders of the Saar, and even Saar officials (who, having been
taken over from the pre-League administration, were, of course,
especially fearful of "post-return" reprisals), played an important role
in attempting to frighten the "enemy" into silence.

Calumnies concerning individuals, and "revelations" gleaned from
stolen documents by using the German Front as transmission belt,
were broadcast from German stations. Besides open attack on single
individuals and campaigns of slander and vilification of status-quo
leaders and their adherents, there was a more refined kind of terrorism
—suggestions of vaguely defined "events" to happen to vaguely defined
groups after the "liberation." Besides, the radio was instrumental in
assisting the campaign against the anti-Nazi press. For instance, a
boycott was inaugurated, people were dissuaded from advertising, subscribers, messengers and sellers were terrorized so that these papers
could nowhere be openly sold, editors were threatened and persecuted,
children of subscribers boycotted in the schools, the authors of outrages,
if arrested, acquitted by local tribunals because of "honorable motives," etc., etc. The function of the radio was to support this campaign
by threatening, "exposing," advising, extolling, and abetting. And the
same was true with respect to the curtailing of other means of expressing opinion and campaigning, e.g. hampering opposition meetings by
terrorizing prospective participants, or boycotting those who wanted to
rent rooms and halls for such purposes. Countermeasures by the Governing Commission were weak and ineffectual and were always hampered by the League Council's readiness once again to accept Nazi
promises to refrain from further intervention.

In this way the radio contributed to the setting up of what the
Governing Commission as early as 1933 characterized as a complete
"*de facto* government" side by side with the legal administration. In this
atmosphere the campaign of propaganda proper worked smoothly
and a majority of more than 90 per cent was gained, a victory which
immensely strengthened the prestige of Hitlerism inside and outside
Germany, because it could be claimed with some plausibility that Germans outside the Reich had "freely" declared for Nazism. Whether the
result of the vote would have been substantially different had real
"freedom" of campaigning existed is, of course, impossible to say.

But it is certain that that minimum of freedom and decency in the preparation of the plebiscite had not been assured which alone would have placed its results beyond doubt, and that in an unprecedented onslaught of terror and propaganda combined, the radio, international in its range and reach, was proved to be a ready instrument in the hands of a regime which was already overstepping boundaries even before it could actually invade its neighbors by the use of military force.

After the return of the Saar the Nazis, despite Hitler's pre-plebiscite assurances that the Saar was the "last territorial question to be settled between France and Germany," erected a powerful station at Saarbrücken which, together with other western German stations, began broadcasting to Alsace Lorraine.[25] The main device of subtle subversive propaganda was the *Hoerspiel,* the radio play. Such plays, usually in the thin disguise of historical or pseudo-historical events, were conceived so as to awaken and strengthen the "loyalty" of Alsatians and Lorrainers to their *Heimat,* the Reich. Everything, whether it dealt with events of Louis XIV's regime, the French Revolution, the war of 1870 or later times, was pictured in terms of struggle of these people against "denationalization" by the French. In these plays Bismarck spoke of Germany's "national revolution" and predicted that "united with Austria we shall march across the Rhine and take the Alsace back." In addition, there was a weekly "Alsatian Program" and a daily "Frontier Echo" which commented on French internal policies in such a way as to stir up the Catholic population of those provinces against their then leftist government.

Nazis and Austria: Defeat and Victory in the First Radio War

In German-Austrian relations between 1933 and 1938 the radio was used as a weapon of foreign policy in various novel ways. For the first time in its history the radio was employed to destroy a sovereign state by means of propaganda launched from outside. Since *Anschluss* was hardly a legal possibility, in that Austria's independence was an important part of the existing international system, and since there existed here a real state organization with a will to defend itself against aggression, Hitler had to move more diplomatically. Hence his propa-

[25] cf. Iwo, *op. cit.*; Friedman, "Alsatian Unrest," *Contemporary Review*, Vol. 155, 1939, p. 215.

ganda became very ambiguous and subtle. Revolutionary propaganda for the overthrow of the Austrian government by force went on side by side with "normal relations"; the dagger was always hidden in the tail of the diplomatic topcoat, and the assassin of yesterday reappeared today as "His Excellency." This situation is admirably reflected in the Nazis' use of radio throughout this period.[26]

When Germany entered the Third Reich, it was hoped that with a little pressure and the help of rightist groups in Austria this country could easily be "coordinated." On March 18, 1933, a high German Nazi personality broadcast greetings to the Austrian "party comrades" and expressed the hope that they also would soon secure their "liberty" from their present "oppressors," adding a hint of German intervention, if necessary. But when the Dollfuss government refused to let itself be destroyed so easily and took strong measures against subversive activities by Austrian Nazis, German Nazism changed its tactics. Official German authorities kept in the background and left it to the leaders of Austrian Nazism, who had fled to Germany where they were allowed to set up headquarters at Munich, there to launch a campaign of terror and propaganda against the Austrian government. Here radio played a major part. Strategically located German stations were put at their disposal, and thus, for more than a year, we have the novel phenomenon of a pseudo-civil war conducted under refugee leadership from beyond the frontier, and with the aid and connivance of a foreign power.

Summer 1933 witnessed the first well-planned campaign. It was inaugurated by Hitler himself, whose "greetings" to the Austrian Nazi leader, Habicht, were read over the radio. The regular "Austrian Service," "to be heard with ease all over Austria," was then announced by broadcasts, in pamphlets smuggled into Austria and even by leaflets dropped from planes. A speech by Habicht on July 5 ushered in regular broadcasts which were continued at fixed hours several times a week. Austria was pictured as German and Nazi, oppressed by a terroristic, "separatist" and "treacherous" minority backed by Germany's enemies. Atrocities were recounted and the people summoned to revolt.

[26] cf. for the following, *The Death of Dollfuss. An Official History of the Revolt of July 1934 in Austria*, translated by J. Messinger, London, 1935; Oswald Dutch: *Thus Died Austria*, London, 1938; M. Ball: *Post-War German-Austrian Relations. The Anschluss Movement 1918-1936*, Stanford, 1936.

Above all, the radio was the transmission belt for conveying orders and advice to followers within Austria and thus helped to organize the internal campaign of terrorism which paralleled that waged from abroad.

But the desired result did not occur, and faced with diplomatic complications, Hitler broke off the campaign at the end of August. It was hoped to make progress by negotiation, and the radio now took over more "diplomatic" functions. Thus, in September, a peculiar mixture of "ultimatum" and offer of compromise with conditions for "cooperation" were broadcast by Habicht, on behalf of the Austrian Nazi Party, showing how an exiled opposition, backed by a foreign regime, considered itself on equal terms with a state government. A new wave of terror, accompanied by a new radio campaign from Germany, started early in 1934. Then the February civil war between Dollfuss and the Socialist workers offered the Nazis a unique opportunity. During the combat they stood aside, going even so far as to broadcast orders to Austrian Nazis not to interfere in the struggle. Afterwards, they tried to capitalize on the defeat of the workers and the weakened position of the government, and broadcast from Munich headquarters a real ultimatum to the victorious party. An armed revolt was threatened unless, before the expiration of an eight days' "truce," the government gave in and opened the doors to Nazism. Upon the intervention of foreign powers, however, Hitler had to retract, and promises, instead of the threatened revolt, followed the famous eight days.

In May, a new, more violent campaign was started which culminated in the abortive July *Putsch* and the murder of Dollfuss. In preparation for the anticipated revolt, hostile broadcasting had assumed a violence unequalled even during the preceding summer. Frauenfeld, exiled Vienna *Gauleiter,* had bluntly called for the assassination of Dollfuss. During the *Putsch* itself, the seizure of the Vienna radio and the announcement, over the air, of the formation of a new government was to be the signal for insurrection all over the country. But this came to nought when the government regained hold of the radio service. And when Mussolini mobilized at the Brenner Pass, Hitler had to accept retreat, actual and moral. For although the German radio, even during the night following the *Putsch,* had broadcast triumphant reports and accompanied the announcement of Dollfuss's death with musical selections chosen to suggest joy over the day's events ("Today the stars glow brighter," "I thought I dreamt," to which the announcer added: "but it is true"), later an "investigation" into the subject of these broadcasts led to the dismissal of Habicht, "responsible for Munich broadcasts," because of "insufficiently careful control of news," an understatement not frequently found in Nazi announcements.

After Hitler had embarked upon a long-view policy of appeasement and boring from within, accompanied even by a formal agreement to abstain from hostile broadcasting, the radio retreated to more under-cover measures such as "historical" *Hoerspiele.* Its main function, from 1935-1938, had been to keep up the "loyalty" of sympathizing groups in Austria until "the day" should arrive. It came when, in 1938, the changed international situation warranted a new attempt at forceful intervention. The "coordination" of Austria, including the Austrian radio service, was already well under way when, at the last moment, Schuschnigg balked. Then, for the first time, the radio was used by Nazism in a way which has become since a standard article of Nazi propaganda: the "strategy of terror." In preparation for an intended coup it was necessary to lay a drum-fire barrage of such intensity as to raise the excitement of the Nazi population at home to a frenzy and cause any will to resist on the part of the adversary and other interested powers to crumble. This "psychological" mobilization started the day Schuschnigg announced his plebiscite. Entirely emotional, it pictured Austria as disintegrating into anarchy, a prey to Bolshevik mobs who, armed by the Czechs, ruled the streets and caused a terrible bloodbath among peaceful burghers, intimating that Germany could no longer abstain from preventing this "slaughter of Germans by Germans." Though pure invention, this campaign, with press and radio in the vanguard, proved to be successful. On March 11, Schuschnigg accepted the ultimatum and resigned. During that night, the radio, transmitting from Vienna to the world the main stages of the tragedy, fulfilled the function of historian. By broadcasting Schuschnigg's last statement that he yielded to force, the radio gave the lie to later Nazi denials and in this respect, at least, served the cause of historical truth. During the following days, 100,000 free radio sets were distributed among the Austrians, in preparation for totalitarian propaganda for Hitler's *post-festum* plebiscite, which was soon to "confirm" the *Anschluss* by an alleged majority of 99.75 per cent of the total Austrian vote.

"Deutschland über alles in der Welt": The Nazi
Short-Wave System

Such was the role of radio as Hitler accomplished his first great coup. But here were only German language broadcasts over long waves, and the Nazis were at least equally enthusiastic in developing a short-wave system of world-embracing power. This was the next step following the creation by various countries of "Empire Services," already referred to.

Tentative transmissions had been made from Zeesen as early as 1929, but a regular service was inaugurated only after Nazism had seized the channels of communication. This was on April 1, 1933, with broadcasts to North America, the overseas region with the "greatest number of racial Germans," and was continued with two hours daily of special programs in German and English. In the following years, the Zeesen short-wave station was organized from the bottom as a separate institution and showed a steady and systematic growth in every respect. Thus, in 1933, 3 wavelengths were used against 15 in 1938; in 1933 Zeesen sent out in but one direction, in 1938 in 6, with 7 specialized regular programs; in 1933 there were only 2 daily program hours; in 1938, 51.25; in 1939, 69 and an average of 126 transmission hours.[27] With the increase in zonal programs the number of foreign languages also increased steadily, including even Afrikaans in the regular daily programs. As to zones, services to Africa, the Far East and South America were opened in 1934, to South Asia, Australia and Central America in 1935. In 1939 a special program zone was inaugurated for Brazil.[28]

An important feature was the attempt to establish intimate contact with the audience. Here Zeesen has been the model for other countries. There is the personal contact with visitors to Berlin from overseas. Such persons are shown around the station, given information and asked for suggestions. They are placed before the microphone to send greetings to relatives, friends, or simply countrymen overseas. Series of such visitors' programs, "Germany as I saw it," "Ibero-America in the Reich," etc., were established, and more or less prominent visitors exploited to

[27] "Program hours" are hours of different programs, while "transmission hours" also contain hours during which the same program was sent over different wavelengths or repeated over the same wave.
[28] Schroeder, *op. cit.*, pp. 72-85; Weinbrenner (ed.): *Handbuch des deutschen Rundfunks*, Heidelberg, 1938, pp. 301ff.

propagandize the Third Reich by giving what might appear to them
and their listeners to be "authentic testimony." Often such visitors
would later become enthusiastic adherents of Nazism and its short-
wave programs.[29]

The next step was correspondence with listeners. "Fan mail" increased
from about 3,000 letters in 1933 to more than 50,000 in 1938, about 60 per
cent in foreign languages (much of it English). Zeesen stresses individual dealing with such letters, studying them, answering them, often over
the air, and quoting suitable passages whenever adapted to propaganda
needs, etc. Questionnaires are circulated abroad soliciting such correspondence (also in foreign languages), contests of all kinds are arranged, such as film or photographic contests with pictures of listeners
or of "significant landscapes," and the interest thus awakened exploited
for other purposes, such as soliciting gifts for the German *Winterhilfe,*
or instigating the desire to visit Germany. In general, the individual
listener's whims and wishes are treated with utmost politeness. As
a result the characteristic reaction of the average listener is: "How great
must be a country which thus responds even to personal wishes of its
members abroad,"[30] or, "If your letters are a mirror of typical National
Socialism, it is regrettable how unfairly Nazis are usually judged
here."[31]

Zeesen has developed an elaborate system of general publicity, sending out advance programs and bulletins in various languages, punc-
tually and without cost to press or individual listeners. They average
75,000 monthly. In addition, there have been picture-placards, maps of
Germany, miniature phonograph records sent out with mailing receipt
and questionnaire; Christmas gifts, material concerning the station, texts
of programs and speeches, and also more general propagandistic material such as Hitler's speeches, booklets containing language lessons,
etc.[32]

A further step in organizing the audience was the founding of listeners' clubs or organizations for group receiving. This seems to have
flourished among "Germans abroad" but was not infrequently found
even among foreign language listeners. Sympathizing owners of res-
taurants, taverns, etc., are important in this respect, since their custom-

[29] Van Gelderland, *loc. cit.,* p. 300.   [30] From a letter from Brazil, Schroeder, *op. cit.,* p. 241.
[31] From a letter from New Zealand, Schroeder, *op. cit.,* p. 254.
[32] Lang, "Berlin Sends Radio Greetings," *New Republic,* January 11, 1939, pp. 279f.

ers regularly listen in. Further devices to keep the individual listener interested are five to ten minutes daily greetings to individuals, such as birthday greetings, special messages to settlers in former German colonies, or greetings by friends and relatives in Germany or friends visiting Germany. It is not only the openly propagandistic side of such messages which is important, as revealed in messages praising the regime, but above all the impression of newly established close contacts, of a "people's community across the seas," which evokes in Germans abroad the feeling that "there must be something tremendously great in this new Germany." This makes such devices of great political significance.[33]

Program exchange, overseas by short wave, has also been considered a valuable means of propaganda. In this respect statistics not only show steady increase but also an "active balance" for Germany, since Zeesen sent abroad much more than Germany took over from abroad. The Nazis have always stressed the importance of transmissions from the Reich in influencing foreign opinion; thus, broadcasting from Linz in Austria, on March 12, 1938, "the tremendous jubilation of the Austrian people," with NBC reportage to America, they boasted of having effectively forestalled "distorting" reports by newspapers of the same event.[34]

The task of German short wave with respect to "Germans abroad"[35] has been first of all to awaken or reawaken their knowledge and sense of the German language. The radio here has cleverly played upon feelings of nostalgia for the old country, passing subtly from entertainment to indoctrination. There are Bavarian, Swabian or Silesian hours, folk music sent from different districts, programs given in local dialects, all dealing with local customs and events. Then there are special programs for German organizations and institutions abroad (for example German schools) and programs specially designed for special events abroad such as "German days" or "reunions," also special programs for German sailors on the seven seas. They deal with "Germandom abroad," its history, achievements, personalities, tasks, struggles, and, guided by suggestions from listeners, use material from overseas, sometimes giving such "foreign-German" artistic or musical creations a first (and, for the most part, last) performance.

[33] Sell, in *Jahrbuch Welt-Rundfunk*, 1937-38, pp. 79f.; Britt: *The Fifth Column is Here*, New York, 1940, p. 55.
[34] Weinbrenner, *op. cit.*, pp. 108, 301ff.
[35] Quotations on the following pages are from fan mail excerpts in Schroeder, *op. cit.*

Fan mail received shows how this system of political indoctrination has frequently succeeded in establishing the same monopoly of opinion which we have observed in the case of the Saar, for people thus won over simply refuse to listen to any other source of information: "We only listen to the KWS and no longer to any other station. . . . At 6:45 P.M. every German in Argentine . . . is at his seat; that simply is a law of nature." Similar reports are claimed from all parts of the globe[36] and demonstrate the power of the short wave as a molder of opinion among "racial brothers." Some such converted listeners would become so inspired that their missionary zeal would express itself in all kinds of propagandizing activities, such as assembling friends, school children and other groups in front of the receiving set, or simply "blasting forth so that the walls shatter" and opening windows so as to enable the neighborhood to hear "Göhring [sic], our dear Hermann"; or constructing sets for fellow Germans or offering them loans to purchase sets, spreading programs by word of mouth or by making copies, copying pamphlets, speeches and other Zeesen material, or writing letters to local papers about these programs and having them published. Some such activities are described in the following extract from a listener's letter: "Goebbels' masterful speech pleased us best. We had invited some American doctors, lawyers and ministers who all understand German. Of our neighbors, 50% are Jews, and what with the heat all had their windows open. At 10:00 P.M. the short-wave station announced Goebbels' speech. Quickly I put the radio at full power. . . . It was high pleasure. . . . The Jews . . . burst with rage and shut their windows. In the street, groups of Americans who understood German had assembled and applauded. . . . My neighbor, minister at an English Church, took the speech as text for his coming Sunday sermon."[37] The general effect of these broadcasts on racial Germans is perhaps best reflected in the ever recurring martial terms in which listeners couch their impressions. As one of them stated after listening to German marches: "We all wished we could see this army march into all parts of the world."[38]

The programs destined for "foreigners"[39] have likewise been charac-

[36] cf., e.g. the account given of the situation in former German Southwest Africa by Bennett: *Hitler over Africa*, London, 1939, pp. 100ff., 178ff.

[37] Schroeder, *op. cit.*, pp. 250ff.   [38] *ibid.*, p. 222.

[39] For the following cf. Schroeder, *op. cit., passim*, and Panton, "Tuning in the Nazis," *Living Age*, Vol. 352, 1937, pp. 316ff.

terized by regionalization and subtle "individualization," always made to suit the mentality of various groups in different zones and regions, and thus, according to the Nazis, "not only turned into foreign language but also into foreign mentality." There is a significant distinction between programs for the educated minority and those destined for the "masses." To attract the former, serious music is offered and from its appreciation the listener is led gradually to a love of all things German and Nazi: "We shall proceed from Beethoven to Hitler."[40] These programs picture achievements of German culture, as embodied in history and art, science and technology, landscape and architecture, language and poetry, and thence proceed to present-day Germany, "victor over unemployment, country of labor service, NS People's Welfare, Winter-Relief, Strength-Through-Joy" and other achievements. The masses, on the other hand, are attracted above all by such features as birthday greetings and personal addresses, light music and entertainment, between which propaganda is cunningly sandwiched. Thus, between weather reports and crop news the listener is told that "the latest statistics show that rape, arson, and Communism have sharply risen in New York City, of which La Guardia is mayor."

In adapting these programs to special regions and groups Zeesen often goes to incredible lengths. Not only are the national holidays and heroes of various countries commemorated but even such local days and events as "Dingaans Tag" in South Africa, or the foundation of Lunenburg, Nova Scotia, of which most inhabitants were not aware. Programs are built for local groups, clubs, schools, colleges, prominent individuals, such as a special broadcast apropos of a Stanford-California football game, or a series of programs directed to American towns and cities bearing names of German ones. Programs to the United States are specialized with respect to all forty-eight states of the Union, commemorating the Texan independence centenary, or sending "Way down in Old Louisiana" or "Beautiful Missouri." Tasmania is approached with a series, "Hello Tasmania, beautiful apple isle," and programs in Afrikaans for the Boers seem to have evoked a warm echo, since until then the BBC had not considered their special wishes and language to be worthy of its attention. To Mexicans Zeesen once did the doubtful honor of declaring them fellow-Nordics through their Toltec ancestors, while in Hindustani it posed as pacifistic, declaring, "We, the German people, respect Mahatma Gandhi just as much as we respect Hitler, who has the same principles as Gandhi; National Socialism, too, teaches non-violence."

Radio and the Spanish Dress Rehearsal for the Second World War

After the establishment of a totalitarian short-wave system, the first great political event in which radio played a major part was the so-called "civil war" in Spain. This was the first instance, since the World War, of European warfare on a large scale and under modern conditions. It offers an opportunity to observe how the various functions of radio foreshadowed many of the stratagems and devices subsequently used in the second World War. In its propaganda aspect, however, this war was important not only for its immediate political and strategic implication in Spain; it was the first instance of the operation of the world-wide "Fascist" revolution against the existing international system. The Spanish struggle was amplified into a matter of general concern as the struggle of "civilization against Bolshevism." By virtue of this diabolically clever propaganda the democracies were split internally from top to bottom and were not only neutralized into "non-intervention" for the duration of the war but for years to come were politically paralyzed by the formation of "appeasement" parties hostile to any action against Fascism. While, with respect to propaganda, the Republic gained only the assistance of Russia, more compromising than helpful, the cause of Franco was furthered by a united front of Nazis, Fascists, Church and City. Ideologically, Fascist propaganda thus won an even greater success than its military intervention, because it led to the total eclipse of democratic policies and morale.

That Spain was purposely made a tool or pawn in this political game is proved by the fact that long before the outbreak of the war Nazis and Fascists worked diligently to undermine the Republican regime and to prepare the uprising. This is the first instance of a system, now notorious through its application in Norway, France, and elsewhere, which at that time passed almost unnoticed even after its results had become apparent. Radio fulfilled certain important functions in this respect. Open propaganda took the form of racialist programs on occasions like the Spanish "Festival of the Race," but more undercover use was made of radio when it served to discover listeners who might be trained for subversive activities and widespread revolt. Listeners were asked to write suggestions to Germany, and some of those responding could be counted on as enemies of the Republican regime.[41]

Lack of space precludes details of the use made of radio during and for purposes of actual warfare. Stations were always among the foremost points of attack and were used to broadcast not only propagandistic "welcome home" programs for whichever side had just conquered but also false orders, either to the enemy to sow confusion, or to the whole population to disrupt enemy administration. Radio was used not only to keep up communication between separate formations and territories but also to keep in touch with "fifth columnists" who worked in enemy territory.

"Loyalist" radio propaganda, though most of the stations and the most powerful were in Loyalist hands, was not as effective as it might have been. A narrow censorship policy prevented the use of radio for reportage by friendly correspondents from Madrid, and exaggerated and inaccurate news reports at first compromised its value, though later the Loyalists turned to a policy of telling the truth even when they had only bad news to report. As to contents, the propaganda was mainly of the "traditional" type, dwelling upon the morale of the army and civilians, the certainty of foreign invasion and, in broadcasts to "neutrals," stressing the common interest of free countries in the face of totalitarian aggression. There was also much effort to refute enemy propaganda, as in the matter of "religious persecution." Propaganda directed to the interventionist countries was often effective, for instance, when Loyalist reports of the Italian rout of Guadalajara forced the Italians to break their intended silence.[42]

In contrast to "traditionalist" Loyalist propaganda, the Francoists, advised by Nazi-Fascist propaganda experts, applied the new technique of totalitarian propaganda. Stamping the Republic with the Bolshevist label and their own cause with that of liberation, nationalism, *hispanidad* and the supernational task of freeing the world from "anarchy," they

[41] Documents found by the Loyalists in the German consulate at Barcelona contain the details of these preparatory activities; cf. *The Nazi Conspiracy in Spain*, by the editor of the *Brown Book of the Hitler Terror*, London, 1937; also *Foreign Intervention in Spain*, documents collected and edited by "Hispanicus," Vol. 1, London, 1937.

[42] Renn: *Warfare*, New York, 1939, pp. 256ff.; del Vayo: *Freedom's Battle*, New York, 1940, p. 151; Sereno, "Italian War Propaganda at Home," *Public Opinion Quarterly*, Vol. 3, 1939, p. 471.

disclaimed responsibility for the outbreak of the war, but at the same time stressed their military superiority and advised the democracies to line up with the stronger side. Besides this totalitarian transvaluation of values, this propaganda is characterized by both its unconcern with logical consistency and its emotional nature. With the approval of the Vatican, religious masses were broadcast to the faithful on the other side, while, at the same time, broadcasts were made "interesting" by constant references to the love affairs and the alleged licentious lives of enemy leaders. In this respect, the broadcasts by Queipe de Llano, the famous "radio general," constitute a unique case in the history of radio. His "harsh voice, often tinged with irony and always threatening" was famous all over Spain and his practices contain a good illustration of this new type of radio "technique." *Strategy of terror:* reprisals are threatened against the families of Loyalists in Franco's control; the actual extermination of active opponents after the victory is announced, or massacres organized by "Nationalists" are frankly used as a deterrent. *Technique of boasting:* the Nationalists represent the "right cause" and are "gentlemen," their adversaries are "criminals." *Technique of vituperation:* the Reds are "ravening beasts," of whom all kinds of atrocities are reported. Thus, the "red militia" is charged with emitting "vouchers for rape" ("each note good for one rape"). *Technique of "humor"* and *appeal to sexual, mostly sadistic, instincts:* the Nationalists show "red cowards" "what it means to be a man," and "incidentally, the wives of the reds, too. . . . Kicking their legs about and struggling won't save them," etc.[43] The effects of such propaganda have been recounted by a noted American author; its destructiveness is only matched by its incredible baseness.

The traditional distinction between "home propaganda" and that destined for "neutrals" does not apply to totalitarian propaganda during the Spanish war. For Franco and his allies there were no "neutrals," but only friends or enemies. As a matter of fact, "Francoist" propaganda often originated in "allied" territory, for stations located in Italy broadcast in Spanish as if coming from Franco territory. German and Italian radio propaganda was entirely at the service of Franco and helped to spread his cause over the entire world. While for internal German or Italian consumption the struggle was pictured as one for

[43] Koestler: *Spanish Testament*, London, 1937, pp. 30ff., 80ff.; del Vayo, *op. cit.*, pp. 153f.; Cardozo: *The March of a Nation*, New York, 1937, p. 56.

combating a Communist uprising (with the same slogans and expressions as those used in their own domestic "revolutions," e.g. "national resurrection"), it was represented to the democratic world as a struggle for traditional values such as family, property, religion. Some Portuguese stations, too, were given over to the use of Francoists. Franco also broadcast in Arabic from Tetuan, in Russian for Russia and Russians fighting on the Loyalist side. Later, he used the short wave, too, mainly in English for America, and in other languages to Latin American countries, where many sympathizing regimes facilitated this type of propaganda even at a time when they still officially recognized the Republic.[44] After the victory, short-wave propaganda from the powerful Madrid station was greatly activated, and gained prestige above all in Latin America as coming from the "mother country" and a regime which the upper classes in most of these countries considered as the defender of their privileges. The Loyalists who, toward the end of the war, also stepped up their short-wave propaganda, proved to be less successful.[45]

Fascism and Democracy Competing, I: Propaganda among the Arabs

Short-wave broadcasting comes again to the fore in another long drawn out propaganda battle—that fought for the minds of the people of North Africa and the Near East. Here, Italy entered first.

Italy's first real radio campaign, planned and concentrated on one single object, started with the preparation of the Ethiopian war. While at first conciliatory toward England, in Italy herself and other countries it was at the same time aggressive with respect to everything British, and when Britain took the lead against Italian aggression, Fascist publicity began an unprecedented campaign of hate against her. This was directed mainly toward the populations in those Mediterranean countries in which Britain's interests were vital, i.e. the Arab population of such countries as Egypt and Palestine, where existing tensions and difficulties could be the most easily exploited. The aim here was to show Mussolini in the stellar role of protector of Islam, while Britain was pictured as imperialistic oppressor. The British were accused of

[44] Riegel, "Press, Radio, and the Spanish Civil War," *Public Opinion Quarterly*, Vol. 1, 1937, pp. 134*f*.; Wolters, "The Menace of Shortwave Propaganda," *Radio News*, May 1938, p. 68.
[45] Beals, *op. cit.*, pp. 161*ff*.; Harris, *loc. cit.*, pp. 121*f*.

revolting atrocities committed in Palestine and elsewhere against the Arabs, while at the same time the Empire was declared "decadent," the fleet "a museum piece," etc.[46]

After the conquest of Ethiopia this campaign did not subside but was even intensified. Broadcasts to the Arabs were now systematically organized. Receiving sets locked to Italian stations were distributed free, above all at "strategic" points such as cafés, the principal meeting place of Moslems. Programs were adapted to popular taste, made as vivid as possible by mixing highly emotional propaganda such as atrocities with attractive entertainments such as amusing tales, Arab poetry and music. Thus Bari engaged the most popular Arab singer for its Arab programs. In range, this station now reached from Morocco to India.[47]

Britain at first took these attacks with extreme unconcern. Occasionally Jerusalem answered certain Italian charges, but very tardily, with great reluctance, and only under the pressure of public opinion and motions in Parliament that the government finally acted by inaugurating the Arabic Service of the BBC, its first foreign language service, in January 1938. Even then the British insisted that they would give "straight news" and did not intend to "retaliate." Thus the broadcasts were "informative," not propagandistic. They consisted of daily transmissions such as talks by Islamic scholars, recitations from the Koran, messages by certain high Moslem dignitaries friendly to Britain, etc., and were characterized by "objectivity turned into extreme dullness," and lack of imaginativeness as compared with the flowery language of the Italians. In short, the BBC dealt with these programs as if they were destined for the British themselves and not for an entirely different audience.[48]

Italy reacted violently and with increased radio efforts, ridiculing the British efforts which they described as entirely unsuccessful: "The ether waves prove to be as little advantageous to British hegemony as the waves of the Mediterranean." Nevertheless, in return for Britain's recognition of the new *Impero* they promised Chamberlain to abstain in the future from hostile broadcasting. Since this "gentlemen's agreement"

[46] A. J. Mackenzie, *Propaganda Boom,* London, 1938, pp. 180ff.; Vernon McKenzie: *Here Lies Goebbels,* London, 1940, pp. 206ff.

[47] Grandin, *loc. cit.,* p. 52; Willert, "Publicity and Propaganda in International Affairs," *International Affairs,* Vol. 17, 1938, p. 823.

[48] Foster, "The Official Propaganda of Great Britain," *Public Opinion Quarterly,* Vol. 3, 1939, p. 269; V. McKenzie, *op. cit.,* pp. 209f.

had been preceded by the resignation of Eden, pictured for years by Italy as the "devil" responsible for Britain's anti-Italian policy, Fascist propaganda could nevertheless celebrate the agreement as a victory.[49]

This was not, however, the end of the radio war. In pursuance of a policy of "division of labor," the two allied totalitarian powers simply changed roles, Germany now switching to anti-British propaganda, while Italy concentrated on France. From Bari and a new station at Tripoli, Fascism now blasted at the French, attempting to undermine their position in North Africa as they had tried to do in the Near East: "Everywhere the natives revolt against the rape of their countries, the French are in danger of being thrown into the sea." Against this sudden onslaught the French eventually answered from Rabat (Morocco), Algiers, and a newly erected station at Tunis.[50]

Zeesen, for its part, thoroughly organized itself for the new task, and from early in 1938 actually dominated the Arab scene. Arab lecturers from German universities were hired, and Arab exiles from Britain-dominated countries engaged as advisors. Zeesen succeeded in establishing effective collaboration with local sources of information or misinformation on the spot, and news from Palestine, in distorted or exaggerated form, was often broadcast from Germany a few hours after its occurrence. Local anti-British newspapers, subsidized and frequently edited by Nazi agents, served as sources of information. These broadcasts were in turn further spread through the offices of the local press, and in these local propaganda activities German embassies took a central part. Local stations also took over material from German news services. Occasionally a bit of comic opera was added to this chapter, as when King Ghazi of Irak, an "amateur" broadcaster who had his private station at Bagdad, sent out anti-British material taken from German services. To British protests the premier replied that "he could not control His Majesty." As to contents, the Nazis followed the usual technique of mixing popular entertainment with highly colored political propaganda, mainly atrocities. According to some observers, this subversive propaganda contributed to the seriousness of the situation during the Palestine revolts of 1938-1939.[51]

The British, although protesting against the campaign and occasionally broadcasting denials of alleged atrocities, otherwise continued

---

[49] A. J. Mackenzie, *op. cit.*, pp. 188ff.   [50] Niessel, *loc. cit.*, p. 839; Grandin, *loc. cit.*, p. 55.
[51] V. McKenzie, *op. cit.*, pp. 199ff.

16420

their policy of "non-retaliation." The radio war thus continued right down to the outbreak of actual warfare between the "radio belligerents." For a time, German racialism and the conclusion of the Stalin-Hitler pact seem to have diminished totalitarian prestige among Arabs, but if the fact that most of the Near Eastern countries lined up with England at the outbreak of the war is adduced to prove that the Axis had failed in its radio efforts, this viewpoint overlooks the fact that the real effectiveness of such propaganda has its crucial test in times of military and political crises, and the recent Irak "incident" may yet prove to have foreshadowed more serious events to come as fruits of long-view disintegrating propaganda.[52]

Fascism and Democracy Competing, II: Latin America

While long and medium wave broadcasting joined with short wave in the Mediterranean struggle, the latter ruled the ether waves in another theater of radio warfare—Latin America. Although totalitarian propaganda here did not originate in a concrete incident and was not as immediately or as openly warlike, the existence of a well-organized campaign with well-defined aggressive aims is proved by the fact that here, as in the Arab contest, the democracies were eventually obliged to resort to defensive measures. Latin America, not directly under the influence of any one great power, offered a fertile field for indirect attack upon the interests of the "enemy." That totalitarian propaganda chose an apparently far-distant region as the field for a major effort testifies to its world-wide revolutionary nature in pursuit of a great plan of world domination. Nazi-Fascist propaganda in Latin America was facilitated by two factors: first, the existence of vast populations of German and Italian origin; and second, the Latin American system of rule through alternating small political *juntas,* which could be exploited for the purpose of winning over native factions, side by side with the organizations of "racial comrades," to stir up unrest and group hatred. "Yankee imperialism" and, with Spain as "intermediary," *hispanidad* also could be used for propagandistic purposes.

It is impossible to go into the details of German Latin American propaganda. It has been "coordinated" and organized as a whole in an extremely thorough manner. Every imaginable device has been

[52] *ibid.,* pp. 170*ff.*; cf. also the interesting report in *New York Times,* October 8, 1939, sect. 4, p. 5.

used, all the way from the totalitarian organization of German "colonies," to "business propaganda" and "cultural propaganda" by the Hispano-American Institute at Berlin and other institutions, student and professor exchanges, the setting up of German schools or German professorships "cost-free" in Latin American countries, the establishment of inter-American airlines, and the financing of the local press and other enterprises. The role of the radio, because of the geographical distance, was particularly vital.

Regular short-wave service from Zeesen to South America was opened on February 2, 1934, to Central America on May 1, 1935, and the two departments were especially organized under Latin American experts. In 1938 Zeesen sent 12 hours daily, and in 1939 a separate program was added for Brazil. Programs were advertised in the usual way: they were announced in the local press, sets locked on German wavelengths were given away or sold cheap, Latin American visitors to Germany appeared on the programs, and "competing" short-wave transmissions were frequently "jammed" or disturbed by "straddling."[53]

However, the Nazis realized that by short wave alone they would reach but a comparatively small number of listeners, in particular in countries with a rather low standard of living. Their main effort, therefore, was directed at bringing their propaganda material to the masses by utilizing the two foremost channels of local communication, the press and the local radio. Such an indirect approach had, moreover, the advantage of being clad in "local," not "foreign," color.

Nazi radio news services were supplied free of charge to the press and local radio stations. Often payments were made for the reproduction of articles. Combining "business" with propaganda, Germans sold an automatic radiotype recording machine. Local stations were often allowed to relay German programs at their own profit, i.e. to "commercialize" them. Stations were provided with records for rebroadcasting, "canned programs" being issued without charge, complete with announcements and talks in the language of the country. Wherever possible, use was made of program exchanges, sometimes so successfully that a government would oblige all local stations in the country to take over the Nazi program during a "National Hour." The system of

[53] N. P. Macdonald: *Hitler over Latin America*, London, 1940; Inman: *Democracy versus the Totalitarian State in Latin America*, Philadelphia, 1938; Beals, *op. cit.* and the same, "Totalitarian inroads in Latin America," *Foreign Affairs*, Vol. 17, 1938-39, p. 81.

private ownership of radio was taken advantage of by subsidizing or controlling stations, or even acquiring them outright. Clandestine stations were also operated by Nazi agents. As for the newspapers, the Nazis had the most success with such local papers as could not afford to subscribe to expensive foreign news services. Their editors were allowed to pick up German news transmissions free of charge and their task was further facilitated by German agents on the spot who would pick up the news, translate it if in German, edit it, and deliver it each day to the editor's desk with headlines all ready for immediate publication, while illustrations in matrix form and other feature devices were added for good measure. Sometimes such agents would deliver material with forged datelines, indicating American or other origin. A further step was the outright acquisition of local papers by German agents.[54]

With reference to contents, Zeesen applied the principles already described, mixing outright propaganda with entertainment, building up programs carefully with a view to "Germans abroad" and "foreign" wishes and conditions, etc. The particular Latin American situation was exploited by attacks upon British and, above all, American "imperialism" and all things "Yankee" and "demo-plutocratic": Unemployment, strikes and labor unrest, "Bolshevism," gangsterism, lynching, maltreatment of minorities, greed of the rich and misery of the masses, failure of New Deal plans, and other problems with which the democracies had allegedly grappled in vain were enthusiastically discussed. "Exploitation" of Latin America by the Yankees, the long history of forceful intervention against "freedom-loving countries," the alleged domination of Latin American public opinion by "Jewish-Yankee telegraph agencies" in the service of "unscrupulous business men eager to increase dollar earnings," "Uncle Sam, the Jewish Shylock," whose most recent device to inveigle Latin Americans was "good neighbor Pan-Americanism"—these were the ever-repeated themes on which Nazi propaganda never tired harping. This type of disparaging propaganda was frequently combined with business propaganda; broadcasts dealt with strikes in the American steel industry at a time when a German firm was competing with Americans for a rail contract, the inference being that there were no strikes in Germany and delivery therefore was

---

[54] Besides authors quoted in note 53, cf. V. McKenzie, *op. cit.*, pp. 261*ff.*; Crowell, "Dogfight on the Air Waves," *Saturday Evening Post*, May 21, 1938, pp. 40*f.*

assured. Besides, popular front or other leftist movements and governments in Latin America were always given special attention, and their activities disparaged as "Bolshevist." Another means of stirring up internal unrest has been the exploitation of Catholic prejudice, in particular during the Spanish war.[55]

Italian Fascist propaganda, though somewhat less systematically organized than the Nazi edition, had the advantage of an even greater number of settlers of Italian origin. Furthermore, the ruling classes in Latin America had a racial, cultural and also Catholic affinity with this "Latin" country which posed as the foremost one in the world. Fascism, moreover, found prestige among the feudal and oligarchic rulers of regimes for the most part only superficially "democratic."

Rome short-wave broadcasting to Latin America began in 1934, but it was only in 1937 that regular daily services were inaugurated. The Italians were heavy buyers of local radio time, arranged for two-way broadcasting, subsidized and owned local stations and papers, etc. Once Mussolini even gave a whole radio station as a personal gift to the ruling "colleague" of one country.[56]

In their propaganda, Italian broadcasts above all pictured "Christian-Latin-Italian" Fascism as a model for Latin Americans in particular. Italy is the great Christian Catholic nation, Rome the spiritual capital of the world in both secular and clerical aspects. Her conquests are missionary and civilizing enterprises, her struggle against Bolshevism in Spain is a fight for Catholicism and the salvation of a country to which Latin Americans feel sentimentally attached. Thus, cultural and religious prestige values were exploited for political purposes. Hand in hand with this type of propaganda went the disparaging kind. The League of Nations, of which most of these countries were still members, was attacked as an instrument of imperialistic power politics and ridiculed as too weak to furnish protection to less powerful nations, an obvious hint to members such as the Latin American states. Yankee imperialism and the democracies in general were objects of attack with familiar Nazi slogans. Thus the Ludlow war referendum proposal was

[55] cf. also Furnas, "The War of Lies and Laughs," *Saturday Evening Post*, February 3, 1940; Hickok, "Developments in International Broadcasting," *Education on the Air*, Vol. 11, 1940, p. 14; Whitaker, *Americas to the South*, New York, 1939, p. 210; Wellner, "Ibero-America im Brennpunkt der Kurzwellen-Richtstrahler," *Zeitschrift für Geopolitik*, Vol. 15, 1938, p. 494.
[56] Inman, *op. cit.*; Beals, *op. cit.*, and "Black Shirts in Latin America," *Current History*, November 1938, pp. 32ff.

ridiculed as an example of what might be expected from spineless democratic regimes, while, with typical unconcern for logic, the defeat of this same proposal was then propagandistically exploited as evidence of how "real" democracy had no chance in America against the warlike aspirations of the ruling group.[57]

Democratic defense developed slowly and hesitatingly. As long as the democracies remained blind to the formation of two ideological and political "blocks," there could be defense, it is true, in the realm of economic competition, and attempts could be made to conserve the cultural prestige enjoyed, e.g. by France. But anything comparable to an active all-out propaganda campaign to uphold the values of democracy was impossible, since this would have presupposed an open campaign *against* the values and systems of Fascism and Nazism.

Britain initiated programs to Latin America in March 1938, after the establishment of a special Latin American Service had been announced in November 1937. There were three hours of daily broadcasts, including two news periods in Spanish and one in Portuguese. Generally, however, only news was given in these languages, while most talks were in English. France came in even later. There had been some Spanish and Portuguese programs over Paris-Colonial, which, however, had been mainly destined for French colonial possessions and were not especially "built" for Latin America. In the spring of 1938, a new short-wave station, Paris Mondial, was inaugurated for general short-wave service divided into four directions or "zones," but only in 1939 did Paris Mondial receive a sufficiently powerful transmitting station at Allouis. One of the four zones, each with special programs, was South America, but how badly organized French short-wave broadcasting was appears from the fact that Central America, a Spanish-speaking region, was included in the French-North American Service, with programs in French, English and German, but none in Spanish! British transmissions were at least sufficiently powerful to be well received in most parts of the Western Hemisphere; in general, before United States broadcasts came in, they ranked best after the German transmissions. French transmissions, however, were hard to receive most everywhere and suffered from interference by other stations.[58]

[57] cf. also Tracy, "Radio and the Monroe Doctrine," *Current History*, November 1938, pp. 29*f*.
[58] "British News by Wireless," *Round Table*, Vol. 29, 1938-39, pp. 726*ff*.; Beals, *op. cit.*; Inman, *op. cit.*

Furthermore, in contrast with the totalitarian powers, neither England nor France paid much attention to spreading their programs through indirect channels. French news at least was not copyrighted, but BBC news was thus restricted for a long time and could not be used free of charge by local press or radio. Later the government intervened and subsidized a free news service, but the British charged their listeners for advance programs. With respect to rebroadcasting, there were, according to one report, about 200 to 300 German relays to one British prior to the outbreak of the war. No extensive use by the local press of British or French radio broadcasts is reported.[59]

Radio and the Munich Crisis

In the case of the Austrian invasion, the "strategy of terror," applied for the first time by a heavily-armed and militarily strong Reich, worked with full success. It was not surprising, then, that it would be applied again in the accomplishment of the next step in German war preparation—the elimination of the Czechoslovakian bastion. Munich, in its moral-psychological implications meant even more than this immediate achievement. As in the case of one addicted to drugs, a country which has once yielded to the temptation to buy temporary peace and safety, bowing before the strategy of threats mixed with soothing promises, will find it ever more difficult, with every new recoil, to return to a more vigorous policy. Munich thus meant the paralysis, throughout a decisive period, of active Western policies.

Anti-Czechoslovak broadcasts over German stations had not been lacking during the years preceding Munich. In tone and content they resembled the anti-French broadcasts destined for Alsace-Lorraine and the anti-Lithuanian broadcasts, which in those years came from the East Prussian stations of Heilsberg and Koenigsberg to prepare the ground for the reacquisition of another *terra irredenta*, the Memel territory.[60] But the broadcasts directed to Masaryk's republic, more than those concerning France and Lithuania, were designed not only for Sudeten-Germans and others inside the country but also for the public opinion of the entire world, as a basis for later accusations and claims. It is significant that, as early as 1935, *short-wave* broadcasts accused the

[59] V. McKenzie, *op. cit.*, pp. 286*f*.
[60] Jonaitis: *La propagande allemande contre la Lithuanie*, Kaunas, 1936, pp. 7, 33*f*.; Iwo, *op. cit.*, pp. 81*ff*.

Czechs of conducting "a passionate fight for extermination" against the German minority, of systematically destroying Sudeten industry and causing such hunger and misery that "thousands have not had any meat for weeks, many children are starving," adding, in the characteristic manner of indirect threats, that even French press reports had expressed "admiration for the unheard-of discipline with which the German people still tolerate the incredible oppression of its brothers across the frontiers."[61]

For the second time the radio became the most deadly of the weapons laying down a drum-fire barrage of terror and propaganda. This time the outside world, a part of which was formally allied with the victim-to-be, could not be expected to remain a passive spectator as it had been during the demise of Austria. Thus this campaign, besides preparing the German people itself for a crisis and causing the immediate "enemy's" morale to crumble, aimed above all at influencing and demoralizing the leading people of Britain and France. The very enormity of the accusations and the very frenzy of the state of mind which they reflected was calculated to produce the desired effect even on "liberal" observers, and still more on those inclined to sacrifice national interests and international obligations for the sake of appeasement. It must not be forgotten that this was the first time that, with events changing dramatically from minute to minute, people in all countries of the world relied for information on the radio, which thus offered itself as an instrument with a range never before available to any propagandist. But the nature of Nazi broadcasting at that time cannot be realized even by those in "neutral" countries who listened regularly to their correspondents' information broadcasts. One must have actually heard those German long- and medium-wave programs destined for Germans and the neighbor-victim—the very tone in which they were voiced during that period of overexcitement and mass hysteria, the scream of the speaker, the rapidity with which "news reports" on alleged atrocities were read, the unintermittent stream of such broadcasts—all this taken together would give the real picture of that campaign.

This campaign, apparently an outburst of passion, was in reality meticulously organized and carefully timed in all details. Accord-

[61] Iwo, *op. cit.*, pp. 83ff.

ing to a later statement by Goebbels himself, "it was of utmost importance during the whole period of the crisis that the so-called situation-reports broadcast by the German stations should not give foreign circles the slightest possibility of seeing through the tactics of the German partner and, perhaps, countering them."[62] Thus, Henlein's proclamation demanding the outright annexation of the Sudeten territory by Germany was broadcast exactly at the time Chamberlain landed at Munich for his Berchtesgaden interview with Hitler.[63] Another device, already used in the case of Austria, was the use of broadcasts to Czechs and, more particularly, Sudeten-Germans given by exiled Sudeten Nazi leaders, who, from headquarters at strategically located Leipzig, communicated with their "comrades" in order to stir them up and convey orders to them. From Leipzig, Henlein thus made frantic appeals to the Sudetens against "the reign of terror of the Bolshevist Hussite criminals at Prague," promised that the hour of liberation was near, asked them to disobey mobilization and other orders, and warned those who dared to obey Prague of committing "high treason against the German nation."[64]

The actual campaign of threats, terror, intimidation and atrocities repeated almost pedantically those of half a year previously. Again, a country was declared to be ruled by "bestial Bolshevists," a "murder-gang" of sadists and cannibals, whence "the whole world is poisoned." Already disintegrating into anarchy this state pinned its last hope on a general European war which would draw France and England into a Bolshevist-Jewish conspiracy to overthrow the totalitarian regimes, and, finally, it was powerless to control its "red mob" which committed massacres and innumerable atrocities among the "German" population. Everything was a detailed repetition of these general themes.[65]

"Sturdy but mild efforts" by the Czechs to counteract Nazi propaganda were overwhelmed by the fury of this onslaught. They were not even assisted by the radio of their "allies" and other countries. The BBC was advised to follow a "cooperative," i.e. appeasement, line of

[62] Quoted by Mathews, "The Radio and International Relations." *Southwestern Social Science Quarterly*, Vol. 20, 1939-40, p. 143.

[63] Ripka: *Munich: Before and After*, London, 1939, pp. 47f.

[64] Gedye: *Betrayal in Central Europe*, New York, 1939, p. 437; Griffin: *Lost Liberty*, New York, 1939, p. 141; Killanin (ed.): *Four Days*, London (without year), pp. 89, 96.

[65] cf., e.g. Morrell: *I saw the Crucification*, London, 1939, p. 174; Seton-Watson: *From Munich to Danzig*, London, 1939, p. 43; Hindus: *We shall live again*, New York, 1939, pp. 208, 243.

policy.[66] This, in itself, testifies to the success of German propaganda and cannot be refuted by the fact that, with respect to the Czechoslovak, and even Sudeten-German and German masses, the effect of the campaign was probably less than expected. Indirect influence upon a minority, even a few single individuals in key political positions, may be more important than its effect on the mass of listeners directly.

Once the campaign was won, however, its result could not but deeply influence opinion and politics. In a "Munichized" world[67] Hitler was now in a position to deal as he pleased with rump Czechoslovakia. It seems that he first hoped through "peaceful coordination" to replace what still remained as an autonomous political entity with an entirely dependent "native" regime. The months between Munich and Prague witnessed the gradual increase of Nazi pressure, evident from the character of Czech broadcasting, which, after Munich, no longer at the service of a free country, turned "factual" and endeavored to further what today, in a similar situation, the Vichy government of France calls "collaboration." The German radio, however, showed itself less "cooperative." Although the rump state after Munich had been set up as a federal union which gave its nationalities wide autonomy, complaints by Fascist groups of Slovaks and Ruthenes and by Sudetens (a small number of whom had been purposely left within the Republic) gave rise to renewed attacks from without and eventually, when the Czechs proved too recalcitrant even in their weakened condition, served as a pretext and entering wedge for the final and outright conquest.

During the intervening months, the Vienna radio had incessantly broadcast anti-Czech propaganda, directed mainly at Slovaks tending toward secession. In March 1939, the leaders of the Fascist-secessionist Hlinka faction, deposed by the "loyalist" Slovak group on orders from Prague when danger of secession had become acute, fled to Vienna, thence to start a violent campaign for Slovak "liberation." Once again the radio was put at their disposal, and for a few days there developed a radio war between Vienna and Bratislava, still in the possession of the "loyalist" Slovak government. It was denounced as "treacher-

[66] V. McKenzie, op. cit., p. 122; Armstrong, "Armistice at Munich," Foreign Affairs, Vol. 17, 1938-39, p. 228.

[67] There is no better account of these effects than Edmond Taylor's The Strategy of Terror, New York, 1940.

ous" by these "Vienna Slovaks" who asked the Slovaks to revolt and called Hitler "Europe's greatest man who holds his protecting hand over the Slovaks." Then the other Reich stations joined the battle in the German language, pounding in the now familiar theme of atrocities and anti-Czech charges and even using the "German minority" as a pretext.[68] When this campaign resulted in the Czech surrender and German troops marched into the remnants of Czechoslovakia, the Czech radio, too, capitulated; its final act was to calm the people and, repeating at five-minute intervals the announcement of the occupation, to warn them to offer no resistance.

All-Out Radio Warfare and the Approach of Actual War

The Munich crisis meant the turning point in the development of a general "radio war" among the major European powers. The democracies at last took the counteroffensive against the long-established totalitarian practice of broadcasting across frontiers to the population of other countries. Although the appeasement mood prevailing after Munich makes it probable that the leading western politicians still considered such efforts on the part of their countries as means of "enlightenment" and propaganda for the peaceful solution of conflicts, they actually constituted a psychological preparation for war, since it was now too late to bring about the fall of the Nazi regime through internal revolution, and there was no chance of inducing it to make compromises. Thus even the well-intended efforts of Europe's "wireless towers of Babel" to bring about "peace in our time" were doomed to failure and became the symbol of the world's inevitable drive toward the abyss of war.

The most significant feature of this new development in radio politics was the all-out effort to reach foreign populations by the use of their own languages. With the exception of certain campaigns by the totalitarian powers, foreign language broadcasting, as we have seen, had been limited to short-wave services destined for overseas countries. Thus Italy, making use of long- and medium-wave transmissions, in 1937 broadcast regularly in 18 languages, and Moscow, including those of certain Soviet nationalities, in no less than 62.[69] But countries like Britain and France had never broadcast to Germany or Italy in the native

[68] Griffin, op. cit., p. 201; Buk: La tragédie tchécoslovaque, Paris, 1939, p. 190; Hanc, "Czechs and Slovaks since Munich," Foreign Affairs, Vol. 18, 1939-40, pp. 102f.

[69] Harris, loc. cit., p. 114; Sharp, "Propaganda on the Airwaves," Christian Science Monitor Magazine, October 27, 1937, p. 5.

languages of the inhabitants. At the height of the Munich crisis, however, the BBC for the first time directly addressed Germans and Italians, news was broadcast in German, Italian, and French, and important speeches of British statesmen were sent out in translation.[70]

After Munich this became a permanent practice, thus bringing to realization, though in an unexpected sense, the adage that "people shall speak unto people." Besides its Empire, Arab, and Latin American services the BBC now established a "European Service" which, at the outbreak of the war, was broadcasting in 16 foreign languages. This service employed foreign translators and announcers and soon was broadcasting 12 hours daily. News and news commentaries were the most significant features of these broadcasts. According to British tradition, they were at first "informative" and entirely unemotional, without special attractions and not trying, in any way, to adapt themselves to the special conditions and requirements of an audience under totalitarian rule. Thus news to Germany was offered at a fixed hour even when there was a Hitler speech at the same time—in other words, when no German could get away from his master's voice even had he wished to. Later in 1939, as the situation became ever more tense, the BBC adopted certain more frankly propagandistic techniques, transmitting, for instance, such special appeals to the German people as a manifesto signed by eighteen eminent Britons, or a plea by the British Mineworkers' Federation to the German miners.[71] The French radio, too, began broadcasting in German, Italian and other languages to the respective peoples but was more poorly organized and likewise hampered by political intervention. Thus during the Italian invasion of Albania on Good Friday, 1939, when a speech by King Zog was transmitted by Radio Tirana in various translations, a French station rebroadcasting it announced the continuation of the program but failed to follow up the announcement after intervention by French appeasement politicians.[72]

Nazi reaction to the democracies' tactics was violent. It was both defensive and counter-offensive. Listening-in to foreign stations had been permitted so far unless it was Moscow. Now, the spreading of news heard over foreign stations was forbidden under heavy penalty,

[70] Tallents, "British Broadcasting and the War," *Atlantic Monthly*, March 1940, p. 365.

[71] *New York Times*, February 5, 1939, sect. 4, p. 4; *New York Herald Tribune*, January 28, July 7, 1939.

[72] Grandin, *op. cit.*, p. 31; *New York Herald Tribune*, June 18, 1939, sect. 2, p. 1.

and the public was warned of foreign radio propaganda, those "brazen poison plots" and "bombs for the mind." Although Goebbels, in an article in the *Voelkischer Beobachter*, ridiculed the "effort to separate the people from its leaders," a note of anxiety breaks through: "For some weeks the English have been putting out news in German over their wireless; they do it very skillfully under the cloak of a desire for truth and a stern, almost scientific objectivity. They do so because they think that this is the best way to obtain a hearing in Germany. . . ."[73]

German counterattack in the form of an English language campaign from Hamburg and other favorably located stations began in March 1939. During the first weeks the English spoken was very bad and news reports ridiculously exaggerated. Then the man who later was to become notorious as "Lord Haw-Haw" was put in charge of the service and the programs at once became humorous, mild, and mixed with entertainment features so as to attract an audience. Thus the ground was laid for the great campaign which accompanied the early stages of the war. That even a totalitarian propaganda campaign has to affirm that it acts in the interest of objective truth, is revealed by the Nazi declarations of intention accompanying the inauguration of these broadcasts: "It is not our intention to try to put up a counterblast to these detestable hymns of radio hate. . . . The truth will be put against the lie, and that is far more effective than Yiddishry at international microphones. . . . Mr. Smith will learn to judge as between news which the English stations give him and the news offered him by Germany. We do not fear the results of the comparison. . . . Lies have short waves."[74]

At the same time, "monitoring" became a more widespread practice. Thus, France set up a center at Bizetre, with a foreign language staff and other necessary equipment. In this Germany had preceded France by several years.

Hostile Nazi propaganda against Poland had long been more undercover than propaganda against other countries. It was indeed realism on the part of Hitler to conclude, as early as 1934, a pact of nonaggression with the country against which the Republic had voiced the strongest and often quite justified grievances, since this not only worked to neutralize a stronger adversary during the period of relative German weak-

---

[73] Translation in Knop: *Beware of the English,* London, 1939, p. 154; cf. also p. 178.
[74] From "*Westdeutscher Beobachter,*" translation in Knop, *op. cit.,* p. 177.

ness, but also served propagandistically as eyewash for those who doubted Hitler's "peaceful intentions." On the part of Poland's leaders it was the worst kind of illusion, since her interests lay with collective security or strong alliances, but they were so blind that even at the time of Munich they lined up with Hitler, extracting a portion from the mutilated body of Czechoslovakia, only to lose it a year later together with their whole country. Poland is the outstanding example of how "nonhostile" totalitarian propaganda worked with as deadly a success as frankly "hostile" propaganda could ever expect to attain.

Although for these reasons "undermining" propaganda could not proceed as openly as it had in the cases of Austria and Czechoslovakia, it had not been lacking during the years of German-Polish friendship. It had in general two main directions: one, as usual, the German minority in Poland; the other, the members of various other national minorities comprised in the Polish state, in particular the Ukrainian peasants, oppressed and miserable under the oligarchic rule of Polish landowners. As long as there was enmity with Russia, this faction likewise formed a tool of interventionist policies against the Soviets, and when Ruthenians got autonomy within rump Czechoslovakia, the hopes of Ukrainian irredentists went high. As one of them remarked: "We don't need a war; all we need is plenty of radio propaganda, an irredentist campaign such as the world has never yet seen, then arms smuggling, a little help from Germany, and the Ukrainians everywhere will do the job themselves."[75] Actually, the turn of Nazi-Russian policies in 1939 prevented Hitler from using the Ukrainians openly or very actively as a lever against Poland, although broadcasts in the Ukrainian language were made at the height of the crisis.[76] Russian neutrality at that time was immeasurably more valuable to Hitler than Ukrainian unrest could be.

The Nazis, in spite of official friendship with Poland and an agreement to abstain from interference in its "internal affairs," succeeded in organizing the German minority in Poland as a Nazi spearhead in much the same way as "Germans abroad" in other countries. Although not the most useful instrument for such undercover activities, the radio was even here employed for various purposes. Thus "German" inhabitants of three lonely mountain villages in the Carpathians, thirty miles from the nearest railway station and far from

[75] Wiskemann: *Undeclared War*, London, 1939, pp. 227f.
[76] V. McKenzie, *op. cit.*, pp. 133f.

the main road or other German settlements, were discovered by Nazi propagandists, who frequently appeared in those distant hamlets with propaganda literature and advised the inhabitants to buy radio sets and to listen to German stations sending special programs to Germans in Poland.[77] When the crisis was on Germany came out into the open and sent direct appeals to the German minority, asking them to collect material and data on Polish "atrocities" and persecutions.

It would be tedious to describe in detail the 1939 anti-Polish campaign of propaganda and terror, since it is a mere repetition of those of 1938 and early 1939, with simply the names of Poland and Polish leaders taking the place, *mutatis mutandis*, of Austria and "Tschechei," Benes and Schuschnigg. Instead, a short outline of the chronological development of the press and radio campaign[78] may convey a general impression. It began suddenly on August 8, when a firm speech by Marshal Smigly-Rydz was seized upon as the occasion for an accusation of "Polish impudence" and "brazen provocation," and the Polish "chauvinists who now are whipping up the masses for a march on Berlin" were warned that they risked their own existence since "there is a limit to German patience." On the next day the campaign continued under such slogans as "Polish war hysteria," "aggressive megalomania born of weakness," "chauvinism which lusts for German soil," and ending up in a solemn "beware Polonia." It was on this day that all German movies were ordered to show the film on the "Invincible West Wall." During the next days the first but still rather mild and vague atrocity stories made their appearance, until on August 16 the campaign suddenly reached a new stage. Thus far it had been a question of certain definite problems and incidents (mainly in connection with Danzig), but now it was said that "the whole Polish question" had to be solved and thus compromise was no longer possible, "German honor" now being involved. During the following days the "barrage" grew more violent and emotional. Polish "atrocities" were now specified, and press and radio came back with reports on mass arrests of Germans who were tortured in jail, many others in desperate panic fleeing across the border, while at the same time British mediation offers were ridiculed as "tubercular coughs of senile sinners." Then stories were told of "bestial torture" of women, children and aged people by "Polish bandits" who have

---

[77] Wirth, "Germans in Poland," *Contemporary Review*, Vol. 156, 1939, pp. 353*f.*
[78] As revealed by reports of the *New York Times* of that period.

"even surpassed the bestial acts of the Benes system," all this mixed with "human interest" stories concerning these "refugees" from Poland. On the twenty-sixth, we hear for the first time of border incidents and "overt acts" of Polish aggression. In the following days until the beginning of war there was a profusion of atrocity stories, alleging such things as slaughter, mutilation and castration of Germans, together with continuing reports of frontier incidents provoked by Polish "insurrectionists."

This time, however, the radio war was not as one-sided as it had generally been. Not only did the Poles reply more vigorously than the Czechs had done a year before, but the Western powers also turned a barrage of radio propaganda on German listeners. The BBC campaign, directed by the new Information Department of the Foreign Office (the forerunner of the present Ministry of Information), not only sent out news and commentaries but also made direct appeals to the German people, such as one by the British Council of Labor to German workers.[79] Thus a battle of words in which both sides took part, preceded, and almost imperceptibly led over into, actual war.

The United States and International Radio Propaganda

In a history of radio in international politics up to the outbreak of the present war the United States deserves very little attention. This concluding section will be more concerned with the reasons why, throughout most of the period with which we have been dealing, this country failed to take part in what had become one of the foremost political activities of other powers. As has been shown in another section, the United States in the 'thirties had become one of the main "victims" of a totalitarian propaganda which was directed not only to its own territory proper but, above all, to a region where it had vital interests at stake, notably the other parts of this hemisphere. But while other powers concerned eventually went over to defense and even counterattack, the United States, if we except a slow and hesitant beginning at the very close of the period considered here, remained passive. This attitude cannot be ascribed solely to the general "isolationism" so characteristic of American foreign policy throughout this era. The reasons why a country which has been foremost in the technical and general evolution of radio, and also foremost in developing "advertising propaganda" into a fine

[79] *New York Herald Tribune*, July 2, 1939.

art, did not make use of this instrument even when national interests were at stake, are probably still more profound. This country, after the disillusionment of the World War, not only wanted to isolate itself so far as possible from "international relations" but wished to build up a "depoliticized" civilization of its own, based upon the spirit of individualistic enterprise—the "rugged individualism"—which had made this nation. Propaganda, in such a civilization, takes the form of business advertising and of cultural and social, or even internal political propaganda, but propaganda in the field of foreign relations requires a centralized direction and organization. This was alien not only to American ideology but also to the peculiar organization of radio as an individualistic enterprise based on private ownership, the characteristic feature of American broadcasting.

Thus it was a peculiar combination of circumstances which, until only recently, prevented American participation in the "radio war." This can best be made clear from the vicissitudes which marked the attempt to organize American defense against attacks upon her interests in Latin America. Prior to 1938 some of the larger broadcasting companies in this country had indeed developed programs directed by short wave to Latin America. These programs, however, had been purely "entertainment" or, at best "cultural," and also contained general economic and special business advertising, though not in the form of "sponsorship," which was forbidden by law. There was but little broadcasting in Spanish and Portuguese, no adaptation of programs to a foreign audience, no effort to have programs rebroadcast or to gain other channels of local distribution. There was no personnel with an intimate knowledge of foreign audiences and conditions, home programs simply being transcribed for short-wave transmission. The transmitters were so defective in power that reception was inferior to that of most European services. The lack of interest in political propaganda is revealed in a statement made at the time, that "the ultimate object of these radio broadcasting companies is to attempt to develop markets to a point where the same programs will have definite value to an advertiser."[80]

With the growth of anxiety and concern over increasing anti-American penetration of Latin America by foreign propaganda, a proposal

[80] On the early history of these broadcasts cf. Beals, *op. cit.,* pp. 288ff.; Inman, *op. cit.,* pp. 28ff.; Harris, *loc. cit.,* pp. 131ff.; and the material in *Hearings before a Subcommittee of the Committee of Interstate Commerce,* United States Senate, 75th Congress, third session, May 12, 18, 19, and 23, 1938, Washington, 1938, *passim.*

was made to counter these efforts by setting up a government short-wave station designed to deal exclusively with this situation. Parallel bills sponsoring such a station were introduced into Senate and House. The hearings before the Senate Committee set up to deal with the so-called Chavez Bill reveal with perfect clarity the reasons underlying the hostility to such enterprises. It was a combination of two main causes which killed the project: first, political isolationism, blind to any possible foreign threat to this country (said Senator Bone, Chairman of the Committee and in charge of those hearings: "I do not want to embarrass this nation in its international relationships; especially with my own isolationist views I do not think we ought to meddle too much with these international relationships. . . . God was good to this nation and put two great oceans between us and the people who might cause us trouble. . . ."[81]); second, the fear by business interests of "state interference" with what they considered their *domaine réservé*, comprising not only the radio companies themselves but business quite generally, which was afraid of setting a "precedent." The whole procedure of these hearings was apparently not a fair investigation into the facts but rather a "propagandistic" attempt to show that there was actually nothing to cause anxiety. Thus the persons testifying before the committee (most of them representatives of the big radio companies) were asked whether, from their own experience, they could confirm that hostile propaganda had occurred, of the kind mentioned in one rather sensational newspaper article which the chairman said he had just happened to read. Most of them denied such knowledge, and this was construed as evidence of the nonexistence of such propaganda! Those in charge of these investigations also completely failed to understand the nature of that bit of propaganda, the existence of which they could not deny. It was played down as ordinary "business propaganda," so much "ordinary Chamber-of-Commerce boosting," ignoring that in a regime subjecting everything, including economic matters, to politics, even business propaganda becomes "political." Such business propaganda was actually played down by dubious methods, as when German export statistics of 1936 were compared with those of 1913 instead of the years immediately preceding Nazism in order to prove that totalitarian propaganda had little effect on commercial relations with Latin America, or when measures of repression adopted by certain Latin American countries against Nazi-

81 *Hearings*, p. 156.

Fascist interference were referred to as evidence of the ineffectiveness of their propaganda efforts.

After having averted this "danger," however, the broadcasting companies, in view of public interest in the matter and probably responding to government pressure, decided to devote more attention to short-wave broadcasting, in particular to Latin America.[82] In 1938, new wavelengths were assigned to several stations and services over these wavelengths reorganized. Several companies created special "International Divisions" with foreign language departments and qualified personnel and began to develop special programs instead of merely sending network material. But these new programs were still "nonpolitical" except for general emphasis on "good-neighborliness" and similar policies; they avoided any polemics and, in particular, all anti-totalitarian propaganda or argumentation. With respect to foreign language news, a recent study has shown that even in the Spring of 1941 news to Latin America in the "totalitarian languages," in contrast with those in English, Spanish, and Portuguese, was neglected and left almost entirely to the respective totalitarian short-wave services.[83] On the other hand, special features such as the reading and answering of fan mail, the commemoration of national holidays and other special Latin American events now received attention, advance programs were sent out, and reception improved. Much criticism, however, was still leveled against the organization of these broadcasts. Thus the best programs originated at stations too weak to be heard clearly, or which could be received in certain parts of Latin America only, while technically the best equipped stations were those avowedly experimental ones operated by the great electrical companies, sending less elaborate and less well-designed programs with much general network material in the English language only.

American short-wave broadcasting to other than Latin American countries followed the same lines but developed even more slowly.[84] Prior to 1938 there were no regular programs at all. In 1938, some com-

[82] Good material on these later developments is to be found in a number of Princeton senior theses. Besides Harris, cf. J. L. Mohler: *Uncle Sam, Radio Propagandist?—A Study of American Shortwave Broadcasting to Latin America*, 1941; D. L. Mulford: *A Study in Shortwave Radio Propaganda*, 1940; G. B. McNeill: *El Amigo se hace Amigo*, 1940; cf. also Wellner, *loc. cit.*, p. 493.

[83] cf. Mohler, *loc. cit.*, p. 125.

[84] cf. *Hearings, passim*; theses quoted above; Church: "Short Waves and Propaganda," *Public Opinion Quarterly*, Vol. 3, 1939, pp. 217f.

panies, within their new International Divisions, established services in French, German, Italian and sometimes other languages destined for European listeners. But there was little adaptation to these audiences, and too much reliance on network material often sent at wrong or irregular hours, and whatever news and talks there were appeared for the most part in English only. Any definite plan to follow a consistent political line has been as much lacking here as in the case of Latin American programs. From time to time, however, "entertainment" was interrupted by foreign language transmissions of important political speeches by the President, the Secretary of State or other prominent persons, notably the transmission of President Roosevelt's "quarantine speech" (one of the earliest of such short-wave transmissions). This was considered as informative only, but as a matter of fact gained a much more political, in fact propagandistic, significance through the simple fact of the prevailing circumstances in the totalitarian countries, where a population cut off from information originating outside and deemed to be "unwholesome" is apt to be impressed in a highly political fashion by such so-called informative transmissions. Thus such transmissions can be said to have gained political importance, so to speak, in spite of the underlying theory and intent. Such broadcasts, during the time of mounting tension in Europe in 1939, became ever more frequent, and it is probable that already those directed to totalitarian countries in their languages became, at least "unofficially," conscious instruments of governmental propaganda efforts. Thus timidly and with hesitation, as if apprehensive whither such activities might eventually lead her, America has at last joined the efforts of those nations whose survival in their life-and-death struggle she is today bound to assure with all means at her disposal.

THE THEORY AND STRATEGY OF NAZI
SHORT-WAVE PROPAGANDA

By Philip E. Jacob

Dr. Jacob is at present a secretary of the American Friends Service Committee. He obtained his A.B. degree from Yale University, an M.A. degree from the University of Pennsylvania, and his Ph.D. degree from Princeton University in 1941. This study and the one entitled, "Atrocity Propaganda," are abridgments of substantial parts of his thesis submitted to the Department of Politics in partial fulfillment of the requirements for this degree of Doctor of Philosophy. During the summer of 1939 and the first weeks of the war he visited Germany and the Low Countries, returning to the United States in the fall of that year as an instructor in the Department of Politics at Princeton. During the year 1940-41 he served as a member of the research staff of the Princeton Listening Center, specializing in the field of German propaganda.

PART I. THE NATIONAL SOCIALIST THEORY
OF RADIO PROPAGANDA

A NOTE of unbounded belief in the power of Nazi propaganda runs through all the writings of National Socialist leaders on the subject. They frankly credit many of their victories both within and without Germany to the superiority of their propaganda technique. Supremely confident that they have accurately grasped the essential principles governing the use of the instrument, and skeptical that others can or will learn the art in time, they count on further victories to come.[1]

Genesis of the Nazi Theory of Propaganda

The Nazi tribute to propaganda stems directly from the now familiar rationalization of German defeat in the World War. Germans after the Armistice of 1918 attributed their country's startling collapse not to the failure of German arms but to Allied propaganda from without, abetted by "Marxist" propaganda from within, an attack to which the German character had proved particularly susceptible and against which German counter efforts were pitifully ineffective.[2]

Whatever its shortcomings from the point of view of historical fact, this thesis gained ready acceptance in Germany. In the years following the Armistice people were "predisposed to attach very great importance to propaganda" because during the war they had constantly been warned to "beware the noxious fumes of enemy propaganda."[3] Many found in the rationalization some measure of compensation for the numbing shock of the collapse. No doctrine "could have been more soothing to the national vanity of a people who had for two generations been taught, and had blindly believed, that its military leaders possessed the secret of perennial invincibility."[4] The military men, for their part, eager to exonerate themselves, seized upon the argument with especial alacrity. Even leaders of the Weimar Republic, according to some writers, accepted and helped promote the rationalization of German collapse which prompted Hitler to study and master the art of propaganda.[5]

---

[1] cf. Joseph Goebbels, *My Part in Germany's Fight*, pp. 250, 285; Wickham Steed, *The Fifth Arm*, p. 89; Herman Rauschning, *The Voice of Destruction*, p. 11.

[2] cf. A. J. Mackenzie, *Propaganda Boom*, pp. 14ff.

[3] Harold Lasswell, *Propaganda Technique in the World War*, p. 3.

[4] Steed, *op. cit.*, p. 53.

[5] *ibid.*, pp. 79, 83.

The rationalization of defeat provided a powerful stimulus to the study of propaganda technique. "Patriotic Germans," reported Lasswell in 1925, "are anxious to understand the nature of the noncoercive weapon which was wielded so successfully to their discomfiture in wartime and there is today a more luxurious flowering of treatises upon international propaganda . . . in Germany than anywhere else."[6]

Two distinct schools of theorists emerged from this inquiry, both of which have taken a hand in shaping the prevailing concept of propaganda in Germany. A group of military experts, in the tradition of Clausewitz, Bismarck, Ludendorff, and the total war strategists, have analyzed the particular use of propaganda in military conflict. The Nazi politicians, whose unquestioned mentor is Hitler himself, evolved their conception of propaganda primarily with reference to the winning and consolidation of political power. The two approaches are by no means contradictory. Rather they complement each other, each focusing its attention upon a different problem and area of application. Hitler indeed seems to fall in both groups. In the days of *Mein Kampf,* he was primarily concerned with the application of propaganda to the political struggle. In recent years, according to some reports, he has busied himself more especially with the military aspect of propaganda.[7]

The character of Hitler's acknowledgments indicates that he frequently failed to assess the true nature of his sources. For instance, his estimate of Allied propaganda needs considerable modification in the light of impartial postwar studies. He greatly exaggerated its achievements and attributed to it principles and policies in which he himself believed but which actually were not followed by the Allies. In probing Hitler's theory of propaganda, however, it is not the actual features of his models, but what he thought they were, which counts. His sources are significant only for the impressions which he derived from them. Having decided that certain propagandists were effective, he studied them until he discovered to his own satisfaction the secrets of their success. On the basis of his conclusions he then constructed and buttressed his theory of propaganda.

[6] Lasswell, *op. cit.,* p. 3. See especially Committee for National Morale, "German Psychological Warfare." 1941.

[7] cf. Rauschning, *op. cit.,* Chap. 1; Otto Tolischus, *They Wanted War*; Edmond Taylor, *The Strategy of Terror.*

The Nature and Functions of Propaganda

The Nazis conceive of propaganda as the art of influencing mass opinion by means of suggestion. "Understanding the great masses' world of ideas and feelings," says Hitler of propaganda, it "finds, by a correct psychological form, the way to the attention and further to the heart of the great masses."[8] It is the process of molding the state of the public mind, which, in the Nazi view, is the mind of the "masses." Propaganda persuades rather than constrains, though, as we shall see, the Nazis consider that physical force can sometimes be used as a technique of suggestion as well as an instrument of constraint.

Three functions of opinion management have been distinguished by the Nazis. Strictly speaking, they apply the term "propaganda" only to one of them. This is the "conquest of the masses" by the propagandist for the "idea" which he is propagating. The task of propaganda in this sense is to spread conviction, win support, attract followers and push them toward action. By propaganda, an idea which one day is unpopular and not recognized or understood by the masses, the next day starts off on a new wave of popularity, declares Goebbels. It transforms the masses' view of life and thus accomplishes an ideological revolution.[9]

The second function assigned to the opinion managers is the "enlightenment" (Aufklärung) of the masses. Its object is to keep the faith burning brightly among the converted, to deepen their conviction, understanding and loyalty, and to ward off heretical notions.

Third, opinion management can seek to paralyze organized opposition to the "idea." Here, its task is not to arouse masses to action, but to destroy the opponent's will-to-resist and produce a state of passivity and apathy. It concentrates on undermining faith, not on building it up. In pursuing the first function, propaganda is evangelistic; in the second, protective and doctrinaire; in the third, disintegrative.

The Nazis draw virtually no line between the peacetime use of propaganda and its wartime functions. They accept Clausewitz's definition of war as the extension of policy and go one step further by turning the definition around—peace is merely a period in which warfare is carried on without the use of military weapons. Good propaganda therefore

[8] Adolf Hitler, *Mein Kampf* (Reynal & Hitchcock trans.), p. 233.
[9] Joseph Goebbels, quoted by Franz Six, *Die politische Propaganda der NSDAP im Kampf um die Macht*, p. 66; cf. also Hitler, *op. cit.*, p. 852.

"should begin in peace-time and operate in such a way that the country reaps its fruits as soon as war is declared. . . . War-time propaganda ought to be merely the more concentrated, and, of course, more vigorous continuation of peace-time propaganda."[10]

In wartime the "conquest of the masses" proceeds in neutral countries, among allies and possibly in the enemy countries as well in order to widen the basis of sympathy and cooperation. In particular, propaganda of the evangelistic type must be used both on the home front and in the army to rally the fullest measure of enthusiasm for the war effort. The "idea" must be made to strike home with such force as to challenge the most heroic sacrifice, and forge the utmost unity of purpose. Enlightenment and censorship also have their place—at home and among neutrals whose support is solicited. While propaganda seeks to stir people to peaks of enthusiasm and devotion, the steady quiet task of maintaining their morale in the face of the strain and disappointments of war must be performed by "enlightenment." News of the war needs to be filtered and interpreted, the ultimate and immediate aims of the war must be constantly clarified, each germ of doubt or hesitation has to be discovered and rooted out, the necessity of every sacrifice must be satisfactorily explained. Finally the strategy of disintegration is applied to the enemy —both to his army and his people. "Artillery preparation before an attack as during the World War will be replaced in the future war by the psychological dislocation of the adversary through revolutionary propaganda," Hitler is alleged to have predicted.[11]

Principles of Mass Suggestion

The masses, believe the Nazis, are primitive and feminine, motivated by feeling and instinct.[12] Mass behavior, however, is not haphazard and erratic, for instincts operate with all the force of laws. These laws are everywhere the same, irrespective of nationality, political system, social conditions or epoch. Even racial differences, so fundamental in Nazi philosophy, do not modify the psychological characteristics attributed to men in the mass.[13] This assumption, that all "masses" are alike, gives the Nazis supreme confidence that their theory of propaganda, having worked in Germany, will work everywhere, at any time and under any conditions.

10 Ewald Banse, *Germany Prepares for War*, p. 75.
11 Rauschning, quoted by Taylor, *op. cit.*, p. 71.   12 Hitler, *op. cit.*, p. 237.
13 Rauschning, *op. cit.*, p. 210.

The Nazis have understood that the "masses" cannot be dominated by force alone. A few obstinate intellectuals may easily be crushed by violence. The masses can never be crushed. They can only be led. Mere force, furthermore, cannot counteract active propaganda. "As propaganda, if applied wisely, influences the will of man, it is more secretive, more forceful, and deeper in its effect than the open force of suppression."[14]

The irrational masses are, of course, easily suggestible. Anything achieved with intellectuals by means of a reasonable explanation may be erased by an opposite explanation. "But what you tell the people in the mass, in a receptive state of fanatic devotion, will remain like words received under an hypnotic influence, ineradicable, and impervious to every reasonable explanation."[15] Here is the leader's opportunity, for endowed with exceptional rational powers, he can understand the laws of mass behavior and by controlling the vast power latent in the masses, he can rule.

The Appeal to Feeling

The fundamental principle of Nazi propaganda is that "suggestion can only be effective in a state of high emotion."[16] The propagandist must therefore appeal to human irrationality—to the longings, drives, impulses, demands, strivings of his audience—and steer clear of intellectual ballast. "The more primitive the methods of propaganda the more intense will be the reaction of the masses which feel and react primitively."[17]

The most significant aspect of man' irrational nature is his longing for faith. It is belief that moves men's souls, say the Nazis, rather than the cool analysis of the mind. "Our people long for an inner meaning of their political life, they long for a political confession of faith and they are ready to subscribe to one eagerly," declared the Nazi propaganda leader Hadamovsky.[18] The "spiritual content" of the propaganda is consequently the fundamental factor in its success. The propagandist's most telling weapon is a challenging idea or "view of life."

But the idea must also conscript in its service the rational powers of man. "The mind . . . must be a critic of faith and strength in order

[14] Eugen Hadamovsky, *Propaganda und Nationale Macht*, p. 16.
[15] Hitler, quoted by Rauschning, *op. cit.*, p. 212.   [16] Hadamovsky, *op. cit.*, p. 18.
[17] Joachim Weinbrenner, in *Handbuch des Deutschen Rundfunks*, 1939-40.
[18] Hadamovsky, *op. cit.*, p. 132.

to produce increasingly convincing formulations." The basic appeal of the idea should be irrational. But the intellect should be marshalled to guide its development and application.[19]

The propagandist need not worry about his idea being too radical and driving people away. The more revolutionary, the more striking the propaganda, the more vigorous the movement will become. Radical and inciting propaganda, especially at the inception of a movement, will frighten off weaklings and irresolute characters and prevent the strength of the first nucleus of the organization from becoming diluted. At the same time, even at the beginning, it will attract attention and tacit agreement among large numbers who fear to come out publicly in its support, but are impressed by a powerful, dynamic movement.[20]

An essential prerequisite of success for propaganda, say the Nazis, is absolute belief in and devotion to the cause on the part of the leaders. "Only a storm of burning passion can turn people's destinies, but only he who harbors passion in himself can arouse passion," declared Hitler.[21]

Simplicity and the Slogan

In presenting an "idea" to the masses the propagandist must make his argument simple, clear and uncomplicated so that it may be easily understood by the untrained mind. "All effective propaganda has to limit itself only to a very few points and to use them like slogans until even the very last man is able to imagine what is intended by such a word."[22] Everything which is not relevant to the issue at hand and which might confuse the chief point of the propagandist must be sloughed off.

The necessity for extreme simplicity and vividness of presentation makes slogans or "fighting words" of crucial importance. The great and overwhelming world view must be summed up and crystallized in a few powerful words. "The fighting slogan of a movement has always and at all times been its most successful propaganda," asserts Hadamovsky.[23]

The Authority of Fanaticism

To avoid confusion, the Nazis rule out "objectivity"—the discussion of any point of view but that of the propagandist. Propaganda must be dogmatic, one-sided, intolerant. "As soon as by one's own propaganda

[19] ibid., pp. 132-4.
[21] ibid., p. 137.
[23] Hadamovsky, op. cit., p. 11.

[20] Hitler, op. cit., p. 856.
[22] ibid., p. 234.

even a glimpse of right on the other side is admitted, the cause for doubting one's own right is laid," says Hitler.[24] The program of a movement
must be given the absolute authority which attaches to an unalterable
creed. The basis of faith should be fixed, though the form of its interpretation and application may vary.

The propagandist should simplify not only the positive ideas for
which he is seeking allegiance, but the objects he is attacking as well. A
cardinal principle of Nazi propaganda technique is to unify the objects
of hate. The opposition, though it may take many forms, must appear
as one and the same enemy. Having set forth one scapegoat for discontent all the others must in some way be related to it.[25]

The Principle of Repetition

Having set forth a few basic issues simply, it is necessary to drive them
home by constant repetition. By sheer bulk of references, the idea will
be kept in general circulation until it is accepted without thinking and
even without awareness of its original source. In the end, reiteration and
concentration of attention will build up tradition and accompanying
symbolism which will solidify the idea in the audience's mind. "Per-
sistency, as in so many other things in this world, is the first and the
most important condition for success."[26]

But repetition does not mean dull uniformity. The essential issues, the
basic slogans must be repeated, but the manner of presentation should
vary. If this is done, repetition will not bore the public.

The Theory of the Lie

Much has been made of the Nazi "theory of the lie" in discussions of
Nazi propaganda. Some go so far as to maintain that the principle of
"the bigger the lie, the more easily it is believed" forms the basis of all
Nazi propaganda technique. Without passing any judgment on the
Nazi practice of propaganda, it does seem that, so far as the theory is
concerned, this point has been misconstrued and Hitler's remarks on
the subject usually taken out of context.

The lie theory, rather than an essential principle in the Nazi theory
of propaganda, is the theory of propaganda which Hitler attributes to
the Jews. It is a direct corollary of his blanket condemnation of the Jews

[24] Hitler, op. cit., pp. 236ff.; cf. also pp. 467 and 485, and Rauschning, op. cit., p. 239.
[25] cf. W. A. Sinclair, The Voice of the Nazi, p. 33.   [26] Hitler, op. cit., pp. 238ff.

as inveterate liars on the one hand, and his charge that they had successfully weaseled their way into key positions of power and influence.
Similarly, when connected with the discussion of Allied propaganda in
the World War, the lie theory sought to rationalize the success of a
propaganda campaign which spread nothing but unadulterated falsehoods, according to the German view. It explained how easily the masses
could be misled.[27]

The fact of the matter is that truth does not figure in the Nazi theory
of propaganda. All the Nazis say in essence is that lies, if they are big
enough, will be believed. The question of whether they should be used
is not one of propaganda policy, but of the ends chosen, and the means
available. The problem of the propagandist is to establish belief, to convince the masses, irrespective of the validity of his argument. Scheid
well sums up the Nazi theory on this point when he says: "Good propaganda does not have to lie, it ought not to lie. . . . It is an error to think
that a people cannot bear the truth. . . . It is sufficient to present the
truth in a form which is accessible to it."[28]

The Spirit of Mastery

The use of force is a vital element in the Nazi theory of propaganda.
The masses are impressed by strength, they enjoy conflict. The process
of mass suggestion is at bottom a conflict of will between the propagandist and his audience. If the propagandist is to succeed in imposing
his will as the stronger of the two, he must make his audience continually aware of his determination and the dynamic power of his will.
"Propaganda and force are never absolute antitheses," maintains Hadamovsky. "Between them are means of every degree to exert influence
from gentle persuasion to wild mass propaganda; from the loose organization of recruits to the creation of state or semi-state institutions;
from individual to mass terror."[29]

The propagandist must constantly attack. Indeed he should seek conflict, for where there is conflict interest is aroused, and an opportunity
presented to demonstrate strength and power. The policy of frontal attack should be pursued even against a hostile public opinion when one's
point of view is totally unpopular. Masterfulness should be carried over
into the conduct of public meetings. Never should one rely upon police

[27] cf. *ibid.*, p. 313. [28] Othon Scheid, *L'esprit du Troisième Reich*, p. 238.
[29] Hadamovsky, *op. cit.*, p. 19.

protection. This "discredits the sponsors in the eyes of the great masses." Instead, the meetings should be protected first by an "energetic and psychologically correct management of the meeting" and second by a tightly organized, highly disciplined "supervision service." Rough, coarse, harsh language conveys the impression of forcefulness, as does ridicule.[30]

The spectacle of cruelty and brutality also finds a place in Nazi propaganda theory. Too much frightfulness produces apathy. But the right dose of terrorism elicits respect. "The people need wholesome fear. . . . They want someone to frighten them and make them shudderingly submissive."[31] The application of force against a minority, furthermore, gives vicarious expression to the verbal concentration of hate on the opponent. It visibly reinforces the impression of the propagandist's superiority and draws the audience into the circle of the superior as against the persecuted ones.

The Power of the Spoken Word

While the Nazis have made it a point to neglect none of the media of communication in their propaganda efforts, they have unhesitatingly indicated which they consider the most significant and influential in the process of mass suggestion. They continually stress the importance of the spoken word. A speaker can much more easily touch the emotions than a journalist or pamphleteer. At a mass meeting he confronts his audience face-to-face. If he errs he "has always before him the living correction." He knows immediately if his appeal fails to catch fire and can change his approach. In a mass meeting, furthermore, an individual finds himself in the midst of a vast community, and loses his sense of loneliness and powerlessness. The approval of the crowd impresses upon his mind the rightness of the doctrine he hears preached. The mass meeting unites and creates *esprit de corps*. The process of thought is diminished as each person merges his individuality in the "mass."

The Function of Radio in the National Socialist State

Their theory of propaganda led the National Socialists to quick appreciation of the unique political potentialities of radio—an instrument made to order for the wholesale dissemination of ideas to the masses by

[30] cf. Hitler, *op. cit.*, pp. 468, 697, 698, 725; also Hadamovsky, *op. cit.*, p. 18.
[31] Rauschning, *op. cit.*, pp. 82ff.

means of the spoken word. By radio, the voice of the propagandist could reach out beyond the limits of the most gigantic mass meeting and touch people in their homes, in their places of work and on the street corner. "Radio," asserted Dressler-Andress, an important Nazi radio leader, "has the advantage over all other means of forming public opinion through its ability directly to impress the whole of the people."[32]

To heighten the Nazis' interest in radio, their arch-enemies presented before their eyes a case study in the use of that instrument for political purposes. The international broadcasts of the Soviet Union and the organization of a widespread and powerful listeners' movement by the Communists in Germany deeply impressed the Nazi propagandists. Though, as usual, they probably exaggerated the impact of this propaganda, the fact that their chief competitors in the fight for mass support saw in radio a means of agitating and forging international solidarity among workers, convinced the Nazis more strongly than ever of its political importance.[33]

Nazi consideration of the function of radio was conditioned by the fact that they had little opportunity to exploit the instrument before their capture of the reins of government. Whereas they developed their theory of propaganda primarily in relation to their struggle for power as an opposition political party, their views on radio applied almost exclusively to its use by a totalitarian state.

The "Political Radio"

The Nazi conception is of a purely political radio completely controlled by the state and serving only state purposes. "Genuine sincere radio," they say, "is simply propaganda. Radio is the representative of propaganda if we understand this word in its full meaning: propaganda means spreading, divulging, assisting, convincing others of ideas and cognitions, it means fighting on the battlefields of the mind, it means to make things fertile, to pass them on to another generation, to destroy, to weed out and annihilate, to build and to abolish."[34]

Under their direction, the National Socialist authorities proudly announce, "radio has been thoroughly politicized and has become the voice

[32] Horst Dressler-Andress, "German Broadcasting," *The Annals of the American Academy of Political and Social Science*, January 1935, p. 62.

[33] cf. Hadamovsky, *op. cit.*, pp. 78*ff*.

[34] Adolf Raskin, "Dramaturgy of Propaganda," *Handbuch der Deutschen Rundfunks*, 1939-40.

of the nation."[35] "The German radio," declares Hans Kriegler, president of the National Radio Chamber, "is a manifestation of the total creative forces of National Socialism."[36] It is, says another Nazi radio leader, "the most modern, the strongest, and the most revolutionary weapon which we possess in the battle against an old, extinct world and in the battle for a new Third Reich. . . . It is the shock troop . . . of the National Socialist world outlook."[37]

Though the total function of radio is political in the sense that it must in every respect serve the national interest, the Nazis draw a distinction for practical purposes between its specifically political, i.e. ideological and governmental tasks, and its broader cultural goals. As a "bearer of culture" radio unfolds the national heritage to the German people and induces them to breathe deeply of the "spirit" therein. In this capacity it serves the further purpose of organizing and directing the leisure time of the people in line with the spirit and ends of the nation. As a strictly "propaganda instrument," radio has to imbue the German people at home and abroad with the National Socialist ideology, act as a link between the political leadership and the people, bind the national community together in times of crisis, counteract anti-Nazi propaganda, and promote friendship and "understanding" for Germany among foreign nations.[38]

The Political Tasks of Domestic Broadcasting

The immediate task of the radio after the National Socialists took it over, was the "creation of a unified political will." The unanimous and wholehearted support of the German people had to be won for Adolf Hitler.[39] Radio was "a means by which to create *psychological infection*" —the infection of the nation with the National Socialist ideology. "Well prepared political broadcasts," felt the Nazis, "can produce such a strong mental current that a community, a people and even groups of peoples may be induced to common action."[40] "The political use of the radio

[35] E. Kurt Fischer, "The German Radio's Broadcasts for the People at Home," *Handbuch des Deutschen Rundfunks*, 1939-40.

[36] Hans Kriegler, "The German Radio—Objectives and Organization," *Handbuch des Deutschen Rundfunks*, 1938-39.

[37] Hadamovsky, *Der Rundfunk im Dienste der Volksführung*, pp. 13, 19.

[38] cf. Joachim Weinbrenner, "The Elements of Broadcasting," *Handbuch des Deutschen Rundfunks*, 1939-40.

[39] Dressler-Andress, *op. cit.*, p. 64.

[40] Weinbrenner, "Radio Knows No Boundaries," *Handbuch des Deutschen Rundfunks*, 1938-39.

made masses out of individuals and a national community out of the mass."[41]

Secondly, radio is conceived by the National Socialists as "a living bridge" between the leader and his people.[42] Hitler "made radio what it is today, the mouthpiece of a determined leadership. He made radio the constant and direct link joining leadership and people."[43] Radio "serves the Government in a systematic campaign of explaining its plans and purposes, in the form of a direct talk by the Leader to every single member of the Nation." It "enables the Government to report at any time and in a direct way on its activities and its measures."[44] In addition the people become familiar with their leaders and learn to trust them because they feel they know them personally. The importance of this function of radio, says Dressler-Andress, was amply confirmed by the enthusiastic approval given the *Fuehrer* in the plebiscite on Germany's withdrawal from the League, November 12, 1933, following his appeal from the Siemens factory two days before. "How could the German people have become aware of the personality of their leader, of his intense and sincere devotion to the service of the commonweal, if there had been no radio to give them this direct communication of his personality?"[45]

Radio becomes of crucial significance in moments of crisis. It enables "all Germans in decisive hours to unite in a solid community of listeners."[46] The support of the people is rallied behind the government, while the sinews of morale are strengthened by judicious appeals from the national leaders, sent by radio into every home and place of work.

The Political Tasks of International Broadcasting

The Nazis have divined both dangerous and "constructive" implications in the fact that "radio does not recognize the frontiers created by Nature or by man" and "slips into the territory of other peoples."[47] "For the first time in history radio affords the opportunity of influencing huge nations through daily and hourly impressions from outside."[48] If such

[41] *idem*, "The Elements of Broadcasting."
[42] Goebbels, "Geleitwort," *Rundfunk im Aufbruch*, p. 9.
[43] Heinrich Glasmeier, "The Reorganization of the German Radio," *Handbuch des Deutschen Rundfunks*, 1939-40.
[44] Dressler-Andres, *op. cit.*, p. 63.   [45] *ibid.*, p. 62.
[46] *ibid.*, p. 63.
[47] *idem*, quoted by Thomas Grandin, *The Political Use of the Radio*, p. 48.
[48] Hadamovsky, *op. cit.*, p. 60.

influence is exerted on Germany by other countries, especially by Russia, the Nazis consider it pernicious interference in their internal affairs and vehemently oppose it. On the other hand, they have from the beginning justified foreign broadcasts by the German radio over long and medium wave to European countries and by short wave to overseas audiences. As a matter of fact, they severely criticized the pre-Nazi radio administration for not adequately developing this phase of German broadcasting.

It is particularly necessary to place the stamp of nationality on international broadcasts, say the Nazi radio leaders, when, as in Germany's case, the primary aim is to revive and strengthen the cultural, political and "spiritual" ties between nationals living abroad and the homeland. "Our broadcasts are addressed to all people who believe in the German language and German culture wherever they may live," states Kriegler openly. They are in response to a great longing for "spiritual and national self-defense" on the part of "racial comrades" who are separated from the fatherland. "Our broadcasters have always realized that they should adapt their programs to the spiritual needs of Germans abroad, thus assisting them in their fight for the maintenance of their national character by furnishing them with spiritual weapons."[49] Specifically, they need, "first, information, then German music and recreation, and finally they must feel themselves united proudly with the Fatherland in its actions, purposes and accomplishments."[50] Germans should also be able to hear the mother tongue regularly no matter what part of the world they live in. Above all, radio must convey to them an understanding of the "revolutionary renewal" of the German spirit which flows from National Socialism and lead them to embrace the Nazi ideology with fervor.

Particularly important was radio's contribution to the "spiritual preparation" of the German territories before they rejoined the Reich. "When our co-nationals returned to the Reich from the formerly separated areas they confirmed the importance of our radio policy," says Kriegler. Thanks to the German broadcasts they had been able to learn the truth about National Socialist Germany despite the lies told by the broadcasting stations of the countries in which they lived, sta-

---

[49] Hans Kriegler, "Radio's Contribution to the Establishment of Greater Germany," *Handbuch des Deutschen Rundfunks*, 1939-40.
[50] Herbert Schroeder, quoted by Grandin, *op. cit.*, p. 48.

tions "entirely under the influence of Free Masons, clergymen or Marxists." Their loyalty to the Reich remained unimpaired.[51]

The National Socialist radio not only speaks to Germans at home and abroad, but represents the German nation before the whole world. In this capacity, its purpose, say the Nazis, is to make Germany understood abroad and to counteract anti-German propaganda. In its foreign broadcasts, the Nazi radio seeks to correct the prevalent false impression of the Reich and to answer "the malicious attacks of the Jewish democratic world" which continue to stir hatred and even war hysteria against Germany. The broadcasts tell "of this new Germany of ours, its work and its plans. . . . However, we never made the mistake of offering National Socialist ideology to other peoples. It was on the contrary stressed by us constantly that National Socialism just like Fascism is no export article. . . . Our greatest political goal has always been to spread the truth about our fatherland and to make others see the difference: over there blissful Jewish democracy, desirous to burn people holding different political views, alive with medieval intolerance, and here a people who want nothing but to work and erect its house according to its own taste."[52]

Although Germany initiated foreign broadcasts purely in "self-defense" against the "hatred campaigns and warmongering attempts" of her enemies, and in the interest of truth and peace, Fritsche is frank to admit that this did not impose impartiality. "No one must complain that today we no longer go on telling the world merely about the work in our country but that we express frankly our opinion on political events. Even now we refuse to send purely polemic broadcasts such as the English and the French have adopted in their programs following the Communist pattern. We do not want to produce explosions in foreign countries through shortwave broadcasts. But we cannot miss the fact that there is plenty of explosive material in foreign countries. And whenever we have to uncover a lie we no longer restrict ourselves to the simple statement of the truth but we try to tell the world who invented the lie, why he did it and whom the liar wanted to deceive besides us."[53]

The specific functions outlined for short-wave broadcasting are merely

[51] Kriegler, *op. cit.*

[52] Hans Fritsche, "Foreign Languages and the Radio," *Handbuch des Deutschen Rundfunks,* 1939-40.

[53] *ibid.*

the functions of international broadcasting applied to overseas audiences: "1. To organize the widespread German communities in the continents of America, Africa, Asia and Australia and to incorporate them into the newly organized national community at home; 2. To influence the overseas countries as a whole with the objective of creating understanding for the new German Reich."[54] The short-wave transmission was created to "demonstrate the will and achievements of National Socialism beyond the German frontiers to the whole world" and to carry "a piece of the German soul and of German thought to all those who follow their professions and duties outside of the boundaries of their homeland. . . . The radio became the great awakener of the mother tongue, in addition to its use as a medium for news and the messenger of the political and cultural life of the homeland."[55]

The desire to forge contacts with people of German descent living abroad seems to have been the major factor behind the inauguration of the North American Service, the first regular "zoned" schedule of the German short-wave radio broadcasting. Schroeder, former director of German short-wave broadcasting, states that this action was taken because North America contained the greatest number of people of German descent in overseas countries.[56]

Broadcasting Principles of the Political Radio

That several qualities distinguish radio from other channels of communication is recognized by the Nazis. Schroeder lists four. First "it speaks to everybody personally, addresses him directly and reaches him in his most private surroundings, in his own home." Second, it makes use of the spoken word, whose "efficiency . . . is greater than that of the written word. It is more immediate, striking, primitive and more comprehensive." Third, a broadcast can accompany an event without a time lag. "It is not a report after the event, but an immediate, simultaneous experience." Fourth, the radio is not restricted as to audience. It "knows no human limits. . . . It speaks to everybody and influences everybody as individuals, groups or masses."[57] The Nazi principles of broadcasting endeavor to harness these qualities to the functions of the political radio.

[54] Kurt von Boeckmann, "German World-Wide Broadcasts on Short-Wave," *Handbuch des Deutschen Rundfunks*, 1939-40; cf. also Schroeder, *op. cit.*, pp. 19ff.

[55] Dressler-Andress, *Die Reichsrundfunkkammer*, p. 13.

[56] Schroeder, *op. cit.*, pp. 73ff. Schroeder estimates a total of 10,000,000 to 12,000,000 "overseas Germans," 8,500,000 of whom he places in North America, 1,000,000 in South America.

[57] *ibid.*, pp. 19ff.

Generalization and Diversification

The radio program must make a general appeal to everyone, say the German broadcasting directors, irrespective of occupation, nationality, or cultural and intellectual level. The level of the program, therefore, should *not* be geared to the lowest grade of intelligence in contrast to the general Nazi injunction for propaganda. Rather it should approximate a golden mean, being neither too low nor too high. It must appeal to the sophisticated and also be understood by the average person.[58]

Thus the sharp dichotomy between masses and sophisticates, so fundamental to Nazi propaganda theory, is virtually wiped out for radio. Radio, as an instrument of the state, must consider the *whole* people as its audience. Radio "must be shared by *all* the people so as to help preserve the interests of *all* people." [Author's italics] Political broadcasts, as well as other parts of the program, must be examined to see if the occasion interests the entire public.[59]

Although the radio program taken as a whole should have general appeal, the schedule must also be diversified to meet the tastes and interests of particular groups and sections of the audience.[60] Directional antennae have made the diversification of the short-wave schedule especially feasible. Broadcasts "beamed" to different zones, or areas of the world, can easily "take into consideration local demands in regard to the time schedule and the composition of the programs."[61]

The German short-wave radio has differentiated seven program zones. Each "has its special characteristics and needs to be dealt with individually." North America is "large, highly civilized, and radio-satiated." Schroeder notes "its hurry, its riches, optimism, hard realism, its belief in progress and its other superstitions." Latin America, though geographically connected with the northern continent, "forms a world by itself." "It is ruled by tradition and formalities." Its small, but highly educated upperclass has higher cultural ambitions than North America, which is "rather primitive."[62]

The programs for the different zones vary both in language and content. The native language of the audience is used in news bulletins and talks. The content of the news bulletins since the start of the war has

---

[58] Goebbels, "Die Aufgaben des Rundfunks," *Archiv für Funkrecht*, September 1936, p. 297.
[59] Harry Teichert, "Political Broadcasts," *Handbuch des Deutschen Rundfunks*, 1939-40.
[60] Goebbels, *op. cit.*, p. 297.   [61] Von Boeckmann, *op. cit.*
[62] Schroeder, *op. cit.*, p. 112.

been diversified, though Grandin reported that as of 1939, "the broadcasts from Zeesen usually give a single authorized version of events to all continents and listeners."[63] Feature programs exhibit the most variety. The National Socialist short-wave radio has carried diversification to the point of planning special programs for each of the forty-eight states in the United States and for individual cities, universities, schools and other groups.[64] It is hoped, for instance, to catch the fancy of residents in Alabama with a weekly broadcast, mainly music, entitled "I Come from Alabama wid my Banjo on my Knee." Musical programs have been dedicated to listeners in Cincinnati and Hawaii. A few days after the outbreak of the war the German radio honored Amherst College and the state of Massachusetts with a forty-five-minute program.[65]

A further distinction is made between programs designed for foreign listeners and for persons of German descent within the respective zones. To "Germans Abroad" go German language news bulletins, programs of German music and art, a series of broadcasts on different features of the new Germany, programs commemorating Nazi holidays, direct "reportage" of great political events and demonstrations, programs in dialect referring to the villages and provinces in Germany whence the listeners originally came, "fairy-tale hours" for the children, broadcasts for sailors and youth groups, and "real fresh humor" instead of the "stupid jokes" of American programs.[66] This material apparently resembles more closely the domestic programs than those circulated in foreign languages. The news comments of Hans Fritsche on the North American Service, for example, are actually broadcast internally, then rebroadcast externally.

Entertainment

Five constituent elements make up the German radio schedule: entertainment, culture, reportage, talks and news. Of these, entertainment is the foundation of the program, despite the fact that the function of radio in the National Socialist State is the promotion of cultural and political objectives. Year by year the proportion of time devoted to musical entertainment has increased until by 1939, 70 per cent of the total schedule was musical.[67] Light music and entertainment serve as the bait of the

[63] Grandin, *op. cit.*, p. 30.   [64] Schroeder, *op. cit.*, p. 120.
[65] Files of the Columbia Broadcasting System Short-Wave Listening Post.
[66] Schroeder, *op. cit.*, pp. 117ff.
[67] The composition of the radio schedule for 1935 is given in Arno Huth, *La Radiodiffusion;*

political radio. They entice the audience and induce it to listen to political and heavy cultural programs. Only after music has first brought the listener to the loudspeaker and caused him to relax, can the radio guide him to a "higher" level. A program solely of political speeches cannot serve the Nazi cause in the right way because the listener "fatigued by his effort of attention would simply switch off." Furthermore, if the German radio failed to entertain, it would also drive its audience to foreign stations, no matter how thrilling the political speeches nor how fine the cultural programs.[68]

According to the directions of Dr. Goebbels the entertainment program of the German radio should be "light but not shallow," a program that pleases the nonintellectual simple man but at the same time has something to offer the artistic and more sophisticated listener. "Therefore no more of these over-intelligent introductions which made a man feel that these works of music are such mysteriously scientific things that one has to be a graduate of at least two faculties in order to understand them."[69]

Culture

Long before the National Socialists took control, cultural broadcasts had established themselves as one of the outstanding features of the German radio program. Transmissions of great music, both classical and modern, including the festivals at Bayreuth, Munich, Dresden and Berlin, as well as concert series of the first order, achieved international renown. Educational programs and regular courses of instruction were inserted in the radio schedule. Readings of fine literature took an important place.[70]

Puissance Mondiale, p. 132; for 1936-37 and 1937-38 in Kriegler, "Der Nationalsozialistische Volks-Rundfunk an der Jahreswende," *Rundfunkarchiv*, January 1939, p. 1; for 1938-39 in *Rundfunkarchiv*, August-September 1939, p. 357.

	1935	1936-37	1937-38	1938-39
Music	61.6%	67.6%	69.7%	69.4%
Literature	4.7	4.0	3.8	3.6
Talks	8.5	7.1	5.9	4.7
Reportage	4.7	5.6	6.0	6.8
News	11.8	8.5	8.7	9.9
Misc.	8.7	7.2	5.9	.5.6

The figures given are per cent of broadcasting time.

[68] Hadamovsky, *Dein Rundfunk*, pp. 50ff.; idem, *Rundfunk im Dienste* . . . , p. 22.

[69] Quoted by Hans Otto Fricke, "The Radio is There for Everybody," *Handbuch des Deutschen Rundfunks*, 1938-39.

[70] Huth, *op. cit.*, p. 132.

During the first year of their administration the Nazis admittedly neglected the cultural side of radio, in favor of political propaganda. By 1935 they claimed to have retrieved the balance.

We have seen, however, that in the Nazi view, culture bears a definite relation to politics. Consequently, the content of the cultural broadcasts is quite restricted. Musical and artistic programs now presented over the German radio are deliberately planned as a means of fostering the German spirit and therefore one can expect to hear only true "Aryan" compositions. Education in Nazi ideology means education for such groups as the Hitler Youth and the Labor Front.

Perhaps because of this self-imposed limitation, the German radio leaders by 1938 admitted they were hard pressed in the production of cultural broadcasts. "The creative power of the German people is not unlimited. . . . Besides, whether we wish it or not, artistic achievements bear a certain ratio to financial means." Furthermore "a theater may play a certain performance for a week, a month or a year. The radio listeners expect something new every night or almost every night. They expect a different program in the morning, another at noon, in the afternoon and at night." "This tremendous demand for artistic and spiritual production," asserts Hadamovsky, "prompts us to follow either of two courses: either complete mechanization and superficiality which is identical with cultural exploitation, or prudent restriction of radio hours, and in case this should not be possible, of the number of programs." Hadamovsky favors the latter course as one "that may well permit constructive cultural work." In addition he proposes that the various broadcasting stations in the Reich take over part of each other's programs.[71]

Reportage

Radio achieves its greatest dramatic and emotional effect, according to the Nazi theory, in the direct broadcasting of events and experiences— "reportage" (*Zeitfunk*). "The listener is given an opportunity, so to speak, to be present at the time an event really takes place. The listener can go through an event from a distance."[72] The National Socialist radio specialists have noticed especially that "the sense of reality, the excitement, the enthusiasm which only surge up in the middle of a united crowd, are effectively produced by radio."[73] A broadcast, they believe,

---

[71] Hadamovsky, "The Goals of German Broadcasting," *op. cit.*

[72] Eduard Robert Dietze, "Radio Reportage in Germany and the Anglo-Saxon Countries," *Handbuch des Deutschen Rundfunks*, 1939-40. [73] Scheid, *op. cit.*, p. 244.

will most forcefully impress the masses when it has the setting of a crowd, when the microphone is taken outside of the studios and a public gathered together around it.

Reportage supplements the news service, but performs quite a different function. The press furnishes information about an event after it has taken place, which the reader can peruse at his own convenience. In reportage the radio announcer must produce something in the nature of "an artistic creation," a vivid, sharp expression of what is actually taking place before his eyes.

In its "pure" form, radio reportage conveys directly to the listener the acoustic impression of an event without the intermediary of a spoken description. Here radio can glory in its sheer technical capacities. The listener hears the applause, the shouts, the shuffling of feet, the gasps of the audience at great public gatherings. He can catch the roll of the waves as a *Kraft durch Freude* steamer churns its way to Madeira.

Usually, however, reportage involves a running account of the event, given by an announcer. To make it a lively experience for the listener, the reporter himself must experience the event he is relating. "The main characteristic of radio reportage is its impromptu quality." It should take the form of a "personal chat," a "dialogue with the unknown, mute listener." The reporter should not read from a prepared manuscript as this prevents him from introducing personal remarks and in other ways conveying the impression of actuality. On the other hand, it is natural that the speaker should help out his memory by having some notes before him. "Catchwords will assist the speaker in devoting himself to the experience he is going to describe and to its presentation before the audience without having to burden his memory too much by remembering everything."[74]

Effective reportage is not necessarily limited, say the Nazis, to "direct broadcast" where the event and the broadcast take place simultaneously. On this point, they claim, German views and practice differ from the American. "What matters is what impressions the speaker had during the time of the event, the strength and sincerity of his feelings. If the speaker was actually impressed and does not merely try to give that impression by empty words and pathos, then the listener will be impressed too even if he hears the report after the actual event."[75]

Reportage is the *chef-d'oeuvre* of German political broadcasting.

[74] Dietze, *op. cit.*   [75] *ibid.*

Sometimes it sets the stage for a major political address, conveying the atmosphere of a mass meeting or demonstration. On historic occasions, political reportage may stand alone as a program feature in its own right. It reached climactic heights when Germany took over Austria and the Sudetenland. But by 1939, according to the *German Radio Handbook,* reportage was in a critical state because good reporters had been so swamped with work after 1933 that their creative capacities were exhausted. In view of this, one writer suggested that the amount of political reportage should be reduced to the point where the right form of dramatic presentation could be devised for each program.[76]

The Spoken Word

The Nazi theory of broadcasting maintains the traditional respect for the spoken word. "All decisive radio effects are due to the spoken word," says one leader. "Without the spoken word there is no radio success. Music alone does not make us happy."[77] The spoken word is of special significance in broadcasts to German people abroad. "The word more than music is a carrier of the national characteristics of a people."

Radio because of its general audibility greatly increases the range of the spoken word and hence its political effectiveness. On the other hand, the German radio theorists maintain that certain grave dangers are implicit in radio's audibility for the user of the spoken word. "A wrong word pronounced at a small meeting can be passed over in silence, a bad advertisement may be destroyed, a false newspaper report may be denied. But the word spoken before the microphone spreads over the entire globe in one second. Enemy and friend alike listen to it and it cannot be taken back."[78]

In order to avoid haphazardness and dullness the radio speaker must select out of the body of material before him, the most "impressionable" items and group them effectively and pointedly. He picks an "acoustic" word with which to start his program, a word which will catch the ear of his listeners.[79] The Nazi radio leaders warn especially against long and boring lectures. Nor will plays with dozens of actors succeed. The most effective radio forms for spoken programs, they feel, are short bulletins, dialogues, interviews, radio plays, and three-way conversations, accompanied or interrupted by music. The fifteen-minute period should

---

76 Raskin, *op. cit.*   77 *ibid.*
78 Hadamovsky, "The Goals of German Broadcasting," *op. cit.*   79 Raskin, *op. cit.*

be the basic unit for the program schedule. The spoken word achieves great dramatic effect if it is used in connection with reportage.[80]

The principles governing the use of the spoken word apply to direct "political broadcasts" as much as to other types of programs. Political talks given over the radio should be brief. For the most part, the radio should present condensed synopses of speeches and events, simply reviewing the high spots. "Only if the Fuehrer speaks do all German stations broadcast the speech."[81] Preferable to talks, in the Nazi view, are political skits and dialogues. The extensive use of this type of program has become a peculiar feature of German broadcasting. The Germans have also applied the spoken word in political reportage, whose development has already been mentioned.

News

The radio news service is considered by the Nazis a channel of information definitely secondary to the press, and largely dependent on the press as a source of news. The radio, they say, should give brief summaries of general interest, rather than detailed reports, which should be left to the papers. Though non-polemical, they should consistently express the Nazi view on world affairs. They should of course be reliable, even at the sacrifice of freshness.

"Radio (news) items," says Fritsche, "must be short and must not be followed up by involved explanations. Besides, they ought to be as variegated as possible and selected from many different fields, so that each of the millions of listeners may find something that interests him in particular." No one interested in the life of his nation will find the radio news bulletins sufficient information. They will merely whet his appetite to read the newspapers.[82]

People should not be annoyed, continues Fritsche, if radio news comes to them after they have already seen it in the papers. The Nazis believe in a standard version of events to be reported over the radio irrespective of the audience. Thus what may be stale news to the city listener, may not have reached the rural villages. The urban dweller must put up with repetition of items he has already seen in the metropolitan press, so that everyone in the country may know about them. News items ap-

[80] Schroeder, *op. cit.*, pp. 125ff.   [81] Teichert, *op. cit.*
[82] Fritsche, "A Commentary About Radio Broadcasting," *Handbuch des Deutschen Rundfunks*, 1938-39.

pearing at noon may have to be repeated at night so as to oblige listeners outside of the Reich. The important thing is to get the standard bulletin across to all listeners no matter how stale it may become for particular groups.[83]

German policy in radio news bulletins, say the Nazis, is to report the truth on important world events but at the same time to make clear the National Socialist point of view. "Our radio does not claim and does not try to pretend that it aspires to a bloodless kind of objectivity . . . our radio declares quite openly: This is the interpretation of National Socialist Germany regarding the background, the character and the true significance of this or that event. . . . This honest admission of one's own point of view is the principal guide that we have in selecting and formulating the radio news that is broadcast to the world over the German shortwave station. Because of the very fact that we admit that our objective is to tell the truth about Germany in these news broadcasts we find it easy never to overstep those borders within which all news to foreign countries has to be kept. These borders are drawn by our own tact and our respect for the other nations and their peculiarities, and, on the other hand, they are inspired by our desire to thwart those efforts that carry destruction beyond the natural borders of the peoples of the earth under the flag of world revolution."[84] In other words, Nazi radio news policy is, at one and the same time, to tell the truth, to give the Nazi interpretation of the news, to respect other nation's sensibilities and to fight Communism!

In Germany's fight for the truth through the radio news service, it is not the radio's policy to answer and deny each and every distortion of the truth which emanates from abroad but to rebut a whole accumulation of falsehoods periodically. "One loses one's sense of direction if one tries to persecute every little swindler. However from time to time we have a big housecleaning and then we wash away the whole fraud as Hercules once did in clearing the Augean stables."[85]

Reliability must never be sacrificed in favor of speed, say the Nazis, even to counteract false news spread by one's enemies. Here is one place where it is dangerous to apply the principle that a good offense makes the best defense, and to attempt to broadcast news before the others do.

[83] *ibid.*
[84] *idem*, "Foreign Languages and the Radio," *Handbuch des Deutschen Rundfunks*, 1939-40.
[85] *ibid.*

"If you make up your mind to dish up news items before anyone else can do so, you will be liable to make numerous mistakes. However, nothing would be a greater mistake than to spread incorrect news during a time of crisis for they will have to be denied later and it is even possible that the events themselves will give them the lie. With one false report of this kind you may lose the confidence of your audience for a long time to come and it is a painstaking business to regain that confidence."[86]

Finally, radio announcers must subordinate their individual personalities to the program, maintain the Reich radio directors, yet present their material with vigor and spirit. "With modesty, simplicity and reserve, must be paired a firm determination and energy."[87]

PART II. THE STRATEGY OF THE GERMAN RADIO'S NORTH AMERICAN CAMPAIGN

IN propaganda, as in industrial organization and military development, the Third Reich entered the second World War holding an initial advantage over the Allies. The British, having enjoyed a large degree of success in their propaganda during the first World War, were not unnaturally content to rest on their laurels. What worked once, should work again. The National Socialists, acutely aware of previous German shortcomings on the "moral" front and attributing to Allied propaganda perhaps greater credit than was its due for bringing Germany to its knees in 1918, struck out to find new methods and conceptions which would enable them to become in the art of symbol manipulation the masters even of the clever British. Dr. Goebbels and his understudies mapped out strategies for radiobroadcasting and for other forms of propaganda as meticulously as though they were commanding tanks instead of words.

At least four avenues of evidence may be explored in analyzing radio propaganda strategy. Occasionally the broadcaster makes a clearcut statement about the policy he is pursuing. Or an opponent may analyze the propaganda and "reveal" its strategy. Both of these sources need to

---

[86] Wagenführ, "The September Crisis over the Radio," *Handbuch des Deutschen Rundfunks*, 1939-40.

[87] Hadamovsky in *Handbuch des Deutschen Rundfunks*, 1939-40.

be viewed skeptically unless supported by other evidence, as they are like all *ex parte* statements subject to bias.

The other two avenues are more reliable. Within the broadcasts there is often internal evidence which shows the purpose which the propagandist hopes his statement will fulfill. Sometimes he feels that to secure an adequate response from the audience, he must clearly express the implications of his statements and make his intentions obvious. Usually, however, internal evidence appears in the relationship of a particular incident or theme to other themes which the propagandist is developing.

The last and most important avenue of evidence is found in the relationship which a particular theme or argument bears (a) to the military and diplomatic movements which preceded, accompanied or followed the setting forth of the theme, and (b) to the opinions of the audience. It is this approach which has been followed in analyzing the strategy of German radio propaganda to North America.

In attempting to reconstruct the strategy of propaganda, the analyst must guard constantly against reading more into the evidence than is actually there, for he may visualize a highly integrated strategy of which the propagandist himself was completely unaware. Analysis must seek primarily for broad lines of policy, allowing for the flares and flourishes of the individual commentator, and for sections of broadcasts which may not have been deliberately planned with regard to policy. Although atrocity stories are one of the most sensitive indices of German propaganda strategy, it is quite conceivable that even some of these find their way into the broadcasts "by accident." German commentators, like Americans or British, must meet the deadline. Having already fulfilled the daily instructions in their script, they may still need "filler" to round out the fifteen-minute program. "When in doubt, use an atrocity," might well be a standing rule for the war broadcaster. So he rummages through his file for an old tidbit, which can quickly be refurbished to meet his immediate plight.

The German Radio's American "Problem" in the War of Words

For the National Socialists, the campaign for American public opinion which they had waged by short-wave radio since 1933, assumed especial importance upon the outbreak of the war. Analysis of broadcasts received from Berlin by the Princeton Listening Center suggests that the Nazi propagandists envisaged three objectives for their North American radio service after September 1, 1939. First and foremost, they wished to neutralize the United States in so far as the furnishing of active aid to the Allies was concerned. They had neither the necessity nor the hope of securing the support of the American people for Germany. Nor were they particularly concerned whether the United States forsook "moral" neutrality and Americans gave their sympathy to the Allies. They did wish to prevent the turning of sympathy into materials of war and the evolution of moral judgment toward economic and possibly military intervention.

While the primary objective of the North American schedule, the prevention of American intervention in the war, was negative in its implications, the masters of Zeesen at the same time continued to pursue their prewar objective of winning and maintaining the positive loyalty and cooperation of German-Americans for the Third Reich.

The German broadcasts also sought to weaken the Canadian war effort by stirring distrust and ill will between the Dominion and England. The Nazis considered this objective a sideline, to judge by the limited attention which they devoted to it on the radio schedule.

In their struggle for American neutrality, the German propaganda strategists were confronted by a curious problem. The odds on the surface seemed to favor their campaign. The deep-rooted isolationist tradition in the United States, reinforced by twenty years of disillusionment with Europe's politics following the first World War, had found legal expression in the series of Neutrality Acts designed to keep the country out of another war. The seeds of skepticism, which still germinated regarding Allied appeasement policies at the beginning of the war, kept American public opinion definitely opposed to military and financial intervention.

On the other hand, the American people were almost unanimously opposed to National Socialism and all its works. Thus when war actually broke out the vast majority were intensely concerned that the Allies should win. A sharp increase during 1939 in the number of those opposed to the arms embargo provision of the Neutrality Act indicated that opinion on material support for the Allied cause was in a highly volatile state where the slightest false touch might turn it heavily against Germany. Perhaps most dangerous of all from the German standpoint was the close tie which had been forged since Munich between American neutrality opinion and the ebb and flow of Allied fortunes. Whenever the security of the Allies visibly deteriorated, Americans tended to throw over their commitment to neutrality.[88]

This confronted the broadcasting strategists of Berlin with a dilemma. Any move which undermined American confidence in an Allied victory would automatically jeopardize the attainment of the chief objective of German propaganda—the maintenance of American neutrality. Yet the basis of German policy had, of course, to be the winning of the war. How to reconcile policy with the condition of American public opinion was the wartime problem of the German radio's North American Service.

The Voices of Berlin

Regardless of the war and its problems, the German short-wave radio, in the words of one of its spokesmen, offered its American audience, "a choice assortment of broadcasting viands, sparkling musical champagne and other tasty delicacies, such as operettas, variety entertainments, dance music and comic bits, as well as regular news features and commentaries." These dishes were served from six to nine o'clock in the morning, and from ten minutes to five in the afternoon to one o'clock in the morning. All played a part in the enticement of American opinion. The heart of the campaign, however, lay in the news bulletins, talks and other spoken programs which took up more than one-third of Berlin's eleven-hour daily North American schedule. In these the *Deutsche Kurzsender* wove the net of words and argument with which it sought to ensnare the opinions of its American listeners.[89]

With minor modifications, the schedule of spoken programs remained virtually unchanged throughout the entire war up to June 1941. Six fifteen-minute periods of news in English are broadcast on the North American Service, four in German and one in Spanish. In addition the notice of American listeners is called to some six bulletins in English, broadcast by Lord Haw-Haw and his colleagues to Britain during the middle of the day and early afternoon, which can be picked up without difficulty on this side of the Atlantic. Short topical talks, dialogues and other spoken features occupy some seven periods of the daily schedule

[88] P. E. Jacob, "Influences of World Events on U.S. Neutrality Opinion," *Public Opinion Quarterly*, March 1940, pp. 57ff.

[89] Harold N. Graves, Jr., "Propaganda by Short-Wave: Berlin Calling America," *Public Opinion Quarterly*, December 1940, p. 602.

and usually contain the most direct and specialized propaganda, as well as the most highly colored with emotion.[90]

Reputedly the chief of Berlin's talking staff is Fred W. Kaltenbach, Iowa-bred German-American, who holds a Ph.D. from the University of Berlin and according to his own testimony, served as a lieutenant in the United States Coast Artillery during the last war. Once a week in his "Letter to Harry," he offers the "folks back home" in Iowa advice on what to think and how to act in regard to the European war and American foreign policy. Thrice weekly he handles a fifteen-minute program preview, one of them specially timed for the Pacific Coast. The rest of his assignment includes a "Military Review," and a series of weekly talks on such topics as "Anglo-American Relations" and "German Contributions to Making America."

In the first winter of the war, Edward Leopold Delaney, Irish-American actor and author of cheap fiction, joined the staff. E. D. Ward, as he calls himself over the microphone, usually delivers three topical talks a week and takes part in the "Political Cabaret," a risqué skit devoted to ridicule and slander of Allied personalities.

Dr. Otto Koischwitz, a *bona fide* German, formerly on the faculty at Hunter College in New York City, is the third member of the triumvirate which dominates Berlin's North American Service. Introduced at first as "Dr. Anders"—translatable as "Dr. Otherwise"—he has since June 1940 used his own name or his initials, "O.K." "O.K. Speaking" comes on the air regularly at 9:00 p.m., five days a week, while on a sixth, Koischwitz delivers an erudite fifteen-minute "College Hour," furnishing everything from a Nazi-approved interpretation of surrealism, to an exposé of the subtleties of Hegelian philosophy.

Catering to a rising American interest in the ineffable "Lord Haw-Haw" which followed upon the excellent publicity given him by the British press, the Berlin radio, on April 12, 1940, began to rebroadcast to North America some of the solicitous messages prepared by His Lordship for the English audience. In April 1941, according to a report in *Time Magazine,* Lord Haw-Haw cast aside the aura of mystery which surrounded his identity ever since his debut two years earlier with the now famous phrase, "To some I may seem a traitor but hear me out. . . ." Confirming rumors that he was William Joyce, a pro-

[90] References to the schedule of German short-wave broadcasts to North America are based on the program for the week of April 6, 1941, as published by the German Library of Information, New York City.

Fascist, American-born, English-bred Irishman, he explained that he had dropped his incognito to answer London press stories calling him a common spy. Whether his father's recent death in East Dulwich, London, also induced the self-revelation, he did not say.[91]

Evidently with special audiences in mind, the Berlin radio provided three feminine parts in its North American production. Gertrude Hahn, as a telephone operator for *The Pittsburgh Tribune* in the weekly dramatic monologue "Hot Off the Wire," appeals primarily to workers. Constance Drexel, introduced as a "Philadelphia socialite and heiress," has periodically assured "culturally-inclined Americans that opera, concert music and the theater are thriving in Germany." Erika Schirmer, in "Interview of the Week," presents German military, economic, political and cultural leaders who tell, usually in guttural, heavily Germanized English, of National Socialist achievements in their fields.

A miscellany of other programs rounds out Berlin's weekly schedule of features in English. As of April 6, 1941, a daily report on "Economic Problems" occupied about four minutes. In September 1940, during the mass aerial assaults on Britain, Berlin introduced "Hot Shots from the Front," using the reportage technique three times a week in broadcasting vivid, purportedly firsthand, descriptions of German forces in action. "Listen and Judge for Yourself" exposes British propaganda once a week. The satirical approach is exploited in the "Club of Notions" as well as in the "Political Cabaret" already mentioned. "A Thousand Years of German History" and "A Thousand Years of German Literature" alternate in a biweekly series which continues indefinitely. Once a week, Germany is seen "Through a Woman's Eyes," while on Sundays, Americans can hear a translation of Admiral Lutzow's opinions on war developments. In the spring of 1941, following a well publicized offer to pay for cablegrams from American listeners criticizing its programs, the German short-wave radio launched a special series —"Democ and Nazi"—in which it undertook a rebuttal. By April, this had become a daily feature. "Jim and Johnny," a dialogue specially designed for Canadian listeners and appealing to a rather low intellectual level, is broadcast weekly.

The German language part of the schedule, though substantial, is by no means so impressive. Hans Fritsche, editor-in-chief of the Berlin station, broadcasts a "Press Review" three times a week. His aggressive

91 *Time Magazine*, April 14, 1941.

and dogmatic manner suggests that he considers his audience already converted to the National Socialist world outlook. Admiral Lutzow speaks in German once a week, while a "sound picture" of the news is presented in "Today in Germany," a daily commentary.

The Arsenal of Argument

The arguments or themes used by the Berlin broadcasters in the pursuit of American opinion during the war, fall into five main patterns: *division* of America from Britain and the Allies, *reassurance* regarding German intentions and conduct, and German-American relations, *futility* of the Allied war effort and American aid, *dissension* within America, and *intimidation* of the United States.[92]

These lines of argument emerged in the first weeks of the war and persisted virtually unchanged in their basic outlines throughout the Berlin radio's campaign up to March 1941. Each news broadcast, every topical talk, while introducing a variety of detail and illustration drawn from both past and contemporary events, fitted the material to one or more of the patterns.

The German radio strategists rarely concentrated on elaborating just one pattern to the exclusion of the others. They mixed and wove them together in different combinations depending on the particular demands of propaganda policy at the moment. Sometimes they mixed them consistently. At other times, they produced confusion by presenting simultaneously, patterns which were mutually contradictory, for instance, reassurance and intimidation. The key to the German strategy of propaganda, as will appear later, lies in the relative emphasis placed on each of the patterns at different stages of the campaign.

The Pattern of Division

The Berlin radio concentrated its major and most consistent attention throughout its North American campaign upon the pattern of division. It sought to present every argument which might possibly breed suspicion of the Allies and implant the view that the war involved strictly European, not American interests.

On England, of course, was pinned the guilt for starting the war and

[92] This analysis is based upon broadcasts recorded by the Princeton Listening Center from November 30, 1939, to March 11, 1941. Except where otherwise indicated, quotations are from the archives of the Center. Dates given in parentheses refer to the day on which the Center heard the broadcast.

for continuing it. England had carefully plotted this war, using France and Poland as the chief minions of her design. Intent on pursuing her bloodthirsty course, she has turned down every German overture to call a halt to the suicidal madness which she precipitated. England, consequently, is responsible for every dead boy, for every cripple that comes back, for all the misery the war has brought. . . ."

In prosecuting the war, Britain respects neither humanitarian nor legal canons of conduct. It was England which instigated the Poles to commit frightful atrocities upon the German minority during the first weeks of the war, British aviators who ruthlessly and indiscriminately bombed civilians and nonmilitary objectives, British soldiers who pillaged in Norway and Belgium, the British blockade which shamelessly violates the rights of neutrals. "Unable to defeat Germany on land, on water or in the air, England has settled down to her old game of making war on those who can't defend themselves, on helpless infants and mothers, on the old, infirm, the sick and the maimed." (April 7, 1940)

Albion, the Berlin radio reminds us, joins barbarism with its perfidy. All that England does takes place in the name of civilization, liberty, justice and the rights of small nations. What hypocrisy! Does England fight "for the glory of God? No one believes that bloody war is the road to heaven. For social improvement? War doesn't improve social conditions. For art, for science, for civilization? War destroys civilization." (April 4, 1940)

Britain's real war aim, now as ever, is protection of its imperial position in the world and the maintenance of an iron dominance over Europe. "While other countries have been satisfied with moderation, England has methodically set about dominating the world. When a nation in any part of the world became powerful and threatened to follow a course which did not conform to the interests of British imperialism, then England made war on that country." (February 17, 1940) She has consistently fought German aspirations for national freedom and has made "encirclement" the keynote of her policy. Both the first World War and the present one were undertaken to implement that policy.

The present war, the world must realize, "is a fundamental struggle between the German social state and the British plutocracy." (February 13, 1940) England's interests are those neither of neutrals, of her Allies, of her Dominions, or even of her own people. "Great Britain . . . lives, works and fights . . . for the well-being of her plutocracy." (March 28, 1940) The war occurred because "a few plutocrats were afraid to lose their power, and saw no other way out than to make war on the new idea." (March 7, 1940)

Behind the plutocrats Berlin in turn saw the machinations of international Jewry. The tycoons of British finance and journalism, who manipulate the strings of British politics, are almost all Jews, maintained the Nazi broadcasters. British politicians, like Churchill, are in effect retained as servants of the Jewish conspiracy for world domination. In return they receive their luxurious country homes, their well-padded bank accounts and the false prestige which attaches to political position. On the other hand, Jews were reminded that British politicians are adept at the double cross as in the case of the "Jewish National Homeland" which was promised in the World War, but somehow never materialized afterwards.

The Berlin broadcasters have concentrated a great deal of their attention on illustrating the wide divergence if not conflict of interests which has prevailed between Britain and the United States throughout the history of the American Republic. A series of talks on "British Disregard for American Neutral Rights" began with 1784 and carried on until it had disinterred the Anglo-American diplomatic tangles of the World War. The great disparity between British ideals and interests on the one hand, and American on the other, has become apparent to many Americans, according to the Berlin radio, which presents every evidence it can of disaffection in the United States from the Allied cause.

The Pattern of Reassurance

In contrast to the Satanic concept of Britain, Berlin's word-etchers deftly drew the picture of an upright, heroic, progressive Germany fighting to rid herself and the world of intolerable injustice and cherishing nothing but the most cordial of sentiments toward other nations. At every opportunity, Germany's cultural heritage was recalled, its industrial and scientific achievements, its glorious natural scenery, the health vigor and honesty of its people. National Socialism had rescued this fine country from the same kind of greedy, plutocratic oppression under which Britain had suffered, and established in its place the reign of social justice, releasing the full creative energy of the German people.

The noble and peace-loving German folk had for years been the victim not only of internal but of foreign oppression, both engineered principally by the one common enemy—the Jew. Yet the victim of abuse was made to appéar an aggressor, with Germany the constant butt of malicious misrepresentation before the world, especially after National Socialism had begun to revive the spirit of the German people. To cap off the dismal record, Germany's enemies once more had forced war upon her against her will.

Germany's aims in this war she has been forced to fight are just, honorable and idealistic. Paramount is the desire for peace, as evidenced by the Fuehrer's frequent appeals to the Allies to stop the senseless conflict. But while "Germany's foremost war aim is peace," this "can only be maintained when the vital interests of great nations are given due respect and consideration." Germany demands "full liberty within the living space allotted to us by nature. We will acccpt no interference and no hint of any domination. We will brook no creation of artificial buffer states along our frontiers, to act as willing tools that foment these disturbances. After a long period of partly enforced separation and particularization, we have united to form the German nation and demand to be recognized as a first-class power. As such we will receive our due share of colonies from which to procure the raw materials necessary to a sound economic existence." (June 16, 1940)

In addition to securing her own interests, Germany seeks to free neutral nations from the stranglehold of British naval and commercial power. "The world must be given freedom of the high seas, which is the right of non-belligerents to continue trading without supervision by a warring power." (June 16, 1940)

Germany is further concerned with the reorganization of Europe on a more just and rational basis, after ridding it of the tyranny of British domination. Though the details of the "new order" are left somewhat vague, the Berlin commentators have at one time or another sketched its main outlines. Kaltenbach has set it forth as comprehensively as anyone. "There is going to be more solidarity in Europe. . . . The old balance of power myth by which England sought to retain a dominant influence will have to be scrapped. Military as well as economic responsibility on the shoulders of small states has proven to be of fictitious value. . . . Let those take responsibility who can carry it and . . . let others accept leadership where it presents itself with convincing power. . . ." "The future is guaranteed to have peace and security. Germany offers Europe a new system of economic life, providing steady markets, just prices, solid money, sound money, and freedom from crises. . . . Capitalistic exploitation of the weaker by the stronger will be impossible. Unemployment will disappear in Europe as class rivalry will also disappear. . . . The laborer will receive his allotted place of honor. The farmer will stand securely. . . . Every individual will contribute to the welfare of the whole. No longer will profit be the guiding impulse, but the creation of values, which will give prosperity to each individual within the scope of his activity." (July 16, 1940)

The immediate war aim, however, is of necessity the military defeat of Britain. Nothing in Germany's aims, however, would affect the British Empire, if England did not for its part cherish ambitions for world domination. The Fuehrer "has stated time and time again that the basic principle of his policy was an understanding with Britain. . . . England must give up her idea of exercising hegemony in Europe and control over the destinies of independent nations. When England gives up this idea, Germany will welcome the opportunity of cooperation with England in a new order of things in Europe. Germany does not want to destroy the British Empire." (June 16, 1940)

Berlin commentators insisted that the U.S. had nothing to fear from Germany which had "no interest whatever in American affairs, neither in North nor in South America, neither in political nor in military matters." (June 16, 1940) America had itself set the precedent for what the Nazis were trying to do. "You have proclaimed your Monroe Doctrine, so Germany declares itself against potentially hostile alliances within Central Europe." (March 28, 1940) Even if Germany did have designs on the American continent, Berlin assured American listeners that "a German attack against the United States is just about as feasible as an attack from Mars." (June 17, 1940)

Aside from the appeal to common idealistic premises, Berlin commentators, especially after the defeat of France, stressed a more hardheaded, materialistic point of view, in line with their preconception of America as a purely money-minded, business-motivated community. "Germany is going to win this war. Why not face the facts and make up to the winner? Why quarrel with the dominant power in Europe . . . when that power . . . is slated to play the leading commercial part on the continent after the war?" (July 5, 1940) In brief, why can't two brigands get along well together when there are enough spoils for both?

The pattern of reassurance included flattery in addition to bribery. America's long tradition of neutrality and current practices and opinions in line with this tradition drew Berlin's most extravagant praise. "President Washington's advice that Americans should steer clear of all entangling alliances was the law of *Real-politik* for America and it was a good law," said one speaker. (January 26, 1940) "We cannot help congratulating the American people on their steadfast, neutral attitude," added another. (March 7, 1940) "Would that there were more Fords in America!" exclaimed E. D. Ward after the motor magnate had refused to manufacture airplane engines for Britain. Germany even thought well of American national defense efforts at times. "Public opinion in Germany, the opinion of the man on the street, rejoices that Uncle Sam is going out on his own to free himself from an alleged reliance on British sea-power. The Germans rejoice that there are . . . additions to the growing U.S. Navy, now neck and neck with Great Britain in the race for the world's naval supremacy. Somebody has to have the world's largest navy, and Germany would just as soon see Uncle Sam the proud owner as anyone else." (June 17, 1940)

German war conduct was consistently presented as legal, moral and heroic. Unrestricted submarine warfare was defended as retaliatory action against England's illegal blockade of all German exports and imports, irrespective of whether they were contraband. German submarines have had to attack without warning because Britain, in violation of international law, armed her merchant ships. Germany's invasions of neutral countries also found justification in international law. These nations allowed their neutrality to be violated by the Allies without protest and frequently had connived with the enemy in these acts. No permanent occupation was envisaged after the war was over and in the meantime the life of the people would be as little disturbed as possible. In the occupied countries, German forces have accomplished a phenomenal job of repairing the ravages of war.

The Berlin broadcasters built up an almost medieval concept of the German warrior—gallant, chivalrous, and honorable. He would never attack anyone except the military forces of the enemy, even under great provocation. Though the RAF pursued the infamous practice of bombing civilians, German airmen, in retaliating, carefully confined their targets to military objectives. The German soldier mixed congenially with the population in the occupied countries and did everything to make their lot easier, from cleaning up debris to serving as a temporary butcher. Berlin told its listeners to discount at 100 per cent all reports of atrocities committed by German soldiers. These were merely propaganda lies, deliberately fostered to arouse hatred of Germany, and embroil relations between her and neutrals, especially the United States.

The Pattern of Futility

The German strategy of argument depended heavily on convincing American listeners that England and the Allies were doomed to defeat. Although in developing this pattern of futility, Berlin commentators often recounted the exploits of German arms and boasted of German invincibility, their main emphasis was negative. Britain, they maintained, was desperately weak and thoroughly demoralized.

Militarily, Britain and her allies were particularly deficient in air power. British and French planes were inferior both in numbers and quality to German, and there was a deficiency of well-trained pilots. This in turn seriously affected the significance of British naval power, for the airplane had demonstrated its unquestioned superiority. The Allied armies were poorly equipped, and especially lacked mechanized units. Strategically, Britain's position was extremely vulnerable, especially after the German conquest of Norway and the Low Countries, which placed German air bases close to the key industrial centers and made Britain completely dependent on extracontinental sources for both war materials and food. The German radio ridiculed the English Channel as a barrier to invasion.

Wherever Britain turned it met defeat, depleting still further its already limited military power. On land, destiny seemed to spell out an unending series of "glorious retreats" for British expeditionary forces before the irresistible Axis armies. At sea, the Royal Navy was futilely trying to enforce a blockade, Britain's chief weapon against a forewarned, self-sufficient Germany, if not the whole continent of Europe. Indeed, England's blockade had boomeranged as the combined action of the German Navy and Air Force took a drastic toll of Allied merchant shipping. In the air, the RAF could not prevent the methodical crippling of British communications and industrial production by the *Luftwaffe,* while over Germany, British pilots seemed to have an uncanny capacity for never hitting military objectives. English preparations to resist invasion did not impress the German broadcasters as likely to change the course of events. "It is clear," said Haw-Haw on August 2, 1940, "that when it comes to her *own* defense, England will be as weak as she was in defending her own Allies."

Britain's economic and financial position was critical. Extremely heavy war expenditures had depleted domestic and foreign reserves, and imposed a crushing tax burden on the common man. Shipping losses had brought about the collapse of Britain's foreign trade, so vital to her life and power. No improvement in domestic agricultural production had occurred to render England less dependent on outside sources for supplies. The number of unemployed kept increasing despite the war, disclosing that "the scarcity of materials forces England to reduce her production constantly." (August 5, 1940)

As the material lot of the Britisher steadily deteriorated under German attacks from sea and air, British morale had crumbled, claimed Berlin. The atmosphere in England had become one of "depression and despair . . . unrest and ill-concealed panic." (July 15, 1940) In their desperate plight, the British people were plagued with incompetent military and political leaders, who "have always believed and even now believe that the stoutest weapon in the world is bluff." (August 26, 1940)

The German radio pointed to the defection or impotence of Britain's allies and of her Empire as further evidence of her weak position. As British weakness and hypocrisy become apparent, "the small countries of Europe are making haste to leave the sinking British ship." (July 1, 1940) The United States likewise would not want to support a losing cause, Berlin stated confidently. Americans were warned to beware of British propaganda attempts to create an "illusion of victory" in order to secure continued American support. England's fate was sealed, however, irrespective of any aid America might give, whether commercial or military.

Meanwhile, in Germany "life goes on normally," undisturbed by the British war effort. Food is plentiful, industrial production at a peak, supplies of raw materials sufficient, trade thriving, the people in good spirits, "thoroughly convinced that under the present leadership they will bring this war to a successful end and that Germany will acquire that place to which she is entitled." (October 13, 1940) The German radio was concerned to point out to American listeners the strength and cordiality of Germany's chief ally, Italy, and harped on the vast implications of the pact with Soviet Russia (now a thing of the past), which had removed all possibility either of a second front against Germany or of a hunger blockade as in the World War.

The Pattern of Dissension

Though arguments directed at stirring dissension within the United States and at undermining confidence in American institutions have occupied a relatively small proportion of time in Berlin's North American campaign, they have been a sensitive index of the campaign's intensity. They have usually appeared in force only at critical moments in the war, in the midst of German military moves or when some phase of German-American relations approached a climax.

German short-wave commentators warned the American people against interventionists, whose determined purpose, they declared, was to drag the United States into war. Harboring "plans for Anglo-Saxon world domination," these tools of London "poisoned relations between great nations," meddling in European affairs to the detriment of all concerned, while trying to whip the American public into a war hysteria. Ambassadors Kennedy and Bullitt had actually goaded the Allies to war with promises that the United States would soon join in. (April 7, 1940) Congressional leaders and cabinet members such as Senators Pepper and Pittman, and Secretaries Knox and Stimson, came under the lash of criticism. (June 22 and 23, 1940) The German radio increasingly shouldered President Roosevelt with direct responsibility for moves aimed at embroiling the United States in the European war. It also attacked "the war-mongering William Allen White Committee" and "that German-hating Amazon . . . that queen of wishful thinkers, Dorothy Thompson." (September 4, 1940)

On several occasions, Berlin commentators suggested that American interventionists might not be motivated by a purely disinterested sympathy for England. Willing, apparently, to attempt an appeal even to those whose sympathies were completely identified with the Allies, the Nazis ingeniously argued that interventionist leaders were actually scheming, cold-blooded imperialists who realized that the exhaustion of Britain and Germany in a long war would pave the road for American world domination. England was "the Poland of United States interventionism." (September 20, 1940)

The National Socialist broadcasters have tried to exploit every note of racial and nationalist discord which they thought might be festering in the heterogeneous American body politic. They specialized in Jew-baiting, elaborating with minute detail the twists and turns of a vast Semitic plot for world mastery. The sons of Zion "visualize a Jewish super-rule in the world, not achieved through a Jewish state, but through open or preferably (secret) Jewish influence and control over the various nations. . . . What a world that would be—Gentiles labor-ing and slaving and the Jews sitting as parasites on top of the world!" (September 22, 1940) To this end, Jewish journalists have secured a stranglehold on the press. In 1917, furthermore, "Jewish influence proved to be of vital importance for drawing America into the war" (June 4, 1940) and the schemers are in the process of repeating their performance in regard to the present war. Though the Berlin radio in its North American Service usually stresses these political machinations of Jewry, it indulges occasionally in the more lascivious items common in domestic German propaganda. "American womanhood," said "Sinister Sam," one of the anonymous Berlin commentators, "will complain about the lewd and offensive (attitude) . . . Jewish men often adopt towards girls and women—or about the often-complained-of Jewish as-sociation with immoral processes and abuses as brought out by the Dewey and other investigations." (July 25, 1940)

Vicious as were the attacks on the Jews, they could hardly stand com-parison with Fred Kaltenbach's remarks about "niggers." He served American listeners a gruesome menu of atrocities which colored troops had inflicted on prisoners and civilians in past and current wars, and asked if Americans wished to abet England and France in their betrayal of white civilization and become party to the imposition of "nigger rule" in Europe, as they had during the occupation of the Rhineland after the World War Armistice. (cf. June 11, 17, 1940) American Ne-groes on the other hand could hear from Berlin of the frightful treat-ment meted out to men of their race in British colonies, and of the charitable feelings entertained toward them by the Germans.

Berlin sought to encourage and guide German-Americans in the face of increasing anti-German sentiment in the United States. Though in-tolerance and blind prejudice were sweeping the country as in World War days, "people whose opinions really count will admire you for sticking up for Germany in a fight which is no concern of the United States." Kaltenbach suggested that if he "were home in Iowa," he would as a German-American "support the Administration 100 per cent in building up American defense . . . refuse to support any measures intended to help England against Germany . . . refuse to support any man for President or Congress who has expressed himself in favor of helping England . . . join up with and take active part in any organization pledged to absolute neutrality and non-intervention . . . urge the Administration to bury the hatchet and face the new European order like a shrewd Yankee business man." (August 19, 1940)

To a lesser extent than in its broadcasts to Britain, the Berlin radio attempted to draw American attention to domestic economic problems and to fan the coals of class conflict. The "Economic Review" on September 23, 1940, claimed, for instance, that most of the money spent by state and county governments to remove slums goes into the pockets of real estate speculators. "Landlords were interested only in collecting substantial profits through rents or sales. . . . Flats and homes proved so expensive that the poor, the small laborer could never anywhere near afford them."

Class against class, race against race, isolationist against interventionist, and everyone against the press—this was Berlin's pattern of dissension within the United States.

The Pattern of Intimidation

Up to the spring of 1941, the German radio was sparing in its use of intimidation against the United States. It reserved this pattern for special occasions when German-American relations reached a highly critical state and other arguments had failed to dampen American ardors for Britain. Even then, it did not resort to the unadulterated terror tactics adopted in many of the broadcasts to Britain and hostile European countries. Warnings were generally mild of tone and threats implied rather than barefaced.

The policy of aid to Britain, Berlin admonished, had led the United States to the brink of conflict just as in 1914-1917. The national defense program was a "palpable subterfuge for goading a nation into a fever of hysteria." (October 18, 1940) But war, Americans were reminded, was not a pleasant experience. The devastation wrought in Poland and the wiping out of Rotterdam were consequences flowing from a foolish baiting of the German war machine. Germany was "using new and ter-

rible weapons, the nature of which you cannot know, which revolutionize the conditions of warfare." (May 18, 1940)

Continued antagonism to Germany, Berlin suggested, would earn for
the United States nothing but lonely isolation in the "new order" and
deprive her of friendly contact with the important nations of the post-
war world. By attempting to "institute a system of purely pan-American
economics," shutting out German trade, America was "clinging to old
forms and wilfully shutting her eyes to new developments." (July 6,
1940) The United States might even face an economic sanction if she
did not adopt a more cordial attitude toward the powers-to-be in Europe.

America's present policy, declared the Nazi broadcasters, had also
jeopardized the "American way." A listener in Dallas, Texas, purportedly wrote that "the joker in the defense bill permits the government
to take over industries and plants, lock, stock and barrel, even in peace
time . . . our government, with the approval of the legislators, if not
of the people, enacts laws that are identical, if not more dictatorial, than
those of dictator nations." (August 29, 1940) E. D. Ward foresaw the
suppression of all political opposition in alleged remarks by Attorney
General Jackson, defining criticism of a nation's leaders as a type of fifth
columnist activity. (August 30, 1940) Thus, unbeknown to most Americans, the national defense program had already placed the United States
on the very threshold of totalitarianism.

The Evolution of German Strategy

The strategy of German radio propaganda to North America from
the outbreak of war in September 1939 to the spring of 1941 generally
evolved in accordance with shifts in military activity, diplomatic relationships and American neutrality sentiment. The campaign falls into
six major periods. In each, the patterns of argument stressed by the Berlin broadcasters reflect to a large extent the contemporary situation of
world events and of public opinion in the United States.

The Impact of War: September 1–November 4, 1939[93]

During this period, which witnessed the crushing of Poland, the
declaration of war on Germany by France and England, and the enig-

[93] The author is indebted to the Columbia Broadcasting System Short-Wave Listening Post
(hereafter referred to as CBS) for access to their transcriptions of German broadcasts covering
this period.

matic action of Soviet Russia in seizing eastern Poland, American public opinion veered sharply away from neutrality. The shock of war seemed to sharpen issues, sweep aside indecision and evoke a more violently belligerent attitude toward Germany, culminating on November 4 in the repeal of the arms embargo from the American Neutrality Act.[94]

German strategy, aimed at placing the Allies immediately on the defensive in regard to the moral issues of the struggle, depended heavily upon the pattern of division. The thesis of Allied war guilt emerged simultaneously with the German invasion of Poland. The attack on Poland, insisted the Nazi commentators, had resulted from British-inspired Polish aggressiveness against Germany. The stubborn recalcitrance with which Poland had refused to negotiate Germany's just demands, her provocative mobilization and her brutal persecution of the German minority would never have occurred without British backing, and made Germany's recourse to force inevitable. Gruesome tales of Polish atrocities at the front accompanied the sweep of the German armies. These dropped out of circulation when Germany appealed for peace following the Polish *débâcle*, but came back strongly as soon as Allied rejection was foreshadowed.

The sinking of the *Athenia* the day after England declared war impelled the German radio to introduce another familiar theme in its pattern of division—the ruthless scheming of the British to get the United States into war. The Germans at first simply denied any complicity, maintaining that none of their submarines were in the vicinity. On October 22, however, Dr. Goebbels personally took the microphone and accused Winston Churchill of engineering the crime in hopes of creating another *"Lusitania* incident."[95] Berlin also charged Britain with spreading "propaganda lies" about German atrocities in Poland and troop concentrations on the Belgian border, in an effort to whip up anti-German sentiment in the United States and influence Congressional debate on the repeal of the arms embargo. "England," said Fred Kaltenbach, "was willing to fight to the last Pole and now she is willing to fight to the last Frenchman. England will be only too glad to fight to the last American."[96]

The reassurance pattern appeared in a "peace offensive" launched by the German radio at the end of the Polish campaign and culminating

---

[94] cf. P. E. Jacob, *op. cit.*   [95] cf. Adolf Halfeld, *The Case of the "Athenia,"* pp. 31*ff.*
[96] Quoted by Ed Johnson in release to *The New York Times,* October 25, 1939.

in Hitler's speech of October 6. Having no quarrel with the western powers, Germany was ready to stop this "senseless and idiotic" war, upon the conclusion of the Polish "incident." Overbalancing the fearsome aims stated by Hitler in *Mein Kampf* regarding France, were the Fuehrer's more recent assurances, especially the cancellation of demands to Alsace-Lorraine, and the concrete evidence of the Siegfried Line, built "to avoid a stupid fight between our two peoples."[97]

The German appeal for peace, however, was no molly-coddle affair, for added to the modicum of reassurance was a double dose of futility and intimidation. Berlin stressed Germany's invincibility. The Russian-Nazi pact, it crowed, put the Reich in a position where she could fight on for years in spite of the British blockade. Consider the fearful results of action by eight hundred bombers against the Polish city of Modlin, suggested Otto Dietrich, Reich Press chief. Then imagine what would happen if Germany sent a similar number of planes against the British fleet and the "strategic shipping ports of England." When Chamberlain rejected Hitler's proposals, Berlin hinted that intervention by President Roosevelt might bring the Allies to their senses before it was too late.[98]

Moves to modify American neutrality policies in favor of the Allies prompted the German radio to a further use of intimidation, coupled with dissension propaganda. "Americans, Americans, LISTEN. The danger of being dragged into this war stares you in the face. Do you really want war? You don't want to send American youths to the battlefield of Europe. Tens of thousands will never come back and other tens of thousands will come back crippled. The billions of dollars it will cost you will never be paid."[99] Berlin quoted the protests of Senator Nye, Father Coughlin and others against repeal of the arms embargo and criticized President Roosevelt for his friendship to England. His assurance that the lifting of the embargo would not send Americans to fight in Europe could not be taken too seriously because this measure alone would not have aroused such enthusiasm in Britain and France. It was a sign of things to come. Washington's agitation about the *City of Flint*, American freighter captured and claimed as a prize by the German Navy, likewise showed that American authorities were heading more and more in one direction—toward war. People in the United States should remember President Roosevelt's speech of August 1936, when he

[97] CBS release, September 18, 1939.   [98] CBS release, October 14, 1939.
[99] CBS release, September 20, 1939.

said that America was pulled into the World War by little wrong decisions.[100]

Hibernation: The "Phony" War, November 4, 1939–April 8, 1940

Despite intensified sea warfare, the quiescent state of land warfare in the west during the winter of 1939-1940 raised doubts in the minds of many as to whether the belligerents were actually engaged in war at all and even led to insinuations that the horrible specter of appeasement was in the offing. An offshoot of the war sprang up in the north, however, when Russia attacked Finland on November 30, 1939. For over three months the deeds of the Finns stole all the thunder from the main struggle, until massive Russian power finally told against them and precipitated a peace treaty on March 12, 1940.

American neutrality sentiment again ran strong, having withdrawn from the excitement of the first weeks of war. Confidence reigned in the ultimate success of the Allies, and in the ability of the United States to stay out of the combat. At one point, however, a dramatic change occurred in the course of public opinion. With their sympathies strongly engaged in the struggle of "little, honest Finland," Americans forsook their compunctions about lending money. A good majority felt that the United States could safely extend credit to the country which paid its debts in the midst of a fight for its very existence.[101]

In this situation, the German radio emphasized the pattern of division even more strongly than in the previous period, with reassurance and futility assuming definitely secondary significance, while dissension and intimidation played very minor parts. Berlin's strategy appears chiefly in its treatment of the Finnish war, the war at sea, atrocities, Anglo-American controversies and alleged British efforts to extend the theater of conflict.

The German radio dealt gingerly with Russia's northern adventure, obviously laboring under considerable embarrassment. It contented itself with brief and matter-of-fact résumés of the official communiqués. Frequently even these were omitted. Details of the bombing of Finnish

---

100 CBS release, October 30, 1939.

101 cf. polls conducted by the Princeton Public Opinion Research Project (hereafter referred to as PPORP). Results of the PPORP surveys of American public opinion on the war are summarized up to July 1940, and presented graphically, by Hadley Cantril in an article, "America Faces the War," *Public Opinion Quarterly*, September 1940. Shifts in opinion from July to October 1940 are analyzed by Cantril and his assistants in the succeeding issue of the *Quarterly*, December 1940. Later figures were unpublished as of May 15, 1941.

civilians, a favorite topic of the British Broadcasting Corporation, were conspicuously absent. Berlin's reticence was understandable. The mate, whom Germany had just taken in a *mariage de convenance*, was now assaulting a youngster which the Reich itself had helped to bear some twenty years before.

Try as they would to soft-pedal the war in the north, Berlin's commentators could not escape without evolving some sort of a thesis on the subject. On the whole, they accepted the Russian version of events, and early in the war advanced the notion that Finland had forfeited Germany's friendship by collaborating with her arch enemies in the League of Nations.[102] By the time peace was negotiated, Berlin had ingeniously hooked up the northern conflict with British designs to widen the theater of war and could therefore interpret Finland's acceptance of peace as a great setback for the Allies. Finland had been victimized through her association with the Allies, but fortunately for herself, had realized in time, not to trust their treacherous offers of help.[103]

As Britain came more and more to rely on the blockade as her major weapon against Germany, and the Nazis in return attacked both naval vessels and merchant shipping by every means at their command, including raider, mine, submarine and airplane, the war at sea became the major subject of discussion in Berlin broadcasts. News of German victories and British losses absorbed some of the attention, while in the encounter of the pocket battleship *Graf Spee* with three British cruisers off Montevideo, the German broadcasters had one of their few opportunities to explain away a German defeat. They declared the British had used poison gas in the attack, the Uruguayans had not granted the ship a long enough period of time in port to make it seaworthy, and the captain had put "an honorable end to a glorious career" by scuttling the ship.[104]

The main concern of the German radio in the argument on sea warfare, however, was moral. It condemned the British blockade as an inhuman attempt to starve women and children, a flagrant violation of international law and a disastrous blow at the rights and well-being of neutrals. It defended German action at sea, first, as in complete accord with international law, and later, as justifiable reprisal against the British blockade—a "counter-blockade." When the British Navy used every

---

[102] cf. broadcast recorded by the Princeton Listening Center, December 5, 1939.
[103] *idem*, March 14, 1940.   [104] *idem*, December 16 and 18, 1939.

means in its power to stop the movement of goods to and from Germany, whether or not they were contraband, why should not German U-boats and airplanes do all in their power to disrupt the British commercial lifeline, even to attacking lightships and fishing smacks which served as patrol vessels?

This counterblockade thesis, with its implication of unrestricted submarine warfare, aroused a storm of protest from neutrals, including the United States. Then, on February 17, 1940, the British obligingly boarded the German prison ship *Altmark* within Norwegian territorial waters, raising both a legal and a humanitarian issue. For aside from the "unprecedented violation of Norwegian neutrality," the British were guilty, according to the German account, of extreme brutality in carrying out the attack.

The incident marked a turning point in the whole debate on sea warfare. Berlin's propaganda strategists temporarily shelved the counterblockade argument and for the first time pressed a sustained moral offensive against the British Navy, diverting attention from German misdeeds. They charged that the attackers had "behaved like savages shooting off their rifles and automatic pistols in every direction while the Germans did not even have a revolver with which to defend themselves. . . . In the wild English shooting, six German sailors were shot down like animals. Their wounds show that they were fired on at close range for the holes where the bullets entered were small and the exits were torn open as wide as six centimeters."[105] In "collecting souvenirs" English sailors had shown special interest in clothes, linen, watches and silver tableware, but generally "robbed and demolished anything they could lay their hands on."

The German radio meanwhile did not neglect to elaborate the implications of the incident for neutrals. "British egotism not only disregards the rights of neutrals but strives to maim, compromise or even force neutral nations in an effort to drag them into the war, even if it means their destruction." How would you feel, a commentator asked Americans, if a German warship sailed into New York harbor and fired on the *Queen Mary*? Berlin became ominously critical of Norway's actions, warning that "no state can be described as neutral that suffers such crimes or limits itself to protests."[106]

At the end of January 1940, the British Broadcasting Corporation,

---

[105] *idem*, February 19, 1940.　　　　[106] *idem*, February 17, 1940.

inspired by the Vatican's condemnation of German conduct in Poland, launched an impressive atrocity campaign against the Nazis. Responding to the challenge, the German radio took up the Polish situation in earnest. It flooded the air with news items and topical talks, reviving and elaborating its earlier reports of atrocities committed by the Poles, telling of exemplary reconstructive efforts carried out under the German occupation and charging the Allies with atrocity-mongering. "The inventive minds of British propagandists have tried to transform murdered German women and children into Poles," it claimed.[107] German actions have been directed solely at the establishment of order and the securing of justice without a spirit of revenge. Berlin also discovered atrocities within the confines of the British Empire to use in its counterattack, eagerly broadcasting news of oppression in India, malnutrition in the crown colonies, and the execution of Arab "fighters-for-freedom" in Palestine. In countering the accusation that the Germans were suppressing Catholicism in Poland, a detailed review of Britain's record of persecution in Catholic Ireland proved convenient. The German campaign of rebuttal continued in full force throughout February and March 1940, except for the week of February 17 when Berlin broadcasters were fully occupied with the *Altmark* incident.

During the period of hibernation, Berlin's broadcasters directed the attention of their American listeners to a series of controversies between Britain and the United States, both contemporary and historical. These proved, they said, the great disparity of interests between the two nations. The American Revolution gave the United States charter membership in Fred Kaltenbach's "British Lion Tamers' Club" composed of those who opposed British domination. Using Secretary Lansing's memoirs as evidence, the German radio pointed out that England had stolen financial and political secrets while searching American mails during the World War. In the current conflict, the dispute between the United States and Britain over mail censorship showed that the "high-handed, long-nosed representatives of Mr. Churchill" were up to the same old tricks.[108]

As the spring of 1940 wore on and approached the fateful date of the German invasion of Scandinavia, the theme that Britain was bent on spreading the theater of war to neutral countries received increasing

---

[107] *idem*, February 6, 1940. [108] *idem*, January 25, 1940.

emphasis in Berlin broadcasts. It appeared in connection with the Finnish war and the *Altmark* affair as already noted. After the Russo-Finnish peace it continued to agitate the German radio as indications appeared that the Allies were determined to tighten up their blockade in Scandinavian waters. A sharper and more urgent tone gradually emerged. British action was impending, Berlin warned, but it would not catch Germany napping. When, on April 8, Britain announced the laying of mines off Norway, German commentators reacted violently. "Whether Norway is going to put up with the rape of her neutrality," said one, "is a matter which we are not to decide; that Germany is not going to put up with this pirate fashion of molesting her Scandinavian trade can be taken as pretty certain." Two hours after this broadcast German troops marched into Denmark.

"Lightning Action": The Attack on the West, April 8—June 22, 1940

The might of the German military machine shaped the events in this period. With sudden hammering blows it snuffed out the national independence of five countries, drove the British Expeditionary Force out of Flanders under a hail of bombs at Dunkerque and smashed France to its knees despite the "impregnable" Maginot Line and the "finest army in Europe." On June 22, representatives of a reorganized French government signed an armistice with the German victors at Compiègne Forest.

Alongside of the dramatic accomplishments on the battlefront, Hitler's armed forces wrought an equally striking transformation upon American public opinion. By the end of June, only a minority of the American people thought England and France could win. Meanwhile, opinion had moved swiftly toward increasing aid to the Allies, even at the risk of war, although the great majority still opposed immediate military intervention by the United States.[109]

The fast-moving military situation virtually overwhelmed the German broadcasts during this critical period. Berlin devoted both its news programs and its talks almost entirely to covering the day-to-day developments of the war. Nevertheless, even when faced with a straight reporting job, the announcers and commentators pursued definite lines of propaganda strategy.

[109] cf. Cantril, "America Faces the War," *op. cit.*, pp. 396ff.

The futility pattern dominates the argument of the period. German troops won the Scandinavian campaign at the very outset and subsequent operations involved merely "mopping up" insignificant pockets of Norwegian resistance and throwing into the sea the motley array of forces which the Allies finally landed in a half-hearted gesture of support. This represented a serious defeat for England, both strategically and militarily. In particular, German air power had proved its superiority over British naval power. As the Nazi attack swung from the north to the west, the Berlin radio staged a repeat performance of this line of argument. It spoke of the invincibility of German arms and the magnitude of Allied losses. It prophesied the imminent doom of the enemy. What hope of resistance remained for Britain with "her army smashed, her mechanized divisions gone?"

The pattern of division also played an important part. In justifying the attacks on Scandinavia and the Low Countries, the German propagandists expounded the now familiar theme that Germany had simply forestalled Allied plans to extend the war to these countries. It had moved into Norway and Denmark to "protect" them against impending British invasions. Similarly, in the light of "incontestible proof" of the imminent occupation of Belgium and Holland by the Allies, the Fuehrer had decided to take their neutrality "under his protection against the Anglo-French aggressors."

Following the announcement on May 2 of the withdrawal of Allied troops from Southern Norway, Berlin broadcasts concentrated unusual attention upon alleged British attempts to "make trouble" in the Balkans. References to such designs had appeared before, averaging four weekly on the broadcasts recorded by the Princeton Listening Center in the previous six weeks. But during the single week of May 3, they totaled twenty-seven in addition to fifteen references to the activities of the British fleet in the Mediterranean. This interlude may have been designed to "camouflage" preparations for the *Blitzkrieg* in the west, by diverting Allied attention to the Near East. On the other hand, it may have been a verbal "barrage" preparatory to a projected German move in the Balkans, which, for some reason was halted and redirected at the last moment.

Some evidence supports the latter view. The German radio has in the past consistently used the "barrage" method to herald its diplomatic and military offensives. No inkling either of a desire or of a capacity to change the method has been noticed in German broadcasts either previous to or since this time. Secondly, German references to the Balkans reached their peak on May 6 and 7 after which they dropped sharply. If camouflage had been intended, one would have expected its continuation right up to the time of the German attack on May 10. As it was, Berlin dropped its attention to this subject at the very moment when the British Cabinet, in response to mounting criticism over the conduct of the Norwegian campaign, was considering drastic changes leading to the appointment of Winston Churchill as Prime Minister. Could it have been that Berlin, fearing the inauguration of a more vigorous British policy in the west, changed its Balkan plans and moved instead against the Low Countries, with no time effectively to redirect its radio "barrage?"

Simultaneously with the march of German soldiers into Belgium and Holland, Berlin directed a ferocious campaign of atrocity stories against the Allies, resurrecting old themes and introducing fresh ones. It bitterly condemned the actions of the Allied air forces and threatened drastic retaliation, while defending the record of the *Luftwaffe* as one of unimpeachable purity in the face of extreme provocation. It accused the Allies of pillaging and destroying the Low Countries in the course of their retreat. Berlin reserved for the French an atrocity specially designed to appeal to American race prejudice—the use of colored troops. For "niggers" to fight in a war between whites, cried Fred Kaltenbach indignantly, "is a crime against the standing of Europeans and the rest of the world."[110] Lord Haw-Haw in his incomparable style deftly touches on the same theme. "These subhuman beasts have taken German prisoners, poured petrol on them, and set them alight to the applause of French soldiers. . . . Such worthy representatives of the old world for which Mr. Churchill and M. Reynaud are fighting!"[111] The art of mistreating prisoners is not limited to the colored man, however. The French, for instance, arrested seventy-two neutral persons in Belgium and took them to Lille Prison, where they were "stripped naked without regard to sex, deprived of all their personal possessions, beaten with a rifle butt, and foully kicked. Some of them were murdered."[112]

In replying to charges of German misconduct, Berlin repeatedly ac-

[110] Broadcast recorded by the Princeton Listening Center, June 11, 1940.
[111] *idem*, June 7, 1940.   [112] *idem*, June 7, 1940.

cused the Allies of "atrocity-mongering." "These London lying reports," suggested an announcer during the first days of the offensive, "are not only designed to promote anti-German propaganda all over the world, but are meant especially as a stimulus for the Netherlands population inciting them to ill-treat German wounded or imprisoned soldiers."[113] To prevent their soldiers from surrendering, the Allies had revived the World War trick of "asserting that the German soldiers kill any man who surrenders and that prisoners of war . . . are being used as screens for tank attacks."[114] The stir that rose over German parachutists was used by Berlin to heap ridicule upon Allied propaganda as well as to level dire threats of retaliation if the parachutists were mistreated.[115]

The German radio gave renewed and urgent warning to the United States of intensified British activity to plunge her into war. It reported a plot of the British and French Secret Services to sink the American liners *Manhattan* and *Roosevelt* on their way back with refugees from the war zone.[116] Instead of hunting for German fifth columnists, Americans should watch "the English agents and propagandists in the United States who have a direct interest in seeing America save the British Empire."[117] "What they earnestly desire," said E. D. Ward of the Allies on June 15, "is that the guns to be shipped from America have with each one a man in Uncle Sam's uniform."

As the fall of France neared, the German radio injected a modest dose of reassurance into its stream of words. On June 14, and for several days following, it gave a detailed summary of an interview between Hitler and Karl von Wiegand, American journalist, in which the Fuehrer remarked, "Germany is one of the few nations which hitherto has refrained in any way from matters concerning the Americas only. I say, therefore, America for the Americans, Europe for Europeans." Berlin, of course, consistently defended the behavior of German armed forces in combat, asserting that with military work to do they did not "fight against civilians or against hospital units." In the occupied territories, German authorities quickly put life back on a normal basis and left no stone unturned to provide for the safety and well-being of the inhabitants.

In the meantime, vigorous dissension propaganda sprang up for the

[113] *idem*, May 14, 1940.
[115] *idem*, May 10-16, 1940.
[117] *idem*, June 3, 1940.
[114] *idem*, May 18, 1940.
[116] *idem*, June 3, 1940.

first time in months. During the Scandinavian campaign, and the first weeks of May, the German radio almost completely neglected any specific treatment of American questions. Aside from having a very full schedule of military reporting, the broadcasters may have thought American public opinion too profoundly shocked by the course of events to sustain any direct manipulation from Germany. After May 25, however, when the tide set strongly and surely against the Allies, Berlin turned to America with acid criticism. It severely castigated the American press for promoting intervention. The broadside hit American political leaders and even touched the American people, whose gullibility for fifth column stories irked the Berlin commentators. "About the first Fifth Column to appear in America," according to Lord Haw-Haw, "was the one which marched through the imagination of the more excitable citizens of Salem" and sent them out to hunt witches.[118] On the other hand, Berlin did not apply outright intimidation to the United States in this period, although it meted out a severe dose to England, France and indeed all the countries in the path of the German attack.

Peace Offensive: June 22–August 8, 1940

This was a period of little military activity and much speculation. While the world waited tensely for the next German move, mystery shrouded the exact state of Franco-German relations, particularly the disposition to be made of the French fleet. On July 3, the British Navy took matters into its own hands. At Oran Bay, off Algeria, it joined battle with French warships and put a number out of commission. France broke off diplomatic relations with England two days later.

On July 19, Chancellor Hitler addressed a "last appeal" for peace to Britain, which elicited no official answer from England, although Prime Minister Churchill had delivered a particularly defiant speech just a few days before. Meanwhile, in the East, Soviet Russia found the occasion opportune to secure Bessarabia and North Bukovina from Rumania and absorb the three small Baltic States. The period ends with the first mass assaults by the German Air Force on the British Isles.

During this time, a surge of confidence swept over the American people that England would win the war and correspondingly, the number increased of those who thought the United States would enter the

[118] *idem*, June 7, 1940.

war. The trend towards further material and financial aid to Britain noted in the previous period continued.[119]

The major subjects discussed by the German radio concerned either directly or indirectly the establishment of peace in Europe. Berlin broadcasters addressed themselves to (1) French relations with England and Germany after the Armistice; (2) an appeal for peace with Britain, stressing the same theme used in the "peace offensive" after the Polish campaign; (3) German efforts at building the new Europe; (4) forceful admonition to the U.S. not to interfere with assurance that the preservation of American interests was compatible with German domination of Europe.

The broadcasters thus made use of all five of the main patterns of argument. The dominant one still remained futility—the hopeless position of Britain and the vast strength of Germany. For reassurance, Berlin presented Hitler's offer of peace, Germany's beneficent conduct in the occupied territories, her fair treatment of France, an attempt to settle old troubles between the Balkan countries, and specifically for the United States, a promise of material advantages in the new order if she adopted a more cooperative attitude toward it. The division pattern included England's "treachery" to France at Oran, her refusal to accept peace, further British atrocities, and continued efforts to get the United States into the war. The dissension pattern was broadened and for the first time since the early weeks of the war, intimidation directed at the United States found a place in the German broadcasts. Criticism of American policy, leaders and people sharpened, and warnings as to the dangers of interventionism became very direct and precise.

The German radio's most significant activity was building up and tapering off Hitler's peace move. Standing alone, "on the eve of a great German offensive," Britain's position was desperate—economically, militarily, morally. Separated only by the narrow strip of the English Channel, she confronted a Germany whose power had meanwhile grown stronger as a result of the Battle of France. England lay imminently exposed to all the ravages which had befallen the war-torn countries of Europe. Against this background, the Fuehrer in his great generosity, again offered Britain a last chance for peace and a guarantee of the security of the British Empire. The rejection of his appeal and the criminal resort to intensified bombing of civilians showed the depth

[119] cf. PPORP ballot, July 20, 1940, in Cantril, *op. cit.*

of stupidity and depravity to which England had fallen and made her doom inevitable. Already German attacks on shipping and strategic centers in the British Isles, although not so dramatic as the military activity of the preceding weeks, were crippling England and preparing her for the final reckoning. On these themes, Berlin drummed incessantly to Britain as well as to America, while Germany made ready for attack.

Battle for Britain: August 8–September 27, 1940

What might be called the first "Battle for Britain" opened up on August 8, 1940, with the unleashing of the German Air Force for all-out attacks on England. The declaration on August 17 of a total blockade by Germany highlighted the maritime phase. Throughout the period, actual land invasion of the "island fortress" loomed constantly as the possible culmination of the battle, which probably reached its climax in the week of September 7 when London received its first major baptism of fire. Developments of greater or lesser importance occurred on other fronts. The Italians had cleared English forces out of British Somaliland by August 18. An Axis-sponsored conference at Vienna at the end of August, led to the cession of large sections of Transylvania by Rumania to Hungary. On September 3, Anglo-American cooperation progressed a long step forward with the exchange of fifty overage American destroyers for bases in British possessions in the Western Hemisphere. The period ends with the signing of the Three Power Pact between Germany, Italy and Japan. Meanwhile, American opinion moved still further toward helping England, though as yet few favored military intervention.[120]

The ebb and flow of the Battle for Britain absorbed the major attention of the German broadcasters. Their strategy of argument generally paralleled that of the period of "Lightning Action." The futility pattern dominated. The Berlin speakers made the same immediate assumption of victory as before, and issued the same boasts about Germany's crushing military superiority. They introduced graphic descriptions of the German forces in action and told of the steady disintegration of Britain under the impact of the aerial attack on the one hand, and of the "total blockade" on the other. They disparaged England's chances of resisting invasion and minimized the effect of American aid. The exchange of

[120] Cantril, *op. cit.*, Chart I.

bases for "old destroyers" indicated, as a matter of fact, that "Britain's need has already reached the crisis point."

The division pattern shared the limelight. The RAF perpetrated even more outrages on hospitals and centers of culture than in the previous period. Britain turned her back on the starving peoples of her former allies, refusing to permit food to pass to them through the blockade. Within England, the plutocracy still ruled but was ready to desert to lives of luxury in America before the sailing became too rough.

Reassurance came in a fairly modest quantity. The *Luftwaffe* carefully sought out only military targets. Germany had not stripped the occupied countries of their food supplies and indeed was trying to feed her former enemies out of her own surpluses. The settlement of Hungarian-Rumanian grievances by peaceful negotiation illustrated the principles of diplomacy to be followed in the "new order." The United States was to be congratulated on its shrewd bargain in the destroyer-base deal. "You can't beat a Yankee in a horse trade or in a real estate deal," remarked Fred Kaltenbach.[121] "America for Americans, Europe for Europeans" was still Germany's motto as regards relations with the western hemisphere, with the offer of the hand of friendship wide open.

The dissension pattern meanwhile had taken over from the pattern of division most of the developments in America's drive toward war. Berlin talked more of "hybrid Americans" than of British agents. It accused the interventionists of being *anti-British*, American imperialists, in addition to tagging them with the customary label of unpatriotic servants of Britain. President Roosevelt received a tongue-lashing or two, especially in regard to the sending of the *American Legion*, a United States boat evacuating American refugees from Finland, through the area of the German blockade. Here and there intimidation cropped up with a warning that the country had moved forward on the road to war and dictatorship. But on the whole, such attempts were halfhearted, and after the destroyer-base deal, all criticism of America dropped off sharply.

In Midstream: September 27, 1940–March 11, 1941

This was a period of indecision on all fronts. Periodically, German airplanes would blast at different parts of England with devastating fury, as at Coventry on November 14. The tempo of German sea war-

---

[121] Broadcast recorded by Princeton Listening Center, September 9, 1940.

fare stepped up in 1941. The RAF steadily pounded at German bases. But the Battle for Britain failed to reach a conclusion. In the Mediterranean, Italy undertook a large program of military adventures which turned sour. By winter, Italian troops found themselves battling desperately to keep from being pushed into the Adriatic by the Greeks. A drive into Egypt stalled at Sidi Barrani and on December 8 the British opened a dramatic counteroffensive which swept the Italians not only out of Egypt but out of Cyrenaica as well. Neither the British nor the Greeks, however, completed their jobs and a virtual stalemate prevailed during the first months of 1941.

Developments in the United States portended a steady move from neutrality to nonbelligerency, especially after the election of President Roosevelt for a third term on November 5. The President's fireside chat of December 29 and above all, his message to Congress on January 8, 1941, calling for passage of the Lease-Lend Bill, indicated that American domestic as well as foreign policy was to be directed at the one objective of assuring a British victory, without regard to cost, or to the forms of neutrality which had hitherto been respected. This development was consummated on March 11, 1941, with the enactment of the Lease-Lend Bill by Congress.

The strategy of the German radio campaign was as indecisive as the military and diplomatic situation which it accompanied. In many respects it appeared to have returned to the state of hibernation of the winter of 1939-1940. Berlin brought forth many of the familiar themes of that period, but no major trends of argument seemed to emerge. As a matter of fact, the broadcasts to North America leave the impression that the German radio wished to avoid extraordinary developments which might react in a wrong way and hasten the United States further towards intervention.

The pattern of futility continued to play an important part in the broadcasts. Aerial activity against the British Isles was steadily grinding out the ultimate triumph. As the period progressed, however, Berlin's emphasis shifted more and more from the air war to the throttling of England's lines of supply by the German blockade. Britain was beset with economic difficulties at home and abroad, and disaffection was rising in the Empire. Furthermore, the Three Power Pact, Molotov's visit to Berlin and other diplomatic developments enhanced both the prestige and the strength of Germany and showed how completely the Continent had shut Britain out of its affairs. British victories in Africa against the Italians could have no effect on the outcome of the war. America's aid was an insignificant particle on the scales of the war.

The Berlin radio introduced a touch of novelty into its pattern of division with a series of exposés of British propaganda, in which it adopted an analytical approach rather than its customary ranting style. For the rest, the RAF furnished some more atrocities, British intrigue led to the Greco-Italian conflict and England persistently denied food to the starving in Europe.

Reassurance absorbed more attention than in the preceding period. The expansion of the "new order" to the Far East in the Three Power Pact, and its consolidation in Europe by German military penetration into Rumania and diplomatic maneuvers with Spain and Russia, need alarm no one, for its spirit is inoffensive and reasonable—always providing its evolution is not interfered with. Life on the Continent, in the occupied countries as well as elsewhere, proceeds normally, with Germany still filling in the dietary gap left by the British food blockade.

Toward the United States, the German radio adopted a considerably more aggressive attitude than during September. Criticism of American foreign policy increased, reaching in October about the same level as at the beginning of the Battle for Britain. By December, attacks on American policy tended to decline in German language programs to the United States. The presidential election, as might be supposed, excited no enthusiasm, but neither did it elicit sharp criticism. Rather, Berlin adopted an attitude of resignation and declared its neutrality in America's internal political affairs. Roosevelt's fireside chat and other pronouncements on foreign policy, however, came in for unadulterated invective. Yet the German radio was still sparing in its use of outright intimidation, casting only a veiled threat in connection with the Three Power Pact.

With the passage of the Lease-Lend Bill, the German broadcasters evidently realized that they stood in a different relationship to the United States than heretofore. Previously an unfriendly neutral, America had now to be considered an active enemy. The strategy of argument to North America, therefore, swiftly underwent modification, and the tone of the broadcasts to the United States came to resemble closely that adopted in the broadcasts to Britain. Harsh, sharp criticism, and outspoken intimidation now issued freely from the Berlin transmitters. No longer did commentators seek to cajole American listeners and soothe their fears. For eighteen months they had tried patiently and with infinite solicitude to halt the mad rush to doom. Now America had put her head into the noose of a virtual alliance with Britain and the German broadcasters were not in a mood to be charitable.

BRITAIN SPEAKS

By Daniel Katz

Daniel Katz, associate professor of psychology at Princeton University, has been a member of the Princeton faculty since 1928. He received his Ph.D. from the School of Citizenship and Public Affairs of Syracuse University in 1928—the first doctorate conferred by the School of Citizenship in the field of social psychology. He has been one of the pioneers in opinion research and attitude measurement and is the author of "A Scale for Measuring Attitudes toward the Law" and co-author with Floyd Allport of "Students' Attitudes." His "Social Psychology" with R. L. Schanck is one of the standard works in the field. A member of the editorial board of the Public Opinion Quarterly, Dr. Katz is concerned in his present research activities with polling techniques and psychological aspects of public opinion.

BRITAIN SPEAKS

The story of British short-wave broadcasts to North America parallels closely British war efforts in general—a lethargic pre-Dunkerque phase and an aroused post-Dunkerque phase.[1] Before the Battle of Flanders the American public was fed the Overseas Service, inaugurated for Empire listeners in 1932 and based upon the Home Service of the British Broadcasting Corporation. To Americans, not very enthusiastic about British cooking, the warmed-up remnants of the original meal were not very palatable. News bulletins were a half hour in length, often containing items of yesterday's American press; the reiteration of pious hopes took the place of adequate and informative stories of the progress of the war; the style of presentation compared to the American radio was dull and the tempo leisurely; and the special talks and features were not infrequently on the stuffy side.

During the Battle of Flanders, however, the BBC began to think more in terms of an American audience. A series of feature talks, called *Britain Speaks*, was instituted and it soon grew from a tri-weekly to a daily affair. Its spokesmen included distinguished authors, artists, journalists and scholars; some of whom were, from the American point of view, genuine radio personalities. The Overseas Service was formally replaced by a special North American Service on July 7, 1940, which was further enlarged on September 29, 1940, to a six-hour nonstop program in the evening in addition to news bulletins during the day. News bulletins were cut to fifteen minutes. Dramatizations and special features supplemented the news reports and the news commentaries. The *Radio News Reel*, "the war in sound," with eyewitness accounts, sound effects, and simulated spot broadcasting became a late evening feature.

These concessions to an American audience were justified in that British broadcasts because of the device of rebroadcasting are technically available to more listeners in the United States than the radio programs of any other foreign power. In the fall of 1940 about 90 American stations rebroadcast BBC programs and this number was increased to about 130 by June 1941. Moreover, the Mutual Broadcasting System has transmitted the BBC news reports twice daily and the two programs *Britain*

---

[1] For a concise statement of the short-wave activities of the British Broadcasting Corporation on both the European and North American fronts see Harold N. Graves, *War on the Short Wave*. New York, Foreign Policy Association, 1941.

Speaks and the *Radio News Reel* once a week. Many Canadian stations also rebroadcast the North American Service with more complete coverage and these rebroadcasts are audible to a fairly large section of the American public.

The Princeton Listening Center recorded British short-wave programs from December 7, 1939, to June 1, 1941. In the following analysis of these transcribed records an attempt will be made to answer two types of questions: (1) What do the British seem to have been trying to do? What have been their objectives? Or more technically, what symbols have the British employed and how were these symbols patterned in relation to the events of the war? (2) What have the British short-wave broadcasts been like? How do they compare in general character with German short wave or with American radio presentations? This second type of question will be considered first, since the general characteristics of British broadcasting to America tell us something of the framework in which their strategy has operated.

Characteristics of the British Broadcasts to North America

1. The High Intellectual Level and Hence the Narrow Audience Appeal of the British Programs.

Unlike the German short-wave propaganda with its mass appeal the British broadcasts have been directed, consciously or unconsciously, at a numerically small audience of upper-income people of better than average education and background. The spokesmen and commentators for Britain were top-flight individuals, many of them experts, authorities or outstanding performers in their field. While they have spoken with the prestige of authority and of fame, they also tended to talk in the tongue of the intellectual and the scholar. And the subject and the tone of the discussion has often been heavy for the average American listener. Many of the talks could have been university lectures, and in fact university professors did appear before the BBC microphone from time to time.

The weighty nature of the political and military interpretation is indicated by the caliber and training of the commentators. Wickham Steed, who has appeared almost every week for extensive analyses of world affairs, is a former editor of *The Times* and the author of a number of historical volumes. Vernon Bartlett, an Independent Progressive member of Parliament who served as diplomatic correspondent for four of the leading English newspapers and was for ten years the London director of the League of Nations Union, has been used frequently on many of the programs. George Slocombe, the author of several books on international affairs, publicly commended by Cabinet ministers for his dispatches from the Hague during the conference of 1929, A. G. Macdonell, a satirical as well as a serious writer, Lindley Fraser, Scotch economist and author, and J. B. McGeachy, former Rhodes scholar, have been at one time or another the regular news commentators. Air Marshal Sir Philip Joubert, in charge of the Coastal Command of the RAF from 1937 to 1939, appeared once a week in the *Britain Speaks* series. In addition to this regular staff have appeared fairly frequently such spokesmen as Philip Noel Baker, author, Dodge lecturer at Yale University in 1934, and Labor member of Parliament; Sir Ronald Cross, Minister of Shipping; scientist Julian Huxley; J. C. Wedgwood, another Labor member of Parliament; Alexander Keith, a Scottish journalist; and H. M. Brailsford, socialist intellectual and author. Many other authoritative names have been added for occasional lectures when the situation demanded, as when John Maynard Keynes, the economist, spoke on Britain's economic position or Donald Tireman talked about the economic significance of the Lease-Lend Bill, or G. D. H. Cole on economic freedom, or Professor Brierly, professor of international law at Oxford, on some legal aspects of the export blockade. High ranking officials also are heard from time to time including A. V. Alexander, First Lord of the Admiralty; Prince Bernhardt of the Netherlands; Malcolm MacDonald, Minister for the Colonies; C. R. Atlee, Lord Privy Seal; Sir Samuel Hoare, British Ambassador to Spain and Sir Hugh Dalton, British Minister of Economic Warfare, as well as rebroadcasts of talks by Prime Minister Churchill and Lord Beaverbrook.

Turning from the more technical aspects of the war to the broader questions of human and social issues, we still find a consistently high standard of performance with such stars from the literary, dramatic and artistic world as the novelists J. B. Priestley, Hugh Walpole, and Ian Finley; the actor, Leslie Howard; and the cartoonist, David Low, carrying the brunt of the broadcasting with single or occasional appearances by Noel Coward, Somerset Maugham, James Stephens, Rose Macauley, and Richard Llewelyn. The literary level which these broadcasters sustain is in keeping with their character, as the opening line of Finley's talk, February 2, 1941, attests: "It was spring and the candles of the chestnut trees stood up white and pink and the road stretched away, a dusty white ribbon into the distance, where the snows of the Bavarian Alps hung like a mirage through the heat haze." The picture which follows of the Bavarian professor representing the best in German culture and scholarship, which the Nazis have repressed, is indeed appealing. But it is more poignantly appealing to Finley's circle than to the men in the mines and the men in the factories.

One bit of evidence of the high-brow character of the American audience for British short wave has come from the fan mail to the BBC which established Priestley as the most popular of the British broadcasters. Now Priestley from many points of view has deserved this popularity, but his analysis has been so profound and intellectual that he would scarcely rank first if the audience were at all representative of the middle and lower classes. Even among a middle-class audience one would expect Leslie Howard (with his sentimental tugging at the heart-strings and his dramatic tales) to be more popular than Priestley.

Nor have all the special features of the North American Service fallen far below the standards of Steed and Priestley. The Listening Post, a regular feature, has reported German short-wave propaganda to all parts of the world as well as other forms of German propaganda. It has brought out contradictions and analyzed propaganda tricks. But again the presentation and the analysis were more for the student than for the man on the street.

Exceptions should be noted to the upper-class appeal of the North American Service. Two of the regular speakers were Herbert Hodge, a London taxi driver, and William Holt, a writer who was once a Yorkshire weaver. These exceptions bring out by contrast the emphasis upon people who count. They demonstrate that the English, self-conscious in their new-found democracy, have not objected to some representatives of those who have not been to public school. That Hodge and Holt carried any genuine appeal for the American masses is doubtful, but they have satisfied upper-class Americans that the English can be democratic without being vulgar or communistic.

The *Radio News Reel*, on the other hand, has achieved a measure of popularization, for it has come closer to American spot broadcasting or reportage than any other foreign radio program. With a very few exceptions, however, it has presented reconstructions of events rather than genuine spot broadcasting. It has been a notable exception to the ex clusive appeal of BBC programs which emphasized the spoken word. Nonetheless it is doubtful that it could have competed at the popular level of American variety programs like those of Bob Hope, George Burns and Gracie Allen, and Fibber McGee and Molly.

The characterization of the North American Service of the BBC as intellectual and, therefore, forbidding to the masses refers primarily to *form*. No evaluation of the *content* of these programs as intellectual in the sense of their originality or their soundness is here intended. The reference to their intellectuality refers to the literacy level rather than to the intelligence of the message. Intellectual form and intelligent content generally, but not necessarily, go together. Will Rogers at times gave an intelligent summing up of situations in nonintellectual form. Similarly, stupid ideas can be dressed up in good intellectual form.

To assume that the British short-wave programs have been ineffectual because their intellectual nature limited the size of the audience is to misunderstand the nature of propaganda and the public opinion process. One of the most important functions of propaganda is to reach the small group of persons who are already sympathetic, to keep up their enthusiasm and interest, and to furnish them with arguments and interpretations so that they can convert others. The radio is a device by which the central source of propaganda can reach directly the fireside of the great masses but this use of the radio has been exaggerated as a propaganda weapon. Fully as important in the opinion process is the interaction of human beings in which they are reinforced or weakened by the expressed opinions of people they know. Mass appeals from a central source need the mediation of many leaders and lieutenants along the line if they are to have much effect.

The BBC has not only furnished information and encouragement to a small group of American friends, it has furnished this information to a very select group of opinion-leaders. The upper-income listeners are politically and socially very articulate and occupy strategic positions for disseminating their views as writers, lecturers, officials of private organizations and as leaders in general.

Whether or not the BBC *deliberately* presented its appeal to reach a small circle of opinion-leaders we do not really know. It is quite possible that the British proceeded *unconsciously* to make their appeal to the people who counted. It may never have occurred to them that the masses needed special courting. On the other hand, if the decision was conscious it could have been justified by these reasons: (1) The upper-income groups are reached more easily by short wave because their sets are better equipped on the whole for short-wave reception and their listening habits are not as firmly fixated upon American variety programs. (2) It is more important to reach the *opinion-leaders* than the masses. (3) The nature of the British case as compared with the German case had more intrinsic appeal for the upper-income groups. The threat of German aggression to the established order, the have-nots against the haves, would arouse less indignation among those who have little stake in the present order than among those who have a great stake. (4) The British sympathizers and potential sympathizers were relatively more numerous among the upper classes because the upper-income groups are more Anglo-Saxon in origin and more identified with Britain in social values.

2. The Individualistic, Relatively Unregimented, Nature of British Broadcasting.

German broadcasts are purer instances of propaganda than British broadcasts in that the Germans have a rigid party line to which all spokesmen must adhere. British broadcasts, on the other hand, have permitted a fairly wide range of individual difference of opinion and expression. The BBC has not turned over its microphone to Communists but it has allowed Socialists, Liberals and Conservatives to give their own interpretations of the causes, the conduct, and the objectives of the war, so long as they have not advocated a negotiated peace with Hitler. In short, the British programs and the German programs have fitted the popular distinction between education and propaganda, for whatever that distinction is worth. The unregimented nature of British broadcasts is evidenced in two ways: first, in the freedom of expression permitted to the speakers and second, in the failure to coordinate the verbal appeals with events. The Germans have made the war of words one weapon in their total strategy of warfare. The English have made much less effort to gear their verbal efforts to planned or unplanned events.

There was no central ideological line imposed upon British spokesmen about war aims. The official point of view emphasized the winning of the war and dismissed peace plans for the reconstruction of Europe as premature and ill-advised. Yet Priestley, the ace of the BBC, has vigorously attacked the government's conception of peace aims, maintaining that it is not enough to destroy Hitlerism but that the conditions productive of Hitlerism must be destroyed as well. Similarly, the liberal speakers have tried to convince their American audience that England is fighting for a better social order, whereas the more conservative-minded broadcasters have interpreted this war as a continuation of World War I.

The interpretation of the parties to the conflict, Germany and England, followed no regimented plan but rather gave scope to the individual construction of the particular speaker. Though some British commentators have shifted from an attack upon the Nazi leaders to a condemnation of Germany as a whole, others continued the older policy of carefully distinguishing between the German people and the Nazi regime. Likewise, in the picture of England presented to American listeners there has been great inconsistency. Hugh Walpole and other speakers have given a Christmas card picture of the charming England made famous by the novelists and poets, with its quaint villages, its venerable traditions, and its conservative customs, like villagers touching their caps. A radically different conception of England was substituted by Priestley in his comment on Alice Duer Miller's poem, "White Cliffs." Referring to Miss Miller's poem, he cried, "But this isn't the England that's fighting the war. This Christmas card caricature of England couldn't fight this war a couple of days. This is a war of machines and of men who make and drive these machines. They don't make 16-inch guns or Hurricanes or Spitfires down in the old family place in Devon. . . . It is industrial England that is fighting this war . . . those scores of gloomy towns half buried in thick smoke with their long dreary streets of little houses all alike and the rather short . . . folk, usually with bad teeth, who aren't much to look at, but who happen to be among the most highly skilled and trustworthy workmen in the world. . . . It is these towns who've produced most of the wealth that enabled the other fancy little England to have its fun and games; and it is this other big England that is having to take it in this war. The bombs fall on Coventry, Sheffield, Birmingham, Manchester, not on the old family place in Devon." (March 9, 1941) Priestley's remarks, addressed to Miss Miller's poem, could have been equally well addressed to the work of some of his fellow broadcasters.

Even the actual conduct of the war by the British government has not always been approved by BBC commentators. Vernon Bartlett took exception in July 1940 to the British policy of appeasing Japan by closing the Burma Road. Though he admitted the tight place in which Britain was placed, he was disappointed in Churchill's statement of the problem. And he goes on to say: "But why didn't the Prime Minister speak out more frankly? After all, frankness is one of his greatest qualities." (July 18, 1940)

A parallel instance of a German broadcaster taking his Fuehrer to task before a world audience has escaped the notice of the writer.

Whatever the ultimate effect of the German regimented presentation of their case as compared with the individualism of the British presentation, there is no doubt that the British with their relatively uncoordinated approach have had the advantage of *interest* and *variety*. The regimented presentation, though it can achieve greater consistency and singleness of purpose, suffers nevertheless from monotony and repetition. As long as the party line remains constant there is no need to listen to the official version because the listener can supply it himself. Especially is this true with the intelligent type of audience which the BBC reaches. And from a long-run point of view variety is essential for holding an audience. In Germany itself the Germans tire of their own press and welcome foreign newspapers.

Another advantage of the individualistic presentation is its greater sincerity. The constant stereotyped praise of the Fuehrer and of German institutions after a time seems much less genuine than the English mixture of criticism and approbation. The clash of individual opinions on the British short wave has seemed living proof of the vitality of English democracy. On still another count, regimented propaganda suffers from a disadvantage. The rigid following of a central ideological line produces ridiculous reversals when events force a change in ideology as has happened with official Communist doctrines. On the other hand, the effect of individualism is to keep interpretation more fluid so that the whole propaganda effort is not forced to do a rightabout-face.

The lack of regimentation and planning in British propaganda, however, has meant that the events were not effectively exploited at the most strategic time. When a great deal is left to individual initiative, every one's responsibility may become no one's responsibility. Thus, after the destroyer deal, about a month elapsed before the British really expressed their gratitude. When praise and flattery might have had some effect upon American listeners, the BBC permitted the weeks to slip away until finally the first Lord of the Admiralty in a gracious speech thanked America and cleverly linked the interests and ideals of the two democracies. Only to some Americans it may have seemed a little like the man whose life has been saved, saying to his benefactor, "Oh, by the way, many thanks for saving my life last month." As a matter of fact, it was an American, working in England, who seemed to sense the necessity for more immediate gratitude, for on October 14, 1941, Edward Montgomery, the American journalist, said in his broadcast: "The British people are grateful for these ships. I thought you might like to know that." A similar error was not made concerning the Lease-Lend Bill.

The lack of coordination between the Ministry of Information and the military services, typical of the partially autonomous functioning of departments in a democracy, has consistently handicapped the BBC and is, of course, one of the reasons why the Ministry of Information has become the graveyard of political careers.[2] The military services have been very cautious in the information to which they are willing to let the Ministry of Information have access. This is one cause for the unreliability of the BBC news bulletins in the Norwegian and Flanders campaigns and for the paucity of news at other times. It is also partly responsible for astonishing interpretations by English broadcasters who have not been in a position to know what is really going on. Thus when Holland and Belgium were being overrun by Nazi mechanized divisions, one of the military experts of the BBC calmly informed his American audience that the British Army was relatively the most highly motorized army in the world—yes, more highly motorized than the Germans who still relied a good deal on horse transport.

In spite of the individualistic nature of the British broadcasts to North America it would be a mistake to regard them as chaotic and utterly lacking in direction and unity. While there may have been no blueprint set before each speaker as is true in German broadcasting, there were, nonetheless, some well-defined policies which have been well observed. For example, British broadcasters studiously avoided taking sides in the 1940 presidential election although they were very eager to see President Roosevelt reelected. Similarly while the Lease-Lend Bill was being discussed, they quietly stayed out of the debate. This practice was in line with the general policy of asking for American help rather by

<hr/>

[2] N. Riley in his *999 and All That* (London, Victor Gollancz, Ltd., 1940) gives an English journalist's criticism of the conduct of the Ministry of Information in the early days of the war.

indirect suggestion than by direct appeals. The British broadcasts derived some unity, too, from the selection of speakers. Obviously only those who were interested in stating the British case to America have appeared before the microphone. But perhaps the greatest unifying factor has come from the forensic leadership of Winston Churchill. His resounding phrases were echoed and reechoed by news commentators and feature speakers alike. Nor has this been due to regimentation of the broadcasters; rather it derives from the Prime Minister's rhetorical skill in expressing what his countrymen feel.

3. The Inferior Character of News Bulletins and News Commentaries Compared with the American Radio and with the BBC Feature Talks.

Both the British and the German radio news services have suffered by comparison with the American radio, primarily because governments in time of war control the agencies of information directly or indirectly. In England the Ministry of Information has had its difficulties with the military services in securing adequate and timely information. As a result BBC news bulletins have frequently lacked novelty and timeliness, a fatal thing in radio presentation. In the history of the Princeton Listening Center there was only one occasion on which the staff felt that it had received information from short wave in advance of the regular American news channels—in the occasion of the Hess case.

Moreover, the optimistic bulletins of the BBC were shown to be grossly unreliable in both the Norwegian and the French campaigns. In the Norwegian campaign the BBC accepted unconfirmed reports from Sweden which led its listeners to believe that the British were winning the Battle of Norway. The resulting news of the British withdrawal came as more of a shock in England than in America where other news sources were available. In the Battle of Flanders and the Battle of France the reporting was not as inaccurate, but again the BBC gave the wrong impression of the course of the battle. The general formula followed in these campaigns was: first, glowing accounts of Allied strength and enemy weakness; second, detailed accounts of minor actions favorable to the Allies; then, promise of great news to come as the major battle is now being joined; but then no account of the major conflict and finally belated explanations of the German victory and its compensating aspects for the Allied cause. One is led up to a major climax with hope of a

British victory, but the climax is omitted and instead anticlimactic accounts of the strategic retreat begin to come in.

After Dunkerque the news bulletins were somewhat more reliable, but there was almost always the expected tendency to present events in a favorable light to Britain. Thus the air raids on Germany were for a long time exaggerated out of all proportion to their military importance. Day after day the BBC recited accounts of devastation to German ports and German military objectives with serious crippling of German industry, and from these highly destructive operations "only three of our bombers failed to return." The listener was sometimes tempted to wonder if one reason why only three planes failed to return was the fact that the original squadron was not too numerous. When the first North African campaign got under way and there was better fare to offer the public, one could almost feel the relief with which the BBC dropped these stories of the British air offensive on the Continent.

Not only have news bulletins suffered from both unreliability and repetitiousness, but the news commentaries in their interpretations of current affairs were also below the best American standards. The commentators were sound in historical background but mediocre in contemporary analysis. Their performance in forecasting developments has been poor. The American public was able to get a better summing up of important events and a better statement of future possibilities from its own commentators. No British news commentator has been up to the standard of Raymond Gram Swing. The lackluster nature of the news commentaries was the more striking when compared to the brilliant work of the speakers in such series of feature talks as *Britain Speaks, Within the Fortress*, and *Democracy Marches*. There was no one who stood out in news interpretation as Priestley did in his general interpretation.

4. The *Indirect* Motivational Appeal of the British Broadcasts.

Compared to the direct stimulation of motives in the modern advertising or political campaign the British appeal for American support has been indirect and remote. In place of the many specific and varied appeals to fundamental motives of security, materialistic gain, and egoism, so characteristic of the American propagandist, the BBC speakers have emphasized the general moral symbols of democracy, decency, humanity and Christianity. They have stated their case in broad, abstract terms and have directed their pleas to the derived or secondary human drives rather than to the appetitive, biological and materialistic urges. In brief, the British motivational appeal was calculated more to enlist casual sympathy than to energize people to definite measures of action.

The British have not, however, left the story at the point of justifying the moral righteousness of their struggle. They have gone on to show that their cause is ours, that if Britain, the bridgehead of democracy, were to be destroyed, America would have to face a Nazi-dominated world alone. Even here, however, the issue was not translated into specific motivational appeals. The threat to the American way of life in a German victory was not implemented by particular instances to show how our daily lives would be affected. Little reference was made in concrete terms to the effect of a German victory upon American living standards, upon American trade, and upon American employment. The implication of the British story has been that with the fall of Britain, America would be the victim of a German attack. But little was done to make this plausible for the American to whom the Atlantic Ocean stands as a great protective barrier. Nor have the possibilities of Latin American infiltration been exploited. Finally, in the event of a German victory, a much more immediate danger to America than military invasion would be the great impetus which Nazi success would give to Fascist forces within the United States. Of this possibility, however, there was only the vaguest hint in British propaganda.

The indirection of the British approach is consistent with the attitude which British propaganda theorists and broadcasters alike have expressed toward propaganda. They have asserted that they are not interested in the high pressure methods of the advertiser with its minor deceptions nor the Machiavellian techniques of deceit practiced by the Germans. They contended that all they wanted to publicize was the truth about the war and that in the long run the truth would win them more support than Goebbels' whole bag of propaganda tricks.[3] While it would be naïve to accept the expressed British conception of their propaganda policy at its face value, it is nonetheless true that many of their practices have accorded with their theoretical position. They have not regimented their spokesmen as do the Germans nor have they coordi-

[3] The British attitude toward propaganda has been recently stated by F. C. Bartlett in his *Political Propaganda* (1940) and is also found in S. Rogerson, *Propaganda and the Next War* (1938).

nated their propaganda with other weapons in their conduct of the war, as has already been observed. Their unreliability in news reporting has produced relatively minor distortions and seemed to flow more from ineptitude and the lack of cooperation between the War Office and the Ministry of Information than from a deliberate attempt to misrepresent the major issues of the war.

Moreover, it is altogether probable that the indirect nature of their motivational appeal will be more effective from a long-run point of view than high pressure techniques and deceitful tricks. In the first place, the truth of the matter does indicate considerable community of interest between Great Britain and the United States. With this solid basis to go on, the British could afford to be ethical in their presentation of the case.

In the second place, by merely stating their case and not directly appealing to us to come into a shooting war, the British avoided the negative effect of alienating our support. Many Americans felt that we had been tricked into entering the last war. They were on the alert for any obvious propaganda tricks which would involve us once again.[4] So it may have been good strategy on the part of the British to enlist our sympathies by general symbols and allow our own leaders to implement the general appeal with concrete suggestions. Thus the Lease-Lend Bill coming from President Roosevelt and backed by Willkie met much less opposition than would have a similar proposal presented directly to the American people by the English leaders themselves.

In the third place, the British may have been more interested in American supplies than in our formal entry into the war. Her need was ships and the munitions of war and hence there was no necessity for trying to stir up the American short-wave audience to the pitch of war fever. If she succeeded in winning sympathy for her plight, American political leaders already converted to her cause could do the rest. Finally, the small audience of upper-income people did not need as direct a motivational appeal as would a mass audience. They were capable of translating the English case into concrete terms themselves.

The Strategy of British Broadcasts: The Pre-Dunkerque Phase

The characteristics of British broadcasting, just discussed, were both a result of the strategy of the British manipulation of themes and a con-

---

[4] Moreover some Americans have a feeling of guilt about the last war which may overdetermine their isolationist behavior in the present situation. Cf. J. S. Bruner, "The Dimensions of Propaganda," *Journal of Abnormal and Social Psychology*, 1941, Vol. 36, p. 316.

ditioning or limiting factor of their strategy. The broader strategy of the British conduct of the total war, which has avoided thorough co-ordination of the Ministry of Information with the military services (thus giving the short-wave broadcasts their individualistic, unregimented character), determines in part the strategy of the broadcasts themselves.

In the first phase of the war, the pre-Dunkerque phase, the characteristics of the Overseas Service of the BBC just discussed appear in their most exaggerated form. The programs appeal to a very small audience not only because of their intellectual character but because of their particular type of intellectualism. Historical background is used in news interpretation in a ponderous way, feature talks are too often cultural in the worst sense of the word, and the academic statement is preferred to the interesting expression. The planless, uncoordinated nature of the programs is distinctly in evidence. The dynamic leadership for the war of words, later supplied by Churchill, is missing. The news features show their most marked inferiority during this period. The motivational appeal is so indirect as to be almost lacking.

The first phase shows little patterning of symbols or plan of campaign. The broadcasts reveal more than anything else the England of Chamberlain, Henderson and Halifax; an England that considered any adjustment to war conditions as the equivalent of an adequate adjustment; a complacent, smug, even senile England; an England that ran its war industries on a peacetime basis, that failed to place adequate war orders in America; the England, so rich and so powerful in its own eyes, that it felt that somehow it could not be really touched by the brutal realities of war.

The reflection of this atmosphere in British broadcasting is clearly seen in its news stories on unemployment. The total unemployment as of December 11, 1939, is reported by the BBC as 1,361,000 and Chamberlain's prediction is cited that workers will be rapidly absorbed by the armament industries. Yet almost three months later, on March 4, 1940, the British news announcer gives the unemployment estimate as 1,500,000 and proudly calls attention to the reduction which this figure represents over the 2,000,000 unemployed in March 1939. In other words, a nation engaged in total war with its existence at stake not only failed to utilize its man power, but was so unaware of its danger that it could broadcast to its American audience that six months after the outbreak of the conflict it still had an army of a million and a half unemployed out of an adult working population of less than twenty million.

It is hard to escape the impression during the pre-Dunkerque days that British broadcasts were an open window through which one could look directly at the thoughts and actions of the British leaders rather than a façade erected to please an American audience. The radio stories are as revealing of Chamberlain's England as Neville Henderson's book, *The Failure of a Mission*. The strategy of British broadcasting in this first phase of the war shows two outstanding features: (1) the temporal lag between events and British themes and symbols and (2) the defensive position of the British in meeting German propaganda.

1. The Lag Between Objective Events and the Themes and Symbols of British Broadcasting.

The British in their interpretations of the war stressed themes which reflected the past. The contemporary scene was neglected and the future was not anticipated. Their symbols in this period were the symbols of the last war. In the specific application of their ideology they were always behind rather than ahead of actual developments. This is true both of their interpretation of the military nature of the war and of the moral issues involved.

The themes which were used concerning the nature and conduct of the war were: the economic blockade as the primary weapon of the war, the superiority of sea power to air power, empire unity and strength as contrasted to German weakness, and Anglo-French unity and strength as contrasted with German weakness. Much space was given to the reiteration of the idea that an economic blockade would force Germany to her knees. Constant reference was made to the war at sea, to German shipping and naval losses, and to the great superiority of the British shipping position. In addition to frequent news items, detailed talks on the topic were not uncommon. Thus on January 8, 1940, Sir Arthur Salter, Parliamentary Secretary to the Ministry of Shipping, gave a fifteen-minute lecture on the *Empire Merchant Marine*; on February 29, 1940, A. C. Hardy talked on *British Shipping*; on March 3, 1940, "Taffrail" spoke on the merchant navy and fishing fleet and the same character appeared from time to time with similar contributions; on March 7, 1940, Roland Bird lectured on the *Export Council*; on March 8 the captain of the *Queen Elizabeth* was heard from; and on March 28 Dennis Powell and Salter discussed our *Present Shipping Strength*. These talks with insignificant changes could all have been made in World War I. There is little recognition that the situation had changed either from the point of view of advantages to Germany or to Britain. No emphasis is placed upon the greater vulnerability of the German economy with its background of years of *Ersatz* living nor is allowance made for the loopholes in the blockade through Italy and Russia. The theme of economic blockade by sea power is used with little relation to the contemporary situation and little anticipation of future possibilities.

An even more spectacular lag appears in the theme of the superiority of sea power to air power. In spite of the demonstrated effectiveness of air power on land in the Polish campaign, the British continued to ignore its possibilities as a threat to the British Navy. To the Englishman the control of the seas is one of the dearest of symbols. To modify his conception of it either for an Empire or an American audience was beyond his emotional horizon. The Norwegian campaign demonstrated the real challenge of the German bombers to the British Navy. But the British commentators continued to lag behind events with repetitions of the theme that Britain rules the waves and with encouraging accounts of the naval victory at Narvik. Though the Dunkerque evacuation was justly hailed as a superb achievement of the navy, the tendency nevertheless was to neglect the role of the RAF in fighting off the German bombers. Vernon Bartlett's statement at the time shows in its phrasing the cherished faith of the British in sea power. He said: "The miracle of this evacuation continues, thanks to Anglo-French cooperation and thanks to the proof that air power has no superiority over sea power." (June 2, 1940)

The themes of British military strength based upon the last war consistently underestimated the importance of the air arm in the war of words as in the war of bullets. For example, Charles Gardner spoke on *Some Aspects of the German Air Force*, admitted the German superiority in numbers, but went on to draw the wrong conclusions. The Germans, he stated, made two mistakes. One is their overfondness for allying the air force with the army. "In consequence the German air force has an army cooperation bias. . . . The result has been that the German pilots are trained mostly for working at short range and in conjunction with moving armies, bombing and dive bombing a path for the mechanized forces on the ground." (April 13, 1940) In effect the British even after Poland and at the time of the Norwegian campaign regarded the German teaming of air force and army as unorthodox because apparently it didn't keep the planes up in the skies where they belong. Finally, however, in November of 1940 the lag between the old symbols and the march of events was partly remedied, for the BBC carried the announcement of the Air Ministry of the creation of a new branch of the RAF to be known as the Army Cooperation Command. This is described as the latest if not the final step in building a system of cooperation between the two services—a policy strongly advocated in the past by experts. And that night Macdonell commented on the lessons not of Flanders nor of the Norwegian campaign, but on the Polish campaign in which there was such superb cooperation between the German ground and air forces.

The lag between actual developments and the interpretation of the war by the BBC is to be found both among its own speakers and in the admissions of British officials recorded in its news bulletins. After the Norwegian evacuation the BBC admitted that the crucial difficulty had been the local air superiority of the Germans due to German control of local air bases. And the news report for May 7, 1940, recounts the speech of Oliver Stanley, then Secretary of War, in the House of Commons thus: "British battalions had been brought up to strength and given all equipment. . . . Had it not been for air attacks, Mr. Stanley said, they might well have maintained their positions for any length of time. . . . Mr. Stanley said that it had been impossible to find out whether there was any chance of getting defense in the air or fighter protection for our troops until those troops had been landed." Stanley's statement that it was impossible to foresee the air problems in the Norwegian campaign, even when it was known that Germany held air bases in Denmark and Norway, is more an admission of the British attitude toward anticipating problems than proof that these problems were unknown and unpredictable.

In the pre-Dunkerque phase the concepts of the last war appear also in the contrast between the manpower and economic resources of the Anglo-French empires and Germany's assets. The strength of the Empire and the united strength of the Anglo-French alliance are recurring themes. The summing up, however, lags behind contemporary realities. The importance of specific military equipment and the specific industries to supply and replace the actual weapons of war enter the picture very incompletely. Figures are given on the comparative naval armaments of the warring parties but other military armament is neglected.

The same lag between objective events and British verbalization can be seen in the moral sphere in this pre-Dunkerque phase. The symbols for which the British were fighting were essentially the same as in 1914. The most frequent moral issues in both the news commentaries and in the feature talks were: (1) the war guilt of the Nazis in their aggression against small nations and in their violation of treaty obligations, (2) Nazi atrocities in Poland and in their air and sea warfare, (3) British democracy contrasted with Nazi tyranny, and (4) British regard for the rights of neutrals, for international law and for law and order in general, as against Nazi illegality. Now it is true that since moral symbols supposedly represent the experience of generations, if not the wisdom of the ages, they are not as easily outmoded by new developments as are the specific concepts concerning the military and economic nature of warfare. Nonetheless, the moral symbols employed by the British in the pre-Dunkerque phase had been worn thin in the last war. American attitudes had changed in the light of postwar events so that the particular formulation of the old themes lacked vitality and dynamic.

The failure of the British denunciation of Nazi aggression to keep pace with the swift German blows can be seen in the British emphasis upon legal technicalities of international law while the Germans marched on to new violations of human liberties. The British justified their export blockade on the legal ground that the Germans had broken the Hague Convention and the 1936 Submarine Convention. And experts on international law went on the air so to testify. During the Finnish war the British accused the Germans of infringing the neutrality rights of the Scandinavian countries, respect for which kept Britain from aiding the Finns. During the Norwegian campaign the British spent some time in trying to prove that their sowing mines in territorial waters came after the German invasion was already under way. A good deal of the British legalistic discussions about German infringements of international conventions would have been more in keeping with prewar events such as the German occupation of the Rhineland and the German intervention in Spain. But now war was on and still the British acted as if what the Germans started in the Rhineland, carried further in the annexation of Austria, continued in the Sudeten absorption and the seizure of Czechoslovakia, were all unrelated events of little moral import.

2. The Defensive Position of the British in Meeting German Propaganda.

British programs during the pre-Dunkerque phase were frequently occupied with attempts to meet German charges. The BBC was distinctly on the defensive from two points of view. First, they allowed the Germans to formulate the issue and they tacitly accepted the enemy formulation of the problem. Second, in meeting the enemy on the battleground he had selected, the British merely entrenched themselves instead of attacking the German positions.

The Germans formulated the issue at stake as a choice between the old system and the new order, between the illusory freedoms of democratic imperialism and the genuine security and equality of national socialism. The British plutocrats had too long dominated and dictated to the rest of the world while they enjoyed the good things of life at the expense of the masses. It is not, the Germans asserted, a war of the English people against the German people. It is the people's war against plutocracy. It is a struggle between the *haves* and the *have-nots*.

In this contrast between the economic benefits of a new order and the fictitious liberties of plutocratic democracy the British took the defensive by their failure to reformulate the problem. Then, within the framework of the issue itself they failed to take the offensive, for they defended the political freedoms instead of attacking the German version of a new order. As a rule it is a mistake to let one's opponent define the points of difference in the dispute, but it is even more of a mistake to defend the role he has assigned you than to attack and expose the role he has assigned himself. In defending oneself the charges of the opponent are publicized explicitly or implicitly and through positive suggestion receive a certain acceptance. Even if one succeeds in clearing himself the emphasis is more upon his guilt than upon the guilt of the accuser. The audience goes away saying, "No, I don't think the defendant was really guilty though he wasn't too bright to have gotten into that mess in the first place." Moreover, to clear oneself of all charges effectively is much more difficult than to hurl accusations. Aside from the sheer factor of time is the inherent fact that since we are not too close to angels an accusation can often have or appear to have a distorting grain of truth in it.

The defensive position of the BBC and the difficulties it involved appear clearly in a series of talks they launched entitled *This Freedom*. The talks emphasized the political freedoms of democratic Britain which were under attack by the German propagandists. They were reasonable discussions which admitted imperfections in democratic functioning but they were colored by a certain complacent acceptance of democratic malfunctioning as inevitable because of the many practical difficulties. Thus Lord Haley explained that India cannot have dominion status because of the Mohammedan minority which is afraid of losing minority rights. "The first attitude of the Mohammedans is to demand guarantees for their protection of a kind which do not seem compatible with a democratic system and a responsible government. Could they get the guarantees by a written constitution under which certain rights of the Moslems couldn't be interfered with? Well, I think their reply would be: the basic statutes of that nature have not proved very successful in central or southeastern Europe. In that respect, the safeguard hitherto has been the existence of the British government." And Beveridge in discussing economic freedom with Cole dismisses Cole's objections as those of a reformer who is trying unduly to hasten the evolutionary growth of democracy.

In effect, then, the weakness of the series *This Freedom* was in the defense of the values of the old system. The Germans had attacked British plutocratic imperialism and enthusiastically described the advantages of their new order. The British reply was, "Yes, our democracy is not perfect, it does not extend sufficiently to the economic sphere, but look at our nice political liberties." This was apparently the issue the Germans wanted to raise and the lines along which they wanted the war of words fought.

Later in this first phase of the war the BBC, though still failing to reformulate the issue, launched a new series of talks called *Under Nazi Rule*, attacking the position of the enemy. This series, though an attempt to carry the war of words to Germany, was so tame and trite as to have little interest or effect for the American audience. It missed many opportunities to bring home the meaning of the fascist dictatorship in the life of the individual. Moreover, it signally failed to explode the Nazi myth of the more abundant way of life of the new order. Effective tales of how the living conditions of the German people were sacrificed on the altar of war to produce guns instead of butter were not told. Though the English at this time carefully differentiated between the leaders and the people and made the Nazi leaders the object of their attack, they nevertheless failed to direct their attack against Nazism. The term Hitlerism was used instead of Nazism and Hitler was singled out as the devil rather than the Nazi system. The British spokesmen either were slow to see the real meaning of fascism or they did not truly hate what they saw. Hence they fell back upon the symbols of the last war and defended democracy casually and unimaginatively.

It is true that an occasional speaker referred to the new order and suggested that England was the genuine source of a new social system. These casual references, however, were merely attempts to exploit the phrase, the new order. They showed no understanding of the issues involved. One broadcaster, for example, pointed out that England was the nation best equipped to develop the new order, since England was always in the process of change. It remained for the second phase of the war to put teeth into the jaws of the British verbal efforts.

The Post-Dunkerque Phase

On June 24, 1940, the day of the signing of the French armistice, Priestley told his North American audience: "Nobody doubts even yet the courage of the individual French soldier nor the sound qualities of the ordinary French people. . . . They have not been beaten, they have been sold out. . . . The strength of the Nazis does not lie in their armaments, formidable though these may be. It comes from the curiously mixed bewildering attack, a technique based on what we might call years of gangster experience. . . . The Nazis are masters of the art of increasing the rottenness in this world and taking full advantage of it. They can spot the weak places and they don't hesitate to pour poison into them. It is this technique far more than the weight of their military machine that makes them dangerous, the most dangerous enemies that our civilization has known for a thousand years.

"They are very fond of describing themselves, as are the fascists, too, as a young and virile people who possess far more of the masculine virtues than the decadent, worn-out citizens of the democracies. A great deal of their propaganda, especially in its photographs showing masses of blond and stalwart young Nordics, is devoted to painting this picture of themselves. And these magnificent young brutes, it is suggested, are irresistible for they belong to a new race of supermen. All this, of course, is a lot of clever humbug designed to impress simpletons. Hitler, Goering, Goebbels, Ribbentrop, Himmler, are these the representatives of a young virile race of conquerors? Take a look at them. Just listen to their talking and screaming. Watch closely all their antics and then judge for yourself.

"... Winston Churchill stands up like a man and openly and honestly tells his people that the road before them will be long and hard. Does Hitler stand up and talk like that? No. . . . He assures them over and over again that they are on to a soft thing, that round the corner is complete victory and they will be able to swallow and bully everybody. Why does he have to feed them this stuff? Because these young, virile all-conquering people haven't the stomach for the hard truth. They have to exist in a kind of opium dream of conquest and grandeur, otherwise they are going to lose heart, their young virile all-conquering hearts. . . . They can't even use their toughest men in the front line. They use them as storm troopers to bully and cow the poor wretches back home.

"... Day and night ceaselessly during those years they jumped to the rotten spots in every corner of the world and the very tolerance and good humor of the democracies provided them with superb opportunities of which they took instant advantage. For these are men who shed all illusions but one: a belief in their own ultimate greatness.

"If you can keep in mind always that gangster background then you have always a clue to their mentality and weapons. Remember, too, that they discovered that sheer impudence pays, so that nothing is too impudent for them. They feel they can't overestimate the stupidity of the world."

Thus opens a new chapter in the British war of words. Gone is the British understatement and reserve; gone is the weak denial that we aren't altogether as bad as the Nazis picture us. Priestley and his colleagues begin to hit out as if they meant it. There is, of course, no sharp line of demarcation, on one side of which all broadcasts are of the pre-Dunkerque character and on the other side of which the war of words is vigorous and definitely purposeful. But Priestley's speech, quoted above, cannot be duplicated before the middle of June 1940, though there are many statements of a piece with it after the June days.

After the inauguration of the North American Service on July 7,

British broadcasts show better program balance and more skilled technical direction. New stars appear before the microphone. The news commentaries improve somewhat. The programs are less planless than before, due to Churchill's leadership and the logic of events. They do not lose their individualistic character, however, and they still are limited to an upper-income audience. As the months wear along, the motivational appeals are not quite so indirect.

The post-Dunkerque phase can be divided into three periods: (1) the period of the invasion threat, from the fall of France through November 1940; (2) the period of Axis reverses, from December 1940 through March 1941, and (3) the period of new strategic retreats, April and May of 1941. Though the general British problem of securing swift, energetic and abundant American aid was the same for all three periods, each period presented its own special problems both on the military and verbal fronts. After the fall of France the urgent problem was to convince the American public of England's ability to survive in any form—instance the line: "There'll always be an England." At first it was a question of immediate survival in the face of the threatened German invasion. When the mass daylight raids failed to give the Germans local air superiority over England, it became a question of lasting through the winter despite the war of attrition in the air and on the sea. The second period begins, however, with the Greek victories in Albania and the British successes in North Africa. The issue shifts from one of mere survival to one of British victory, and Churchill is able to cry, "Give us the tools and we'll finish the job." The third period sees another change in the complexion of the war as Yugoslavia is quickly subjugated and the Greeks and British are pushed back into the sea. Somehow the new Dunkerques must be symbolized into other than a defeatist meaning.

In the following discussion the three periods will first be examined separately from the point of view of the special problems presented and then the constant problem of motivating America to active cooperation will be considered for the whole post-Dunkerque phase.

1. The Period of the Invasion Threat: June through November 1940.

After the fall of France, England's capitulation seemed a matter of time.[5] The British needed desperately to persuade America that they

[5] About 32 per cent of the American public thought England would win the war after the fall of France, whereas before the invasion of the Low Countries over 60 per cent were of that opinion. H. Cantril, "America Faces the War," *Public Opinion Quarterly*, 1940, Vol. 4, pp. 387-407.

could and would hold their island against invasion. The themes employed to accomplish this objective were: (a) Britain's *will to win,* her iron determination to see the war through; (b) her human resources to do the job, notably in the toughness of English character; (c) the unity of all her people in their will to win, and (d) the strategic difficulties of a German invasion especially in the light of Britain's all-out preparations to meet it.

Winston Churchill's famous words of June 1940, set the tone for other British spokesmen with respect to Britain's will to win: "We shall not flag nor fail. We shall go on to the end. We shall fight in France and on the seas and oceans; we shall fight with growing confidence and growing strength in the air.

"We shall defend our island whatever the cost may be; we shall fight on beaches, on landing grounds, in fields, in streets and on the hills. We shall never surrender and even if, which I do not for the moment believe, this island or a large part of it were subjugated and starving, then our empire beyond the seas, armed and guarded by the British fleet, will carry on the struggle until in God's good time the New World, with all its power and might, sets forth to the liberation and rescue of the Old."

The essential toughness of the British character is brought home to the American audience by precept and example. Brian Meredith starts his description of an air raid as follows: " 'Please pass the marmalade,' said the little old lady. I was having breakfast in a small hotel in an English south coast town a very few hours ago. At this moment the air raid sirens began to wail, and the man at my elbow looked up at the clock. 'A little ahead of himself this morning,' he remarked; 'they were three minutes ahead of their schedule yesterday.' I drank my coffee and tried not to gulp it. No one around me budged. 'Would you please pass the marmalade?' said the little old lady again, more firmly this time as the warbling siren died away." (July 4, 1940)

In the pre-Dunkerque phase the theme of Empire unity as a source of Allied strength had been a favorite topic of the BBC. With the threat of invasion hanging over them, the British spokesmen shifted their emphasis to the internal unity of the British island. Empire cooperation still was the subject of news items and of speeches, but during the period of the invasion threat the solidarity of all classes of English society came to the foreground for the first time. The toughness of English character and the will to win are true of *all classes and creeds* within England

Priestley visited the factories and brought back reports of the high morale of the factory workers. Native Scotchmen and Welshmen were brought to the microphone to add their voices to the cause of unity. Old and young, men and women, shop owners and factory hands, farmers and lords, were all pictured as completely resolved to repel the invader. Even pacifists in the past war took the air to tell of their militancy in this one.

Allied to this theme of island unity were the descriptions of the preparations to make things hot for Jerry, for the accounts of these preparations stressed the many organizations of the people, official and semi-official for defending England. Priestley's phrase, *this island fortress*, was not only repeated by other commentators but it was given substance by stories of the building up of the army, the growth of the Home Guard and the barriers and obstacles being erected to prevent successful invasion. In addition, the RAF came in for its share of attention as both a defensive and offensive weapon. Finally, the British control of the sea was never lost sight of in these attempts to show America that Great Britain had both the will and the weapons to repel a German invasion. The net effect gave a heartening impression to England's friends of the strategic difficulties confronting the Germans.

The period of the invasion threat in 1940 took on a somewhat altered aspect as the RAF drove back the enemy air fleets or took a heavy toll thereof during the mass daylight raids of late August and early September. Though official spokesmen warned of the constant imminence of invasion, other speakers directly or indirectly took the attitude that before actual invasion Germany would have to gain local air superiority over England. The blasting of the invasion ports across the Channel also figured prominently in the calculations of the commentators. The feeling grew that prior to invasion the Germans would try to wear the English down both through incessant pounding from the air and from the increasing shipping losses. Moreover, the air victories at long last gave the BBC a genuine success story.

During these months of attrition warfare the British settled down to meet the demands of the situation on the verbal front. Home morale, including considerations of the will to win, the unity of the people and their ability to take it, remained the dominant themes. The subject of the enduring rock of British character became more important than ever. But the British began to object to their own phrase, *England, the beleaguered fortress,* for it gave the impression that England was wholly on the defensive. Hence the offensive efforts of the RAF against occupied Europe and Germany assumed new proportions in short-wave transmission. The bombing of distant objectives had long been a staple commodity of the BBC, and as these raids were stepped up the subject received unusual attention. It was, in fact, the only story the British had of an offensive weapon against the Germans. The blockade was less spectacular in that there was no news of the sinking or capture of important Axis ships. Indeed, it had become a question of who was being blockaded—the Axis powers or Great Britain. The huge Allied shipping losses received very little attention from June 1940 to December 1940 in the BBC short wave to America, though before June there had been a detailed account of these losses at sea.

According to the British account of their excellent home morale four main propositions are apparent: (1) the extent of the damage caused by German bombs is relatively slight; (2) the nature of the damage is non-military as compared with the precision bombing of military objectives by the RAF; (3) the German losses in machines and pilots outweigh the military value of the damage caused, and (4) the greater the intensity of the German raids the higher the morale of the English people. The first of these propositions was not consistently presented since the air raids themselves increased in intensity as the Germans took to night bombing. As the weeks went by, the admission of the destructiveness of the air attacks grew. The gradual admission probably accorded with the facts of increasing damage, but it also had the desirable effect, from the British point of view, of accustoming their American audience to the problem by degrees so that they would not feel that the English cause was hopeless. At times, too, the inconsistency in reporting air raid damage was due to the varying purposes of particular speakers. One man was eager to reassure America that England cannot be knocked out of the war by German bombs. Another speaker sought to enlist American sympathy for the British, subjected to the ruthless Nazi attacks on their churches and homes. Consequently, they told somewhat different tales of the extent of the damage. Hugh Walpole did not exactly reconcile these conflicting versions when he stated on November 17, 1940, "Here once again I reflected on the extraordinary fact that everyone, absolutely everyone, in London had escaped death by a shade."

The second proposition of the nature of the German damage concentrated on the point that the German bombing was indiscriminate, and deliberately so for terroristic purposes. Again and again admissions of the destruction caused by the German planes were accompanied by the claim that the destroyed properties had no military value. They were workers' homes, churches, historical treasures, hospitals, and shops. The bombing was wanton, inspired by the Nazi lust for destruction and murder. It was asserted, in contrast, that the British bombers, if they could not find the assigned military objectives, returned home with their bomb loads. Two purposes were served by this interpretation. The audience might be impressed by the failure of the German air attacks as a military weapon and, also, they might become indignant over the senseless destruction of these attacks. On the other hand, some observers might not follow the British logic in that the so-called indiscriminate bombing might seem to them a blunderbuss weapon but still a military weapon in total war.

The loss of German planes and pilots received much more emphasis in September 1940 than in November 1940, partly because of objective facts. Total German air losses were announced repeatedly during September and October. But as the Germans turned more and more to night bombing their losses were smaller. The British frequently called attention to the German losses in trained personnel. The comparative figures on German and British air losses were even more strikingly favorable to the British when stated in terms of pilots and crews than when stated in terms of planes. The Germans were losing bombers as against fighters; bombers carry crews and fighters often a single flier. Moreover, the British pilot who loses his fighter plane is often able to bail out and come down into friendly territory. The account of the air war thus revealed both the spirit of the RAF and its superiority to the German air force. The prediction was confidently made that just as the quality of the RAF both in men and machines had been proved far superior to the Luftwaffe, so in the course of months with American help quantitative superiority would be achieved. The war, far from being lost, our American friends please note, was already being won in the air and in the factory.

Admissions of the intensity and effectiveness of the German air raids were woven into the theme of the aroused fighting spirit of the whole British nation. We were not only shown an England subjected to brutal pounding of bombs but we were shown a people who responded to this ruthless savagery with the courage of heroes. Their courage was presented not as self-conscious, dress-parade bravery but as the simple, unaffected heroism and self-sacrifice of the common people struggling to preserve their homes and liberties against the Nazi felons. Sidney Horneblow, for example, tells the story of the St. Thomas hospital in London which had been hit by German bombs on four separate occasions within a few weeks. "I talked," said Horneblow, "to the sister in charge of one of them [an improvised basement ward]. 'Aren't the patients a bit nervous in the bombing?' I asked. 'No, they are simply marvelous,' she says. 'They seem so happy and they say they feel safer here than in their own home.' 'And what about you?' I asked, 'Wouldn't you rather be away with the others in the country?' 'No,' she says, 'I would sooner stay here and see it through.' "

I would sooner stay here and see it through was the key line in the BBC stories of English morale. It cropped up among the workers going about their appointed tasks, as in the case of the nurse in Horneblow's account, among the shop keepers, and among the lords and ladies. Even Leslie Howard and Priestley in answer to their American friends, who wondered why they went back to England and the bombing, simply said that they wanted to see it through.

2. The Period of Axis Reverses: December 1940-March 1941.

The Greek repulse of the Italians and the victorious campaign in North Africa gave the BBC new and welcome material for its American audience. It had tried to use the bombing of Germany as the basis for the theme that Britain was carrying the war to the enemy, but now the Allies were really on the offensive. Now, in place of the stereotyped communiqués of bombing operations in Europe, there was definite news of advances, of the occupation of specific territory, of prisoners and matériel taken. American listeners heard in detail the reports of particular victories and the confident prediction that the enemy was at last on the run and it was only a matter of time before ultimate victory would be ours.

Again during this period British courage under air raids was stressed. More analysis was made of German propaganda; there was more questioning of the meaning of the new order in Europe, and more discussion was devoted to peace aims. The main development, however, besides the victory theme was the increasing attention given to Anglo-American cooperation.

The victory theme of the North African campaign employed similar concepts to those used in the air war, namely, the quality of the personnel of the English fighting forces compared to the Axis forces. Both the Italian planes and the Italian mechanical equipment are no match for the British. But more important, the English or Australian soldier is a far superior fighter to the Italian enlisted man both in terms of morale and in terms of sheer fighting ability. When the news is first given of the beginning of an engagement, it is charged that the Italians are masters of the art of retreat. After the victory is won, the BBC, however, says the Italian troops fought bravely enough, but their generals were incompetent cowards who betrayed them. The emphasis upon *the superior quality of the democratic citizen fighting as an individual against the numerically superior masses of totalitarian robots has come to be symbolic of the British interpretation of the war in general.* It is their explanation of their success in the air, their success in North Africa and their hope for ultimate victory. It is the result of the facts in the matter in that the Axis powers have been able to use superior numbers of men and have had superior quantities of mechanized materials, a result also of England's historical position of conquering and ruling in spite of her small man power and a result of the conflicting ideologies of the war: democratic individualism *vs.* totalitarian regimentation.

The victory theme also made a good deal of the role of sea power and the cooperation between sea, air and land power. The naval successes in the Mediterranean vigorously reinforce the English argument that Britain in its continued domination of the seas is still a military power of the first rank.

Another aspect of the victory theme concerns the new defensive role of the Axis powers. *The Axis has lost the initiative* is the key phrase in this interpretation. Thwarted in its attempts to subjugate Greece, pushed almost out of Albania, the Axis faces mounting difficulties in attacking the Suez through the Balkans. Yet with the Italian Empire crumbling and Italy itself insecure, Hitler must take steps to save the situation. Thus Hitler's hand is being forced. Instead of following out his own schedule of war operations, he must now move to check the Allied offensive.

From the time of the fall of France the spokesmen for Britain had linked the destiny of Britain, *the bridgehead of democracy*, with the destiny of the United States. They had spoken of the community of interest of the democratic nations. They had attempted to create the impression of the essential identity in race and culture of the American and English peoples. In this period of Axis reverses the theme of Anglo-American cooperation increased in volume and in intensity. The visits of Willkie and Hopkins to England were played up conspicuously. Daily reports of Willkie's activities were broadcast. Lavish praise was showered upon Willkie and Hopkins by more than one BBC speaker. Gerald Barry, editor of the *London News Chronicle,* in the *Britain Speaks* series commented: "For the British public it has been almost a case of love at first sight. Mr. Willkie has been hail fellow well-met with everybody and the average Englishman's opinion was well summed up by a private soldier who declared, 'You may be a Republican but you are the best Democrat I have ever met.' . . . As for Mr. Hopkins, I personally was familiar already with that irresistible slightly wry smile of his, those shy shrewd eyes and that charm of manner. So I can't pretend that I have been surprised to find that wherever he has gone he has won warm friends." (February 5, 1941)

3. The Period of the New Strategic Retreats: April-May 1941.

The success story of the opening months of 1941 was cruelly interrupted by the Axis recapture of Bengazi early in April. From this point to the end of our study on May 30 the events of the war are a succession of disasters to the Allied cause with the recapture of Libya, the swift subjugation of Yugoslavia, the fall of Greece and finally the crowning blow of the loss of Crete. The British commentators had now the immediate problem of explaining away the German victories and the fundamental problem of reconciling this series of British defeats with the assumption of the ultimate victory of the British cause.

The immediate problem was met by three arguments: (a) the heavy price paid by the Germans in men and matériel, (b) the moral victory of the Allies in their glorious resistance to superior military weapons, and (c) the minor importance of the Balkan campaign compared to the main objectives of the war. The first argument fell back upon the old military maxim (which hardly applies to opponents unequal in armaments) that the attacking side loses much more heavily than the defending side. The story was told of German infantry being mowed down by

British gunners until they had to stop from sheer fatigue. British losses were small both relatively and absolutely, the total loss in Greece not exceeding 15,000 men.

The second theme is the moral victory of the British and their allies. The British went to the aid of the Greeks realizing fully the strategic dangers of the action but determined not to abandon their comrades. The Greeks and the Yugoslavs by their refusal to capitulate before the demands of Hitler, backed by his Nazi hordes, set a glorious example for the world. And the Greeks and the British fought valiantly and skillfully.

Finally, though the German success is admitted, its strategic importance is denied. To win the war Germany must destroy England herself. Compared to this essential objective the Balkan situation is a side issue. To have placed an army numerically comparable to the German troops in Greece and to have kept them supplied would have required transports and warships already needed for the defense of England. The British did not make the major strategic error of denuding their home defenses for a minor success in the peripheral Balkan front. The German conquest of the Balkans brings her no closer to her real goal, the British Isles, and further extends her problems of controlling rebellious peoples.

The same themes are elaborated to show how it is possible for the British to lose battles and still win the war. The moral argument of the heroic resistance of the Greeks and Yugoslavs is exploited for its future possibilities. The Germans, because of this resistance, entered Yugoslavia and Greece not as *collaborators*, as in Rumania and Bulgaria, but as *conquerors* with all the difficulties that conquerors ultimately face.

The losses of the Germans are integrated with the theme that time is the ally of the British. The Allies are fighting a delaying action for the purpose of harassing the Germans and gaining time. As their own war effort gains momentum and as the arsenal of democracy assembles its weapons the Nazi hope for ultimate victory grows slim. But before Britain is on a parity with Germany in machines and munitions every diversion in the Balkans which takes German time and effort is a success whether or not its immediate outcome is the loss of territory.

Allied to this reasoning is the frank admission that the Germans have a seven-year head start on the British in building up a war economy. In the fall of 1940 English speakers were optimistic about matching the

Germans in planes and armaments in a very short time. In 1941, however, the long period of German preparation is borne home to the American audience with the implication that it will take some time before the British can abandon their defensive role and their strategic retreats. The English prophecy is that it will be a long war. Germany with her seven-year preparation will win initial successes but will ultimately lose unless Britain herself can be quickly destroyed. The advantage of this argument is that the passage of time itself, no matter what news it brings, is interpreted as a victory, for it means a long war and hence a German defeat.

Another aspect of this final period is not without significance. The British indirection in asking for American help begins to break down. The cry for ships and more ships becomes in the voices of some speakers almost frantic. "It all depends on the strength that we can draw from overseas *now* into this great armed camp here. Therefore, our cry to our friends in America today is for this one thing: give us *ships, ships,* and *ships.* If you cannot give us your own ships, give us the ships of your enemies that you have interned; build us ships; help us repair our ships in your ports and docks; speed the repairs and hasten our fleets home to us with the stores of war. We are a Jonathan, fighting a battle with a giant, and we need the strong arm of a brother." (Frank Owen, editor of the *London Evening Standard,* on April 9, 1941.)

The Major Problem of the Post-Dunkerque Phase

Though military and political events after Dunkerque created special problems from time to time for Britain's spokesman, their one over-all objective has obviously been the stimulation of all American help short of an actual expeditionary force. This objective imposed a harder task upon British propagandists than the German objective of neutralizing our war effort imposed upon the German propagandists. All the Germans had to do was to slow up the pace of our preparations by techniques of confusion and by appealing to our natural dislike for participation in another shooting war in Europe. On the other hand, the English enjoyed the strategic advantages of being closely related in actual blood, in language, in culture and in foreign policy. American diplomacy has looked to Downing Street for leadership even more than Princeton and Harvard have respected Oxford and Cambridge.

Indirect Solution Through Techniques of Identification

Both the Germans and the British have played their hands according to their intrinsic strength. The Germans have taken full advantage of their easier strategic objective, whereas the British have capitalized upon their cultural closeness to the United States. Since Dunkerque the English have made many efforts to destroy the in-group and out-group barriers between Great Britain and the United States so that American listeners would feel completely identified with the English in one large in-group or family. Thus the BBC has used many speakers who have lived in the States and have friends or a following here and are to some extent already identified with us—for example, Leslie Howard, Ann Dvorak, Vivien Leigh, Lawrence Olivier, Priestley, Somerset Maugham, Noel Coward, and Ian Finley. These broadcasters employ American expressions and American slang. American newspapers and American leaders are frequently quoted. Priestley used the remark of the *New Yorker* about Mussolini waiting to jump in to help the upper dog. Much time on the air was given to the visits of Willkie and Hopkins as has already been indicated. Then, too, Americans now serving England in a military or war capacity of some sort are brought before the microphone. Thus pilots serving in the Eagle Squadron of the RAF recount their experiences in fighting German planes and bombing Germany. American equipment receives conspicuous mention and praise, beginning with frequent reference to the excellence of the Lockheed bombers, and continuing as additional types of equipment reach England. Generally the inference of the identity of the two great English-speaking peoples is left to the audience, but on occasion it is more specifically implied as in the following comment on the destroyer deal by A. V. Alexander, the first Lord of the Admiralty: "The white ensign will fly at their ensign staffs in the future, but many of us will in our minds' eyes see the stars and stripes still fluttering there as well. After all, these ships and all their consorts in the Royal Navy today stand between the Western democracy and the ruthless aggression of the Nazi dictator." (November 2, 1940.)

Moreover, our English cultural heritage is frequently cited. England is presented as the England of Shakespeare, of Dickens and of Thackeray so that it is not alone the living Britishers who are being bombed but our cultural ancestors as well. The parental relationship is further emphasized in a special series of broadcasts by stories of English towns with the same names as American towns. England is described as the fountainhead of democratic institutions. American democracy stems directly from the Magna Charta, about which Americans know more, says Finley, than native Englishmen. The English Parliament is the mother of the American Congress.

The identity of the two nations is also emphasized by the common fate of the two peoples. German propaganda is quoted which ties together the corrupt democracies of England and the United States and their lying leaders, Churchill and Roosevelt. ("The servile and degenerate character of Britain and the United States.") The BBC itself seizes opportunities for linking together Churchill and Roosevelt as the great democratic leaders. ("The free peoples of the world listen now only to Churchill and Roosevelt.")

Devices of identification were used sparingly in the first phase of the war during which little attention was paid to a potential American radio audience. After Dunkerque, however, there is an abrupt rise in the attempts to achieve a psychological identity of Great Britain and the United States. Relatively more time was given in the summer months of 1940 to the English origins of the American culture than in the fall and winter months which followed. Then, the emphasis is placed relatively more on the American aspects of the English struggle. In the summer the BBC was saying: "The destruction of England means the destruction of your parent, for we begot you, you must remember." In the months which followed, however, the BBC said: "American weapons and Americans themselves are fighting with us in the Anglo-Saxon cause against the Nazi tyranny."

Direct Solution Through Appeals to Common Values and Interests

The building up of a we-feeling through techniques of identification was, however, only an indirect way of suggesting the essential community of interest between the United States and Great Britain. The broadcasts from England, both in the news commentaries and the feature talks, advanced reasons and arguments for American participation in the war in everything except men. These appeals calculated to rally support to the British cause seemed clearest in their stimulation of the negatively toned emotions. The BBC portrayed the menace of the Nazi *Wehrmacht* to democratic institutions and to life itself. They pointed out that nation after nation had fallen through failure to unite in the common cause; that Hitler meant to rule the earth; that the British fleet was the protective barrier for the United States as well as for England, and that England as the bridgehead of democracy had to be held if western democracy were to survive. This appeal to fear of the aggressor was not well implemented nor vividly presented but its import could not be mistaken.

Along with the danger of the German threat went the appeal to the dislike of and anger against the common foe. This theme was perhaps more concretely and picturesquely presented than any other appeal employed by the BBC to enlist American support. Churchill, with his verbal scourging of the Nazi gangsters, was ably seconded by Priestley and Finley. *The super policemen, the super bullies, the super gangsters, the lie factory of Goebbels, the pack of ravenous wolves, the brutal Nazi system, the whole blackmailing, murderous, Nazi-Fascist gang, the double cross which is their national emblem,* are some of the labels employed. Moreover, a convincing picture of the calculated cruelty and the callous contempt of the Nazi leaders for any humanitarian values is presented. And this portrayal furnishes a good object toward which the aggressive impulses of the audience can be directed.

The British broadcasters have been more consistent, and perhaps more effective, in arousing the unpleasantly toned emotions of fear and dislike of the common foe than in suggesting positive motives. Definite goals for which the war was being fought, other than defense against aggression, lacked clear definition and authoritative pronouncement. Like a political campaign in which people vote against an enemy rather than for their champion, the British have seemed to do better with their negative symbols in the war of words than with their positive themes.

The positive themes for which the British are fighting, according to their short-wave spokesmen, are essentially four in number: (1) the symbols associated with the rise of democratic national states after the French Revolution, the symbols of political democracy; (2) the universal symbols of morality supposedly transcending epochs and cultures, the eternal verities, justice, truth and decency; (3) the symbols of Christianity, the Christian values of Western civilization—as against Nazi paganism; and (4) the symbols of social democracy stressing economic equality, security and collectivistic values. This profusion of ideological sources[6] could conceivably strengthen the British case, but as a matter of fact it weakened the unity and coherence of the British argument. All these symbols may not be necessarily irreconcilable, but England's spokesmen failed to fuse them into a consistent set of positive peace aims. They were vague and even inconsistent in describing the type of world for which they were undergoing sacrifice and privation. Each spokesman stressed the particular values which appealed most to him. The Conservatives talked about morality, the old-fashioned Liberals about democracy, the progressive Liberals about social democracy, and the occasional religious representatives about Christianity.

Perhaps more serious than the lack of unity in the British idealization of their cause was the greater emphasis given to symbols of political democracy than to social democracy. The political freedoms for which the first World War was fought have come to be rather overworked symbols. Excellent as they may be from an idealistic point of view, it must be remembered that they are the product of an older period. The enthusiasm with which they fired the middle classes during and after the French and American Revolutions cannot be easily recaptured. When the democratic states were young and expanding, the political freedoms symbolized both a freer life of the mind and a more abundant material existence. Compared to the socialistic symbols which the Germans have seized and distorted in their master phrase, *the new order*, the older democratic phrases lack emotional dynamic. They have been contaminated, moreover, with the power politics of imperialism.[7]

As the post-Dunkerque phase wore along, however, an interesting development in the use of different types of symbols can be observed. More and more attention was given to the social changes occurring in England and the social changes which the British want in the post-war world. At first many of these attempts to depict the social democracy in England produced by the war bring out only the rigid class nature of English society. For example, a true story is related of how a real English lady, billeted by mistake to the same house as a tradesman's wife,

---

[6] In an earlier analysis of the Listening Center's British material its director wrote: "Their symbols—Christianity, civilization, democracy, freedom, honor—are broad enough to spread umbrella-like over a multitude of geographical sections and political attitudes." H. N. Graves, "Propaganda by Short Wave: London Calling America," *Public Opinion Quarterly*, 1941, Vol. 5, p. 42.

[7] It is true that like most wars World War I was represented as the people's war, but the symbols employed did not emphasize economic or social democracy. Cf. J. R. Mock and C. Larson, *Words That Won the War*. Princeton University Press, 1939.

actually sits down at the same table with her and the merchant's wife even sits at the head of the table. This occurred during the time they occupied the same house. And Sir Ronald Cross describes how the war has destroyed social barriers: "We actually talk to complete strangers in the street; companions in air-raid shelters become bosom friends in a few minutes. *It's all very extraordinary*, but I think it a very good thing." (October 9, 1940; italics, the writer's.) To some American listeners the truly surprising thing may have been Cross's exclamation, *It's all very extraordinary*. In short, the tales of the charitable spirit of the English upper classes under the pressure of war are a far cry from a convincing account of English social democracy.

Gradually, however, the efforts to set up the goal of a better social order improve. This is accomplished in part by the use of progressives like Brailsford and Wedgwood and by the political development of men like Priestley. The goals of social democracy become more concrete. They include a world of economic security in which unemployment will be unknown and an economic system with more opportunities for the masses and smaller differentials between income groups. The war is interpreted not as a struggle between rival imperialistic regimes but as a people's war against their oppressors. In a talk entitled *Is this an Imperialist War?*, H. N. Brailsford points out that people are making the same mistake in basic issues as in military matters in regarding this war as a repetition of the last one. "The most old-fashioned of us are our radicals. . . . They are opposing the last war in the old ideological trenches which they so stubbornly defended then. . . . The German conquest of Europe would . . . turn Europe into a vast colonial dependency subject to the merciless exploitation of the master race. But that is the *least* thing it could do. It would enslave the entire working class of this continent, which would lose at once its rights of political and industrial organization." (January 7, 1941.)

In spite of the growing recognition among British spokesmen of the necessity of symbolizing war aims in harmony with the mass aspirations of the times, the BBC never achieved a well-formulated program of positive goals of dynamic value for the common people during the period of this study.

This failure is not necessarily an indictment of the British propaganda policy. Propagandists are limited very much in their appeal by conditions over which they have no control. A new dynamic program

for a social order in which there would be no Hitlers may have been too
advanced an ideology as far as America itself was concerned. Such a
program would have alienated many upper-income Americans as too
progressive and too revolutionary. And the American middle classes
might not have been ready for it. The fact is that the American people
do not reflect a homogeneous spirit which will unanimously and enthusiastically accept either the philosophy of the old or the philosophy of the
new. The old philosophy of nationalism with its emphasis upon political
rather than social freedoms and its imperialistic orientation may be as
strong as the social philosophy of the New Deal. It is also true, however,
that the English failed to furnish the proper leadership for even a
definitely limited ideology. They failed to go as far, for example, as
President Roosevelt in his formulation of the four freedoms. The favorable reception of these symbols shows that the English definitely missed
a trick here.

One reason for the failure of the English leaders to exploit the ideological situation can be found in the many practical considerations of
the moment. The Foreign Office was trying to hold as many of the
neutral countries in line as possible. It was trying, moreover, to maintain
the support of the governments in exile, such as the Polish and Dutch.
Hence it would have opposed any propaganda policy of a revolutionary
nature with a broad program for a revised Europe which would not
guarantee the restoration of the national independence of the many
small states. England, fighting for her very life, was in no position to
offend any possible support she saw in any quarter. Moreover, with the
war presenting so many unpredictable factors there was some advantage
in keeping the ideological line as fluid as events themselves. It is a
mistake to confuse ideology and power politics, as Stalin has shown in
his colossal errors. Ideology has to be kept stable and fairly constant if
it is to have motivating value. If the English had adopted a definite
positive ideology, they might have encountered many difficulties. As it
was, in "sloganizing" the war as a conflict of Christianity against paganism they ran into trouble when the atheistic, pagan Russians were attacked and became their allies.

In short, in an uncertain world, with America rather unprepared for
a progressive ideology, with power politics still an important element in
the British will to survive, with self-preservation the all-important factor
at the moment, it is not to be wondered that the English were content

to take an ideological line that was essentially *negative*. This accorded most with the pressing need of the moment; it could be adhered to in spite of unpredictable changes in the social scene and thus save great contradiction; it rallied some support from America; and it offended few, if any, vested interests.

THE STRUCTURE OF ROME SHORT-WAVE BROADCASTS TO NORTH AMERICA

By Bruno Foa

Dr. Foa is at present Director of the Bureau of Latin American Research in Washington, D.C. A native of Italy, he was for several years a member of the faculties of a number of Italian universities as a professor of economics. In 1938 he was appointed Research Fellow in the National Institute of Economic and Social Research, London, subsequently joining the staff of the European News Service of the British Broadcasting Corporation. At the end of 1940 he became a member of the staff of the Princeton Listening Center, and at the same time carried on research work for the Office of Public Opinion Research at Princeton, and the War Documentation Research Project at the Library of Congress, Washington, D.C.

THE STRUCTURE OF ROME SHORT-WAVE
BROADCASTS TO NORTH AMERICA

As befits the land which gave birth to the genius of Guglielmo Marconi, Italy is endowed with a most impressive radio setup, and has been among the pioneers in the field of international short-wave broadcasting.

Prato Smeraldo was, until a few years ago, a solitary tract of that beautiful and melancholy countryside to the south of the Eternal City. At the present time it is the seat of the streamlined "Imperial Short-Wave Radio Center," whose powerful transmitters carry the voice of Rome, in some twenty-five languages, to the remotest corners of the earth. Prato Smeraldo, and to some extent the ultra-short-wave station of Monte Mario, on the very outskirts of Rome, stand thus as the Italian counterparts of Daventry and Zeesen.

The Italian broadcasting services, both domestic and international, are run as a monopoly by a nonprofit government sponsored and controlled corporation, the E.I.A.R. ("Ente Italiano Audizioni Radiofoniche"), known to listeners in English-speaking countries as "Radio Rome."

Radio Rome, for all practical purposes, is just a branch of the Italian Ministry for Propaganda (officially styled "Ministry for Popular Culture") though other government departments have also their say as to its management and policies. And to the extent to which the Italian Ministry of Propaganda is "coordinated" with its Berlin partner, it can be considered as a semi-independent unit of Dr. Goebbels' outfit.

The Nature of Radio Rome Propaganda

The principles which underlie Fascist radio propaganda are, accordingly, closely connected with the Nazi philosophy of broadcasting. Unlike the Nazis, however, the Fascists have never felt the need of an articulated and "scientific" theory of radio propaganda. They have used the radio as best they could, on various occasions, as a weapon for implementing political and diplomatic offensives, for example by stirring up trouble, as by Arabic broadcasts from Bari during the Palestinian troubles of 1936-1938. But one would look in vain for a Fascist "master plan" of radio propaganda in theory or in practice.

There is, of course, a great deal of similarity between Italian and German radio techniques. Both are frequently characterized by an inordinate degree of violence—and by what one might call a "black-and-white" technique, based on elementary crude contrasts, extremes of flatteries and threats and a few highly simplified symbols and slogans. Radio Rome, like the German network, never does things by halves; it knows only friends or enemies and is never embarrassed when it is a question of branding yesterday's friends as today's mortal enemies.

It is true that Nazi propaganda, just as much as Fascist radio propaganda, is departmentally planned even in its minutest details. But German propaganda draws vigor and strength from its close association with all-inclusive political and military strategies which are planned by the German Reich independently and are backed by the tremendous resources of the country, military and otherwise. Fascist Italy, on the other hand, which has consistently played second fiddle in Axis policies, is a junior partner of the German Reich, and her attempts to wield some kind of independent initiative (as against Greece in the fall of 1940) have been far from successful. It follows that while German propaganda can always boast of the power of the Nazi Empire and give out hints as to various fresh developments and initiatives, Radio Rome and Fascist editors such as Gayda and Ansaldo can only refer to "Axis" strength and "Axis" power and to what Germany, and occasionally Japan, can do to make the world safe for the totalitarian dictators.

Besides, whereas Dr. Goebbels employs a staff of highly intelligent and politically-minded broadcasters, most of whom are capable of identifying themselves fully with the policies that their scripts advocate, Fascist radio speakers usually act as unimaginative bureaucrats, bent on "safety first"—that is to say, on avoiding all *faux pas* which might provoke the wrath or the censure of their chiefs.

This is why Radio Rome, in several years of activities in the field of both domestic and international radio, has failed to produce a single radio personality, or even one "broadcaster" in any real sense. No trace can be found in its broadcasts of the oratorical and intellectual gifts which Italians possess so profusely. By and large, Fascist political broadcasts have the irritating mechanical quality of electrical transcriptions; they are all "canned" broadcasts in a very fundamental sense.[1]

The Peculiar Significance of Radio Rome

Were the behavior of Radio Rome invariably shaped on the Berlin model, with a customary time lag, it would hardly deserve independent attention. But, as we have indicated, this is by no means entirely true.

First of all, there have been occasions when Radio Rome definitely took the lead in Axis radio policies. The anti-American Axis campaign of the last eighteen months is a very good case in point, for while Berlin for a long time pursued a rather cautious and ostensibly detached attitude toward the American moves in aid of Britain, Rome came out in the open as early as the fall of 1940. Whether this was due to the Fascists' desire to obscure their military defeats in Greece and Africa by a cloud of international controversy, or whether Radio Rome was employed as some sort of scouting craft by Berlin strategists is, of course, in the present stage of our knowledge impossible to say.

What is even more important, Italy, from the first day of her intervention, had to face the initiative of both ally and foe. With the exception of the short-lived battle waged at the French frontier in June, of the occupation of British Somaliland in August, and of Marshal Graziani's

[1] Most of the talks and commentaries broadcast from Rome are delivered anonymously by speakers described as "staff lecturer," "member of our staff," or with pseudonyms such as "the Italian Pimpernel" or "Machiavelli, Jr." The Radio Rome English-speaking staff is understood to include mainly people, both men and women, of Anglo-Italian or American-Italian extraction. Judging from the volume of references to monetary and banking affairs, it is permissible to infer that it must include a disproportionate number of amateur or "crank" economists, and it is not difficult to make plausible guesses as to the ultimate source of the peculiar brand of muddled thinking which characterizes Radio Rome's economics.

Major James Strachey Barnes, a veteran member of Mosley's fifth column, delivered a series of addresses to the British public during the fall of 1940, thereby gaining the distinction of attaining a degree of violence almost unequaled even in the annals of Radio Rome.

Other well-known propagandists of the Fascist gospel to Anglo-Saxon countries, such as Professor Luigi Villari and Mrs. Olivia Rossetti Agresti, are often featured in the Rome broadcasts to England and North America.

In so far as this country is concerned, however, the trump card of Radio Rome is Ezra Pound, who is invariably introduced as "the well-known economist and poet." Mr. Pound is a fanatical admirer of Mussolini, and an all-out champion of Fascism, totalitarianism, and anti-Semitism, although, for some unexplained reason, he never tires of quoting Jefferson, John Adams, and Lincoln, strange bedfellows indeed of the Fascist dictator! It is difficult to apply standards of judgment to his broadcasts, which, incidentally, were the despair of Princeton transcribers. Perhaps it was not a mere coincidence that his first talk on the American program of Radio Rome (February 6, 1941) bore the title *The Limits of Human Understanding*, and indeed traveled far beyond those limits, however widely or loosely defined.

thrust to Sidi Barrani at the beginning of September 1940, Italy has always fought on the defensive. At the same time, all major military offensives of the period—the air blitz on England, the drive through the Balkans and the invasion of Russia—have been the responsibility of Germany.

Accordingly, and no matter how aggressive they may have been in appearance, the strategies of Radio Rome have been so far mainly defensive. The complacent expectations which were entertained in the first phase of Italy's intervention had to give way to a more grim outlook. Radio Rome had to readjust its policies over and over again, under the impact of quite a few unpleasant shocks. To that extent its behavior reflected, far more than the unperturbable self-confidence of the Nazi stations, the ebbs and flows of BBC strategies in the first year of the war.

Conditions, Expectations, Techniques—The Intervention Trend

Radio being a mirror of foreign policy, it will first be necessary to recall the political developments which conditioned the strategies of Radio Rome. Those during the period extending from September 1939 to June 1940 can be briefly summarized as follows. From the outbreak of the war to the end of February 1940 Fascist Italy followed an ostensible policy of "nonbelligerency" which, so far as an outside observer could have judged, was hardly distinguishable from neutrality. No doubt a pro-German bias existed and was apparent, but it was mostly confined to the press, while the radio, especially foreign language radio programs, gained an unexpected reputation for fairness and impartial reporting. For the first time in two years the Russo-Finnish war marked a certain divergence in the radio policies of Berlin and Rome, for while Berlin was cold and detached, Rome sponsored the Finnish cause as if it were her own. It even looked as if Italy might take the lead, under the auspices of the Holy See, in promoting a joint "European" front against the Bolsheviks, and only timid anti-German references were allowed to appear in the Rome newscasts. It was significant, however, that the scathing denunciations by the Vatican Radio of the German rule in Poland, which occurred at about the same time, were carefully ignored.

The turning point in the official Fascist policies came on March 2,

1940, when the Anglo-Italian coal dispute was featured very prominently by the Italian press and radio and used as a peg for a violent, if short-lived, anti-British campaign. A few days later, Von Ribbentrop came to Rome, and the two dictators met at the Brenner Pass. This led at once to a revival of symbols such as "Axis" and "German-Italian alliance" which had for long been kept in the icebox. The invasion of Norway marked the beginning of an open and complete identification of Italian with German interests on the part of Radio Rome. Unmistakable signs, including authoritative pronouncements, indicated that Italy had decided to enter the war and that the only question still open was the actual date of intervention. On May 11, just twenty-four hours after the beginning of Hitler's offensive in the west, Radio Rome started its own private blitz against the Allied Powers. Great prominence was given to a report by an official of the Italian Foreign Ministry, which raised the whole question of the blockade and declared that the British had created an intolerable state of affairs for Italy. During the following days, the voice of Radio Rome became louder and ever more threatening. It was pointed out that the British fleet had made a poor showing off the coast of Norway and that in the near future it could not be expected to do better in the Mediterranean. On May 31, Radio Rome quoted a Berlin source as saying that Italy was "on the verge of entering the war." On June 4, one of its announcers coolly stated that "Italy remains perfectly tranquil on the eve of entering the war." On June 10, at 6 p.m., Mussolini appeared on the balcony of Palazzo Venezia, in Rome, and announced that the die had been cast.

Looking back on those developments, it is quite clear that Radio Rome had a definite place and function in the Fascist international strategies of the period. Up to March, it was used to mislead the Allies and to suggest that Italy took a detached and impartial attitude and might even be prepared to bolt to the democratic side. From April onwards, the broadcasts of Radio Rome, together with many other devices, were meant to convey the impression that Italy's intervention might take place at any moment, thereby distracting and immobilizing a part of the Allied land and naval forces. The part played by Italy in keeping some of the Allied forces busy, by the threat of immediate intervention, was openly admitted by Radio Rome later on, and German acknowledgments to that effect were gratefully noted.

Expectations of a Short War

It is plain that Mussolini and his associates banked on a very short war and the immediate surrender or invasion of England. This appears quite clearly from the predictions made by Radio Rome. It also seems possible that the immediate intervention of Spain was expected.

Dr. Giovanni Ansaldo, the star commentator of Radio Rome in the domestic programs, had already prophesied with glee, as early as April, the invasion of England in the summer. On June 3, one commentator scoffed at the suggestion that the war might be long and hinted at "new forces, including Italy, which may furnish the necessary impulse for a decisive stroke with such speed that the prophets of a long war will be stupefied."

On June 17, the day of Petain's surrender, Radio Rome predicted that "the capitulation of England is not far off." On July 7, and we quote merely at random, it was stated that Count Ciano had gone to Berlin to prepare "the last phase of the war against England." On the fifteenth, the authoritative *Giornale d'Italia* was quoted as writing: "Germany is preparing to inflict a final blow on her enemies from the North Sea and the Atlantic, and Italy is preparing a similar blow against Great Britain in her imperial territories. Within *a few days* these preparations will be finished, and Great Britain will be called to settle the final account. She will have to choose between submission and a hard war, *whose phases will not be marked by years or months but by days and hours.* Germany and Italy are nearing this *final phase. . . .*"

On August 12, while great daylight battles were taking place in the skies over England, Radio Rome declared: "Great Britain has been closed in a ring of fire by the German air forces, which are now *ready to stage the final attack.* . . . The German air force is achieving the dominion of the air even on British soil. . . . Britain's fate *will soon be decided by effective action on the part of the Axis Powers.*"

The first disappointment came when the much advertised date of August 15 passed and Dr. Goebbels was unable to flash throughout the world a single picture of Hitler standing in front of Buckingham Palace. Radio Rome felt that some sort of apology was due its listeners and on the sixteenth declared as follows: "The British propaganda machine has declared that Signor Gayda and other prominent Italian journalists had given August 15 as the date that would be fatal to Britain. Now that August 15 has passed, and Britain is still standing, the British propaganda hails this as a victory. As the date was invented by Mr. Duff Cooper's imagination, the victory is fictitious . . . and although the Italians had (yesterday) no reason to rejoice over the fall of London, they could find enough matter for joy in the news of the Italian victories in British Somaliland."

On August 25, Gayda was quoted as warning the British "not to jump to the conclusion that Germany's Blitzkrieg has failed. . . . The British will face new surprises *before many days elapse*." A few days later, Radio Rome made a remarkable change of front, and belittled the very significance of a possible invasion of England: "It is safe to say that *the decisive stage of the war will be fought out not in the United Kingdom but in the Mediterranean*. By losing one link with her Empire, Britain loses her prestige and becomes once more what she had been in the Dark Ages, *an island that anybody can invade*." (August 30)

The trouble, of course, was that though on paper anybody might have invaded England at that time, nobody actually took the trouble to do so. As a consequence, the dreams of quick victory fast disappeared, and after another spell of joyous expectations, which coincided with the German air attacks on London, the guns of Radio Rome had to readjust their range, and the prospects of a war of attrition had to be openly discussed.

Expectations Concerning the United States

There is no evidence that Radio Rome overlooked America's policies and moves or failed to take account of their possible implications. Already on June 1, one commentator said: "Even if Uncle Sam thought to interfere, he is unprepared to come in immediately. . . ." And two days later: "To counter Italy's attitude, the Allies have pointed to the possibility of American intervention in the war. Assuming that she may, it is still interesting to examine the facts. Italy is here on the scene and fully prepared, while America is far away. Italy can throw in her weight immediately, while it will be a long time before America can commence to give active aid to the Allies. . . ."

Besides, it was assumed that American opinion was overwhelmingly isolationist and that America would not "commit the folly of letting herself be beguiled and enticed by the Allies." (June 7)

Throughout that summer, Radio Rome relied on the comfortable assumption that America would avoid all further commitments and that her help to England would be too small and would come too late. The state of unpreparedness of the American defense industry became a favorite theme.

The destroyers-naval base deal was hinted at very early in the Rome broadcasts, the name of Colonel Donovan being linked up with it. When the deal was concluded, Radio Rome tried to minimize its significance and stated that it indicated both American imperialism and the perilous state of the once proud British Empire. But, once more, a certain readjustment of assumptions and techniques had to take place, and the signing of the Tripartite Pact was hailed both as barring the path of American intervention and as a safeguard for the Axis Powers in the event of a long war.

Reverses in Greece and Africa

The brief but violent anti-Greek campaign staged by Radio Rome in August 1940 was a classic of Axis bullying tactics at their worst. It flared up suddenly and reached at once a wholly artificial peak of violence. The Greeks were charged with the "brutal assassination of an Albanian patriot," and almost in the same breath Radio Rome proceeded to dress up a full indictment against the whole Greek nation. It was stated that "Greek megalomaniacs" had the "mirage" of a Greater Greece, which would include Albania within its frontiers. The Greeks were described as satellites and acolytes of the British. Great indignation throughout the Balkans was reported owing to the "savage murder," and apparently it reached new heights after the report that "another Albanian had been assassinated by the Greek authorities."

A few days later, however, Radio Rome denied that Italian troops were being concentrated at the Greek frontier and described that report as one of the "usual manoeuvres" which "might help Britain to draw Greece into the war." Very soon the tension subsided, and Greece was as good as forgotten.

On October 28, the Italian forces suddenly crossed the Greek-Albanian frontier and the opening bars of the fanfares of Radio Rome on the Greek war followed very closely the familiar theme of the "preventive" and "defensive" war. Italy, it was stated, had no aggressive intentions, and was going to protect Greece against the British and against herself. It was declared that England was already making use of Greek naval and air bases and that the British "were so sure of Greek cooperation that they considered a material occupation quite unnecessary." The firm resistance of the Greeks was described as "a proof of the aggressive intentions of Greece."

The campaign, as we know, turned out to be a complete failure, and Radio Rome had to make the best of a rather difficult situation. It was explained, naïvely enough, that the setback indicated "in an incontrovertible manner that Italy had no aggressive intentions against Greece because should she have entertained any such ideas, she would have massed enough troops and raw materials to overrun Greece immediately after the first clash."

As was inevitable, Radio Rome tried to focus attention on the individual bravery of Italian soldiers who, it was explained, were fighting a better armed and more numerous foe, and on the exploits of the Italian Air Force, which was said to be ruling the skies of Albania. The analogy between Greece and Finland was dismissed because "Finland," it was said on December 10, "fought single-handed, while the Greeks are fighting in close cooperation with the British forces." Finally, consolation was sought and found in the Duce's assurance that sooner or later the neck of the Greeks would be broken, and there the matter was allowed to rest.

Marshal Graziani's drive from the Libyan frontier to Sidi Barrani, at the beginning of September, had been hailed by Radio Rome as the first stage of a general offensive against the Suez Canal. It was eventually pointed out that a period of preparation was necessary, in view of the formidable difficulties of the enterprise. But rumors that the British might seize the initiative and strike back were dismissed (October 24) by statements such as the following: "The British are probably unaware that the Italians seldom lose a position after they have conquered it."

At the beginning of December, Radio Rome gave out signs of an impending fresh Italian offensive and pointed out (December 3) that "a successful offensive by Italy in Africa might well be sufficient to bring the British Empire to its knees."

The brilliant campaign waged by General Wavell, therefore, took

Radio Rome by surprise no less than the Italian High Command. A certain natural hesitation was accordingly exhibited when it was a question of acknowledging the enemy successes. Disquisitions about enemy advances which might well prove to be blunders and the irrelevance of mere territorial gains began to creep in; one even heard much of "lengthening lines of communications." The BBC could not have handled the job better. Later, and when it became apparent that the British offensive had not been stalled after its initial thrust, Radio Rome took a noble and defiant attitude. It gave up its previous attempts to minimize the losses and admitted that Italy was taking severe punishment. But, it was added, Italy could take it. Attention was called to the heroism of the Italian soldiers, especially the stubborn resistance of the Bardia garrison, and to the strength of Italian morale. Mr. Churchill's Christmas speech to the Italian people, and obviously exaggerated reports about the collapsing of Italian morale published in England and this country, enabled Radio Rome to distract attention from the battlefield and concentrate on the issue of morale. Italian morale, it was declared, had emerged from the trial unscathed, and the British effort to knock Italy out of the war had been a failure.

Explaining Defeats

The technique of explaining away defeats is bound to follow certain ironclad rules which are very much the same for totalitarian and democratic propagandists. First, you ignore the setback. Next, you deny it. Later, you defiantly admit it, but call attention to the gap between the alleged aims of the enemy and what has been actually achieved. The center of gravity of the discussion shifts from the enemy to the "self," from details to general principles, from the battlefield to the home front. But, clearly faced with adversity, totalitarian propaganda finds itself in a particularly bad predicament. Democratic governments do not claim the distinction of infallibility, while totalitarian philosophy is based on the assumption of complete and uninterrupted success. Loss of face is not so damaging to democracies as it is to totalitarian countries, for the emphasis of Fascist and Nazi propaganda is on the smooth and clock-like work of their political and military machine, so that a slight setback risks the overturn, at least on the psychological front, of the whole apple cart. A democracy can admit that it has been wrong— a dictatorship never. On the other hand, the totalitarian propagandists have an advantage in that they have fewer compunctions about hiding the truth behind false claims and accusations.

This shows why totalitarian propaganda cannot explain a setback without resorting to some preposterous types of rationalization—note the extravagant lengths to which Radio Rome was forced in its search for an "explanation" of reverses suffered by the Italian armies in Greece. The weather, British "perfidy," and the fact that Italy was fighting on many far-flung fronts were all invoked. An anti-American barrage was started as early as November and increased in coincidence with the fall of Koritza and Argyrokastron—possibly as a hint that the Americans were really somewhat to blame for the plight of the Duce's armies. The African defeats were handled by Radio Rome much more cleverly, and, taking a long view, one can even say that it made as good a job of its task as was possible under the circumstances. Nevertheless, a number of damaging admissions had to be made, and these involved a striking change of front as far as propaganda strategies were concerned.

The main change occurred with respect to Britain. The weary British lion, badly battered and indeed on its deathbed, which had been one of the favorite similes of Radio Rome until December 1940, gave way to a quite different picture. It was suddenly discovered that Italy had to stand the armed might of the most powerful empire of the world, which had thrown into the struggle, as it was alleged, "no less than 1,500 airplanes, 425,000 men, and half a million tons of warships." (December 20) Italy was proud, it was declared (February 10, 1941), "to have to face this great and desperate offensive of the British Empire," and no less an authority than the Fascist National Directorate was quoted as having praised in a message to the Duce (March 23) "the daring of Fascist Italy in throwing herself against the most powerful empire in the world."

This was all very well in so far as it helped to heal the wounds inflicted by the enemy on Italian prestige, but it meant that Radio Rome had traveled far from the supreme contempt and disdain it had exhibited along with the other media of Fascist propaganda during the palmy days of the intervention. It had pretty thoroughly scorched its own earth on the propaganda front.

Under the circumstances, it was natural that the hopes of Radio Rome should turn toward the future. In the words of one commentator (January 5): "The coming of Spring and the invasion may write the last act of the British Isles forever."

Rome Broadcasts to North America

Radio Rome has paid increasing attention to its audience in this country ever since the spring of 1940, when regular commentaries were added to the short-wave newscasts for America. In October, the North American Service of Radio Rome was expanded to 2½ hours; the number of daily news bulletins was increased from 2 to 4, and 2 talks in English were scheduled as a regular evening feature. This did not include the short-wave programs in Italian, intended for the American community of Italian origin, which also featured 2 commentaries each day plus a number of news bulletins. In addition, Rome short-wave broadcasts addressed to the British Isles have also been available to possessors of short-wave sets in this country.

There is no doubt that the volume of references to American affairs and of direct propaganda during the first year of Italy's intervention grew altogether out of proportion to the increase in the actual number of hours of broadcast. During the summer of 1940 the United States was pretty much out of the picture. But, already in the fall, references to this country had grown from a few scattered bits of news and comment to a regular coverage of news from Washington, and to full-dress commentaries on America's attitude. And though for a while no overt attempt was made to appeal directly to the American man on the street or to evoke from him some kind of definite response, this practice was later sharply reversed; the American listener was treated no longer as an onlooker, but as a protagonist in the drama who had to be persuaded and won over.

Trends of Broadcasts to the United States

The main trend of Radio Rome broadcasts to this country, in the year under review (May 1940-May 1941), can be divided into three successive periods. The first phase covered the summer of 1940. Comparatively little attention was paid to American moves in aid of Britain, and though there were occasional references to the isolationist trend in domestic opinion, to American imperialism, and American unpreparedness, there was no such thing as a coherent and well-knit strategy

The second phase coincided, roughly speaking, with the fall and the presidential election, but, once more, although there was intensified stress upon American isolationism, with ample quotations from Senator Wheeler, Colonel Lindbergh, etc., Radio Rome kept a fairly detached and moderate attitude.

Some anxiety, however, developed soon after the election, finding expression in an increasing volume of blandishment and bait held out to this country, which clearly implied the desire to exercise a sort of mild pressure. It was insinuated that the collapse of Britain would pave the way to important territorial aggrandizements by the United States, and there began to be much talk, at the same time, of the Monroe Doctrine and "Europe for the Europeans."

The third phase opened towards the end of 1940 and involved a drastic rearrangement in assumptions and techniques. From the time of President Roosevelt's December fireside chat, Radio Rome apparently assumed that the United States was already in the war, and its North American broadcasts were accordingly shaped along the lines of broadcasts to an enemy country. This is proved by the fact that the general character of Rome broadcasts to the United States became identical with that of the broadcasts to England. The same themes cropped up, the same targets came under fire. President Roosevelt shared with Mr. Churchill the ignominy, or shall we say the honor, of being Public Enemy No. 1 of the Axis.

The Problem of Initiative

As we have already hinted before, unlike Berlin, which stuck as long as possible to the fiction of "friendliness" towards the United States, the Rome radio abandoned fairly early its complacency regarding the attitude of this country in the war and showed little hesitation in pinning on the United States the label of an enemy country. This may have been due not only to a desire to distract attention from Greece and Libya, but also to offer some sort of justification for the fact that the war was still dragging on. In fact, much in the same way as Radio Rome justified the Italian failure against Greece on the ground that the Greeks were being assisted by the British, it implied also that the Axis failure promptly to crush Britain was to be imputed to American aid to Britain.

In some way, therefore, it can be said that Radio Rome took the initiative in opening hostilities against this country. But in a deeper and far more fundamental sense this was not true. The most significant fact in the history of Axis-American relations ever since the destroyer deal has been that this country has wrestled the political initiative from the dictators and has kept it ever since. In other words, the United States has moved forward steadily, finally aligning itself in the anti-Axis camp, while Germany and Italy have found it expedient to refrain from openly hostile initiatives, with the single, though important, exception of the Tripartite Pact with Japan. This state of affairs compelled Radio Rome, as well as the German radio, to be on the defensive throughout the period—defensive in the sense that the Axis was deprived of the careful and convenient choice of its target, of freedom of choice in the timing of its outbursts, and was reluctantly forced to acknowledge a succession of rather hard knocks. It was only in later months that Radio Rome attempted to seize the initiative and shift the ground of debate to American domestic conditions, resorting thus to what might be called offensive strategies. But, again, while Rome and Berlin could only increase their fulminations and threats, this country was *acting*—and action, as Germany has taught the world, is the most effective weapon of propaganda.

Basic Themes

Let us now turn to examine the structure of Radio Rome broadcasts to the United States and its basic themes. These themes can be summarized as follows:

1. ATTACKS ON PRESIDENT ROOSEVELT AND THE ADMINISTRATION. These have been and are the keynote of Radio Rome broadcasts—the idea being, as usual, to discredit the leaders of the "enemy country" in the eyes of the enemy population. The anti-Roosevelt campaign followed, with a lag of three to four months, a parallel anti-Churchill campaign for English consumption.

2. STRESS ON AMERICAN ISOLATIONIST FEELING. The strategy underlying this theme is too obvious to require comment. It aims to give the picture of a disunited nation in which unpopular policies are being forced through by the Administration against the will of the people.

3. AMERICAN (or ANGLO-SAXON) IMPERIALISM. This is a theme based on two notes: American exploitation of the British, and joint Anglo-American exploitation of the world.

4. UNCLE SAM TAKING ADVANTAGE OF BRITAIN. It is suggested that under pretense of "helping" John Bull, Uncle Sam is bent on strangling him and picking up eventually the broken pieces of the British Empire.

5. YANKEE IMPERIALISM IN LATIN AMERICA. It is alleged that Uncle Sam is making the best of the opportunities afforded by the war and the British blockade in order to: (a) expand its trade with Latin America at the expense of both Europe and England; (b) establish bases and exercise a complete military and economic stranglehold over Latin America; (c) take over the bulk of British investments in Argentina and other Latin American Republics.

6. ANGLO-AMERICAN RIVALRIES, PAST AND PRESENT. It is explained to American listeners that the British are snobbish and have always hated and despised Americans. References are made to English "ingratitude" after the last war.

7. INTERVENTION WOULD BE RUINOUS FOR AMERICA. The Axis Powers and Japan are described as an invincible combination.

8. INTERVENTION WOULD MEAN THE END OF DEMOCRATIC LIBERTIES IN AMERICA. This theme sounds, to say the least, strange on totalitarian lips; yet, it is pressed home very strongly by Ezra Pound and other commentators.

9. THE UNITED STATES IS UNDER JEWISH DOMINATION. This is, of course, a staple theme of Axis propaganda and is also incessantly harped on in the Rome broadcasts to England, with reference to English conditions.

10. THE UNITED STATES IS UNDER PLUTOCRATIC DOMINATION. It is stated that this country, far from being a democracy, is dominated by a small clique of plutocrats and moneylenders. The same is said about England.

11. AMERICA IS UNPREPARED. This theme, which figured very prominently in an earlier phase, was later played down.

12. AMERICA IS VIOLATING HER NEUTRALITY. The Monroe Doctrine is, of course, the stock symbol featured in connection with this theme. What is apparently overlooked is that "nonbelligerency" was not an American but a Mussolinian discovery.

13. PREDICAMENT OF THE AMERICAN UNEMPLOYED AND OF THE AMERICAN WORKING CLASSES. The theme of class warfare played a dominant part during the winter and spring months, obviously in an attempt to bank on the silent Soviet-Axis partnership which appeared to exist at that time.

14. AMERICAN LABOR TROUBLES. This theme is nothing else but a specification of the previous one.

15. THE INVASION OF AMERICA IS IMPOSSIBLE. This theme is meant to reassure American listeners that they have nothing to fear from the Axis.

16. BAITS. It is stated that the Axis would be glad if, as a result of the fall of England, this country would annex Canada and all British possessions in the Western Hemisphere—possibly even Australia and New Zealand.

17. AMERICA WILL STAY OUT OF THE WAR. Appeals are made to "Yankee common sense," and confidence is expressed in the hope that the American people will realize that they have nothing to gain by intervention.

18. AMERICA IS ALREADY IN THE WAR. This statement, of course, is hardly consistent with the previous one, but it is often made, possibly in an attempt to discount the effect of fresh impending moves of this country against the Axis.

19. THE JAPANESE ARE VERY STRONG. Great stress is laid on the strength of the Japanese Navy, and it is suggested that if necessary Japan will take care of the United States just as effectively as Germany will take care of England, while Italy will "wear down" the enemy in Africa and the Mediterranean.

20. WE SHALL WIN ANYHOW. It is made quite plain that the Axis Powers will win the war—in fact, they have already won it—even if America fights.

Basic Patterns

It is not difficult to discern the basic patterns of argument which underlie the themes just indicated. They are:

First, an attempt to drive a wedge between the American people and their Administration, and to promote *disunion*.

Second, an attempt to intensify domestic disunion by pitting group against group, race against race, and class against class, and to promote *disaffection, religious and racial hatred, and class war*.

Third, an effort to drive a wedge between the United States and Britain and between the United States and Latin America.

Fourth, an attempt to persuade the American people that the issue of the war has already been settled, whatever this country may do, and that American intervention would thus be *futile*.

Fifth, an effort to frighten the American public into submission to Axis policies, by stressing the strength of the Tripartite Powers and uttering other threats designed to engender *intimidation*.

Sixth, what Dr. Philip Jacob calls the pattern of *reassurance,* which is based on the profession of Axis friendship and the denial of aggressive intention, occasionally supplemented by "baits."

Seventh, what might be called a pattern of *hostility*. Forgetting all nice distinctions between American people and Administration, "warmonger mentality" and "Yankee horse sense," Radio Rome very often turns the metal of its broadsides against the United States, the Anglo-Saxon nations, and the English-speaking peoples as a whole.

Finally, there is a pattern of *inevitability,* in the sense that Radio Rome appears to have made up its mind as to the unavoidability of a clash between the Axis and the Anglo-Saxon Powers (and this country in particular), and seems ready to face the fact, much as it deplores it.

The Roosevelt Symbol

The name of President Roosevelt stands first and foremost among the symbols of hatred disseminated by Radio Rome in its North American broadcasts. During the first phase, the line taken by Radio Rome was that the President was hostile to the Axis, but that his policies of aid to England were severely conditioned and held in check by the state of domestic opinion. "President Roosevelt," said one commentator on November 25, 1940, "is a very astute politician. However great his sympathies may be in favor of Great Britain, he pays a great deal of regard to American public opinion and naturally *places American interests before anything else*. This is why he is standing firm on the neutrality law. . . ."

The December fireside chat, besides disillusioning Radio Rome, induced its stage managers to abandon all pretense of moderation, so far as the President was concerned. An anti-Roosevelt trend set in and soon reached an unparalleled climax of violence. The President was described as: a man intoxicated with the notion of power (February 6), a puppet dictator pulled by the strings of international finance (February 6), a man enamored of power (February 21), a man who cares only for the limelight (March 11), the most dictatorial of dictators and the most intolerant of dictators (March 17), a real dictator (March 25).

It was also alleged that: he nurtures aggressive designs against Europe, particularly against the elementary rights of European liberty; he identifies the interests of America with those of the international moneychangers of New York and London; he wants to impose institutions on Europe which the latter does not want, notably the American international credit and banking system based on the gold standard; he identifies himself with the preservation of the gold standard, for the benefit of the Jews as well as of those Gentiles who have sold out their Christian principles.

It was added that, being "a slave of the money power," and being "moved by an insatiable ambition to rule," he wanted "to irritate the European Powers," and he did not want to "stop this blood business" (presumably the war unleashed by Hitler and later joined in by his acolyte Mussolini) "because it means 200 billion dollars of debt and the end of American liberties." He was further charged with the desire "to inflame the masses of the American population," lending "support to a propaganda of terror and fear," with "following dishonest tactics," and with "backing a filthy system which he disguises under the names of justice and liberty."

This little catalogue of name-calling could be extended almost in-definitely, but what is of most interest is *why* that barrage of abuse should be heaped upon the head of the American president.

No doubt Radio Rome has tried to make as much capital as possible of the political controversy which surrounds Mr. Roosevelt here at home. That this is so is confirmed by the fact that Radio Rome has taken great pains to stress the type of criticism which is likely to appeal to certain sections of opinion in this country, as by accusing him of harboring dictatorial ambitions, despite the fact that, to all except the most gullible, the anti-dictatorial fulminations of Radio Rome can only arouse scorn and contempt. It was indeed very edifying to listen to Fascist broadcasters and hear from them the eulogy of balanced budgets, representative government, and democratic institutions; charity, how-ever, begins at home, and the Fascists might well begin by setting their own house in order. But consistency and logic have never bothered Fascist or Nazi propagandists.

Appeals to the American people, inviting them to take matters in their own hands and take direct action against the President, were not lacking. One quotation will suffice (April 17, 1941): "No previous act of the Administration," one speaker said, commenting on the seizure of sabotaged Italian ships in American ports, "has disgusted the *right mind of Americans* as greatly as this unwarranted breaking of both international law and the ancient law of hospitality, which . . . *is respected even by savages*. But *disgust* on the part of its citizens *is not enough. Stronger measures* than these must be taken by those who can-not stomach those blots *on the fair escutcheon of the Stars and Stripes.* Only one President, Andrew Johnson, has ever been impeached . . . (and) it would seem about time that the good people of America harkened to the voice of Senator [*sic*] Hamilton Fish, who declared that *if Roosevelt drags the American people into this war, he too should be impeached.* Would it not be still better to weigh this act before America is thrust into the stream?"

After all, this was nothing else but a fresh example of the traditional Hitler-Goebbels technique—followed as usual by Rome, usually in its slovenly way of singling out a personal target as the symbol of all that was corrupt in the eyes of the Axis and against whom some sort of immediate and direct action was suggested. It was the technique which worked against Schuschnigg, against Benes, against Paul

Reynaud and Mandel—the same technique which has been engineered against Churchill.

It was a strategy of disunity—and, ultimately, terror—which aimed both at the base and the apex of the social pyramid. At the base it was meant to sow the seeds of disunity and to play up the animosities which a statesman has inevitably aroused during his tenure of office. At the apex it conceivably aimed at the nerves of Mr. Roosevelt himself, so as to add sinister threats of personal insecurity to the heavy strain of his responsibilities. President Roosevelt has been singled out as the strongest link in the world anti-totalitarian alignment. At the same time he is vulnerable, for after all, he is only an individual, and as such—who knows?—he may be susceptible to the effects of a concentrated barrage of threats and attacks.

Plutocracy, Class War, Religion

While President Roosevelt and his Administration have been attacked by Radio Rome on account of their "totalitarian" and "demagogic" policies, they also have come under fire on altogether different grounds: antilabor leanings, neglect of the interests of the American working classes, and identification with plutocratic and Jewish interests. Capitalism is declared to be the arch enemy of the Axis "New Order," and although this will come as a distinct surprise to some sections of the American public, Mr. Roosevelt is its standard-bearer.

Thus, as usual, Axis propaganda wanted to have it both ways: to discredit the President in the eyes of conservative circles, branding him as a demagogue, and at the same time to alienate the working classes, who have been told that he is a reactionary.

It must be added, however, that in the first half of 1941 the class war and a frankly subversive line of argument gained the upper hand in the broadcasts from Rome, committing the Axis Powers, at least for the time being, to social revolution and the destruction of capitalism. This is a point which it is important to stress, especially since the totalitarian leopard tried once more after the invasion of Russia to change the color of its spots.

A myth which was particularly dear to Fascist broadcasters asserts that America wants to fight for the preservation of the gold standard and is otherwise striving to make the world safe for the "creation of money by private banking interests." It was apparently forgotten that in Italy itself discussion of the gold standard, up to 1933-1934, was tabu, so that no criticism against it was permitted, and that the expansion of bank credit has been proceeding in the Fascist countries at least as fast as in England and this country. Frequent references were also made to the "gold debt system," which was described as the chief weapon of Anglo-Saxon exploitation throughout the world.

Profuse tears were regularly shed by Rome speakers over the alleged plight of the American working masses, while Italy was described as a paradise for workers and labor unions. Typical of this theme was a commentary delivered on March 18, 1941, at the time when the strike situation was attracting much attention over here: "Italian Labor Federations," it was said, omitting to explain that there are in Italy no such things as labor unions or federations in the English or American sense, but government-regimented associations, "are closely watching the trend of events which characterize the serious social conflicts *that are jeopardizing industrial life in the United States* at this very moment. According to the American press, these conflicts are caused either by refusal on the part of employers to raise the salaries of the workers or by refusal to recognize the labor unions. *Italian labor federation circles are of the opinion that such a raise is certainly justified, while the refusal to recognize the labor unions is judged a violation of the very fundamental principles of* [blank in the transcript]. . . . Democracy evidently has still a long way to go before doing what totalitarian fascism has done 15 years ago. *Italian circles here are following with profound sympathy the sharp conflict started by American labor.*"

Here are a few more samples of Radio Rome demagogy: "American democracy has joined hands with its English counterpart. The plutocrats and the great industrialists have determined to rule labor, and *to keep workers in a state of slavery,* glossed over by the thin coating of liberty." (March 21, 1941) "America and Britain are so far behind (in social legislation) that these countries look positively *medieval* in comparison with Italy or Germany." (May 28, 1941) *"Fascism and National Socialism* are labor regimes. They *have overthrown capitalism.* . . ." (*ibid.*)

Very little needs to be said about anti-Semitic propaganda, though this has played a great role on the short waves of Radio Rome, for its characteristics, faithfully borrowed from the Nazi model, are now well known.

As one might expect, there has been much talk of "Christianity" from Rome and also of Roman Catholicism, though references to Vatican City pronouncements and to Papal documents were extremely scant and invariably expurgated. One day a commentator went out of his way to pay homage to paganism, no doubt with an eye to the "Aryan" devotees of Wotan on the other side of the Alps. Nor was that just an obiter dictum, for already several months before (December 10, 1940), Major Barnes, speaking as "a sincere Catholic" had stated that he preferred "an honest, virile Pagan to the wishy-washy purveyors of unbelief who are so characteristic of Great Britain and the United States today," and the same pronouncement has been reechoed at different times in the speeches of several other commentators.

The Protestant churches, naturally, have come under the fire of Radio Rome nearly as often as the Jews. But one really curious and persistent feature to be found in references to religion was the charge that this country is unchristian, and that Christians make up only a minority of the population of the United States. One commentator referred to "your Christian minority." And, at least three times (December 8, 1940, April 2, 1941, and May 28, 1941), figures were quoted in support of that extravagant contention, to prove that only 53 million out of 126 million inhabitants of the United States had recorded themselves as Christians.[2]

Democracy

One of the most significant and indeed striking characteristics of political broadcasting in wartime is that, after a certain time, it is quite normal to find both sides paying at least lip service to the same values, and speaking, to some extent, the same language. Thus, there is no doubt that "Lord Haw-Haw," with his emphasis on the inequalities of the English social structure, had something to do with the line adopted by BBC speakers, such as J. B. Priestley, in later months. In their turn, Axis broadcasters often have found it necessary to boast that Germany and Italy are, after all, democracies in their own ways. To the extent that this has been true, it would be difficult to have a better proof of the effectiveness, despite the thinking in some quarters, of the symbols and slogans of freedom and democracy.

[2] So far as this writer has been able to find, the figure of 53 million covers only persons of 13 years of age or more who have declared themselves to be members of an actual church or congregation, thus leaving out children and all those who, though Christians, are not actively connected with a denominational congregation.

Europe and America

Another effective symbol used by Axis propaganda has been "Europe," and so long as the BBC and other British media continue to harp on the theme of restoration of the "sovereignty" of the individual European states, Berlin and Rome will continue to have a clear advantage over London. But this problem does not need to detain us here.

It is interesting, however, to point out that Rome and Berlin have not only identified "Europe" with the "Axis," but have done their utmost to dress up a united "European" front of hostility and antagonism against the English-speaking nations, and America in particular.

Typical of this trend are the following excerpts: "If, after the British collapse, America still wishes to continue the fight . . . she will find herself up against a *united Europe*, far more populous, *more civilized*, more highly skilled and industrialized than the whole American continent put together." (February 12, 1941) "It is quite clear that the Axis is prepared to fight for the *collective interest of Europe*, and the day will come when Europe will be united. As from that day, the Axis becomes the universally recognized *champion of Europe.*" (February 17, 1941)

As to Yankee "honesty," "intelligence," and "common sense," the following solitary pearl, picked out of a talk delivered on May 6, 1941, may be noted: "At least, one cannot but regret that when Columbus did set out to discover America, he never foresaw, alas, that it would become filled up with what is proving to be in many ways *the stupidest and certainly the most strong-headed white race the world has ever known*, the Anglo-Saxon, which is so much the prey of mere instinct and so little led by reason that the philosopher Keyserling felt inclined to class it as *a kind of subhuman species.*"

Identification of the United States and Britain

One of the favorite themes of Radio Rome was that Britain and this country have entered some sort of tacit and sinister compact, aiming at the permanent exploitation and subjugation of the rest of the world. Britain and this country have thus very often been lumped together, under the common denominator "the Anglo-Saxons." Here are a few quotations: "The Anglo-Saxon race is responsible to the rest of the world for having forced on it a war of the most terrible description. . . ."

(January 4, 1941) "The United States stand behind England to help her against the peoples in the war against Anglo-Saxon hegemony." (*ibid.*)

The war aims of the "Anglo-Saxon-Jewish" world were outlined by one commentator (February 13, 1941) as follows: "The political and economic aims of America and Britain are few, and they have to follow traditional lines. Europe is to be kept divided, each different part in economic and political opposition with the other. The Anglo-Saxon-Jewish world is to continue to control the bulk of raw materials and a universal banking system based on gold. . . . The Anglo-Saxon world is to finance all economic developments by the creation of debts by prolific races. Italians, Poles, and Germans are to be employed as hewers of wood and drawers of water for their wage masters. These are the war and peace aims of Britain and America."

Driving a Wedge Between Britain and Uncle Sam

While, for most practical purposes, Radio Rome has completely identified this country with Britain, consistent attempts have also been made to drive a wedge between the two English-speaking nations. These attempts were based on three techniques: (a) the Americans were told that the British hate and despise them; (b) America was encouraged to step in and seize the British possessions in the Western Hemisphere; (c) the British were "warned" against the designs of American imperialism.

The last two techniques call for some details and a few words of comment. The crux of the matter is that while Radio Rome has tried to sell Britain the notion that Uncle Sam does not really mean to help but only to get ready for the moment when he will inherit his fat share of the British Empire, the American people were being told almost in the same breath that nothing would be more natural and more agreeable to the Axis powers than the annexation of Canada and other British lands by this country. Here are a few examples: "Uncle Sam would not mind exchanging his 50 destroyers for the possible inheritance of the British dominion of the sea." (Broadcast to England, August 8, 1940) "The Axis would welcome the idea, if it could be realized, of Canada and Newfoundland ceasing to have any connection with Great Britain. Nor, as far as the Southern Pacific is concerned, would there be any objection whatsoever . . . if Australia and New Zealand elected to place themselves under the protection of the United States and Canada instead of

Great Britain, together with all Southern Pacific islands at present belonging to Britain and France. *It would be difficult to say anything more loyal to America....*" (Broadcast to the United States, December 30, 1940) "The first principle of Axis policy toward America is the Monroe Doctrine. . . . We go even further. We are prepared to count as the New World not only the two American continents, but also Australia, New Zealand, and all the islands of the South Pacific." (Broadcast to the United States, January 8, 1941) "The only way in which Britain will be able to pay her bill to America will be by handing over to America the rest of her Empire in the New World. Perhaps Mr. Roosevelt foresees this, and this is what he has in mind. . . . But *this can hardly be regarded as a very friendly act towards Britain.* Every day the British propaganda machine is pouring out tributes of praise to the United States, and perhaps all the time *Mr. Roosevelt is secretly planning to give the British people . . . a stab in the back, a real stab in the back,* after Britain is knocked out, and after calling her his friend. *The British people deserve to be put on their guard.* If they want to save a goodly portion of their Empire, they had better sue for peace quickly. Otherwise, they will be called not only to redress the balance of power of the old world, *but they will also witness defeat at the hands of their own friend in the new.*" (Broadcast to England, January 8, 1941)

It is worth stressing that the last two broadcasts went on the air *on the same day.* Instances of the same type could be easily multiplied. They require no comment, for the debased Machiavellism which underlies them is bound to be instinctively distrusted on both sides of the ocean and to offend every standard of moral and political judgment in both English-speaking countries. It ought also to be added in fairness that it has little to do with the true spirit of pre-Fascist Italy. It is the voice of Von Ribbentrop, duly recorded and rebroadcast by the Rome branch of the Berlin Ministry of Propaganda.

Latin America and the Good Neighbor Policy

The same duplicity has characterized Radio Rome propaganda in so far as the United States' relations with Latin America are concerned. Occasionally Rome appeared to acknowledge the special interests of this country in the Western Hemisphere. One commentator stated (November 25, 1940) that "the Axis wants a united Europe and would like to see a United America."

United States economic expansion in the South has been occasionally described as a natural and indeed inevitable development: "If the Powers of the Axis increase their influence in Europe and in that part of Asia which gravitates towards the Mediterranean, and if Japan looks to the Far East ... *it stands to reason that the United States cannot possibly ignore their own continental economic expansion.* The United States have also a problem of space to consider." (December 18, 1940)

Yet, in that same broadcast, clear hints were given, accusing the United States of attempting to encroach on the autonomy of her neighbor republics. Reference was made to the *monopoly* of South American agricultural products and raw materials which the United States was said to be organizing, through the Export-Import Bank and other agencies, and to the alleged request for the use of air and naval bases, and it was concluded that "some of the countries of Central and South America will have to come to terms with the United States. Should they be forced in the process to sacrifice their absolute autonomy which is so dear to their hearts, they will have only England to thank. The United States want to drive England out of Central and South America, forcing her to liquidate the colossal holdings that have ever been a thorn in the flesh of North American finance."

On January 28, 1941—once again we are quoting at random—Radio Rome stated that North American plans for Latin America were growing "ever more ambitious and huge" and foreshadowed the "economic conquest of Central and South America." It also referred to the question of the Falkland Islands, which were said to be "justly claimed by Argentina."

A synopsis of the philosophy of Radio Rome on the question of United States relations with South America was to be found in a commentary (March 25, 1941) entitled, *The War and Latin America,* from which a few excerpts may be appropriately quoted: "With the cession of a first group of destroyers to England, the United States acquired the right to set foot on Latin American soil. . . . Other agreements would have to be concluded in order that she (the U.S.A.) succeeds in her aim of taking possession of air and naval bases in Brazilian, Uruguayan and Peruvian territory. . . . *The imperialistic policy of the United States is very evident,* and very evident too is the fact that they would like to make preparations in order to become a dominant power in the New World. In fact, one wonders whether the Latin American countries, especially *Brazil and Argentina, have understood the game. . . .* A plan for a Pan-American economic system had been made, but that plan died before even being started. If it had been carried out, it would have marked the end of the economic independence of Latin America, which cannot let herself be dragged into the game. The United States are monopolizing the markets, profiting from the battle in which Germany, Italy and England are engaged, even though *this is disastrous to Latin America.*"

Some Conclusions

It has been pointed out in previous sections that Radio Rome has always been very lavish with "reassurances" to this country. It may be desirable, in these concluding paragraphs, to find out how far these reassurances are consistent with the Axis war aims, *such as are to be evinced from the pronouncements of their own propagandists.*

It seems clear, to begin with, that the "Monroe Doctrine," which was so often invoked by Dr. Gayda, Ansaldo, and Radio Rome, implied, to Fascist commentators, much more than the convenient slogan "America for the Americans" and its counterpart, "Europe for the Europeans." It has been seen, in fact, that "Europe," according to Radio Rome, includes "its natural complement Africa," as well as the Near and probably the Middle East. The United States is expected to give up all interest in the Far East in order to make room for the Japanese-controlled "Greater East Asia." Incidentally, it would be interesting to know the Japanese reaction to the generous territorial offers in the South Seas made to this country, on certain occasions, by the Rome broadcasters. Finally, we have been invited to identify ourselves with "North America"—namely, the United States and Canada—and to leave untouched the great area south of the Caribbean Sea, so that the Axis Powers may engage untrammeled in their "legitimate trade relations" with the South American Republics, whose economic interests are described as complementary to those of Europe.

It may be safely concluded, therefore, that the "vital space" allotted to this country by Axis radio geopolitics did not really amount to much.

What, then, of the control of the seas, those highways of American trade and the ramparts of American security? Radio Rome has made no bones of the expectation that the Axis—rather, the Tripartite Powers—

will put an end to Anglo-Saxon supremacy over the seas, once and for all: American, as well as British.

It is therefore quite clear that all the Axis soft talk of a new "hemispheric order" boils down to something quite different: namely, Axis control of three continents, Europe, Africa and Asia, as well as of the high seas; some kind of "open door policy" in South America paving the way to an Axis "closed shop" at an early date, the United States living in enforced isolation, in the space from the Bering Strait to the Caribbean Sea, and encircled on land and sea by the most formidable combination of powers ever seen in world history.

A pertinent question is, why has Radio Rome been so interested in the United States, as is apparent from both the volume and intensity of its propaganda?

The answer is not difficult to find. First of all, Italian propaganda may have hoped, probably mistakenly, to capture a large audience among the four to five million United States citizens who are of Italian origin or extraction. Secondly, and what is more important, despite all the narcotics of official and party propaganda, the bulk of the Italian people was presumably pretty well aware of the dangerous implications of the stand taken by the United States in the war, and there are reasons to suspect that the concern which Fascist propaganda has clearly shown since the end of 1940 over developments on this side of the water, may reflect grave anxiety as to the impact of American policies on the morale of the Italian people.

Much nonsense has been written and said in this country about the state of morale in Italy—and in totalitarian countries generally—owing to the fact that most people overlook that public opinion, in a dictator country, is thoroughly "conditioned," and cannot react quickly to developments except in rare and special circumstances. Thus, some commentators wrote Italy out of the war during the winter of 1940-1941, which was sheer wishful thinking; and others, starting from the correct assumption that Italians hate the Germans and dislike this war, drew the wrong inference that the average Italian was ready to join in a revolution, utterly forgetting that the ideals of political and personal freedom associated with the British war aims only appeal to a selected fringe of opinion.

But when all this has been said and allowed for, the fact remains that for Italy there is no power in the world with greater prestige than the

United States, and that the ordinary Italian feels and knows that Uncle Sam may have the trump card of this war right up his sleeve. It follows that every fresh move of this country is bound to affect Italian morale very considerably, and cause serious headaches for Fascist propaganda managers.

PARIS-MONDIAL

By Arturo Mathieu

Mr. Mathieu, as an undergraduate, studied at the Universities of Pisa, Florence and London. In 1934 he obtained his A.B. degree from Swarthmore and has subsequently studied at the Universities of Pennsylvania and Princeton. He joined the staff of the Princeton Listening Center as a Rockefeller fellow in December 1940 and remained with the Center until June 1941.

PARIS-MONDIAL

I T was in advance of the other great powers that France inaugurated short-wave broadcasting, for in conjunction with the Colonial Exposition at Paris in 1931 a short-wave station was established at Pontoise to service the French Empire. Unfortunately this pioneering spirit was neither correctly evaluated nor exploited by the French government, which seriously underrated the function of radio propaganda in a modern political system. The development of radio broadcasting in France is similar to, if it does not parallel, the development of the French aviation industry and military organization in general. France soon started to lose ground from an advanced position after the end of World War I in 1919 until she was ultimately lagging far behind the other countries.

An amazing succession of decrees rather than a single statute formed the "constitution" of the French radio system. The result was that often the work was badly obstructed by contradictory and obscure rules, the bureaucratic routine suffocated almost all initiative, and even the functions of the personnel were not clearly defined. As if this were not bad enough, the French radio was also very poorly equipped. Insufficient funds were allocated for radio expenditures by the government, and in consequence, the organization lacked material, a central broadcasting house, and could not even hire the necessary staff for efficient functioning. To complete the picture, the State Broadcasting System, not unlike the whole French Republic, was divided into various factions each absolutely independent of the others and all irreconcilable enemies, to the extent of having a different address, a separate budget, and a separate staff of personnel.[1]

Given this situation, it is understandable why the French international radio propaganda during the present war was characterized throughout the period from September 1939 to June 1940 by a lack of continuity in direction, which in turn suggests the absence of a formulated theory of propaganda.

During the years 1935, 1936, and 1937, when the national network was being better coordinated and increased in power, not much progress was being made in the field of short-wave broadcasting. The power of French transmitters was surpassed by those of every important nation

[1] Georges Duhamel, French radio official, *Figaro*, April 9, 1940.

in Europe. At the end of 1937, however, the French government began to organize a new, more powerful setup for international broadcasting.

By April 1938 a new short-wave station of 25 kw power was completed at Essarts-le-Roi. The old station at Pontoise (Paris-Colonial) was brought to 15 kw,[2] and both began broadcasting under the new name of Paris-Mondial (which was substituted for the old one of Paris-Colonial).[3] Later during the summer of 1939 a new transmitter of 100 kw was to be completed at Allouis, but in effect the coordinated services of the three transmitters for Paris-Mondial began only in October 1939.[4]

France's position was improved considerably by the construction of the new transmitter at Allouis, but she was still in many respects behind Great Britain and Germany. The French transmitters were so deficient in power that the broadcasts were disturbed by the thirteen transmitters of Zeesen which possessed greater power and had a frequency very close to the transmitters of Paris-Mondial.[5] The quality of the programs was poor and the news coverage very limited.[6]

By 1940 France was supposed to add to the short-wave network of Paris-Mondial eight new transmitters of 100 kw each, four at Allouis and four at Issoudon,[7] but presumably they had not been completed at the time of the armistice on June 22.

Parallel to the improvement in the short-wave network and organization during the years 1939 and 1940 a more definite movement towards better coordination of all the national broadcasting services took place. In March[8] the broadcasting in the colonies was reorganized to compete more effectively with the Italian and German programs in Arabic which had again begun to attack France after a period of calm following the Munich agreement. Among other measures taken, a new station at Tunis of 120 kw was erected to cover the whole North African French Territory together with the already existing stations of Algiers and Rabat.[9]

[2] *Broadcasting Year Book*, 1939, p. 351.

[3] The issue of April 1 of *World Radio Magazine* has the French short-wave station still listed under the name Paris-Colonial. The issue of April 8 of the same magazine has the same station listed as Paris-Mondial.

[4] As announced by the P.T.T. Administration in the April 1939 *Bulletin of the Union International de Radiodiffusion*.

[5] Zeesen: DJB, 15200 kilocycles; DJP, 11855 kilocycles; DJA, 9560 kilocycles. Pontoise, 1524 kilocycles; Pontoise, 11885 kilocycles; Essarts, 9550 kilocycles.

[6] Thomas Grandin, *The Political Use of the Radio*, Geneva, 1939, p. 56.   [7] *ibid.*, p. 56

[8] Decree of March 26, 1939 (*Bulletin*, November 3, 1939, *of U.I.D.R.*).

[9] Grandin, *op. cit.*, p. 55.

The first steps toward the nationalization of all broadcasting were finally taken during the summer of 1939 when war was already imminent. At the end of July 1939[10] there was instituted the office of the Commissary General for Information attached to the President of the Council, whose task was to "coordinate the work of the information and expansion departments in the different ministries."[11] A National Broadcasting Administration was created[12] and it was made responsible to the Commissary "for those functions connected with radio information and expansion."

The decree of August 29, 1939,[13] referring to the broadcasting organization in times of crisis, may be considered the first drastic attempt to nationalize all French broadcasting. Article II of the same decree reads as follows:[14] "All the broadcasting stations which do not fulfill a national purpose will be suppressed." Finally the decree of September 15, 1939,[15] defined the structure of the Commissary of Information which was to be composed of five departments: the first for the direction and general services; the second for documentation services; the third for information services for France and the colonies; the fourth for information services for foreign countries; and the fifth for press and censorship services.

Jean H. Giraudoux was appointed General Commissioner for Information. A well-known novelist, he had been in the Diplomatic Service from 1912 to 1928, had been the head of the Press Service in the Foreign Office and was considered to have a thorough knowledge of foreign countries.

This new organization for broadcasting coordination and control lasted until April 1940. After the fall of the Daladier Cabinet on March 19 a new arrangement was made. By the decree of April 1, 1940,[16] a Ministry of Information was instituted to take the place of the Commissary General for Information more on the pattern of the totalitarian ministries of information. Article II of the decree, in fact, reads as follows:[17] "The function of the Ministry of Information is to collect and disseminate, by all methods, all such elements as are susceptible of af-

10 Decree of July 30, 1939 (*Journal des Télécommunications*, August 1939, p. 249).
11 *ibid.*, p. 249.
12 Decree of September 1, 1939 (*Bulletin*, September 22, 1939, *of U.I.D.R.*).
13 *Bulletin of U.I.D.R.*, September 1939.   14 *ibid.*
15 *ibid.*, February 1940.   16 *ibid.*, April 1940.
17 *ibid.*

firming and propagating French thought and policy and of defending the vital interests of the Nation." France was at last awake to the necessity of the times. On April 10 a Council of Information attached to the Ministry was set up with Giraudoux at the head.

In addition to this council, a Committee of Information was created on April 11 with the purpose of studying "methods of spreading news of French origin within the country and abroad." Monsieur Brillouin was appointed head of the unified national broadcasting services as the supreme authority and general director. He replaced Giraudoux who had been transferred to head the Council of Information attached to the Ministry of Information. The effort made under the energetic direction of Monsieur Frossard, the new propaganda minister, and of Brillouin was indeed intense in all directions. Programs were improved, a better propaganda technique adopted, and the broadcasting personnel increased. Had France been able to withstand the German attack for a longer period, the new organization might have been more effective in directing French public opinion and influencing opinion abroad in favor of the French cause. As it was, the French organization of radio propaganda, like that of her armament production was undertaken too late. When France woke up, the Germans already had a decisive advantage.

Paris-Mondial to June 1940

Soon after the construction of the transmitter of 25 kw at Essarts-le-Roi in April 1938, Paris-Mondial began to broadcast regularly to North America. From a cultural standpoint the programs in general were of a higher type than the average American program and the news broadcasts in particular were excellent commentaries—although not comparable with the American programs in up-to-the-minute news coverage. It is difficult to determine now how many listeners these programs had in the United States before the war and what their influence was on the audiences. We know that after the outbreak of hostilities in September 1939, some of the programs were rebroadcast.

At the beginning of the war, in September, Paris-Mondial was broadcasting for 5¼ hours daily to the United States and the length of the broadcasting time was not increased to any great extent up to June 1940. At that time the broadcasting schedules were extended to 7¼ hours daily. One extra hour was added in February when Paris-Mondial began to broadcast to the Pacific Coast, via Saigon, and the other hour was added in April 1940 after the reorganization.

From the outbreak of hostilities to the reorganization of the French broadcasting services and programs in April 1940, the character of the broadcasts from Paris-Mondial remained fundamentally the same. That is, the music offered was of the type often played on the Continental state networks—rather conservative. The talks were predominantly of a cultural and educational type and the news broadcasts were for the most part intelligent commentaries on the international situation. During this time, naturally, the stress was on the news programs, and after April 1940, the extra time added to the programs was taken up mainly with news and commentaries. During this second period, from April 13 to June 18, the nature of the programs changed considerably. The news programs were longer and better organized, at least as to form; the talks were less intellectual but more to the point. On the whole, the change in government and the new life injected into French propaganda by the creation of the Ministry of Information was reflected in these programs of the last two months.

If we had tried to imagine a lapse of time ideally adapted to a study of French political broadcasting in war time, we could hardly have produced anything better than the actual situation between January and June 1940. This for three different reasons: in the first place, it was the first time in history that the radio had been used so extensively for political purposes during a conflict of major dimensions. It was used in the Spanish civil war, and to be sure, in the long war between Japan and China, but never on such a scale.

In the second place, the nature of the present war is social as well as international. A new doctrine contemplating the complete eradication of the old social order is behind the Nazi and Fascist armies. *Mutatis mutandis*—this type of war recalls the Napoleonic wars; now as then, it is a question of conquering first and then transforming the conquered government in accordance with new principles, rather than a question of winning the war for certain economic or political advantages.

In the third place, because of the rapid succession of events of exceptional importance, the first six months of the year 1940 make a unique background for a campaign of international radio propaganda—the Russo-Finnish war, and the capitulation of Finland in March, the German invasion of Denmark and Norway on the ninth of April, the

German invasion of the Low Countries on the tenth of May, the surrender of the king of the Belgians on the twenty-eighth of the same
month, the entrance of Italy into the war on the tenth of June, and
finally the collapse of France and the armistice on the twentieth and
twenty-second of June.

When we consider the task facing the French radio propagandist
during this period in planning his national as well as his international
broadcasts, we cannot help being impressed by its appalling difficulties.
In the first place, he had no successful military incidents of any consequence to exploit, with the possible exception of the *Altmark* incident
and the second battle of Narvik, both of which were British successes
anyway, and the former complicated by an alleged British breach of international law. On the other hand, there were many defeats both in
diplomatic strategy as well as in military operations to defend and explain. It was necessary to explain the Allied failure, after so much vocal
support, to help Finland in time; there was the fiasco in Norway and
the inexplicable blunders and mistakes made in the defense against the
German invasion through the Low Countries.

Broadcasters, as well as reporters, were well aware of the weakness
of the government caused by the bitter antagonism existing between the
political parties of the right and of the left which, unlike their predecessors in 1914, did not cooperate in face of the danger from without.

They were also aware of the lack of airplanes and of mechanical
equipment for the army. The Maginot Line and the Allied fleets were
the only two symbols of strength left to oppose the acknowledged for-
midableness of the German Army and Air Force. To perform this task
we find at that time an organization that was, to say the least, inadequate. To quote Georges Duhamel, member of the French Academy
and ex-director of the National Broadcasting Administration:[18]

"The French radio lacks sufficient offices, material, personnel and
money . . . the work is paralyzed by the interpretation of the mysterious
and inextricable decrees . . . and inventive intelligence . . . is always
hampered by the most deadly routine. . . . Any man who accepts work
there must consent to waste 90% of his effort in vain and absurd quar-
rels."

We must bear in mind these conditions of the French broadcasting
services as well as the extreme difficulty of the task, when evaluating

[18] *Figaro*, April 9, 1940.

French international propaganda during the first nine months of the second World War. There is evidence that during the first six months of 1940 some programs directed to the United States were translated at the microphone from French texts, already broadcast to the French public. Apparently at that time no care was taken to distinguish between propaganda directed to foreign and domestic audiences: a poor match for the totalitarian technique.

The nature of the programs directed to the United States changed around the middle of April. The reasons for this change, as explained above, are to be traced immediately to the reorganization of the radio broadcasting services that followed the institution of a new Ministry of Information and more remotely to the new, more aggressive policies of Reynaud, who had succeeded Daladier on March 19 as President of the Council.

During the first period, the situation was certainly more favorable to the French propagandist. It was a period of relative calm during which a well-organized campaign could have been directed at leisure to the United States without having to dedicate a good part of the news programs to admitting military reverses or describing the ever-changing military situation.

The French radio, however, did not take advantage of this opportunity. In the news, a great deal of time was given to the Russo-Finnish military operations, and the talks were definitely of such a nature that they must have appeared much too intellectual and farfetched to the majority of listeners. Perhaps this reflects more on the type of audience than on the type of program, but as things are, a discussion of the hitherto little appreciated patriotism of the poet Ronsard[19] or a talk on the origin of pipe smoking[20] was bound to have little or no effect on the majority of potential American listeners.

The following programs broadcast in the week of March 7, 1940 are fairly representative of all talks transmitted by Paris-Mondial during the first period:[21] For Saturday: *Kant and Peace*, talk by Leon Bruschwig. For Sunday: *From Douanier Rousseau to Diego Rivera*, talk in Spanish. *How the French Academy Works*, talk by Monsieur Savarin. For Monday: *An Interview about French Folklore and How It Is Made*

[19] January 30. Talk by E. Henriot on Ronsard, 8:17 p.m., Station TPC.
[20] February 10, 8:15 p.m., Station TPC. Talk by Paul Archinard, weekly program.
[21] Announced on March 7, 8:15 p.m., Station TPC.

Available to the Public in the French National Museum of Popular Art and Tradition, and a talk by Professor Sargeant on *Laënnec and the Invention of the Stethoscope.* For Tuesday: a talk by André Gide on *The Latest French Books.* For Wednesday: *A Moroccan Legend,* by Titaina, *Remarks from a Parisian,* and *Books and the Empire.* For Thursday: finally, a play by Claudel and a talk on Whistler, and for Friday a talk by Madame Titaina on *The Woman's Point of View* and a pastoral talk by the Reverend Worden, head of the Reformed Churches in France.

Among all these and similar talks only two of a more pertinent nature were announced: one, a discussion of *Socialism in the Third Reich,* by Monsieur Lefranc and another, a talk in French from a Czechoslovakian camp somewhere in France.

In the news programs of the month of January the general tone was one of satisfaction, confidence and even buoyancy. It was taken for granted then that the war was going to last a long time. The Maginot Line was protecting France as an insuperable bulwark, and in the meantime the Allied navies were going to force Germany to yield. Time was in the Allies' favor. With this general attitude prevailing, most of the broadcasting was given over to the Russo-Finnish war, the major military event of the period, and the discussion of diplomatic developments in Europe and elsewhere. More attention was being paid to German "intrigue," and to propaganda than to Allied and French affairs, and several "defensive" attacks were launched against the Nazis. The programs were usually short, read in about ten minutes, and followed no particular pattern. At times they began as straight news reports and ended as news commentaries or propaganda talks.

Of particular interest during January were the frequent references in the Paris broadcasts to German diplomatic intrigue and propaganda. The attitude that the French propagandist took in respect to these German activities was more or less comparable to the German attitude towards the "intrigues" of the "international Jewish bankers." The Goebbels organization was painted as a diabolical machine present everywhere and responsible for many events unfavorable to the Allies all over the world. Even certain moves by Russia and by Japan were interpreted as having been originally caused by German propaganda efforts.

The conception of German propaganda one would have derived from listening to Paris-Mondial was of something that transcended the word *propaganda* in its generally accepted meaning. It was a combination of fifth column, propaganda, and diplomatic pressure, but mostly fifth column. Among other targets of French attacks on Germany were German internal conditions and German war aims. A great deal of time was consumed in presenting pictures of a Germany in serious difficulty over food and raw materials shortages, and with very low morale: "According to information recently received in Italy," said the announcer on January 2 in a typical passage, "and from all coming [*sic*] neutral personalities who have stayed recently in Germany, the situation in Germany is anything but brilliant. The food is very poor; the population sadness and uneasiness is considerable; the National Socialist party is divided, as the advanced section is going towards Bolshevism. Restrictions are more numerous every day, and the population is showing its discontent openly. Nowhere may be found the slightest enthusiasm for the war. In a general way the morale is very low. Even in the Army the state of mind is often bad. Officers do not hesitate to declare openly that they do not approve of the war. . . ." This, incidentally, was also a good example of the poor technique of the French "attacking" campaign. This type of general and sweeping statements about the enemy's disastrous conditions are too transparent and old-fashioned. After listening to this "crescendo," one would have been quite justified in doubting the veracity of the broadcaster without further consideration.

News Programs

During the month of February the general tone of Paris-Mondial did not change noticeably. The programs had the same character of news commentaries; scripts were translated at the microphone as in January, and the English was, as usual, rather poor. In that connection, a proof that the announcer had to resort to the practice of translating at sight from the French was recorded on February 10. At 8:05 p.m. on that day a news program was broadcast in English, read by an American. The same program was rebroadcast at 11:30 p.m., this time read by an Englishman. The two translations were different, and incidentally, the translation of the Englishman was far superior to that of the American.[22]

22 This practice of sight translation and also the practice of using the same programs for French and American audiences has been lately confirmed to the author by Miss Marion Dix, who was from January to June 1940 on the staff of Paris-Mondial.

The main preoccupation of Paris-Mondial all through this month was apparently to stress that the Allies were strongly against any peace offensive. This was repeated again and again, not only in connection with the visit of Mr. Sumner Welles, but also in connection with certain rumors about a Russo-Finnish peace agreement and on the occasion of some restatements of Allied war aims.

In the attack on Germany, the attention of the propagandist was concentrated on the following issues: (1) to "answer" the contentions of the German "propaganda" and to expose its dark schemes; (2) to point out and stress the poor economic conditions of Germany and the low morale; (3) to stress German cruelty in the campaign for "extermination" of the Poles; (4) to point out the ruthlessness of the Nazis in their attacks on neutral shipping and in their attitude toward neutrals; (5) to stress the illegal position of Germany in the *Altmark* case and in the prohibition of neutral shipping; (6) to minimize the importance of the Russo-German trade treaty of the twelfth, and, finally, to expose German war aims.

One significant argument advanced by Paris-Mondial in February is worth mention: the reaffirmation of the unity of the French political parties at the time of the secret meeting of the Chamber on the ninth and tenth and the resulting vote of confidence given to the Daladier government. Said the anonuncer on February 12 in answer to the "insinuations" of German propaganda: "The French Chamber of Deputies, after two days of secret session, unanimously adopted the order of the day, giving confidence to Mr. Daladier's government. This unanimous vote proved that *the union among Frenchmen was stronger than ever*." In this case at least, the "professional liars" of the German propaganda bureau were being given a few pointers by the French radio propagandists.

Up to the ninth of April the war in the west continued on its "quiet," uneventful course, and aside from the Russo-Finnish peace and the definite turn of the Italian policy toward the Axis there were few items of major importance to report. Paris-Mondial concentrated its attention on the last phase of the Russo-Finnish war and the peace negotiations, on Mr. Welles' tour of the European capitals, on attacking Germany, and on discussing the changing attitude of Italy.

At the beginning of April the French radio, like the French press, dedicated a great deal of time to arguments in favor of tightening the blockade and to the controversy between the Allies and the Scandinavian neutrals on the subject.

On the eighth the Allied mine-laying operations in Norwegian territorial waters were emphasized, and from the ninth on the invasion of Norway and Denmark naturally absorbed the attention of broadcasters.

In reporting the Russo-Finnish war, Paris-Mondial maintained the same tone of optimism to the end. The importance of the Russian successes was minimized continually even when the peace negotiations had already started.

There was still hope in the broadcasts of the ninth that Finland was not going to capitulate to the Russian demands. It was solemnly declared among other things that: "Great Britain and France will not abandon Finland. They both have the desire to compensate for the default of Finland's neighbors. The Allies are at war and fear nothing. *If Finland should decide to pursue the battle she will never demand anything in vain from the Allies.*"

On the twelfth, however, Paris-Mondial did not fail to give the report of the peace agreement. "After 104 days of the Russo-Finnish war an agreement has been made putting an end to the hostilities" were the first words of the 8:04 p.m. broadcast. And all programs were devoted to comment on the Russo-Finnish peace.

In all these broadcasts the main preoccupation of the French propagandist was to explain why the Allied help did not arrive in time and to stress the fact that the reason Finland was in an advantageous position in the peace negotiations was because of the hovering threat of Franco-British intervention.

Of major importance from a propaganda standpoint was Mr. Welles' tour which attracted considerable attention in March as well as in February. On the occasion of his visit to Berlin on March 1, three-fourths of the broadcast of 8:05 p.m. was dedicated to recalling the speech made by Hitler at the Reichstag on April 28, 1939, in answer to a message from President Roosevelt.

The broadcast, however, seemed directed to Sumner Welles rather than to a radio audience. It was a reminder of all the promises that Hitler had not kept in the past, intended as a warning to Mr. Sumner Welles against accepting any further promises.

The attack on Germany continued in March mainly in connection with the reporting of the following events: (1) German interference in the Russo-Finnish war and subsequent peace negotiations; (2) The German peace offensive on the occasion of Mr. Welles' visit to Europe; (3) German violation of the Belgian sky; (4) the controversy between Britain and Italy over the German coal; (5) Von Ribbentrop's visit to the Pope and the talks between Hitler and Mussolini at the Brenner Pass on the eighteenth.

Most of the attacks were, as usual, directed against the "lies" of "German Propaganda," against the German war aims, and painted the economic conditions of Germany in dark colors. This was the last month in which French radio propaganda spent most of its broadcasting time in attacking and criticizing the enemy. The rapid succession of unfavorable events later prevented such a concentration of attention on German affairs. After the ninth of April most of the news programs were focused on describing the Allied positions or on defending the Allied conduct of warfare rather than on attacking Germany.

Incidentally, it must be observed here that the word "attacking" implies only a *comparative* degree of aggressiveness on the part of Paris-Mondial, not an *absolute* one. The French radio, for instance, attacked German propaganda exclusively in order to refute its contentions. And these were widely publicized in lengthy quotations. French attacks were usually provoked either by previous assaults, by German propaganda, or by unfavorable events which needed a prompt answer.

Comparatively speaking, however, Paris-Mondial was more aggressive in its March news reports than in those of any other month considered in this study. It would be a safe conclusion to say that had conditions remained calm, the French radio would have probably reached a higher level of technique in its news programs by June 1940. But, as it was, any improvement was severely hampered by the rapid succession of unfavorable events during most of April, May and June.

From April 1 on, Paris-Mondial widely publicized in its programs the Allied war plans in relation to an intensification of the blockade measures against Germany. In connection with these campaigns, several attacks were launched on the first, fourth, fifth, sixth and seventh against Germany's attitude towards neutral states. This was a prelude to the long expected Allied action of mine laying in Norwegian territorial waters in order to stop the flow of Swedish iron ore by the Narvik route. While the Germans were preparing in all secrecy a well-planned, definite attack on Denmark and Norway, the French radio was openly publicizing the plans of the Supreme War Council a week ahead.

During the second period the news broadcasts were longer and better organized, following more closely the American pattern. But unfortunately from the very beginning great confusion reigned at the various sources of European news and this lasted for the greater part of May. Also the nature of the events was anything but favorable to the French propagandist.

From the ninth of April to the tenth of May, Paris-Mondial concentrated its news programs principally on reporting the military operations taking place in Norway. From the tenth of May to the eighteenth of June the German invasion of the Low Countries and the attack on France naturally attracted all the attention of the Paris radio.

These two main events "molded," so to speak, the character of French radio propaganda during these seventy turbulent days, and in a certain sense, dictated its arguments. During the first three months of the year the French propagandists had had ample opportunity to choose what events they would report and emphasize, and how to fit them into a pattern of propaganda arguments. They failed then to take advantage of the opportunity, and by the time that the reorganization of the French propaganda services was giving some reasonable hope that a better effort would be made, the events held the French radio chained to a "reportage" of perhaps the most rapid and unfavorable sequence of events that any propagandist ever had to cope with.

Up to the tenth of May, Paris-Mondial held its own as best it could. After the thirteenth of April the news programs were longer and better organized. A serious effort was made to present the Norwegian campaign in the best possible light. From the tenth to the twenty-eighth of May great confusion ensued in the news programs.

Paris-Mondial has been accused of harboring fifth columnists on its own staff. It seems that some news reports were broadcast giving the German version of the news rather than the French. It will not be an easy matter to ascertain the truth of such rumors. One thing is certain, however, that either consciously or unconsciously all the French news reports and in particular those of the month of May may have played into the hands of the Germans. And the same could be said of some talks. Poor technique and poor propaganda strategy might have accounted for this fact. Whether and to what extent this was intentional, we shall probably never know.

As a whole, the German move into Norway was considered a natural "turn" of the war. In general, Paris-Mondial during the six days that elapsed between the German invasion and the landing of Allied troops in Norway had the following aims: (1) to make the German invasion appear like a desperate move to escape from the mortal grip of the blockade, and an indirect demonstration of poor economic conditions in Germany; (2) to minimize the importance of the event and its character of surprise; (3) to stress the enormity of the German "crime" and to point out the reactions all over the world which for the most part were favorable to the Allies; (4) to present the German aggression against the two neutral countries as proof that the Allied position in their controversy with the northern neutrals was justified and to picture it as a lesson to all neutrals; (5) to paint the German plan of invasion as a strategical error; (6) to stress the rapidity of the Allied reaction and the effectiveness of the Allied naval action; (7) to emphasize the resistance of the Norwegians and the heroism of their king; (8) to present the position of Sweden as critical and to emphasize her difficult relations with Germany. The main preoccupation of Paris, however, was to answer point by point the German contentions about the reasons for the invasion in order to "fix responsibilities" for the future.

The news of the landing of Allied troops at Namsos on the fourteenth was broadcast on the fifteenth and from that date up to the twenty-third the tone of Paris-Mondial remained confident and optimistic.

On the twenty-third, the date on which the Germans claimed an important victory at Lillehammer over the Allied expeditionary forces, the tone of Paris-Mondial changed perceptibly in its reports of the military operations in Norway. The German success, of course, was not mentioned, even to be denied, and the war reports became more vague and noncommittal than usual.

A few sentences here and there betrayed an unfavorable situation. In general, however, the tone of the news broadcasts remained optimistic, except that the German expedition was no longer presented as a complete failure. Beginning on the twenty-sixth, several references appeared in the news broadcast to the effect that "the Nazi expedition did not turn out as the leaders of the Third Reich expected and hoped."

From the twenty-sixth to the thirtieth the attitude of Paris-Mondial remained unchanged, and, aside from lengthy and meaningless reports on the Norwegian situation, little more news was broadcast. On the twenty-seventh and twenty-eighth a speech by Von Ribbentrop was answered point by point, and in connection with it the usual attack against the vicious lies of the German propaganda was launched. The German contentions were, however, widely publicized in the course of the attack. On the thirtieth, in relation to the Italian position, Paris-Mondial finally conceded that the Fascist government was definitely on the German side, but a new argument was introduced emphasizing the divergence of attitudes between the Italian government and the Italian people. Declared the announcer in the 8:30 broadcast: "The Italian public is *not* particularly attracted by the possibility of entering the war . . . to a great majority it still remains sincerely anti-German."

While up to the twenty-ninth of April, Paris-Mondial had remained fairly consistent in its standard propaganda policy of reporting only favorable military operations, of minimizing or suppressing unfavorable reports, or of reporting them late when of major importance, on the thirtieth the first instance occurred of a simultaneous announcement by the German and the French radios of a German victory.

In the middle of the 8:30 p.m. broadcast the announcer curtly said: "In the past forty-eight hours the German pressure has increased in Norway. . . . A communiqué issued by the German agency D.N.B. announces that Dombaas has fallen into German hands and that, therefore, communications are now established between Oslo and Trondheim." Not a word of comment was added to this unprecedented announcement. The Germans had not preceded the French by many hours in announcing their success.

On the first of May the attention of Paris-Mondial was focused on several other events of a secondary nature and discussion of the situation in Norway was avoided as much as possible. On the second and third the Allied evacuation of Namsos and of Andalsnes was suddenly revealed simultaneously by the French and the German radios. The Norwegian campaign, however, was not yet reported as a failure.

Between the third and the tenth of May the reports of the Norwegian campaign took up less time. The evacuation by the Allies of all southern Norway was admitted, but their firm stand in the north and around Narvik was repeatedly emphasized.

At the same time more attention was paid to the position of Italy and to the Mediterranean situation. The attitude of the Paris radio towards Italy did not change perceptibly. Still a distinction was made between the press and the Fascist government on the one hand, and the Italian people on the other.

There were no unfavorable remarks about Italy and the tone of the broadcasts remained hopeful. The friendly relations between Italy and the United States, and between Italy and the Vatican were stressed to offset the continuous pro-German utterances of the Fascist press. A great deal of attention was also paid by Paris-Mondial during this week to the Balkan situation. The main object of the French propagandists in this connection was to present the political and commercial relations between Germany and Russia as becoming more and more unsatisfactory. To this end several reports from the "Slovakian frontier" were broadcast with rumors of German-Russian dissension. The Balkan countries, on the other hand, were reported as looking toward Russia for protection against the German menace.

On the eighth, in the broadcast of 8:30 p.m., Paris-Mondial again presented a report that could easily have been taken for a report of German origin: A good part of the program was devoted to emphasizing vividly the dissension existing in the British House of Commons over Chamberlain's war policies. The criticisms of the opposition rather than the government defense were given prominence—in particular the speeches of Herbert Morrison and Lloyd George.

Up to the tenth there were no signs in the French short-wave broadcasts that there was in France even a slight suspicion of what was to happen on that day. On the seventh the defense measures of the Dutch government were reported without comment and all the commentaries seemed to indicate that a German thrust in the Balkans rather than an invasion of the Low Countries was seriously expected.

From the tenth of May up to the eighteenth of June the reports of the operations on the western front took practically all the time of the Paris news broadcasts. The Norwegian campaign passed to second place and henceforth very little time was given to it or for that matter to any other event.

All the news broadcasts of the tenth, the eleventh, twelfth and thirteenth were completely disorganized and the reports were confusing and read without any order. Reports were broadcast that the Germans were advancing in Holland and Belgium but few details were given.

On the fourteenth, the German capture of Rotterdam and the surrender of the Dutch armies north of the Maas were announced, and from this date on Paris-Mondial adopted the practice of announcing faithfully most of the German successes at the same time that the Germans themselves did.

The confusion in the reports from the battlefront grew worse, and the tone of the announcers became more dramatic and alarming. On the seventeenth the Germans captured Brussels, and on the eighteenth, Antwerp. Both captures were promptly announced by Paris-Mondial. On the seventeenth the order of the day of General Gamelin was transmitted and its alarming tone was assumed by all the news broadcasts. Gamelin was quoted as commanding that "Any troop units which cannot advance must die on the spot rather than surrender the smallest part of soil which has been entrusted to them. As it has always been in the serious moment of our history, today's standing order is 'win or die.' We must win." At the same time, several German reports were transmitted and then flatly denied.

After the "order of the day" of General Gamelin, Paris-Mondial tried to assume an heroic attitude and to revive the spirit of 1914 in its broadcasts. As a result the keynote of the Paris programs became confusion and alarm.

The scant knowledge of what actually was going on was openly confessed by the announcer on several occasions. Sentences like the following were often heard: On the nineteenth: "In this sector it is rather difficult to give any details on any front line. The operations are extremely confused. . . ." On the twenty-first: "Towards the South the situation is still confused. . . ."

The alarmist attitude of the news broadcasts increased sharply on the twenty-first after the reports of the speech by Premier Reynaud in the Senate. As quoted by Paris-Mondial he warned: "The nation is in danger; my first duty is to tell the Senate and the country the truth." Some mistakes on the part of the General Staff were then openly admitted, followed by dramatic appeals to the French people and by professions of faith in the "miracle" that was going to save France. Sentences of this nature followed: "The entire region behind Cambrai has been systematically set afire not only by bombs but also by para-

chutists carrying torches and even flame throwers. The railroad stations at Arras, in Amiens and in other cities are in flames."

From the twenty-fourth on, even the official communiqués transmitted by Paris-Mondial contained open confessions of ignorance of
the actual situation. "The violent combats which for several days have
been going on in the North, in the regions of Cambrai and Arras and
which have extended as far as St. Omer and Boulogne *make it impossible to establish the exact line of the front*," the official communiqué
confessed tersely on May 24.

From the twenty-fourth to the twenty-eighth Paris gave up reporting the movements of the fronts and the actual extent of the operations
and concentrated almost exclusively on emphasizing the probable
heavy German losses and on reassuring the listeners that whatever
victories the Germans might have obtained, the strength of the Allied
Empires was still considerable.

On the twenty-eighth the capitulation of the King of the Belgians
gave the French radio a chance to present his action as one of the most
important causes for the serious situation of the Allied armies, and at
the same time offered an opportune subject for comment at a time
when reports were scarce and unreliable. Practically all of the broadcasts of the day were dedicated to accusing the king and to praising
the stand of the Belgian government.

On the twenty-ninth the announcement of the Allied capture of
Narvik began to give a more confident tone to the Paris broadcasts
and from then on to the fourth of June there was more order in the
news programs and the dramatic tone disappeared almost entirely,
perhaps in imitation of the style of the "orders of the day" of General
Weygand, whose elevation to commander-in-chief may have produced
a temporary revival of confidence reflected in the radio appeals.

After the appeal of Reynaud to President Roosevelt on the thirteenth,
however, Paris-Mondial assumed again a theatrical tone influenced undoubtedly by the highly dramatic speech of the Premier. Also following
his example, direct pleas for help to the United States began to be
transmitted in the news broadcasts. And so to the end.

If the improvement that took place in the news broadcasts from
Paris-Mondial after April thirteenth was somewhat impeded by the
nature of the events, the talks, on the other hand, undoubtedly represented the best effort of the French propagandists during the present

war. After the reorganization of the broadcasts in April the inadequacy of the highly intellectual appeal was apparently realized along with the necessity of producing programs adapted for American listeners and transmitted by Americans.

To give an idea of the transformation of the French radio talks to the United States during this second period, the daily program of talks from Paris-Mondial on June 3, 1940, is presented here:[23]

8:20 Dr. Charles Godlin, reporting on his second visit to the French Air Force at the front.

8:40 "Bombs over Paris," radio reporting of bombing of Paris with sound effects.

9:00 "To students of America," André Morize, formerly professor at Harvard University.

9:30 Dr. Donald A. Lowry, Director of Northern Y.M.C.A.

9:45 Interview with officials figuring in the capture of some parachutists.

10:00 Social work among refugees by a Red Cross nurse.

10:08 "How the U.S. would suffer in any case from a Hitler success."

10:20 "Today in France," survey of the French press.

10:30 American Legion program.

10:45 Interview with eyewitnesses of the bombardment of Paris, by Gladys Delmar.

As it appears from the schedule, by June not only was the nature of the talks considerably improved with respect to effectiveness, but also more time was dedicated daily to both talks and news.

Although the highly intellectual lecture did not disappear, most of the programs mentioned in the above schedule were a far cry from the Olympian disquisitions on French literature transmitted in January, February and March. The new talks were interesting, and were read by American voices in a familiar way. Life in France was made more real to the audiences in America, and great effort was expended to revive that France which so many Americans of the A.E.F. had known. That in itself constituted a rather strong appeal. The tone of most talks became less apologetic and more dramatic. Among the interesting talks about actual events were: on the twenty-ninth of April, an account given by the secretary to the Norwegian radio of the German invasion, and on the eleventh of May a broadcast from Brussels transmitting the speeches of Mr. Spaak in Parliament on the tenth. There were several Americans on the staff of Paris-Mondial, all with experience in radio and dramatic work, and after the reorganization of April apparently more attention was paid to them and more time was given to their programs. The American Legion programs in particular were an innovation of the last three months. Among the Americans on the staff were Howard Claney, Paul Archinard, Percy Noël, Vincent Schmidt, Marion Dix, and Gladys Delmar.

Howard Claney had been an NBC announcer with a great deal of experience on the stage and on the air. Paul Archinard was an NBC representative in Paris and Percy Noël had been an American newspaper correspondent in Paris and Tokyo. As to Vincent Schmidt, he was introduced on the fourteenth of May with the following words: ". . . American soldier of fortune who is a veteran of many wars. He flew recently for the Spanish Loyalists during the Spanish civil war, later for Chiang Kai-shek in China, where he was commander of the foreign volunteer squadron. . . . He is now engaged in reporting world war news for American newspapers." His speeches were usually commentaries on military operations, direct to the audience and very interesting.

The principal aim of all the talks was apparently to interest American audiences in the affairs and life of the French people and of their allies; eventually to convince the American people that the Allied cause was also the American cause and that the United States should send help. As in the news programs, however, the plea for help became explicit only in the end. The arguments advanced in the talks were for the most part the same as those advanced in the news broadcasts and press reviews, with more stress on the high morale and calm determination of the French people.

A great effort was made in all talks to revive the spirit of Franco-American solidarity of the last war. Significant in that respect were the American Legion programs.

In the long series of talks on "German Propaganda" read by Howard Claney, Paris-Mondial continued to attack the "vicious lies" of the "Goebbels gang." In these programs, as usual, Paris-Mondial disputed the German version of events point by point and attacked the German system of "false propaganda" and Hitler's propaganda theory. These programs were well connected with immediate events and comprised a series of very plausible, if too explicit, arguments against Nazi theories and practices. Although if judged on the basis of their content the talks of the last seventy days must be considered good, they must have lost much of their effectiveness when received together with the newscasts of the same period.

Techniques

Even if we appraise the arguments and technique used by the French propagandists without relating them to the elaborate systems of German and British propaganda, we must conclude that the French propaganda effort during the first months of the second World War was inadequate and the strategy primitive. Several were the faults and very slight the improvements over the technique of the French World War I propaganda. Considering the six-months period as a whole, the statement of Georges Duhamel[24] to the effect that the French propagandist was at least ten years behind the Germans, must not be considered as too severe. On the contrary, it was a rather conservative estimate.

Most of the propaganda material studied could easily pass for propaganda of the last war, judging from the technique, the symbols and the slogans used. The following statement by Frossard which appeared in *Le Temps* of April 13, explains to a certain extent the reasons for this technique and gives an idea of the French attitude towards propaganda: ". . . To send propaganda abroad? It's a word that I do not like. I do not intend to introduce here German methods. We do not need to undertake an ideological crusade. Justly attached to its liberties, our democracy . . . chooses in its own way, under the hegemony of popular sovereignty, among ideas and doctrines. It (democracy) does not impose its choice on anybody. It does not offer its choice to anybody. We shall not borrow any of the German methods. We shall *answer* the gross untruth that the German propaganda diffuses without scruples, with an honest and loyal *information, à la française*. When one speaks in the name of France . . . one knows of what incomparable patrimony of spiritual and moral values our country is heir and guardian."

[24] *supra.*

Apparently no effort was made, in accordance with these explicit directions, to broadcast news and talks on any "scientific" plan of the German type. Rather, the entire effort was centered around refuting enemy propaganda. The main preoccupation was not to "propagate ideas" but to "answer contentions."

Among the most serious faults in the French technique, we might suggest the following: (1) *Arguments were directed at random* and they were not properly coordinated in relation to final objectives. Many arguments were used in the North American broadcasts which were obviously meant for French or other neutral listeners, and the consequence of this practice was that even if the argument was well presented and perfectly valid, it could not possibly serve two opposite purposes.

To explain further, let us consider first the nature of the task facing the French radio propagandist in his broadcasts to the United States and how he approached it. The principal task admittedly was to transmit news programs and talks apt to produce in the listeners a feeling of sympathy toward France and the French cause in the present war, a feeling of disgust and hatred against Nazi Germany and her cause, and, eventually, a determination to help France and her allies.

In order to undertake this task properly the propagandist should have considered as one of the most essential factors the condition of public opinion in the United States, and more particularly, the American conception of and attitude toward France, Great Britain and Nazi Germany.

Then he could have sent various appeals related to the ultimate aims, based on the events, adapted to reach the type of audience to which they were directed and ready to be most effectively accepted, given certain conditions of public opinion. From all evidence, it appears that the French radio propagandists did not give much thought to the receiving end of the broadcasts. On the contrary, they concentrated on the content, and broadcast indiscriminately to the French Empire and to the United States. This was done on the assumption, perhaps, that the function of the radio propagandist was to transmit to all listeners news reports passed by the French censor and patriotic talks, without any consideration for the attitudes of the radio audiences. Or, perhaps, there was no differentiation for simple reasons of economy, for paucity of funds was always a serious handicap to the French radio.

Several times in the news reports as well as in the talks, Paris-Mondial emphasized the invincible strength of the Allied Empires, obviously for the benefit of French listeners. In many other instances arguments broadcast to the American short-wave radio audience were clearly meant not only for French audiences, but also for Scandinavian, Dutch and Belgian audiences. Typical of these were the warnings transmitted after the German invasion of Norway and Denmark. A news broadcast or a talk was really a collection of arguments for universal consumption. Only certain talks during the latter part of April, May and June, had the appearance of being directed exclusively towards American listeners.

(2) In the attacks against German propaganda Paris-Mondial invariably stated first *in detail* the arguments of the German propagandists and then briefly refuted them. This practice was very dangerous and apt to give much more publicity than necessary to the enemy propaganda, especially when the German arguments were quite plausible. For instance: On February 10 in reporting the secret session of the French Parliament, an announcer declared in the 8:05 p.m. news program, "Germany's propaganda has tried these last few days to make use of the secret session by presenting it as the indication of serious disagreement between the political parties and the government. The unanimous votes that sanctioned the debate gave the Nazis still another smashing denial." Considering the actual bitter antagonism between the French political parties and the government, this was playing with fire.

(3) The coverage of the news was very poor and Paris-Mondial was usually behind the other European short-wave stations. The result was that other news broadcasts were listened to rather than those from Paris. Also, during the months of April and May too many alarmist news items were given out and too many losses admitted—so much so that even the French press protested unanimously on the first of May.

(4) Paris-Mondial, as well as the other French radio stations, has been accused by the French press of often revealing the intentions of the government to the public and of giving away military movements. With respect to this accusation, certainly the campaign for the adoption of more severe blockade measures that culminated with the actual mine-laying operations of the eighth of April is characteristic. Typical

was that sentence broadcast on the seventh: "We are now at the eve of a Franco-British counter-offensive."

(5) Whenever the Paris radio attacked, it usually did so in order to defend rather than to effect an offensive technique of its own. The main object of French verbal attacks, German propaganda, was criticized and exposed whenever there were German contentions to refute. With the exception of the series of talks on *National Socialism in the Third Reich*, there was no concerted systematic attack on Germany or German institutions and conditions. This, perhaps, was due to the fact that the French had inadequate knowledge of internal conditions in Germany, so that they could not criticize with the effectiveness of a Lord Haw-Haw or of "The Traitor of Stuttgart."

(6) The military strength of Germany was *never* questioned. In fact, it was definitely overemphasized. The answering claim that the Allies were much stronger economically and in naval power must have been poor compensation for the damage already inflicted not only on the morale of French listeners but also on the confidence of American supporters.

(7) To repeat our simile—Paris-Mondial was fighting *a propaganda war of position* during a time when the enemy countries were fighting *a war of movement*. For the French propagandist the world had hardly progressed, and he gave the impression of living in a false atmosphere years behind the times. The symbols, whether referring to the enemy or to the Allies, were obsolete. So were many of the slogans. Paris-Mondial, with few exceptions, had not many *new ideas* to present to the public to captivate their imagination, as new things usually do; on the other hand, Nazi Germany did—and to a large extent.

The symbols, of course, were not obsolete in the sense that they had lost their appeal to the human mind; they were obsolete in that they did not correspond any longer to existing conditions as they had when they were first spontaneously created. These were some of the symbols constantly used in discussing Allied war aims: *freedom, cooperation freely consented, democracy, European federation, independence, humanity, justice, liberalism, durable and just peace, civilization.* These symbols, aside from sounding familiar to the point of losing much of their significance, become ironic when connected with Franco-British history of the last twenty years, and with the actual conditions of the democratic government in France—in particular, *durable and just peace, justice,* and *liberalism.*

Of course, it is true that new significance was added to the symbols by the nature of the Nazi regime and by the excesses of the Nazi doctrine, but these symbols were emphasized at a time when the French public was more than anything else conscious of the necessity for *efficiency* and *honesty* in government and of the abuse of the French liberties, and when part of the French press[25] was clamoring for a more *energetic* conduct of hostilities. These symbols were more apt to inflame a 1917 public than peoples weary of the tragic experiences that followed the other war fought for the same ideals.

The idea of *sacred union* of French political parties was also constantly stressed by the Paris radio. Even the term was borrowed from the last war: *Union Sacrée,* but this time it did not correspond to reality as it did then.

It is true that all these symbols were also used in broadcasts directed to the United States, and that they may have influenced some people idealistically inclined and with scant knowledge of French affairs. The dissension between the French political parties, however, and the general conditions of the French Republic were not a complete mystery to most well-informed American listeners. One must also keep in mind that American radio audiences are propaganda-conscious to a fault and not readily inclined to accept again the broad idealistic symbols of the last war.

Among the symbols most used with reference to the enemy were some that had a new significance: *Nazis, New Order of Vassal States, slavery, Hitler, the mental case, gangsters,* and so forth, but the old list of symbols and slogans of the last war was, nevertheless, added to them. *The German propaganda, the professional liars, barbarian methods, illegal conduct, infraction of international law, scrap of paper, piracy, Belgium 1914,* were frequently recurring symbols. So much so that some passages of the broadcasts taken from our recorded files read as if they belonged to propaganda literature of the last war.

(8) Finally, a last fault in the technique of the French broadcasts was the poor English of the translations at the microphone. At times programs were nearly unintelligible on account of the peculiar construction

---

[25] *Figaro, Petit Journal, Matin.*

of the sentences and the usage of ill-adapted words translated literally from a French text.

In concluding, we repeat that it is obviously highly improbable that the French radio propagandists formulated their programs in accordance with an elaborate theory of propaganda consciously applied. Apparently, the declarations of Frossard were a good synthesis of the fundamental attitude. "We do not need an ideological crusade. . . . We shall *answer* to the gross untruths. . . ." That has been the main pre-occupation of the French radio propaganda. The problem was over-simplified. Too much was taken for granted, and instead of following a course of its own, Paris-Mondial tagged along *answering* and *defending*.

ATROCITY PROPAGANDA

By Philip E. Jacob

ATROCITY PROPAGANDA

T HE atrocity story, trusted servant of Allied propaganda in World War I, has enjoyed an adventuresome career in the radio broadcasts of the present belligerents, with the Germans, even more than the British or French, finding the weapon to their liking. Radio atrocity campaigns have in effect become vital strategies of conflict. Broadcasters rarely present instances of brutality haphazardly or as isolated news items. They weave them into themes which are used in various patterns depending upon the military, diplomatic or propaganda activity of the opponent, the attitudes of the particular audience in mind, and the immediate and long-run objectives of the belligerent. Atrocity stories thus serve as a sensitive barometer of the war. In addition they illustrate vividly the techniques employed by the propagandists to intensify emotional appeal and establish credibility, for these techniques were exploited to the fullest in order to assure the success of the atrocity campaigns in the face of indifference and skepticism.

What Is an "Atrocity"?

An "atrocity" is an abnormal occurrence; i.e., behavior which departs from the accustomed patterns of human activity. It is, however, behavior which so violates the deep-seated standards of social conduct, the ethic of those witnessing or hearing about the incident, as to shock them, cause acute nervous discomfort, and arouse the emotion of horror. It may or may not involve material injury to persons or property. It must, however, if it is to be considered an atrocity, injure some institution, convention, practice, attitude or value which a particular audience considers basic to its whole way of life.

Social standards or norms are not fixed entities and furnish no absolute criterion by which to judge what constitutes an atrocity. They change as new forms of behavior establish themselves as normal and normal forms of behavior become out-of-date. Social standards also vary with the circumstances surrounding the act. What is gangsterism in peace, becomes heroism if carried out against the enemy in wartime. They vary further with the cultural background of the audience. The social standards invoked in a given incident depend, finally, upon the relationship between the participants and the audience. If the enemy executes civilians it is "brutal murder." If one's own side does likewise, the state is "protecting" its citizens against criminals.

Considering these variations in social standards, an atrocity must be defined as an act which horrifies a particular audience at a particular time, and under a given set of circumstances. The reaction may be either an unexpressed attitude or overt action. Within limits, an opinion poll helps to uncover the former. With regard to the latter, one can conceive of a "conscience level" in an audience, a point at which the emotional tension aroused by an event breaks out into public expressions of horror, oral or written; into pressure group activity; and ultimately, into government action. An atrocity, then, is an event which crosses the conscience level of an audience to a greater or less degree and elicits various forms of overt response. As the public's view of atrocities changes, the conscience level shifts up or down. If the conscience level declines, acts formerly considered atrocities, occur without affecting the audience's conscience significantly enough to produce overt reaction on its part. If the conscience level rises, some acts which formerly occurred without a flurry of comment now occasion an outburst of public indignation.

The post-World War period witnessed a definite lowering of the conscience level in every part of the world. This was reflected in the general breakdown of international morality and a lowering of standards of humanity in warfare. National policies, whether democratic or totalitarian, hardened a widespread conviction that in the face of alleged national necessity, there was no "law," and the human conscience, brutalized by two decades of war and violence, grew numb to horror. In particular, a deep-seated skepticism arose with respect to all atrocity stories—a legacy of World War propaganda and of the post-war muckraking which followed.

Though the public's conception of an "atrocity" has steadily become more limited since the World War, the propagandists of the present war have adopted, virtually unchanged, the definition of their predecessors in 1914-1918. The belligerents, furthermore, whatever their differences in ideology or conduct, have agreed almost completely with one another as to what constitutes an atrocity. At least by implication they have accepted certain "laws" as criteria of human conduct in wartime. This does not mean that they feel obliged to obey these laws. They merely use them in judging atrocities committed by the other side.

Broadcasts from belligerents in this war reveal two major groups of such laws—laws of nations and laws of humanity. Neither are laws in the sense of being enforceable by a regular authority. Essentially they are two different ways of looking at norms of conduct—one legalistic, the other moral; one dealing with fictitious collective personalities, the other with human individuals. From the first point of view, the subject of the action—a nation—is a group personified as a distinct entity in itself. From the second, though the propagandist may attempt to show that the actors are typical of a whole people, he approaches them as human beings, not as an impersonal body.

Although belligerent broadcasters have talked at length about international law, it is only violations of *laws of humanity* which they label *bona fide* atrocities. A "code of humane law," based on the consensus of the rival propagandists as to what constitute crimes against humanity, would include the following principles. Human life is valuable and should not be indiscriminately jeopardized. Belligerents should not inflict unnecessary physical suffering upon human beings or attack institutions and persons devoted to the alleviation of suffering. Women are ordinarily inviolable. Combat should be conducted chivalrously, granting an opponent is gallant, respects the "honors of war," and refrains from attacking the weak and defenseless. Those innocent of hostile intent or action should not have to suffer the effects of war. Private property and religious institutions and practices should remain unmolested. Acts which transgress these standards are considered atrocities by short-wave propagandists on both sides, and will be accepted as such in the course of this analysis.

The Strategy of Atrocity Propaganda

On February 27, 1940, three months before the Allied armies met defeat in Flanders, Winston Churchill, then First Lord of the Admiralty, virtually admitted the failure of British atrocity strategy. Though the British Broadcasting Corporation had for over a month been conducting its most vigorous atrocity campaign of the war, Mr. Churchill asserted before the House of Commons that "German illegalities and atrocities are coming to be accepted as if they were part of the ordinary day to day conditions of war." Paris-Mondial, the French short-wave radio, met with even less success when it tried its hand at atrocities during the German invasion of the Low Countries.

The Berlin radio, however, conducted a series of major atrocity offensives in a variety of situations, satisfied apparently that its strategy was achieving the desired results.

The BBC's Strategy of Compensation

The atrocity propaganda of the British Broadcasting Corporation evidently followed the strategy of compensation which worked so successfully for the Allies in the first World War. This involved the substitution of a moral offensive for military effectiveness by crying "unfair" at the enemy. The aim is to strengthen morale on home and battle fronts, to enlist neutral support, and to undermine the morale of the enemy by touching the "conscience" of his people. The strategy of compensation uses atrocities, first, to arouse fear and hate of the enemy and pity and sympathy for friends or allies, and second, to release dangerous emotional tensions which are always a by-product of war. The ravages, sacrifices and irritations that war imposes create a body of "floating resentment" which sometimes explodes in times of military defeat or inactivity, unless guided into safe channels. The strategy of compensation seeks to direct this resentment as it arises on the home front into abuse of the enemy and to deflect some of the hatred in the enemy population from one's own side onto the enemy's leaders.

Most of the atrocities in the broadcasts from England recorded by the Princeton Listening Center up to June 22, 1940, were concentrated in the period of slight military activity from January 20 to April 8, 1940 (see Chart I). Morale both at home and among neutral sympathizers was at a low ebb. Talk of a "phony war" was at its height, although at sea Britain was suffering her heaviest merchant shipping losses since the outbreak of hostilities. Criticism of the vagueness of British war aims mounted. Demands for a negotiated peace spread. In this situation the British Broadcasting Corporation launched two atrocity offensives, one directed at the German conscience, the other at the flagging morale of its English-speaking audience.

The attack on the German conscience represented the second stage of British radio propaganda to Germany. At first the BBC had assumed that the German people were not responsible for the actions of their leaders, that they longed for peace, and that this desire could easily be stirred to an effective repudiation of those who had led them into

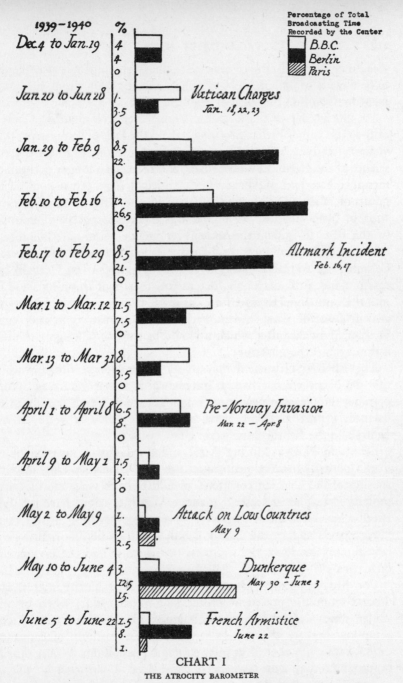

Percentage of Total
Broadcasting Time
Recorded by the Center
☐ B.B.C.
■ Berlin
▨ Paris

1939–1940	%
Dec.4 to Jan.19	4
	4
	0
Jan.20 to Jan.28	1.
	3.5
	0
Jan.29 to Feb.9	8.5
	22.
	0
Feb.10 to Feb.16	12.
	26.5
	0
Feb.17 to Feb.29	8.5
	21.
	0
Mar.1 to Mar.12	11.5
	7.5
	0
Mar.13 to Mar.31	8.
	3.5
	0
April 1 to April 8	6.5
	8.
	0
April 9 to May 1	1.5
	3.
	0
May 2 to May 9	1.
	3.
	2.5
May 10 to June 4	3.
	12.5
	15.
June 5 to June 22	2.5
	8.
	1.

Vatican Charges
Jan. 18, 22, 23

Altmark Incident
Feb. 16, 17

Pre-Norway Invasion
Mar. 22 – Apr. 8

Attack on Low Countries
May 9

Dunkerque
May 30 – June 3

French Armistice
June 22

CHART I
THE ATROCITY BAROMETER

Legend: This chart shows the proportion of time devoted to atrocities, during the periods indicated, in short-wave broadcasts from the British Broadcasting Corporation, Berlin, and Paris-Mondial, recorded by the Princeton Listening Center from December 4, 1939, to June 22, 1940.

war. In other words, the conscience of the German people was thought to be already at odds with Nazi policy, needing only slight encouragement to ripen into the spirit of revolt.

But the failure of the German people after five months of war to rally to this call of British propaganda and the lack of impressive Allied victories set back the BBC's propaganda timetable. Perhaps the conscience of the Germans was dormant and required a longer preliminary massage than had previously been anticipated before it could yield germs of rebellion. The condemnation by the Vatican on January 22, 1940, of Nazi atrocities in Poland was therefore eagerly seized upon by the BBC to initiate the strategy of compensation. It thought the censure of the Holy See would carry especial weight with German Catholics. In addition, news of "murderous attacks" by German submarines and airplanes upon "defenseless merchant shipping" was fed into the campaign. Every effort was made to pin the responsibility for atrocities on the Nazi leaders. Perhaps the German conscience could be shamed awake, after which it would be time to talk again of direct action against the government.

The BBC supplemented the appeal to conscience with a warning that the Nazis' conduct was as impractical as it was inhumane. World opinion, the German people were assured, could weigh heavily in the balance against German arms, and Nazi atrocities were driving neutrals to the British cause.

Events in Norway during April and the German invasion of the Low Countries in May again upset the BBC timetable. Obviously the rousing of the German conscience would have to wait upon German military defeat or at least stagnation. Atrocities could have but little effect when German armies were sweeping everything before them. "Propaganda against the enemy is only deadly when he is tiring and is beginning to doubt the rightness of his cause and the invincibility of his arms."[1]

The BBC's appeal to German conscience is of special interest as it departs from the precedent of the first World War, when atrocity stories were almost exclusively designed for home or neutral consumption. Perhaps this is a case where a new medium of communication, radio, has opened up new strategic possibilities. Where atrocity propaganda may not have been considered a particularly efficient

[1] Sidney Rogerson, *Propaganda in the Next War.*

means of attacking enemy morale when the difficulties of its dissemination over the enemy lines limited the dose which could be applied, now the availability of the ether has made possible experimentation in its use on a broad scale without sacrificing attention to other themes.

On its English language programs, the BBC used atrocities chiefly to define the "barbarism" against which Britain claimed to be defending civilization. As in the German language programs, a clear line was at first drawn between the Nazis and the German people. Only the former incarnated the spirit of aggression, brutality and evil. On January 26, 1940, however, Wickham Steed initiated a broader indictment which viewed Nazism as the fulfillment of German nationalism, and identified the nation with its leaders.

Some BBC commentators drew inspiration from German atrocities for confidence in ultimate victory. Steed, for instance, elaborated the thesis that "German abominations" ranged "the ultimately decisive imponderables against the aggressors." Atrocities served further to widen the scope of permissible military conduct. The arming of merchant ships was defended on the basis of Germany's alleged submarine and air attacks on peaceful fishing vessels and lightships. Atrocity reports were also used by the British as direct and indirect appeals for neutral support. The BBC concentrated on establishing a correlation between German atrocities at sea and the degree to which ships were protected. It claimed that the Germans primarily attacked and sank unarmed neutral vessels which were not in convoy. Under such conditions, suggested the BBC, it was to their own self-interest for neutrals to join the British war effort by placing their ships under convoy.

During its atrocity campaign, the BBC remained almost continuously on the offensive. On both the German and English language programs, charges against German conduct greatly exceeded answers to the countercharges which the Berlin radio hurled against the Allies (see Chart II). One major interruption occurred in the offensive, following the attack on the *Altmark* on February 17, 1940. In German language programs a marked shift occurred from offensive to defensive items, while the total amount of time devoted to atrocities dropped quickly. Evidently this incident and the vehement reaction of German propaganda stalled the BBC's strategy *vis-à-vis* the German people. The atrocity offensive could not be continued until the German charges had been answered or allowed to spend their force.

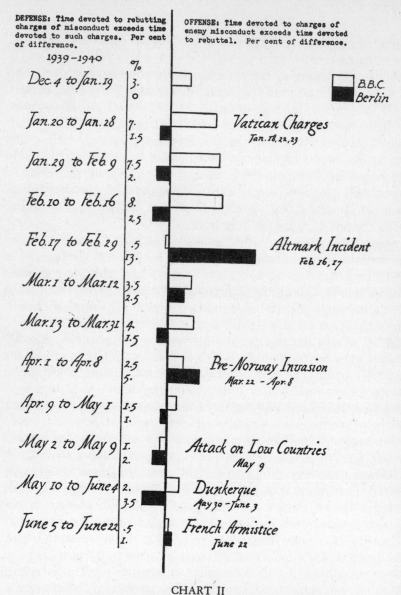

DEFENSE: Time devoted to rebutting charges of misconduct exceeds time devoted to such charges. Per cent of difference.

OFFENSE: Time devoted to charges of enemy misconduct exceeds time devoted to rebuttal. Per cent of difference.

1939–1940

Period	%	
Dec. 4 to Jan. 19	3.0	
Jan. 20 to Jan. 28	7. / 1.5	*Vatican Charges* Jan. 18, 22, 23
Jan. 29 to Feb. 9	7.5 / 2.	
Feb. 10 to Feb. 16	8. / 2.5	
Feb. 17 to Feb. 29	.5 / 13.	*Altmark Incident* Feb 16, 17
Mar. 1 to Mar. 12	3.5 / 2.5	
Mar. 13 to Mar. 31	4. / 1.5	
Apr. 1 to Apr. 8	2.5 / 5.	*Pre-Norway Invasion* Mar. 22 – Apr. 8
Apr. 9 to May 1	1.5 / 1.	
May 2 to May 9	1. / 2.	*Attack on Low Countries* May 9
May 10 to June 4	2. / 3.5	*Dunkerque* May 30 – June 3
June 5 to June 22	.5 / 1.	*French Armistice* June 22

☐ B.B.C.
■ Berlin

CHART II

OFFENSE AND DEFENSE IN ATROCITY PROPAGANDA STRATEGY

Legend: This chart shows the difference between the per cent of time devoted to charges of atrocities against the enemy (offense), and the per cent of time devoted to answers of charges made by the enemy (defense), on BBC and Berlin broadcasts recorded by the Princeton Listening Center. The unit of measurement is per cent of total time recorded by the Center from the given station in the given period.

For the strategy of compensation to succeed, atrocities must be both intense and credible—a difficult task for the British to accomplish, with widespread skepticism of "propaganda," general acceptance of the idea that war was bound to be "total," and the powerful counter-tactics employed by Germany. In the end, military considerations proved the basic determinant of the British strategy of atrocity propaganda. The British moral offensive stopped short with the beginning of the German military offensive in Scandinavia. No atrocity campaign could compensate for a military situation which deteriorated so rapidly and seriously as that of the Allies in Norway, and later in Flanders.

The German Strategy of Confusion

The Nazis have developed a strategy of atrocity propaganda which does not necessarily depend for its success upon the atrocities being believed. The aim is to disintegrate the will of the audience and make it passive, not to strengthen its morale and stir it to action. The method is to confuse attitudes rather than to arouse or release the emotions.

This "strategy of confusion" opens to its users a wide variety of situations in which atrocity propaganda can be used effectively, even in the face of contemporary public skepticism. The propagandist, not having to establish conviction to accomplish his purpose, need only give enough impression of truth to his material to raise doubts and muddy the clearcut conceptions of his audience. The "unstructured" audience then becomes more or less amenable to his own will, or at least sufficiently unnerved to offer but feeble resistance to the pursuit of his objectives. In a world where the line between peace and war becomes increasingly obscured and nations which are technically neutral are nevertheless viewed as potential enemies, this strategy can be applied to advantage at any time, and against all nations, not only an immediate enemy.

The German radio has employed atrocities in this strategy as a "barrage," a "counterattack" and a "holding attack." Before the start of the second World War, the Nazis had developed the tactic of an atrocity "barrage" to pave the way for diplomatic or military intervention in the Saar, Austria, Czechoslovakia and Poland. These bursts of atrocity stories in the German press and over the German radio usually started in earnest about one or two weeks before the final "coup." Between the outbreak of war and the Franco-German armistice, June 22, 1940, the atrocity barrage appeared only once—before the invasion of

Norway. This time it was coupled with a marked rise in references to Britain's intention to spread the theater of war and thus foreshadowed fairly clearly the initiation of a major move on the diplomatic or military fronts (see Chart I). The barrage came into the picture again before the aerial Battle for Britain in August 1940. The fact that no atrocity barrage developed before the invasion of the Low Countries in May suggests that this attack may not have been decided upon until the last moment.

The Nazis employed atrocities in a "counterattack" against the British atrocity campaign of January-March 1940. They supplemented defense of their own actions with a series of charges against the Allies designed to divert attention from the British accusations and throw the enemy propagandists themselves into the position of defender. They sought, first, to substitute Poles for Germans as the object of antagonism and, second, to divert hatred onto British imperialism and British leaders. The onslaught against British conduct rose to a climax following the attack on the *Altmark,* when Berlin magnified the "brutal naval action" into a *cause célèbre* (see Charts I and II).

Immediately upon the invasion of the Low Countries the Berlin radio used atrocity stories preventively as a "holding attack" (see Chart I). It repeated the tactic during the Battle for Britain. In contrast to the counterattack, atrocity propaganda here accompanied a German military offensive. The objective of the holding attack is to thwart enemy action on the moral front while the German army and air force blast out a military victory. Atrocities charged against the Allies might dull the shock to opinion abroad which would inevitably follow upon the sudden initiation of total warfare and break up by doubts the concentration of fear and hatred which might be expected to form against Germany.

In their attack on the Allies in May and June, the Berlin broadcasters charged the bombing of nonmilitary objectives and the killing of civilians in Germany. They told of the devastation wrought by Allied armies during their retreat through Belgium and Holland and of the mistreatment of prisoners. They reviled the French Colonial "nigger" troops. References to British imperialism recurred. The practice of the counterattack was followed by saddling blame for the ravages of war onto the Allied leaders, especially Churchill, who, according to the Berlin radio, epitomized the policy of ruthlessness.

French Strategy

Paris-Mondial paid little attention to atrocities until the invasion of Belgium and Holland on May 10. Then the British strategy of compensation was applied with vigor. The theme chiefly emphasized was the horror of the German *Luftwaffe,* which, without mercy, attacked refugees to clog the Allied military communications, destroyed hospitals and Red Cross units, and devastated open cities. That the campaign ended abruptly with the evacuation of Dunkerque was probably the result of the increasing desperateness of the military situation which absorbed more and more of the focus of attention, while disorganizing the planning of programs. Berlin's holding attack may also have contributed to the spiking of Paris-Mondial's effort (see Chart I).

Italian Strategy

Nothing resembling an organized full-fledged atrocity campaign appeared in Italian broadcasts to the United States up to June 22, 1940, so no clear line of strategy can be depicted. Nevertheless, atrocities offered Radio Rome a medium for the expression of its venom against Russia during the Finnish war. The vehemence and color displayed in the descriptions of Russian bombings stood out sharply from the rest of the program schedule, which moved on with its customary dull objectivity.

Atrocity Themes, 1940

Seven major atrocity themes emerged in the short-wave broadcasts of the belligerents in 1940. They fall roughly into two categories—atrocities occurring within an area controlled by the enemy, and atrocities of war conduct, occurring on the fringe of the area of control. The former includes acts of brutality alleged to have occurred in Poland, in Czechoslovakia and other German-occupied territories, and in the British Empire. The latter includes atrocities in the war at sea, those wrought by the airplane on land, brutal army behavior, and the mistreatment of prisoners.

The development of these themes has been analyzed both qualitatively and quantitatively for the period from December 1, 1939, when the Princeton Listening Center started to record broadcasts, to June 22, 1940, when the Franco-German armistice was signed. In addition to finding out what the broadcasters of the various belligerents said about the atrocity themes, the amount of time which they devoted to each on their daily schedule was measured.

Both offensive items (i.e. charges against the enemy) and defensive atrocity propaganda were included in the analysis. Defense is the reverse side of the atrocity picture, "normal" as opposed to "abnormal" behavior. It is direct when the propagandist answers specific charges made by the enemy. It is indirect when evidence of correct conduct is presented, showing the humaneness of the belligerent, without, however, relating this to the answering of a specific accusation by the other side.

The distribution of emphasis upon the various themes in the course of the period appears in Table I. It will be noted that the atrocities of control and of the war at sea formed the bulwark of the BBC's major atrocity campaigns, and the German radio's counterattack between January 15 and March 15, 1940. The other themes enter the stage principally after the German attack on the Low Countries, occurring in Paris-Mondial's offensive and Berlin's holding attack.

Murder at Sea

During the first World War, the Allies continuously sharpened their atrocity weapon upon the horrors of the war at sea. This same issue embroiled the United States with Germany. On September 4, 1939, the day after England again declared war on Germany, the theme was rechristened with prospects of a long life by the sinking of the British steamer *Athenia,* loaded with American passengers homeward bound from the war zone.

The relatively small loss of life, the immediate German charge that England was responsible for the crime and the spectacular *Blitzkrieg* in Poland stunted the early growth of sea war atrocities, but occasional incidents in November and December kept the theme alive. By February 1940, with German attacks intensified against both Allied and neutral merchant shipping, the British Broadcasting Corporation had developed its full-grown offensive on the subject.

The Berlin radio defended German sea policy vigorously but did not launch its sharp counterattack on British naval conduct until February 15, several weeks after the first extensive British charges. The theme then rose to a climax when Germany virtually declared unrestricted submarine warfare and the British destroyer *Cossack* attacked the German prison ship *Altmark* in a Norwegian fjord on February 17. Tension declined very gradually during March with the British more and more taking up a defensive position. After the start of active military operations with the invasion of Norway on April 8, the theme practically disappears. Altogether the BBC devoted 40 per cent of its atrocity material, up to June 22, 1940, and Berlin over 35 per cent, to the atrocities of the war at sea.

The British Case

Repeating almost identically the charges of the first World War days, British broadcasters have pictured German action at sea as the deliberate destruction of peaceful merchant shipping and the "cold-blooded murder" of those on board. Neutral ships suffer even more than Allied, being sunk "without law or mercy, not only by the blind and wanton mine, but by the deliberately aimed, coldly considered torpedo." Even surface raiders are accused of sometimes attacking ships without cause and without providing for the safety of the crews.

The appearance of the airplane as a weapon of sea warfare furnished a group of British atrocity charges, noticeably different from those of World War I. German planes callously bomb and machine-gun "harmless fishing vessels," considering it "fun to see a little ship crackling in flames like a Christmas tree." Even more reprehensible are attacks on lightships and lighthouses which "serve no war purpose" and "whose only object is the safety of the shipping of all nations." German planes make a special target of neutral ships not in convoys, as they are unarmed and unprotected.

British conduct in the sea war is defended as honorable and in accord with the strictest standards of decency and chivalry. Crews of German merchant ships are always safely provided for when the ships are sunk or captured. Submarines do not attack without giving due warning. No neutral ships are sunk or attacked.

When sterner measures have to be adopted against Germany and towards the neutrals, they are justified, according to the BBC, by the greater lawlessness and brutality of the enemy, in comparison with which British actions appear on an infinitely higher plane. British merchantmen and fishing trawlers must be armed in self-defense because Germany has broken "every convention of civilized warfare and every tradition and custom of the sea." Germany has no cause to complain about the attack on the *Altmark*, "for the Germans, by the crimes they have committed on the high seas, have put themselves outside of the law."

Though the blockade may force severe hardships both on neutral shipping and on the civilian population in Germany, says the BBC, it is after all, a humane means of bringing the war to a just end, through economic strangulation rather than bloodshed. It keeps needed supplies from the enemy's military forces. As for the neutrals, their ships can gain protection by traveling in British convoys. Further, they should remember that none of their ships and none of their citizens' lives have been lost as a result of British action and that in the long run, British victory means their security against German aggression.

The German Case

The Berlin radio, like the BBC, at first defended German conduct in sea warfare as conforming strictly to the accepted rules of international law. Only "legitimate" objectives were attacked—ships which were armed, ships which were in convoy, or ships which were used for naval or military purposes. Fishing smacks, even if not armed, act as patrol boats for the British Navy. Lightships are similarly accused. Submarines are obliged to attack British merchantmen without warning because an attempt to stop and search such armed vessels would be suicide.

To justify its increasingly rigorous action against neutral shipping and further defend the air attacks on British lightships, the German radio, starting about February 15, 1940, supplemented its first argument with the thesis of counterblockade. This argument claimed the necessity of broadening the scope of sea warfare beyond the limits of strict "legitimacy" in retaliation against the enemy's criminal and inhumane policy. The English blockade which aims to "strangle" Germany, that is to starve German women and children, has made the sea around the British Isles a theater of war. Germany has had to blockade England in return. Neutral ships carrying goods to England or stopping at British ports must expect to be treated as blockade runners. Losses should either be charged to England, which forces them into danger by the contraband control system, or to their own greed for risky profit. The German radio has referred to the United States as a model of neutral behavior in wartime and insists that Germany's ultimate aim is to establish the right of all neutrals to trade where they please and the freedom of the European continent from the continual threat of starvation by which Britain enforces her domination. Lightships whose purpose is to assure the safe arrival of England's import traffic cannot claim immunity from the measures of the counterblockade.

When the counterblockade thesis aroused the ire of neutrals, the German radio introduced countercharges against England's conduct of sea warfare, past and present. The British Navy brutally attacked defenseless German vessels and machine-gunned crews which surrendered and took to the lifeboats when their ships were captured or scuttled. In outright naval combat against the German pocket battleship *Graf Spee*, it was guilty of using an unfair weapon—gas. Neutral shipping suffered from English mines and sometimes from English airplanes. Britain even stooped to the sinking of one of her own ships, the *Athenia*, with the loss of both British and American lives, in order to forward her war policy. The climax of British brutality at sea came with the ruthless attack on the defenseless German prison ship *Altmark*, sailing peacefully in Norwegian waters.

The French Case

Paris-Mondial played a very secondary role to the BBC in the discussion of the atrocities at sea. Its interest was mainly limited to the legal issues involved. It dismissed the German claim to legality for the counterblockade as "not only dangerous but untrue," founded on an international agreement which was never ratified (London, 1909). At the same time, the German policy absolved the Allies from any further obligation to respect international law in the conduct of naval warfare. Protests against Allied violations of neutrality are "laughable" when brought forward by Germany which herself has a long record of such violations.

Terror from the Air

By the time of the Franco-German armistice, the exploits of the opposing air forces had become a major atrocity theme over the German, British and French short-wave radios. Aerial abominations appeared not only in the war at sea as previously discussed, but also when the airplane was released for full-scale operations in connection with land warfare, especially during the *Blitzkrieg* in the west. Attacks on land, considered by themselves, furnished the subject matter for 16 per cent of the BBC, and 13 per cent of the Berlin atrocity items recorded between December 1, 1939, and June 22, 1940. Paris-Mondial's atrocity stories, concentrated between May 10 and June 4, 1940, were almost exclusively concerned with the terror from the air.

The dreaded offspring of modern war was nurtured in Poland. Bombs dropped with devastating effect on Warsaw and other Polish cities in September 1939. Rumors circulated in France and England that the Germans had used mustard gas in their air attacks and had dropped poisoned chocolates. Berlin denied the use of gas, as well as other "lies spread by anti-German propaganda during the Polish-German conflict."

The terror from the air appeared again in the Russo-Finnish war. The BBC took a vicarious interest in the Russian air raids, broadcasting the vivid atrocity accounts given by the Finns, as well as eyewitness reports from its own observers. In its news broadcasts the BBC fully reported attacks on nonmilitary objectives and the high toll taken of civilians. The Italian radio, indulging in its only major set of atrocity stories, during the period under consideration, condemned "the horror of the Russian aerial bombardment of civilians in Finland" with a viciousness unsurpassed by any of the other broadcasters. Rome reported one case where Soviet fliers attacked a group of small boys fishing through the ice. "When they finally nosed their planes up into the sky again, they left behind them only a black patch of little bodies rapidly growing cold and another unforgettable landmark on the path of Soviet civilization." Paris-Mondial paid only slight attention to these as to all other atrocities at this time. Berlin ignored the war except for an occasional official Finnish communiqué, always accompanied by the corresponding Russian one.

In the west, reality did not at first measure up to anticipation in regard to aerial atrocities. Neither side unleashed its air force for the "all-out" war advocated by General Douhet and his school. Each was evidently loath to incur the risk of reprisal by a strongly equipped opponent.

Berlin, in spite of its scanty reference to the conduct of the war in Finland, yielded the first comment recorded by the Center, dealing with the air war policy of the western powers. On January 25, it accused H. G. Wells of advocating "the ruthless bombardment of Berlin and of other cities of the Reich because he says it would have a salutary effect upon the German people." The first actual civilian casualty on land in the west caused a flurry of condemnation and exoneration from London and Berlin respectively, though both admitted it was a by-product of a German raid on the naval base at Scapa Flow on March 17, 1940. The great reluctance of the belligerents to offer even the slightest provocation for extended air raids, is again shown by the BBC's vigorous denial of a German charge on April 12 that the RAF had bombed railroad yards in Schleswig-Holstein. London immediately called the story "imaginary" and suggested that Berlin might be trying to set up an alibi for air attacks of its own.

Tension rose during the Norwegian campaign as the BBC, largely on the basis of Stockholm reports, charged German fliers with machine-gunning women and children, razing peaceful Norwegian villages and attacking Red Cross units. On April 19 and thereafter the attention of BBC and Paris-Mondial was focused on reports from Norwegian sources of the bombing undergone by King Haakon and his ministers at the town of Elverum shortly after the beginning of the invasion. The German radio, of course, upheld the honor of the German Air Force in Norway and charged the RAF with a few indiscretions of its own.

The opening of the *Blitzkrieg* in the west stirred Paris-Mondial to its only concentrated interest in atrocities. Vividly, often through the mouths of refugees and other alleged eyewitnesses, came the descriptions of German bombings of open towns, machine-gunning of refugees, attacking of hospitals, hospital ships and Red Cross ambulances. The gloves were off. The bombing of Paris on June 3, however, furnished the occasion for Paris-Mondial's last major explosion in atrocity propaganda. "Paris has been bombarded and the civilized world is shocked. . . . There is to me a revolting sound in these two words, the bombardment of Paris . . . like seeing a beautiful, charming and venerable woman slapped in the face. . . . Scores of houses were destroyed, and more than two hundred individual victims have been counted. Among them, of course, were women and children and while I am speaking, mothers in Paris are at the bedside of a dead child, killed by a German bomb."[2] With this peroration, Paris-Mondial virtually drew the curtain on atrocities, and turned the focus of its attention increasingly toward the seriousness of the task of resistance, positive confidence in the capacity of France to measure up to the job, and later, direct appeals for aid in the face of its desperate straits.

The BBC had temporarily shelved its interest in atrocities when the Germans launched their attack in the west. Quantitatively it contributed only a mild reenforcement to Paris-Mondial's campaign. What it did have to say, concerned the air war and followed the lead of the French radio. As the troops began to flow back to England from Dunkerque, however, the BBC went out on its own, presenting first-hand impressions of the German terror. "One French officer told me he had seen a group of women and children machine-gunned from the air. They were near no military objective. They were out in a field and one woman was having a baby. She and her baby were killed." After Dunkerque, the BBC shifted its attention markedly from atrocities committed by the German Air Force to the effective reprisals of the Allies—reprisals, however, which it insisted were limited strictly to military objectives.

The German radio at the very outset of the military campaign in the west launched furious charges against the conduct of the Allied air forces. The Allies were the first to bomb an open town, said Berlin. On May 10 they attacked Freiburg, in the Black Forest, killing children at play. In Hamburg and Bremen, the British "hit nothing but hospitals, blockhouses and a large training school for nurses." Retaliation is promised for "every attempt of the enemy to turn this war into a total war." "All these attacks on peaceful cities," warned Haw-Haw, "are being carefully registered and at the proper time the enemy will learn that these cowardly attacks have not been forgotten."[3]

Although the conduct of the German Air Force was, on the other hand, "impeccable," it nonetheless became the subject of Allied atrocity-mongering. Allied defeat at Dunkerque under skies darkened by the German Air Force, was apparently Berlin's cue for a full-scale dissection of Allied atrocity reports. Duff Cooper, it said, argued in the following manner. "A German bomber flies over France. It reconnoiters

---

[2] Professor André Morize, in a broadcast recorded by the Princeton Listening Center, June 5 1940.

[3] Broadcast recorded by the Princeton Listening Center, June 3, 1940.

targets worthy of its bombs. Columns of French soldiers are not attacked by the German planes. Suddenly, however, they spot a cemetery which apparently is a more interesting target. Only in the last minute, one of the Germans notices that this is a French cemetery, upon which the Germans say to each other: No, we are not going to bomb a French cemetery. What we try to find is an American cemetery or maybe a Canadian war memorial for our bombs."[4]

As each successive stage of the Allied defeat in the Battle of France was reached, the Berlin radio achieved a new climax in the development of its theme of air atrocities. Both the accusations it leveled against the enemy, and the aspersions it cast upon the Allies for atrocity-mongering were timed to coincide with the most striking deeds of the German Air Force, and the most stunning setbacks of the French and British. The tactic of "holding attack" was therefore carried out not only in the atrocity campaign as a whole, but in the specific integration of this principal theme with the major military moves.

On the March

Many of the atrocities of land warfare which were current in World War days have been notably inconspicuous in the broadcasts of the present belligerents. Gas warfare and dumdum bullets have rarely been mentioned. Few references have appeared to indiscriminate artillery shelling except for the siege of Warsaw. The horror theme built up around the airplane seems to have replaced the terror formerly inspired by Big Bertha and her lesser sisters. The emphasis in atrocity propaganda, as in the actual strategy of combat, has been upon the demolition of enemy resistance from the air rather than from the ground.

Nevertheless, the behavior of the armed forces in the conduct of land warfare has again furnished some classic atrocities. The Allies, on the whole, have refrained from exploiting the theme in their radio broadcasts, perhaps because debunkers so thoroughly exposed the *chefs-d'oeuvres* which they concocted in the World War—the German corpse factory, the crucified Canadian soldier, the chopped-off hands of Belgian children. The same cannot be said of the Nazis, who have stripped themselves of the legalistic frame of mind which cramped the German style in 1914-1918, and have resurrected many of the traditional tales of barracks and battlefield. Berlin devoted 14 per cent of

[4] *idem*, June 4, 1940.

its atrocity material between December 4, 1939, and June 22, 1940, to this theme, as opposed to 3½ per cent for the BBC.

Long before hostilities in the west had reached the point of tension at which such stories usually sprout, the BBC found it necessary to deny a Berlin story that French and British soldiers in the Ardennes had been quarreling over the ravishing of a French girl by the Tommies. During the Norwegian campaign, although the American public, through its own newspapers, became familiar with an imposing record of misdeeds attributed to the German Army, few such references appeared in the Allied broadcasts. On the other hand, the British were faced with a gamut of German accusations following the landing of their own expeditionary force, and on April 22 the BBC had to plead that "so far nothing, nothing at all has been destroyed in Norway by the French or the English." The Berlin radio maintained that "wherever the English fought they took hold of houses and farms in a country which was not theirs anyhow and they let these houses become prey of the flames caused by German arms which of course had to smash such houses."[5]

Souvenirs of Retreat

As part of its atrocity holding attack accompanying the military invasion of the Low Countries, the Berlin radio charged that "while Belgian soldiers bled to death for the sake of the Anglo-French plutocrats, British mercenaries in Belgium pillaged, burned and plundered Belgium as if they were engaged in a colonial war." British troops collected truckloads of silver spoons, knives, forks, jewelry, clothes and other "remembrances." The gold and silver reserves of the Belgian National Bank were carried off to London. Paintings and other works of art were stolen.[6] Similar accusations, though nowhere near so intense, are leveled against the French troops in Holland.

The British were further accused of firing on Belgian troops to compel them to continue fighting, while after the Belgian capitulation, the British and French refused to give refugees food.

Perhaps the most clever *tour de force* of German atrocity technique was the charge that the British set fire to the library of Louvain. This town, destroyed in the course of the German advance in 1914, had

---

[5] *idem,* April 30, 1940.
[6] *idem,* May 28, 1940.

been one of the Allies' most effective Belgian incidents during the first
World War. Americans had expressed their sympathy after the war
by voluntary contributions to rebuild and equip the library. A few
days after the start of the *Blitzkrieg* the Allies once again accused the
Germans of annihilating the city, including the American-donated
library. They soon dropped the subject but the Berlin radio developed
the gutting of the building into one of its most prized examples of
British barbarism, adducing evidence observed at first hand, to prove
that the library had been deliberately fired from within before German
troops entered the city.[7]

"To France's Eternal Shame"

The Berlin radio accused French colored troops of the most vicious
behavior. At first, references concerned the occupation of the Rhineland after the Armistice of 1918, when "40,000 French niggers . . .
made even the sidewalks unsafe for the German population." Turning
to the contemporary battlefront, Haw-Haw told how these "wild
beasts . . . ambushed their prey, single German soldiers" and "inflicted
terrible wounds on their victims with their arm-long knives." Their
barbarity was not limited to their opponents, the Nazis charged. They
plundered Belgian and even French villages in which they were
quartered.

The Noble German

The German radio, of course, denied that any breach of conduct
was committed by German troops in the course of their advance. "The
German forces took every possible consideration for the lives of the
population and the preservation of property." The destruction caused
by the invasion was consequently relatively slight, considering the size
of the conflict. "The German purpose," declared Berlin, "is to wage
war against combatant armies and to defeat them decisively, whilst at
the same time conforming with those conventions laid down by international law for the proper treatment of prisoners and civilians."

"The British Art of Lying"

The German radio repeatedly charged the Allies with "atrocity-
mongering." "The present article," alleged Berlin, "is so similar to that
proved absolutely false after the World War that one needs only to

[7] cf. *idem*, June 20, 1940.

change the date and place to have a 1940 tale." Few of the stories attributed by Berlin to the BBC actually appeared, however, in the broadcasts recorded during this period from England. The German radio may have deliberately put these charges into the mouths of the British, creating straw men which could be knocked down effectively. Thus it could undermine the reliability of the Allied information services, and further the German strategy of confusion.

One of the most striking instances of the disparity between atrocity reports by the Allied radio, on the one hand, and by the German radio on the other, is the stir that was raised over parachutists. The BBC and Paris-Mondial scarcely commented on Germany's spectacular application of a new military tactic. For the Berlin radio, however, the parachutist stories, probably blown up by deliberate exaggeration, quickly became a major dish on the atrocity menu. They served as an important vehicle for heaping ridicule upon Allied propaganda as well as for leveling dire threats of retaliation if the parachutists were mistreated—a procedure calculated to confuse civilians and soldiers alike in their resistance to the German advance. These efforts of the German radio may have been materially helped along by the similar, though without doubt, unwitting exaggerations in the sensational accounts given by American newspapers.

Prisoners of Barbarians

The mistreatment of prisoners by the enemy formed a familiar atrocity theme in the first World War, some charging that it was used deliberately to frighten soldiers into more desperate resistance. Both the story and the countercharge have appeared in the atrocity campaigns of this war, though sporadically and usually with some fairly obvious and specific purpose.

The BBC offered a gruesome picture of the treatment of English prisoners on the *Altmark* in justification of the British attack on the ship. What the Nazis maintained was a harmless merchant vessel, was a "floating concentration camp," where Britons, buried alive under closed hatches, lived for weeks on tea, bread and water.

For several days before the *Altmark* incident, the German radio vaunted the model policy followed by Germany toward prisoners. Its extensive attention to the subject at this particular time arouses the suspicion that Berlin anticipated the British move and was preparing to offset the accusation that prisoners on the ship had suffered mis-treatment: In addition, the discussion tied in closely with the rebuttal of charges which were being made against German conduct toward Polish prisoners. Following the attack on the *Altmark*, Berlin insisted that the prisoners had received the same rations as the German sailors and that "they were so correctly and honorably treated that they thanked the Captain of the *Altmark* for his honorable treatment."

It is during the height of the Battle of France that the Berlin radio brings this theme into its own. French colonial troops are singled out for specially dishonorable mention, being charged with mutilating German prisoners, cutting their throats and sometimes burning them alive. Stories of the mistreatment of prisoners are not limited to the colored man, however. French officers allegedly ordered their men to shoot German soldiers wearing the Iron Cross, and put a price on heads of members of German tank units. Even neutrals were arrested, mishandled and executed by the Allies. The German record, of course, continued spotless despite the calumnies of Allied atrocity-mongers, who tell their soldiers lies about the fate of those who fall into German hands, "so that desperation if not conviction will keep them fighting." Germany is maintaining her old tradition of treating those who lay down their arms "with the respect due to a brave enemy."

The Killing of a Nation

Poland, taking the place of Belgium in the World War, has furnished the Allies with the chief source for atrocities of occupation. It has also been fully exploited by the German propagandists, who seem to have done a more thorough and adequate job in this field than their prede-cessors in 1914-1918. The BBC used the Polish atrocity theme as part of its strategy of compensation. Berlin used it to counterattack the British as part of its strategy of confusion. Each charged its enemy with brutal actions as part of a deliberate policy of extermination. Each claimed the other had fabricated its atrocity stories out of its own misdeeds. Altogether Berlin devoted 20 per cent of its total atrocity material be-tween December 1, 1939, and June 22, 1940, to the Polish theme; the BBC, 26 per cent.

On January 22, 1940, the Vatican radio broadcast a condemnation of German acts of oppression against the Polish population. The next day a detailed report of the persecutions was published in Rome, which, according to the BBC, was submitted to the Primate of Poland, "by a Roman Catholic priest who escaped after being in prison in Poland." This launched the second part of the BBC's atrocity offensive, paralleling the sea war brutalities. The campaign continued at white heat until the *Altmark* incident on February 17, after which it tapered off. Paris-Mondial contributed a few selections to the repertoire with its customary punch, but on the whole took only a minor interest.

Three days elapsed without comment by Berlin after the BBC first announced the Vatican charges. Then the German radio attacked the Polish situation with vigor. Throughout February and March, except for the week of the *Altmark* incident, it told of Polish atrocities, German efforts at reconstruction and Allied atrocity-mongering. The Norwegian campaign and the war in the west did not prevent repeated though brief references. With its characteristic capacity for integrating all of its propaganda material, the Germans wove the Polish theme into other atrocity subjects, such as the parachutists and the treatment of prisoners.

The Allied Case

The BBC and Paris-Mondial charged Germany with brutal oppression of the Polish people as part of a general, deliberate policy of annihilation—economic, cultural and moral. "Jews and Poles are being herded into separate ghettos, hermetically sealed and pitifully inadequate for the economic sustenance of the millions destined to live there or to die there," stated Wickham Steed. Food supplies have been confiscated by the Nazis and starvation looms in the Gouvernement General, now overcrowded with refugees. Secret orders issued by Governor-General Frank virtually decree that all Polish economic resources should become the property of the Reich. Men and women are seized by press gangs in the streets and sent to work in Germany virtually as slaves. Forced labor of another variety is imposed by the German authorities. According to a Paris-Mondial broadcast, "several hundred young girls . . . were sent to the Western front to be 'employed' in public houses which are reserved to the German soldiers. . . . In Warsaw military patrols carried out similar kidnappings for their own purposes."

"They do not only kill the Polish people, they also destroy Poland's culture and tradition," declared the BBC. The Nazis have closed the universities and thousands of schools, shot many of the professors, sent others to concentration camps, robbed and destroyed libraries and laboratories. "The crowning iniquity," in the eyes of the Vatican as reported by the BBC, "is the suppression of all religious practices among one of Europe's most devout people."

That the Nazis themselves were uncomfortable about the stream of condemnation flowing against them for their conduct in Poland, is alleged by the BBC to be evident from their reaction to it. The fact that neutral correspondents are not allowed in the Polish territory and that the Nazis won't agree to the administration of relief in Poland by a neutral commission "tells the story of the conditions that must obtain." Indeed, Poland has been one of the most difficult jobs of the German propagandists and discrepancies constantly appear in their efforts to counteract the Allied charges.

The German Case

The Berlin radio countered with "irrefutable" documentary evidence, including eyewitness accounts by both Germans and Poles, and the testimony of medical experts who had allegedly conducted autopsies, to show that Poles were guilty of frightful atrocities against the German minority in Poland during the military campaign in September 1939. Kaltenbach and Haw-Haw gave detailed and vivid descriptions of the atrocities. Here is the Kaltenbach style. "The Polish soldiers seized the defenseless civilians lying on the ground . . . and regardless of whether they were wounded or not, led them to a boat landing and pushed them into the lake. Then they opened fire on the helpless men struggling in the water. When one of the unfortunate Germans tried to grab hold of the boat landing, the Poles gouged at him with their bayonets. Finally the bodies lay so thick in the shallow water that they formed a pile. The Polish murderers then started a motor boat and backed it into the heap of bodies so that the propeller further mutilated them."[8]

Though the Poles are "inclined by nature to deeds of violence and to outbursts of cruelty," most of the massacres, according to Berlin, were not haphazard occurrences committed by isolated individuals amidst the chaos and fury accompanying the Polish retreat. "The extermination of the Germans after the outbreak of the war was

[8] *idem*, February 28, 1940.

carefully prepared by the Polish government with the guiding support of agents of the British secret service." The French Yellow Book, in Berlin's view, proves that "the Western Powers knew and tolerated the aggressive attitude of Polish jingoism and the brutalities to which the German minority was subjected" and yet did nothing about it.

The Germans would have been justified in every kind of revenge, maintained the Berlin broadcasters, but instead they have only been interested in restoring order and prosperity. The forces of occupation are reconstructing the country under the greatest of difficulties, with due justice both to the Polish population and to German claims to the western part of Poland. A heavy burden has been placed upon the German authorities in these efforts. In addition to the incredibly low standard of living prevailing under Polish rule, the country was hard hit by the campaign when the retreating Poles wantonly and systematically destroyed roads, bridges, electric plants, etc. In spite of this, "over 400 miles of destroyed railways have been built, 1500 miles of roads have been repaired. . . . In Warsaw alone, the German authorities have made 600,000 vaccinations against typhoid. . . . Germany is continuing pensions and paying unemployment insurance. . . . Almost all the primary schools have been reopened." Agricultural laborers are now receiving better wages than under the Polish regime. The Jews receive official support and no one prevents them from earning their living and running their businesses.[9] Herr Frank, the Governor-General, was reported to have declared it his intention "to inaugurate a new gardenlike block in the Polish districts. If the Gouvernement-General would go back to Polish rule some day then it would be his proud conviction that all Polish valuables remained in their place."[10]

The German radio attacked the Allies for their charges against German conduct in Poland. "Atrocity story propaganda seems to the responsible men in Paris and London to be one of the most effective means of drawing the neutrals onto the side of the Western Powers." In contrast, Berlin passes over the Vatican's denunciations in almost complete silence. Only two brief references to these were noted in the Center's recorded broadcasts, the first coming almost two weeks after the original Vatican broadcast. Berlin claimed the Pope had been the victim of false information.

[9] *idem*, February 13, 1940.   [10] *idem*, April 3, 1940.

Under the Shadow of the Swastika

The BBC reenforced its attack on German atrocities in Poland with similar accounts of Nazi policy in Czechoslovakia. These accusations, started a few days after the publication of the Vatican report on Poland, clustered in the first half of February 1940; they were crowded off the air by the *Altmark* affair, but came back strongly in March to commemorate the debacle of Czechoslovakia the year before. The BBC devoted surprisingly little effort to decrying Nazi terror inside Germany.

Intent on Germanizing the Czechs, the Nazis had followed much the same tactics as in Poland, declared the BBC. They were attempting "to destroy not only the economic but the spiritual life of the Czech nation." A reign of terror under the Gestapo had displaced the harsh, but disciplined control of the German Army. Both the BBC and Paris-Mondial disputed the Nazi claim that German "protection" had been sought by the Czechs. "For all these unhappy people the German regime is one of terror, and an abominable one."

Instead of conducting a counter-atrocity campaign against the Allies on this theme, the Berlin radio simply denied the charges as "fairy tales" and maintained that the people appreciated the benefits of German protection. The initiative for the German occupation had come from Prague, according to President Hacha himself. The Protectorate now is the safest and most peaceful country in Europe. Czechs "volunteer" for work in Germany, draw good wages, and send a large amount of their income back to their families. On the first anniversary of the ending of the "Versailles shackles," President Hacha expressed Czech gratitude to the Fuehrer for protection and above all for sparing the Czechs the ravages of war.

The German radio accompanied each successive extension of German military authority, after the beginning of the war, with elaborate exposition of the beneficence of German rule. The fall of Paris called for special assurances from Fred Kaltenbach to his American listeners that "the German government and military authorities are fully aware of the responsibility to the world as trustees for the city and its treasures. Paris will after the war be returned to the people of France in an undamaged condition."[11]

[11] *idem*, June 14, 1940.

The Brutality of Empire

The German radio has specialized in discovering atrocities within the confines of the British Empire, using them especially to counteract the Allied charges of German brutality in Poland and in the war at sea. Berlin has eagerly broadcast news of British oppression in India and signs of Indian discontent. Extreme poverty and disease prevail among the exploited population whom the British consider an inferior race, hardly human beings at all. Other parts of the Empire suffer under similar conditions. The grants made by the British home government to the colonies are nothing but a *pourboire*, says Haw-Haw. Their purpose is to induce "His Majesty's badly treated subjects overseas to join the war against Germany." The British persecute the Arabs, committing "the most atrocious crimes in the name of morality."

Berlin found it convenient to review the record of British-Irish relations as a means of countering the BBC's Polish atrocity offensive. While Britain raised a hue and cry against the German methods in Poland she continued her traditional persecution of Catholic Ireland. Two members of the Irish Republican Army were executed without satisfactory evidence of their guilt, according to the Berlin radio. "They represented Ireland's will to freedom, a will which seven hundred long years of oppression could not wipe out."

Britain's cruel and ruthless methods of imperial warfare belie her vaunted moral aims and conduct. The Transvaal experienced "Lord Kitchener's scheme of universal devastation and depopulation, organized pillage and destruction." "The Danish fleet was annihilated for the sake of protecting the liberty of small nations. All the while, the world's bloodiest conquest was proceeding in India under the banner of civilization and Christianity. One hundred years ago, that same ruling class forced opium on the Chinese Empire by war, also conducted in the name of eternal principles."[12]

The BBC replied that British rule in the Empire was beneficent and that the peoples of the British Empire know that "should they fall under German domination they would be treated like slaves and inferior men, just as the Poles and Czechs are treated now." India had freedom in everything except politics. "Granting political freedom would mean destroying other freedoms ... interfering with the present

---

[12] *idem*, March 21, 1940.

absolute freedom of religion, thought and private life and the right of minorities." Britain does not exploit her colonies. She spends money on them and promotes extensive plans for their welfare. Forced labor exists in only eight British colonial territories, and is carefully regulated, being permitted only for work of direct importance to the community. Safety, peace and quiet prevail throughout the Near East. The Arabian countries joined the Allies at the outbreak of the war, despite prewar attempts to stir up disaffection, because they know the Allies fight for freedom and equality, that their own future is tied up with the democracies, and that only in that way can they preserve their own independence. The IRA men who were executed were tried with "the objectivity and fairness for which British justice is famed throughout the world."

Techniques of Presentation

Two problems have chiefly concerned the belligerent broadcasters in the presentation of atrocities to their audience—intensity and credibility. Intensity is the excitement value which attaches to an item, the capacity to produce "stirredness" in an audience. Intensity enables the appeal to win a place in the audience's focus of attention in competition with other events and to arouse not only interest but active concern. Credibility is the impression of truth. It appeals to the rational faculty of the audience, satisfying its "canons of critical veracity."[13] Actual truth, or validity, is irrelevant to credibility, except in so far as it may help to induce belief.

The standards, both of intensity and of credibility, which an atrocity propagandist must meet to make his appeal effective have risen since the first World War. Because people now expect war to be horrible, it is not so easy to shock their sensibilities. An incident must be much more intense than before to qualify as an effective "atrocity." On the other hand, in the face of widespread consciousness of and resistance to propaganda, and a heightened skepticism of atrocity propaganda in particular, the task of establishing belief is also much harder. Many of the requirements of credibility, furthermore, conflict with those of intensity, creating an added dilemma. The more intense the news, the greater are the efforts required to induce belief. Yet incidents which are easily believed, are not likely to meet the tests of intensity.

[13] Harold Lasswell, *Propaganda Technique in the World War*, p. 205.

British broadcasters in this war have usually resolved the conflict of credibility and intensity in favor of credibility. Research into English propaganda methods in the first World War has put the British on the defensive, especially in regard to the reliability of atrocity stories, and provided German propagandists with excellent material for effective counterattack. Consequently, the British have discussed atrocities with great caution and little emotion.

The Nazis have had an even greater reputation for unreliability. Their strategy, however, aimed at confusing attitudes rather than rousing strong emotions, has enabled them to place less emphasis on the attainment of belief. While they have by no means neglected the use of devices to establish credibility, they have also reached high levels of intensity, comparable in many cases to British standards of the first World War. Lord Haw-Haw and Fred Kaltenbach in particular have become atrocity specialists of the first order.

A detailed quantitative analysis has been made of the techniques used to enhance intensity and credibility in German atrocity propaganda for the period between January and April 1940. The German techniques differ but little from those of the other belligerents.

Techniques of Intensifying an Appeal

To make their atrocity propaganda intense, the broadcasters have employed six techniques: actuality, emphasis, variety, abnormality, individuality and integration with the audience's frame of reference.

ACTUALITY

The great mass of the atrocity material in the short-wave broadcasts of the belligerents has concerned events declared to have taken place. The broadcasters have rarely reported hypothetical atrocities, ones which were proposed or attempted by the enemy, but had for one reason or another, failed to come off. These, they evidently assumed, were less effective than incidents which had actually occurred.

EMPHASIS

Emphasis brings an incident or theme into prominent focus in the audience's attention area. The extensive visual or oral presence of an item before the audience makes it more likely to receive physical notice. Emphasis also conveys to the audience a sense of the item's importance.

TABLE I

Distribution of Atrocity References as to Theme

(in % of total time devoted to atrocities by each belligerent, from December 4 to June 22, 1940)

(Paris-Mondial from May 10 to June 22, 1940)

| | TOTAL | ATROCITIES OF WAR CONDUCT | | | | | ATROCITIES OF OCCUPATION | | |
| | | The War at Sea | | The War on Land | | Treatment of Prisoners | Poland | British Empire | Other |
		Naval Conduct	Air Conduct	Air Conduct	Army Conduct				
BBC	100	23	17½	16	3½	4	26	7	4
Berlin	100	19	7½	13	14	9	20	11½	6
Dec. 4–Jan. 19									
BBC	20	2½	3½	3½	0	1	8	½	*
Berlin	6	1½	1½	*	*	*	2½	*	*
Jan. 20–April 8									
BBC	66	20	13½	3	*	2½	18	6	3
Berlin	53	15	6	1½	*	2½	16½	9½	2
April 9–May 9									
BBC	3	*	0	3	*	*	0	0	0
Berlin	5	*	*	1½	1	*	1	*	*
May 10–June 4									
BBC	8	0	0	5	1½	*	*	0	0
Berlin	25	*	*	6½	9½	4	*	*	1
Paris	94	0	0	90	1	1	1	0	0
June 5–June 22									
BBC	3	*	*	1½	*	0	0	0	*
Berlin	11	1	0	2	3	1½	*	*	2½
Paris	6	4	0	0	1	1	0	0	0

NOTE: * = less than 1%.

On radio programs, the amount of time absorbed by a given item furnishes a rough quantitative measure of the emphasis placed on it by the broadcaster. A more precise test is the extent to which the broadcaster concentrates his attention upon one subject as opposed to other subjects. Chart I shows the proportion of the broadcasts recorded by the Princeton Listening Center, which was devoted to atrocities in different periods. It is therefore an index of concentration upon the subject as a whole. Table I shows the distribution of time among the different atrocity themes. It brings out the interesting fact that attention usually centers upon not more than two themes at any one time and indicates that the belligerent broadcasters follow a principle of concentration of emphasis even in dealing with individual parts of a general topic. The interest of the audience is not to be dissipated by presenting it with too extensive a menu for digestion at one sitting.

VARIETY

The atrocity propagandists use variety in their presentation to offset staleness and dullness likely to result from overemphasis.

In reporting a previously mentioned incident, they achieve variety by placing the incident in a new context or by deriving fresh implications from it. When the Berlin radio referred for the second time to H. G. Wells's proposal in *Liberty Magazine*, to bomb German towns, it used as its point of departure, the alleged fact that other periodicals were now taking it up. The impression of a fresh development was thus given to an old item.[14] By February 19, 1940, the Berlin radio had talked to death the details of the attack on the *Altmark*. One of the commentators thereupon produced a lengthy and novel peroration on traits of English character as revealed by the affair.

Sometimes the themes themselves vary. Those which are worn out are dropped. Some, which suddenly seem timely, are revived. Occasionally an entirely new theme appears. The subject of Polish atrocities disappeared almost completely from the broadcasts of the belligerents by the end of March. The subject of the blockade dropped out of sight during the invasions of Norway and France, but was brought back when agitation started in the United States for the distribution of food under neutral administration in the occupied countries. References to

[14] Broadcast recorded by the Princeton Listening Center, February 7, 1940.

atrocities committed by the Allied armies burst into the Berlin broadcasts during May with scarcely any previous treatment of the themes.

Variety is also sought through vivid and expressive language. Lord Haw-Haw, a master in the use of words, referred to Britain's leaders as "architects of disaster" and asserted that British propagandists, "like conjurers who have repeated their tricks too often . . . are finding a dwindling and unresponsive audience."[15] Notable lapses have occurred, however, at the point of using fresh terms of language. Berlin commentators talk *ad nauseam* of "cold-blooded murder" at sea and in Poland, and of the "starvation of women and children" as the aim of British war strategy. Some of this may have been deliberate with a view to emphasizing a particular phrase through repetition. If so, it shows the frequent necessity of choosing between emphasis and variety as the most effective tactic of suggestion under given circumstances. It is more likely the result of lack of imagination on the part of the second-rate propagandists.

Broadcasters gain variety, finally, by presenting their material in many different kinds of programs. In reporting the *Altmark* affair, the Berlin radio used at one time or another the forms of news bulletin, feature talk, press review, interview, dramatization, report by an observer from the scene of action, recapitulation of events as a fictitious story, an imaginary transposition of the affair to New York harbor with a reversal of the roles taken by Britain and Germany, talk by a participant (the Captain) and comments by a speaker of prominence (Admiral Raeder). In this way, without causing too much monotony in its presentation, Berlin hammered away at the incident for a week, with occasional references creeping out later.

ABNORMALITY

In the case of an atrocity, the degree of abnormality is a fundamental determinant of intensity. Abnormality can only be determined in reference to the particular social norms or standards of conduct prevailing at a given time, in a given place and under given circumstances. In Table II an attempt has been made to erect a rough scale of abnormality by which to judge "atrociousness." This has as its point of reference the standards of conduct which now appear prevalent under conditions of war in what might be called Western civilization, particularly in Eng-

15 *idem*, May 14, 1940.

TABLE II

SCALE OF ATROCIOUSNESS
(based on degree of abnormality)

I. VICTIM

	German Radio Atrocity References Jan. 20-April 8
A. Proximity to human level of life	
1. Inanimate	34
2. Nonhuman	0
3. Human	150
B. Military significance or use (degree of "innocence," defenselessness and expected risk of harm)	
1. Of inanimate objects	
a. permanent and direct military use	0
b. temporary but direct military use	8
c. indirect military use	0
d. no military use—in vicinity of military objectives	2
e. no military use—not in vicinity of military objectives	10
f. no military use—objects belonging to neutrals	14
2. Of animate objects	
a. the armed forces	5
b. hostile civilians (armed)	11
c. occupation or residence near military objectives	27
d. prisoners	6
e. civilians generally (enemy)	63
f. " " (neutrals)	5
g. " " (perpetrator's own side)	8
h. workers	2
i. women, children, aged	23
C. Symbolic significance	
1. National	1
2. Humanitarian	0
3. Religious	7

II. EFFECT

A. Number of victims	
1. One object	7
2. Several objects	64
3. Many objects	48
4. The whole of a class of objects	41
B. Extent of damage (property)	
1. Partial destruction	9
2. Total destruction	10

TABLE II (continued)

German Radio
Atrocity References
Jan. 20-April 8

C. Character of the injury (persons)
   1. Civic disability, robbery, etc., causing social or mental discomfort 20
   2. Physical discomfort, indirect injury to life and limb 37
   3. Death or normal wounding 92
   4. Mutilation 11
   5. Sexual mutilation 4

III. WEAPONS OR PROCEDURE
(degree of impersonality)

A. Impersonal (perpetrator and victim not face-to-face)
   1. Policies 53
   2. Projectiles
     a. long-range artillery, bombs 14
     b. torpedoes (directed at specific object) 0
     c. machine guns (increasingly specific object of attack) 5

B. Personal (perpetrator and victim face-to-face)
   1. Formal procedures 16
   2. Nonformalized procedures
     a. general 45
     b. indirect attack (without use of perpetrator's hand) 12
     c. weapons used against victim at a distance 27
     d. weapons used directly on victim 13
     e. body of the perpetrator used 3

IV. INTENT OF PERPETRATOR

A. Accidental 5
B. Uncontrolled 16
C. Indiscriminate 32
D. Deliberate
   1. Deliberateness alleged or implied 61
   2. Deliberateness inheres in the act 52

land, Germany and the United States. The attempt is necessarily in part subjective in that it is based on *a priori* estimates of the extent of overt audience response which different types of atrocities will arouse. On the other hand, an objective quality is present in that the opinions of the belligerent broadcasters as to degrees of atrociousness have been scrutinized.

The scale rates the victim of the atrocity, the effect of the act, the weapons or procedure used and the intent of the perpetrator. The victim is measured according to its proximity to the human level of life, the degree of "innocence," defenselessness and expected risk of injury as indicated by its military significance and use, and finally, according to its symbolic significance. The effect of the atrocity is measured by the number of victims involved, the extent of damage to property, and the character of the injury sustained by persons. The weapons used are rated according to the extent of direct contact involved between perpetrator and victim. This is based on the assumption that civilization has depersonalized human intercourse and that the personal, or face-to-face weapon or procedure, has become the primitive, hence the abnormal. The intent of the perpetrator is graded according to its deliberateness.

The scale as applied to the German radio's atrocity propaganda from January 20 to April 8 shows a high degree of abnormality in the atrocities reported, though not what would be called extreme in most cases. The German broadcasters apparently build up from the more normal and less thrilling incidents toward the most abnormal and striking. A high concentration of abnormal incidents occurs in the two-week period following the attack on the *Altmark* on February 17. This parallels closely the curve of emphasis already outlined and also correlates with the development from general to specific incidents discussed below. The net effect is to produce a campaign which accumulates intensity both quantitatively and qualitatively until it reaches its climax.

INDIVIDUALITY

To achieve intensity, the broadcasters have often striven to individualize atrocities and lift them out of the general run of events, thereby enabling them to make a more profound and lasting impression on the audience. Individuality is imparted to an event if it is concretely and vividly described and if it is personalized, i.e. identified with specific human beings.

Table III indicates the degree to which atrocities have been individualized in a group of German broadcasts, by showing the extent to which the victim, the perpetrator, the locale, the time, the circumstances, methods and effects of the incidents have been specified and described. German atrocity propaganda on the whole has fallen more on the side of generality than individuality. Nevertheless a rather clear pattern of development from the general to the more specific appears in the course of the different atrocity campaigns over the Berlin radio. The campaign

TABLE III
SCALE OF INDIVIDUALITY

	German Radio Atrocity References				
	Jan. 20-Feb. 16	Feb. 17-29	March 1-31	April 1-7	Total
I. The victim					
A. Unspecified or general	33	10	17	6	66
B. Class or group designated	26	25	16	6	73
C. Particular victim or number of victims designated but not identified	31	17	11	1	60
D. Identity established	3	22	8	4	37
E. Descriptive terms used	2	5	1	0	8
F. Human interest material used	1	6	1	1	9
G. Symbolization (personification)	3	0	3	0	6
II. The perpetrator or person ultimately responsible					
A. Unspecified or general	41	30	20	7	98
B. Class or group designated	15	21	12	4	52
C. Particular individuals designated but not identified	5	11	5	0	21
D. Identity established	6	5	4	1	16
E. Descriptive terms used	1	0	1	3	5
F. Human interest material used	1	0	0	0	1
G. Symbolization (personification)	1	3	0	0	4
III. The locale					
A. Unspecified	47	19	29	10	105
B. Specified	17	34	7	3	61
IV. The time					
A. Unspecified	52	20	29	11	111
B. Specified	10	28	7	2	47
V. The circumstances, methods and effects					
A. Unspecified	38	23	20	5	86
B. General descriptive terms	8	6	1	1	16
C. Details given	19	30	11	7	67

between January and April, 1940, reached its climax of emphasis and abnormality in February, following the *Altmark* incident. At this time the largest proportion of specific incidents and descriptive details is also produced. After the climax is passed, the great majority of incidents are again described only in general terms.

Strangely, the German radio has rarely used the dramatic form in the presentation of atrocities. Sometimes German atrocity propaganda has appeared in the less imaginative dialogue form. "Smith" and "Schmidt," on February 26, 1940, discussed British imperial oppression for a few minutes. The BBC on the other hand, has produced numerous and elaborate dramatizations of the alleged German atrocities in Poland.

INTEGRATION WITH THE AUDI-
ENCE'S FRAME OF REFERENCE

The atrocity propagandists have consistently tried to integrate their appeal with an audience's frame of reference. The frame of reference comprises all the aspects of environment and experience of which an individual or group is actually or potentially conscious. It is a series of triggers attached to the audience's area of awareness and concern. If an appeal touches a trigger it excites a point of familiarity in the audience's consciousness, thereby capturing attention and interest and conveying meaning. The frame of reference thus acts as a counterpoise to individuality. It is the general setting within which specific incidents can achieve significance for an audience.[16]

The broadcasters have appealed to six aspects of the frame of reference of their American audience—geographical, chronological, social, experiential, cognitive, and attitudinal.

They have integrated atrocities with the average American's *geographical field of reference* by telling of incidents whose scene of action lay close to the United States or in some area which, though relatively remote, was of particular concern to Americans. The Berlin radio made much of the British attack on the German merchant ship *Waccama* off the coast of Brazil, and within the American "neutrality zone." Sometimes the propagandists attempted to reach the geographical field of reference by artificial means. The Berlin radio substituted New York for Joesing Fjord, Norway, as the scene of action in a hypothetical recapitulation of the *Altmark* incident.[17]

Most of the atrocities were reported as having just happened and therefore fell within the *chronological field of reference* of the American audience. In general, the present and the predictable future form the area of greatest concern to individuals and their interest usually slackens as an event recedes into the past. References were made occasionally to

[16] cf. Muzafer Sherif, *The Psychology of Social Norms*, Chap. III.
[17] Broadcast recorded by the Princeton Listening Center, February 20, 1940.

atrocities which took place earlier in the war. A few incidents of the first World War were dug up as a background for contemporary ones.

Appeals have been brought within proximity of the *social field of reference*, the circle of individuals in whose activity the American audience was interested. If the audience is acquainted in some way, either with the participants in an event, the announcer, or the reputed source of the news, its concern will be more actively engaged.

The most intimate relationship exists where either participant or announcer is identified as a member of the same primary group as the audience, i.e. a group in which face-to-face contact has been maintained. This rarely happens, and if it does, of necessity involves only a tiny segment of the total audience which the broadcaster is trying to reach. The range of face-to-face contacts of an individual is comparatively small even in our highly mobile civilization. So the announcer frequently tries to create the impression of a primary group relationship with his listeners by talking to them as though they actually were, or at one time had been, face-to-face. He uses primary group terms and language—"you," "I," "our"—and treats his audience like old friends.

If identification of participant, announcer, or source of news with a common primary group seems infeasible, the broadcaster may point out a common secondary group relationship with the audience, i.e. membership in an interest group in which contact is not face-to-face. The most usual secondary group chosen for this purpose is the nation. The Berlin radio eagerly discussed the stopping of *American* ships by the British at Gibraltar, which were carrying food to Poland donated by the *American* Quakers and the *American* Red Cross.[18]

So important do the broadcasters consider the establishment of a secondary group relationship between the announcer and the audience, that special efforts have been made to secure the services of persons whose nationality and even whose manner of speech are identical with those of the audience to be addressed. On the whole, audiences want to hear the "lingo" to which they are accustomed.

Social proximity may be secured to some degree even if the participants, the announcer or the source of news are not members of the same primary or secondary groups as the audience, but are well known to the audience. An American is familiar with Winston Churchill and action attributed to him will excite his attention. Lord Haw-Haw, thanks to

18 *idem*, February 8, 1940.

free Anglo-Saxon publicity, built up a reputation which undoubtedly induced many to listen to him just to see what he was like. When the *New York Times* is quoted, many will take notice, although they may never have seen a copy of the paper.

A very fundamental aspect of the audience's frame of reference is its *field of experience*. If the propagandist succeeds in connecting his presentation with the events in which the audience has been, is, or may be a participant, his appeal is likely to have a profound effect. If he is unable to relate the subject at hand to an actual or potential experience of the audience itself, he can delve into experience of the primary and secondary groups with which the audience is identified, for the audience will be inclined to consider this to a certain degree an extension of its own field of experience.

The broadcaster frequently tries to make the audience feel that it is an immediate participant in the contemporary incident about which he is talking. The audience stands to suffer as a victim, or is directly or indirectly responsible as the perpetrator. The American people appeared as the victims of arrogant British action in the Berlin version of the seizure of American mails.

The propagandist can secure a high degree of intensity by vicariously satisfying the sexual or sadistic impulses in the audience which make it crave, perhaps subconsciously, to take part in an atrocity as perpetrator. He need not fear that the audience will react with sympathy for the criminal instead of the victim. The craving to go and do likewise cannot be given even vocal expression if the audience is to retain its status in the conventional society of which it is a part. The suppressed desire then seeks compensation through the expression of extreme horror at those in whose shoes the audience secretly longs to be.

The announcer may ask his audience to project itself into a hypothetical experience or to imagine itself in the place of the participants in a given experience. "Try to imagine your own womenfolk being chased through the streets by a mob of frenzied degenerates intent on rape and violence; then you will begin to have some idea of the circumstances which moved Adolf Hitler to take action in order to save his own flesh and blood," Haw-Haw pleads.[19]

In the frame of reference there is a large and varied *field of knowledge* to which the propagandist can attach his appeal—the "facts" of which

[19] *idem*, February 28, 1940.

the audience is aware, aside from its own personal experiences and relationships.

One important branch of this field is familiar current events. When a reference is integrated with these events it appears "timely." The *Altmark*, either by luck or foresight, climaxed intensive discussion by the Berlin radio of British naval atrocities and the honorable treatment which Germany was according to its prisoners. Berlin's whole propaganda campaign was thus neatly integrated with the apparent course of events.

The propagandist can, within certain limits, mold the audience's field of knowledge to facilitate the acceptance of his appeals. Unlike the other fields of reference so far discussed, this one is flexible. The body of general facts of which an audience is aware at any moment, fluctuates rapidly because it is exposed to a constant bombardment of fresh stimuli, some of which drive out items originally present in the audience's attention area. A skillful propagandist can guide the introduction of new facts or call up old ones which had been forgotten, thus deliberately changing the contours of the field of knowledge in such a way as to create new areas of meaning receptive to his appeals.

One of the most effective techniques of providing the propagandist's appeal with a hospitable reception in the audience's frame of reference is the integration of incidents into themes. Either by implication or by direct reference, an incident is placed in a stream of similar incidents which has been accumulating as part of the audience's field of knowledge. The incident consequently fits smoothly into an already well-structured pattern and it at once means something to the audience. Furthermore, the progressive development of a theme exerts a cumulative impact upon the audience which isolated or unintegrated incidents could never have. The Nazis have been particularly adept at this task of integrating incidents into themes. In British propaganda instances do occur where atrocity stories crop up in relative isolation from a consecutive theme. This may be the result of some special purpose which the item is designed to fulfill as in the case of a BBC dramatization of German atrocities in Poland on December 28, 1939, when the low point of British fighting spirit was causing concern. It may, on the other hand, be purely haphazard. In either case, it would appear that much of the potential impact of the item is lost by being sprung suddenly on the audience without the building up of a background.

A further step in integration is achieved when one theme is inter-related with another. This also is a finely developed art among the Nazis. The primary purpose of British Empire atrocities told by the German radio was to counteract the Allied stories of German terror in Poland. Yet the material was so handled as to reenforce simultaneously at least three other motifs which the German radio was developing at the time—the attack on British war aims, the evidence of weak ties within the British Empire, and the justice of German colonial demands.

The themes of one side can be further integrated to advantage with those of the opponent, for the latter are quite likely to be included in the audience's field of knowledge, and will serve as a point of reference. The Berlin radio could present charges that the British invented the concentration camp during the Boer War, with confidence that an audience educated by Britain on the score of Nazi terrorism would understand what was meant.

The manipulation of the field of knowledge so as to facilitate the acceptance of an appeal within the audience's frame of reference may, in the case of atrocities, temporarily detract from the intensity of the initial impact. The audience is to some extent immunized to shock because it has been led, in the course of the development of an atrocity theme, to think in terms of a long record of comparable incidents of which the perpetrator was guilty. The atrocity no longer appears so atrocious just because it is not so exceptional. Yet, if this happens, it means that the more fundamental objectives of the atrocity campaign are being accomplished. The enemy has sunk to so low a point in the scale of social values that anything will be believed about him. The propagandist can then concentrate on drawing out the necessary implications for action against him.

Out of the fields of experience and knowledge grows a *field of attitudes* which forms the broadest and most significant aspect of the audience's frame of reference.[20] Attitudes are a prime determinant of action and as such are of particular concern to the propagandist. The line between the fields of experience, knowledge and attitudes cannot be sharply drawn. An appeal to the fields of experience and knowledge almost inevitably involves at least an indirect appeal to the field of attitudes and is, in fact, a most effective avenue of approach to attitudes.

[20] cf. Sherif, *op. cit.*, Chap. VII, for a comprehensive discussion of the development of social attitudes and values and their relation to the frame of reference.

Nevertheless a distinction is useful because attitudes gradually divorce themselves from particular experiences and facts and come to enjoy a more or less independent existence of their own as general sympathies, prejudices and other mind-sets or concepts. A multitude of experiences and facts will then touch upon a given attitude, not just the ones with which it was originally associated. Furthermore, the attitude becomes identified with certain verbal symbols through which it can be approached. One can conceive of an attitude attached at one end to the experience and knowledge from which it derived, and at the other to the symbols with which it has become associated, and the propagandist is at liberty to approach it from either side.

In reaching the audience's attitudinal frame of reference by the avenue of symbols, the propagandist tries to discover and appeal to stereotypes—words and concepts to which the audience has already given a positive or a negative value. The propagandist often links new concepts, toward which the audience has not formed an attitude, with symbols which are already charged with a strong value content, hoping that the audience will uncritically transfer its attitude from the old symbol to the new. When Kaltenbach talks of the French "nigger" troops he hopes that the variety of attitudes from contempt to hate which the term "nigger" elicits in many Americans will come to embrace the French as well. When he talks of Polish national feeling being "largely a denominational matter" and attributes the massacre of Germans by Poles to the difference in religious faiths, he seeks to attach to his appeal the support of antisectarianism and of the belief in separation of church and state which prevails in the United States.

The Weakening of Intensity

To nullify opposing atrocity propaganda, the broadcasters have applied several techniques of weakening intensity. They tone down emphasis on unfavorable items by ignoring them completely or for a period of time. The BBC frequently omits all counterreference to German charges. The Berlin radio, in the case of the charges made by the Vatican regarding German atrocities in Poland, delayed rebuttal until the initial shock of the onslaught had spent itself. A lapse of time without reference will enable other news to crowd the obnoxious items further back in the audience's focus of attention and ultimately they may die out of their own accord. If the enemy keeps up the reference all by himself, without any opposition to lend variety and interest, he runs the risk either of boring the audience or of over-intensifying his appeal.

The intensity of an event is weakened if the audience expects it to take place. No matter how horrible the act or charge, the initial shock is dulled if the audience has anticipated it. Before Germany declared unrestricted submarine warfare around the British Isles, the Berlin radio had fully developed an argument in behalf of the counterblockade and warned of its imminent invocation in view of the British blockade policy. The mass air attacks on England were preceded by an extensive and increasingly intense series of charges against the RAF, some of them coupled with very specific threats of reprisal "when the time comes."

The propagandist may sometimes unwittingly weaken the intensity of his own appeal. He may overintensify, producing a state of satiation in the audience when its norms are so shocked as to be dulled or even destroyed. Something like this may have happened in the later stages of Paris-Mondial's atrocity campaign. Or he may build up such an anticipation of horror in the audience that the atrocities fail to live up to expectations. The Nazis have been played up as beasts with such low standards of humanity that BBC accounts of their atrocities often appear anticlimactical.

Techniques of Enhancing Credibility

The atrocity propagandists have used three major techniques in trying to enhance the credibility of their material—consistency, establishing confidence in the speaker, and referring to sources for authority.

CONSISTENCY

In seeking to establish credibility, the propagandist faces a basic tactical problem in deciding the extent to which he should tell the truth in order to convey the impression of truth. The absence of contradiction, rather than the actual presence of truth, seems to be the fundamental condition of credibility.[21] This means that where the audience has extensive opportunity to find out about events from the enemy or from impartial sources of news, the propagandist will have to preserve external consistency, that is, make his argument hew close to the line of truth. Within an area of effective censorship, he can depart from the truth, but must in any case preserve internal consistency.

[21] cf. *idem*, pp. 83, 84.

In short-wave atrocity propaganda, the broadcaster is in a peculiar position as regards the maintenance of external consistency. Material goes into areas where the opportunity for contradiction by the other side is usually present and the audience profoundly skeptical. On the other hand, the nature of the subject makes it difficult either of absolute proof or absolute disproof. It is largely a question of one side's word against the other. Only rarely do events, verifiable by the audience or by independent investigation, enable the validity of the atrocity reports to be conclusively established or denied during the course of the war. This gives the atrocity propagandist rather wide freedom from restraint by canons of truthfulness.

Whether or not the belligerent broadcasters on one side or the other have taken advantage of this freedom to spread "cock-and-bull" stories, cannot very well be ascertained until the war is over and the facts run down. Independent, impartial reports by neutral observers and journalists, while few in number, tend to corroborate many of the charges made by both sides.[22] It is quite possible that the propagandists have not had to err far from the truth because the facts have been adequate for their purpose.

Although on the whole, the propagandists have carefully preserved internal consistency, instances of self-contradiction have occasionally appeared in the broadcasts of each belligerent. The BBC condemned the Germans for attacking harmless British fishing vessels and denied the Berlin radio claim that British fishing smacks were used as naval patrol boats and were therefore legitimate objects of attack. But then it turned around and admitted that ten thousand fishermen had joined the naval patrol service. Although Berlin indignantly denied that the Estonian ship *Linda* was sunk without warning, it admitted that a man who had been taking a bath had had to jump into the icy cold ocean water, and subsequently died of heart failure.[23]

Some students of the Nazi technique have asserted that large inconsistencies appear if the German programs broadcast to different zones are compared, though the version presented to a given country may sound convincing by itself. W. A. Sinclair, a commentator of the British Broadcasting Corporation, alleges that on December 21, 1939, the Ger-

[22] cf. John Maloney, "Intrigue over Sweden," *Saturday Evening Post*, November 23, 1940; M. W. Fodor, *The Revolution Is On*, pp. 37, 40; and others.

[23] Broadcast recorded by the Princeton Listening Center, February 20, 1940.

man radio sent out a news bulletin charging abominable behavior by British crews at the funeral of German sailors killed on the pocket battleship *Graf Spee* in its encounter with British cruisers off Montevideo. The British spat on the coffins, made catcalls during the funeral service, and threw the body of a dead dog on the grave of the German sailors. This bulletin, says Sinclair, went to Asia and the Far East at half past nine in the morning, was broadcast in Dutch at midday, in Spanish at two in the afternoon, in Arabic at half past four and in French at a quarter past eight. For countries where cats were regarded as unclean, a dead cat was substituted for the dog. Then the same evening, the English language announcer denied that the story had been broadcast at all and accused the BBC of lying.[24]

ESTABLISHING CONFIDENCE IN THE SPEAKER

To enhance credibility the propagandists have tried hard to establish confidence in the speaker. Sometimes they attribute to him the authority of direct observation. Paris-Mondial, at the height of the Low Countries invasion, interviewed Francis P. Hamlin, a wounded volunteer ambulance driver of the American Field Service, who claimed he had personally witnessed the bombing and machine-gunning of Red Cross units by the *Luftwaffe*.

The speaker assumes the aura of impartiality if he is introduced as a neutral. The BBC has repeatedly exploited the services of friendly American journalists and commentators such as H. B. Ellison of the *Christian Science Monitor*, Edward Murrow of the Columbia Broadcasting System, and Warren Irving of the United Press.

In choosing speakers for their cause, the British, following the first World War precedent, have particularly sought the authority of prestige. The BBC has presented over the air such figures as J. B. Priestley, Leslie Howard, Vernon Bartlett, Wickham Steed and Richard Greene.

The speaker may claim the authority which comes from identity with the audience, stressing his social proximity to it and maintaining that he shares its interests and its outlook on the world. Or he may try to secure the confidence of the audience by giving an appearance of honesty in his approach to the subject. He can perhaps disarm the audience's suspicions by frankly admitting bias. "Sure, this is propaganda." "This is propaganda; it is also the truth." On the other hand, the speaker may

---

[24] W. A. Sinclair, *The Voice of the Nazi*, p. 27. For similar references, see also Vernon Mackenzie, *Here Lies Goebbels*.

try to reassure his audience by denying bias. E. D. Ward now and then maintains that he is freely expressing his own opinions without interference by the Nazi authorities.[25] "This is the truth, it is not propaganda," say others. "This is the truth; what the other fellow says is propaganda," is the usual approach of Berlin commentators.

REFERENCE TO SOURCES FOR AUTHORITY

The most common device for enhancing credibility is reference to some source other than the speaker as authority for the reliability of the statements made.

The most convincing source is, of course, the enemy, for to him attaches the least suspicion of bias in regard to references unfavorable to himself. The broadcasters often attribute their information to specific persons on the other side—eye-witnesses, officials, prominent personages. The enemy's press is carefully perused for incriminating evidence. Berlin regularly quotes *The New Statesman* and *The Nation* as the source of information on British imperial atrocities. Special attention is devoted to analysis of the opponent's radio programs for admissions of guilt. The BBC claimed to have picked up an order sent over the German radio to the *Luftwaffe* to harass refugees behind the Allied lines in order to impede the movement of troops.

Next to the enemy himself, the neutrals are the most impartial source of statements unfavorable to the enemy. The broadcasters quote extensively from persons, radio and press in a variety of neutral countries. On the other hand, a very large number of the sources used by the broadcasters are persons or publications in their own camp. A good part of the Berlin menu is made up of quotations from the German press. The news programs indeed often give the impression of a mere rehash and digest of press comment, suggesting that the German radio, rather than gathering its own news, acts as an outlet for news originally collected by other agencies.

A variety of general or cover-all statements of the source are used. Berlin delights in reporting "it is officially stated," exhibiting the proper Teutonic respect for administrative authority. "According to neutral sources," "it is reported on good authority," "high political circles," and all the familiar rubrics of journalistic documentation put in their appearance. Sometimes in using a cover-all source, the propagandist en-

---

[25] cf. broadcast by E. D. Ward, recorded by Princeton Listening Center, August 29, 1940.

gages the audience's desire for prestige, and ego enhancement, as when he announces, "every intelligent person knows." Or he may appeal to universal or general knowledge as his source, i.e. "everybody knows," counting on the timidity of the audience to secure its acceptance.

In referring to a source for authority, the propagandist frequently distorts and twists the original statement to suit his purpose, or even fabricates a reference and attributes it to the source. The BBC claimed that the German radio had recanted on its charge that the British had used gas in the attack on the *Graf Spee*. No such admission was uncovered by the Princeton Listening Center in the broadcasts it recorded from Berlin.

Techniques of Destroying Credibility

To destroy the credibility of an opponent's atrocity propaganda, the broadcasters have used the techniques of denial, exposure of fallacy, exaggeration, attack on the source or speaker, and the presentation of an alternative version of events.

The simplest, most frequently used, but probably the least effective method is denial. The trouble with the technique is that competition for credibility ensues between the allegation of one side and the refutation of the other. The latter can rarely emerge completely victorious. It may weaken the credibility of the opponent's case but can hardly destroy it.

A much more telling blow is leveled if the audience can be convinced that the other side is self-contradictory or has subsequently admitted its error. The broadcasters are consequently always on the alert to find fallacies in the opponent's argument and if none can be found, they are sometimes made to order.

A particularly effective technique of discrediting the opponent's case is to present it in such a way that it exceeds the audience's most extreme limits of reasonableness and appears ridiculous. If this cannot be done with the case as actually stated by the other side, nothing prevents its distortion and exaggeration by misquotation or removal from context, into a form utterly wild and inconceivable, nor indeed the complete fabrication of a fanciful tale alleged to have come from the enemy. The German radio has applied this fine art in attributing to the BBC highly dubious atrocity stories which the BBC apparently never broadcast. Berlin commentators would then indignantly call the British broadcasters atrocity-mongers, and gleefully set about ridiculing the veracity of the reports.

Credibility is undermined by attacking the other side's propagandist or sources. The accuracy of their observation or information is questioned. Doubt is thrown on the impartiality of the speaker or source, and suspicion aroused as to the honesty of their motives. The prestige of the propagandist or source is attacked, either *ad hominem*, or by pointing out a record of past unreliability which destroys his reputation for trustworthiness. A claim to identity with the audience made by the propagandist on behalf of himself or the source of his news may be attacked.

To destroy credibility, a propagandist may also introduce within the audience's frame of reference a pattern of ideas which is incompatible with the opponent's story and consequently, if firmly enough established, rules it out. He can present an alternative version of events to that given by the enemy, either in reply to the enemy's charge or preferably in anticipation of it. In the early days of the Low Countries invasion, the Berlin radio repeatedly emphasized that the German Air Force attacked exclusively military objectives. Instead of directly denying Allied charges, it concentrated upon this attempt to displace them with a substitute story more favorable to the German cause. The German propagandists have gone further and tried to fix in the audience's frame of reference a picture of the German soldier as a gallant, heroic, almost medieval warrior, incapable of anything but honorable conduct. If they could successfully implant such a conception, they would have accomplished the ultimate in refutation, for the listener would be defended by impenetrable armor against the infiltration of British slurs into his consciousness.

To all these forms of refutation—denial, exposure of fallacy, exaggeration and ridicule, attack on speaker and source, alternative version—the techniques of enhancing credibility which were previously discussed can be applied to advantage. Consistency, establishing confidence in the speaker, reference to other sources for authority, are as important in getting an audience to accept a refutation, as in putting across an attack on the other side. A refutation has to measure up to the same standards of credibility as an attack, and the techniques which help one kind of an appeal to meet these standards will serve others as well.

TECHNIQUES OF PERSUASION

By Edrita Fried

Dr. Fried is at present a research assistant with the Office of Public Opinion Research, Princeton. A native of Austria, she did her undergraduate and graduate work at the University of Vienna from which she received her Ph.D. degree in literature and psychology in 1933. For several years thereafter she was engaged in journalistic and adult education work in Vienna. In 1938 she came to the United States, was for a time associated with the Office of Radio Research at Columbia, and in 1940 joined the staff of the Princeton Listening Center, specializing in propaganda content analysis and symbol research.

TECHNIQUES OF PERSUASION

The Problem of Persuasion

GERMAN and British short-wave broadcasts to North America during the period of the Listening Center's recordings were not calls to action. They were designed for persuasion. They supplied ready-made interpretations of world events; they attempted to modify the listener's background of attitudes and beliefs; they sought to build an attitudinal framework for future action. Thus short-wave propaganda followed the pattern of most propaganda in its emphasis upon persuasion rather than incitement to direct action.

The listeners reacted to this propaganda in a variety of ways, which, however, fall into three general categories. The *first* is passive acceptance of material according to its credibility, much like the schoolboy's acceptance of information in his textbooks. The *second* is the incorporation of material into the person's pattern of beliefs, as in the case of the child who develops a personal prejudice against certain races out of the stereotypes of his culture. The *third* is overt action, as in the crowd's response to the suggestion of its leader.

Roughly speaking, short-wave broadcasts to the United States up to the time of this writing are primarily directed at the second type of reaction. Their purpose is to modify the beliefs and thinking habits of the American public in favor of the broadcasting country. Old stereotypes of American listeners are to be gradually undermined and finally replaced by new attitudes.

Naturally exceptions do occur. In its propaganda to some American groups of German descent, for instance, the Reichssender hardly needed to modify the attitudinal background of the listeners. This audience already thought in the desired terms and, moreover, took whatever statements were made as the truth. Hence overt action of one kind or another could be suggested more directly. The BBC, on the other hand, often gives considerable attention to presenting information as factual material of the textbook sort, thus being mainly concerned with the first kind of reaction that we discussed.

The success of propaganda depends in part upon the correct diagnosis of the kind of response an audience is prepared to make. An audience which has already begun to think in terms of the symbols of the propaganda-making country needs to be addressed differently than people who have remained completely aloof. The propagandist who conducts a campaign of some duration will want to know how his listeners are responding so that he can shift his emphasis accordingly.

In general the techniques for securing acceptance and conviction (the first and second types of reaction) approach the individual differently than the techniques inciting to immediate action. In the former case much attention is given to the way in which the human mind operates as a *learning* and *cognitive* mechanism. In the latter instance the appeal is loaded with heavy *emotional* content. In other words, it is possible to distinguish between *formalistic techniques* of persuasion based upon the laws of learning and reasoning and the *motivational devices* related to the nature of the appeal.

This distinction does not imply a dualism between ideas which men accept on a logical and rational basis and ideas which are accepted on an irrational or emotional basis. Rather it distinguishes between the mechanisms of the human mind and the motives which energize these mechanisms. In considering the logical or formalistic techniques we are not assuming a purely rational man. We are assuming, however, that either reason or a semblance of reason must be maintained if individuals are to accept statements as true. Thus the following discussion of formalistic techniques is concerned with the principles of both logic and psychology.

The Superior Position of the Propagandist

Compared with his audience the propagandist is in a superior position. Frequently the public senses its disadvantage as soon as the propagandist starts to pour forth his material. Therefore, people often react with irritation when they believe a piece of communication to be propaganda. Sometimes they go so far as to refuse flatly to lend their attention. Or they lapse into a cynical attitude and continue to point out that "it" is "only propaganda." Their behavior seems to reveal that they do not trust their own emotional firmness and critical ability.

Indeed the propagandist does have the better of his audience. He is an expert, familiar with the laws and aberrations of reasoning and the psychology of human reactions. The invitation extended to his listeners to pass judgment on the matter put before them is to a great extent illusory, for the character of his presentation has already determined the trend of their opinion. A skilled propagandist influences his audience through indirect suggestion, and once they have consented to listen, the law of action has been placed in his hand, and the very fact that the audience is confined to passiveness while he is active may be interpreted as his advantage.

Radio, An Additional Help in the Task of Persuasion

During recent years of turbulent political events the public has come to expect important and objective news announcements over the radio. Moreover, most of the epoch-making declarations of the leading statesmen of the world are made by radio so that it has become a public duty to listen in on certain occasions.

Some of the authoritativeness which attaches to such information is transferred by the public to political matter in general if it is broadcast. The panic produced by the Orson Welles broadcast of a Martian invasion in the fall of 1938, after the Munich crisis, was partly due to the habitual acceptance by the public of spectacular news over the radio.

Further, the very fact of radio propaganda's impermanence increases the chance of its acceptance by listeners. As a rule the listener is not in a position to examine critically what he has heard, nor can he go over an item a second time to obtain more insight and see whether it agrees with the requirements of consistency. Yet the item, once perceived, may leave an emotional impression on him.

Because of the closeness of the radio to primary sensory cues its chances of impressing and persuading people often are greater than those of the printed page. The microphone can be carried to many scenes of action. A baseball game, described by a sports commentator on the field of action, assumes practically the aspect of reality. The actuality is so great that the listener is stimulated much more forcefully than through a written report of the same game.

The swiftness with which news and ideas travel by radio is also likely to add to its prestige. In this war of startling surprises some decisive events were first divulged by radio. Thus the landing of Rudolf Hess in Scotland was reported over the German short-wave station before other media of communication picked up the item. It follows, naturally, that greater timeliness is attributed to news and comments presented over the radio than to announcements made through other channels.

Again such prestige is transferred to other forms of political information reaching the public over the radio.

FORMALISTIC TECHNIQUES OF PERSUASION

Manipulating the Stigma of Propaganda: The Enemy Lies—We Are Telling the Truth

The distrust which the public exhibits toward anything they sense to be propaganda is constantly anticipated by the propagandists. They try to forestall such an attitude toward their own broadcasts and, at the same time, attempt to direct it against enemy communications.

Speakers have frequently bid directly for belief in their own arguments. They simply declare that *they* are *not* putting forth propaganda but merely telling the truth. Simultaneously they either imply or state explicitly that listeners should beware of the irresponsible and misleading statements of the enemy.

"Charming Ray Beveridge," as the German announcer has introduced an American woman commentator, emphasized repeatedly the truthful nature of her sugar-coated accounts of the new Germany: "I prefer radio speaking to any other trade . . . and I've never felt so thoroughly alive in my life as I do at present. For it is my privilege to tell the truth about Germany to my friends overseas." (April 17, 1941.)

Among British speakers, Leslie Howard and J. B. Priestley have made much of the British reluctance to use propaganda. They have contrasted the English restraint with the practices of the German propaganda machine, which Priestley has referred to as "Goebbels' lie factory." "Most English people," Leslie Howard declared, "are very shy of advertising or propaganda and are not by nature very good at it. . . . The English take the view that if anything is good it speaks for itself. . . . Our enemies, on the other hand, believe profoundly in propaganda and have organized it to a unique degree." In the same broadcast Leslie Howard thanks Americans for "their resolution to supply us (Britain) as quickly as possible and as much as possible with anything we need for ultimate victory. Your resolutions," he tells American listeners, "have been like great beacons of light, sustaining the people of this island on their dark and perilous way. . . . We are getting stronger every month, you see, and you are giving us much of our strength. . . . The day will dawn when we shall be victorious if, if you do not waver

... if you speed your great organizations to send us what we need. A historic responsibility lies in American hands today. *Is this propaganda?* Well, *if a prayer for the survival of free institutions* among free peoples ... *if that is propaganda*, I must have become a publicity agent without knowing it." (December 16, 1940.)

Classification of German programs according to topics has shown that references to the lies and fabrications of British propaganda constitute one of the Reichssender's most popular themes. The repeated German accusations against "British lying reports" have an almost maniac ring. Here is a topic of which German propaganda can never get enough. Perhaps most effective, because of the use of widely known and incontestable evidence, was a series of references which began around the middle of April 1941. After the announcement of the news, broadcasters introduced a review of British reportings during 1940 with the words: "It seems to us that in these days of hectic British propaganda and optimistic trick-reporting it is well to remember what political prophets in London had to say a year ago."

Then followed old extracts from English papers and comments from the BBC Service on the Norwegian invasion, the campaign in the Netherlands, etc., which in the light of later events proved to have been out of place.

Attempts to Establish Authenticity

Unceasingly the radio stations of belligerent countries quote documents, expert opinions, eyewitness reports, all types of news sources and other evidence to authenticate their statements. The reasonable assumption is that the more or less enlightened and rather skeptical listener of today distinguishes between confirmed and unconfirmed facts and opinions. Yet the effort to place propaganda on a rational and authoritative basis contrasts often so vividly with the disputable nature of the documentation that the *reader* of the propaganda material finds the attempts fruitless. Here is a case where the transitory nature of radio information is being most successfully exploited, for obviously *listeners*, eagerly following the swift flow of speech, are prone to skip a critical examination of the source of origin.

Frequently the sources of information quoted within one and the same broadcast are of uneven quality regarding their reliability and authenticity. British broadcasts, whose record of truthfulness is notably higher than the German, offer sometimes within the short time of a few minutes such a varied menu as a quotation from an official army communiqué, extracts from a broadcast of a small Balkan station, a Reuter message, brief statements introduced by phrases such as, "it is generally known," or, "it has been reliably reported," and an announcement by the News Service of the Air Ministry. While the British, if they quote at all from newspapers, usually cite their own or American papers, the German radio has a great taste for corroborating its statements and views by the "weight" of some obscure Bulgarian, Brazilian or Danish paper, or by quoting from Swedish, Belgian, French and Italian journals which are both Nazi controlled and generally inaccessible.

Interesting is the German radio's attitude toward the American press. There is no stability in the evaluation of reports from the United States. Passages from American papers and magazines are either quoted triumphantly as "tops" in authority—that is whenever they have something favorable to say—or German propaganda has nothing but a contemptuous sneer for "the plutocratic journalism" of the United States. Passages from *The New York Times* and the *New York Herald Tribune,* for instance, have been quoted as the height of documentary evidence by Haw-Haw, Kaltenbach and many other broadcasters. Intermittently the two papers were referred to jeeringly. E. D. Ward displayed the latter attitude when he declared that one could hardly expect a decent attitude from *The New York Times*, this paper "being owned and controlled by an alien-affiliated group, opposed to all that is German or Fascist, and being the official Wall Street agency in America for the British Foreign Office."

The authority of eyewitness accounts and of expert statements is also exploited for the purpose of persuasion. One would expect radio propaganda to make extensive use of eyewitness reports because of the practically unlimited mobility of the microphone. Yet neither of the warring nations have proved ingenious enough to make the best of this circumstance. Although the BBC has done much better than the German radio, on-the-spot comments, such as American audiences know them, for instance in connection with baseball and football games, are comparatively rare. Instead, the practice of referring the audience to anonymous secondhand eyewitness accounts is very popular with the Reichssender. The BBC often emphasizes the neutral origin of a report or still more readily transmits reports by individuals from the enemy's own camp. Such testimonies seem to rank highest in the scale of trustworthiness because obviously any slips or difficulties reported by enemy subjects deserve belief on account of the reluctance with which they must have been divulged. An illustration of the practice of quoting the unpleasant experiences of enemy subjects is the story of a German traveling salesman in Turkey: "He exercised all his art of persuasion, all the native charm for which Germans are so justly celebrated, and he was booking a certain number of orders. Suddenly he got a telegram from his head office in Germany ordering him to stop his work because the British RAF had completely destroyed the factory and they could no longer supply any goods at all."

The German verbatim renderings of eyewitness reports are not always convincing. Usually they are cloaked in such generalities that they are neither illustrative nor do they sound very sincere. On September 5, 1940, the "vivid account of a young member of the German air force in Berlin on leave" was presented. Its supposedly vivid language was contrasted with the matter of fact wording of the German special news bulletin. The young flier, however, indulged in a pretty stereotyped description himself. He said: "Considerable activity is evident on the airdrome . . . a quarter of an hour later and these young knights of the air are again on their way across the Channel. What a glorious morning! . . . German pursuit planes circle on the lookout for the British defenders. . . . Suddenly the British chasers appear on the horizon, but apparently they cannot quite make up their mind what to do. . . . As soon as their German adversaries swoop down upon them, the Britishers take up the fight. The result is fierce dogfighting with the planes whirling about madly. . . ."

German eyewitness accounts directly from the lips of the observer himself suffer frequently from the anonymity which envelops speakers, introduced as "a sailor," "a soldier," "a war correspondent." Frequently the staff speakers themselves travel around the country and report what they have seen to their listening public who can judge their sincerity on the basis of preceding broadcasts. Many German speakers have actually displayed too much false sentimentality to sound convincing as, for instance, when reporting on the battlefields of Flanders and France. Nor have their exaggerations, such as accumulations of superlatives, contributed to the credibility of their accounts.

As regards expert opinion, radio propaganda has behaved in much the same manner as other organizations and individuals who have tried to enforce their pleas through the weight of expert statements. If first-class commendations are not at hand, some kind of expert opinion can always be dug out from somewhere. Thus again the authority level of the various statements differs widely. The British radio has on the whole made wide use of first-class authoritative statements.

Repeatedly British and German propagandists assert mutually exclusive interpretations buttressed by the views expressed by alleged authorities. Thus, for instance, the oil supplies of the Reich have been the subject of opposed interpretations by experts on the situation.

The BBC quoted the comment of an oil expert who had said that "Germany is facing a serious shortage of lubricating oils, necessary for her aircraft and other war machines." (July 16, 1940.)

The man who had expressed this view was one of the "50 British subjects who arrived in Istanbul after expulsion from Rumania where he worked until the Rumanian government took control of the whole Rumanian petrol industry."

Other oil experts, quoted equally firmly by Germany, stated, on the other hand, that the oil supplies of the Reich were ample and that Germany could go on fighting practically for an indefinite period.

Creating an Atmosphere of Consistency

The importance of consistency as an implement of persuasion may be overestimated by the logician and underestimated by the propagandist. The logician in demanding adherence to the canons of consistency forgets that men have weak memories and strong emotions. The practical politician may forget that men are governed by the reality principle as well as by the pleasure principle.

Two principles of totalitarian propaganda, partially opposed to each other, bear decisively on this matter of consistency. The first principle asserts that different stories be told to different interest groups; namely, such as will conform best with their particular value systems and interests and which will, therefore, be most readily believed. While this practice has already led to considerable contradiction on the home front, it was bound to produce even greater confusion when applied to international propaganda. For, naturally, Nazi propaganda had to legitimize and dress its policy according to democratic standards, if it was to have any chances of success in the United States.

Practices and theories that were openly lauded before the population of the Reich had to be denied or at least rationalized where the American public was concerned. To give an example; the German radio in its addresses abroad, particularly to the United States, has shed crocodile tears over the fact that the Fuehrer's deep desire for collaboration and peace is being steadily frustrated by the British government, especially by the "super-warmonger," Winston Churchill. Yet in its talks to German listeners the propaganda of the Reich has frequently jeered at the idea of international solidarity and at pacific tendencies. Instead, the praise of armed might is sung. Dr. Rust, Minister of Education, told his radio listeners in the spring of 1941 that "it is the will of the creator that the earth should be a battlefield. It is the deepest conviction of Hitler," he went on, "that militant action is the fulfilment of divine law." (Listening Post, April 21, 1940.)

It is hardly an exaggeration to say that German propaganda in faithful fulfillment of this first principle has produced the most startling collection of mutually inconsistent assertions ever to be divulged by one and the same source.

The other totalitarian principle bearing on the concept of consistency presents propaganda with the supreme task of establishing conformity between the actual political decisions and events of the day and that widely known set of concepts and principles that make up the Fascist philosophy. By a process of stretching, pulling and distorting, German propaganda has always managed to produce such versions of political happenings that a kind of forced conformity was established. Each new act of German aggression, such as the invasion of Norway, or the campaign against Yugoslavia, was accompanied by protestations of German propaganda against so-called British intrigues which, as the case was presented, made German action necessary. British intervention, so claimed German propaganda, had to be forestalled. In these and similar propaganda campaigns the German Propaganda Ministry tried to create a congruity between Hitler's aggressive acts against small nations and the much publicized Nazi "principle" of national self-determination.

The British radio systematically exposes these German inconsistencies. A special series of short broadcasts, entitled *The Listening Post*, has been inaugurated to make audiences aware of the contradictory character of Nazi statements addressed to divergent groups. These broadcasts transmit mainly compilations of excerpts from German broadcasts to Czech, Greek, French, Austrian, Norwegian, Arabian and other listeners throughout the world. On April 4, Marcel Deat, a French Fascist, was quoted as having said to French listeners over the Nazi-controlled Paris-Mondial: "There are two million French prisoners in Germany. These two million men represent two million hostages. Germany must keep these hostages . . . why the hell should Germany show us confidence when we do all we can to make her doubt us? . . . when urchins write on walls, when the petty bourgeois admire the BBC, when idiots stare at the sky when a plane is circling . . . when the barbed wire which surrounds the prison camps is thickened."

The Listening Post program thereupon goes on to point out the discrepancy between this and a report to German listeners who "heard nothing of barbed wire and the fate of war prisoners." Instead they heard an account of a conversation "between a radio commentator and one of the 1,300,000 foreigners now forced to work inside Germany. . . . They had to admit," said the commentator, "that Germany was giving them more in wartime than their own fatherland could give them in time of peace."

Obviously the BBC feels that the exposure of such discrepancies between various German-inspired accounts will discourage American listeners from believing what the Reichssender has to tell them.

Yet the offenses of the Reichssender in the field of consistency are by no means exhaustively described by stating that it frequently divulges pronouncements that conflict with each other. For German propaganda to the United States is probably rejected just as much on the basis of an artificial and overemphasized internal consistency as on the ground that its announcements are out of keeping with one another.

The totalitarian principle of establishing at all costs, even at that of credibility, a conformity of events to a set of National Socialist doctrines has made German propaganda appear very unrealistic to those who have a sense of the natural incongruity of life. The extremely tight censorship of the Third Reich has also played its part in this connection. Misled, perhaps, by the false assumption that the performance character of radio presentations would help them get away with it, German radio propagandists have vested their descriptions with a superconsistency and synthetized items in an unnatural manner.

When Fred Kaltenbach, for instance, returned to the microphone after a visit to Compiegne Forest where the Franco-German armistice was signed, his broadcasts betrayed the order of the German Propaganda Ministry to coordinate the signing of the treaty with the German principle of military honor. The Germans were to be presented as gallant and generous victors. Kaltenbach, among other remarks, told the following story in order to persuade his audience: "A French officer came out of the car in which the negotiations were taking place, walked up to a German for some bit of information, no doubt, and the German officer, a very large man by the way, put his arm affectionately around the smaller Frenchman. This little gesture," says Kaltenbach, "was characteristic of the spirit in which the negotiations took place." (July 1, 1941.)

Similar sugary tales make the world as described by German propaganda appear too consistently white or too thoroughly black to stimulate belief in an audience familiar with the practices of realistic description.

As regards the question of consistency, the BBC's procedure is diametrically opposed to that of the Reichssender. The BBC in its broadcasts to the American audience does not have a good record of factual reporting. It has had to perform many "strategic retreats." On the other hand, much of the success of British propaganda in this country is due to the impression of intrinsic sincerity which it has succeeded in giving.

Injudicious BBC reports during the Norwegian campaign have been quoted too often to be mentioned again, but even during the fighting in Yugoslavia and Greece, British speakers could not desist entirely from overconfidence. It is true, unpleasant admissions were made, such as, "It cannot be denied that they've (the Germans) moved with utmost swiftness." On the other hand, there is again the dangerous note of over optimism creeping into remarks like the one made by Lindley Fraser on April 7, 1941, following the German invasion of Yugoslavia and Greece: "In my personal view he (Hitler) has made the wrong choice. If he had been guided by purely military considerations rather than by the question of his own personal prestige, I think he would have decided to conserve his resources for the main struggle against the British Isles. . . . Hitler by this time is like a Far Eastern potentate, he daren't lose face; and if he fails in this latest campaign, he has suffered a major, perhaps a decisive loss."

Yet on the whole it may be that the initial blunders of the first six months of warfare have been forgotten, and that speculations like the one just quoted are tolerated by audiences as the only vent left to a nation that has had bad luck in the field of arms. Moreover, there is a very well-dosed mixture of praise and criticism in British propaganda reports about the English home front that appeals to American listeners. The BBC, although it constantly describes the excellent morale and the confidence of the British people in final victory, has been extremely skillful in adding a gentle dose of self-criticism and irony to its stories. It has been admitted that there was much injustice in British prewar conditions, that the old schooltie tradition ought to be broken up, that British housewives are poor cooks, that the necessity of composing war menus does them good, and that in general a lot of mistakes have been made. Vernon Bartlett said, for instance, on July 21, 1941: "We have plenty of disasters and if we are not unusually brave, perhaps (the war) is making us so."

Furthermore, it must be said that the performance character of radio presentation used by the British radio propagandists has been very good. Frequently their offerings impress one with the compact structure of an artistic performance. Where the German radio has been led into exaggeration and oversimplification that belie a true internal consistency, the British radio has found descriptive phrases of heightened reality.

Repetition

Among its first commands the propaganda creed of National Socialism places the practice of repetition, the importance of which has always been recognized by groups whose professional task includes persuasion and conviction. German propaganda, more than that of any other nation, pays constant tribute to the fact that without repetition the average mind neither learns nor remembers. Among the veritable flood of words that flows daily through the channels of communication, according to National Socialist calculation, only repeatedly exercised and forceful verbal stimuli are likely to leave a mark, while the effects of isolated and gentle stimuli are blotted out by more frequent and ponderous impressions.

British propaganda, on the other hand, is concerned with the importance of repetition to a lesser degree. While the propagandists of the Reich, with their sometimes nauseating plugging of the same theme, obviously follow the central instructions of the Propaganda Ministry, British speakers enjoy a fairly wide latitude in most subjects. When the same point of view is presented it takes different forms according to the imagination and personality of the individual speaker.

Exact repetition, as everybody knows from experience, is boresome. It is repetition through variation that is effective. Not only is it unnecessary but it is even injurious to express a thought complex identically every time it is brought up. The supreme effect, as far as expression is concerned, will be achieved if the following three points are observed: *first,* that an idea be strikingly reformulated for the purpose of repetition; *second*, that it be highlighted by individual key words, which by symbolizing the entire idea may also be called symbol words and which because of their compactness permit repetition. The symbol word "plutocrat" is used, for example, very effectively, from the point of view of persuasion, in incessant German discussions of the British money class system; *third*, that ideas be linked to other thought complexes.

In some respects the conditions of radio broadcasting help to offer variegated repetition. The entertainment character of the radio performance and the personality element which oral delivery necessarily involves make it possible to give new nuances and inflections to themes. The fact that various forms of presentation stand open, such as the drama, the interview, the straight narrative and the factual report, adds an element of variation.

Before discussing other important purposes of the technique of repetition it may be helpful to glance at some German themes and at the way in which they are handled. The war guilt theme, it appears, is one of which the German propagandists can never talk enough. For the sake of variation and reemphasis they have grafted it upon a number of other themes, such as the "balance of power," "the plutocrat," and the "Churchill" themes. Britain, so Goebbels and "his little men" assert, wanted the war to preserve the balance of power in Europe. France and Britain "declared war on Germany and interfered in a private quarrel between Germany and Poland. Germany is thus fighting a purely defensive war, a war of self-preservation, against the avowed aims of Britain and France to cripple her permanently." (Kaltenbach, March 18, 1941.)

Other times the accusation is raised that it was the British plutocrats, "the apostles of Mammon" (July 6, 1940), which dragged England into war "to preserve the status quo." (August 8, 1940.)

Of course, Churchill, from whom all evil flows, is held responsible for this war more often than any other individual or group. He, "the super-warmonger Winston Churchill," "this incredibly debased wretch," "the dictator of Britain" (June 23, 1940), alone wanted this war.

Notably effective, because it gained belief among some groups within and outside France, was another cry which German radio propaganda reechoed eagerly. The British, it was asserted, had first lured France into the war and then left her in the lurch. In one and the same broadcast on July 1, 1940, Kaltenbach fused this accusation with the plutocrat and the Churchill themes. "The big wigs and stuffed shirts across the Channel," he said, ". . . egged on France against Germany. . . . The biggest stuffed shirt of them all, that show case of British plutocracy, the honorable Windsy Churchill, heavyweight champion of international morale and Lord Protector of the rights of small nations . . . unlimbering his powerful 16-inch vocal artillery shot the brave French nation in the back." The BBC, as has been noted, is less concerned with the practices of repetition and reiteration of stock-in-trade ideas.

From the point of view of persuasion two English themes deserve particular attention. The first one comprises the concept of this war as a phase within the life of the British nation which will finally lead to decisive social changes. "It seems," says Noel Coward, "that for the first time people of all shapes and sizes and classes and creeds are getting to know one another." (July 18, 1940.) Another remark on this topic was made by a journalist of *The London Times* who thought "that the intermingling of all classes in the fighting services may well lead to a new understanding between classes after the war." (February 10, 1941.)

The second theme, the repetitive discussion of which betrays its purpose, is that of bombings by the Royal Air Force on enemy territory. Daily the British radio assures its listeners that "British bombings have wreaked havoc on Germans towns," as those who have followed the British war communiqués may anticipate. A schedule of compensation paid by the German government to munition workers who lose their time during air raids (July 17, 1940) is quoted as proof of the effectiveness of the British raids. Coupling the topic of British raids on German territory with British home front reports, propagandists give it a new slant: "As for your wondering how long we can stick this hammering at our centers of production, as you call it, how about us doing a bit of wondering how long the Germans can stick what we are handing out to them in that line? In the Ruhr, for instance, and to their transportation system! We have messed that system up nicely already and we intend to go on making it much worse. They haven't messed us up yet and they are powerless to stop us working and fighting. . . . (December 7, 1940.)

Such constant reformulations and rearrangements of the same fact or idea are naturally intended to achieve more than the mere enforcement of a bit of information in the mind of the listener. British propaganda by constantly mentioning the destruction of enemy military objectives by the RAF hopes to accomplish something beyond mere fact-telling.

Through constant reiteration audiences are often persuaded to take mere impressions for objective facts. They become habituated to the source of suggestion and, in their minds, reports assume the quality of *actuality*. British propaganda by its daily reports on the effects of the British air raids improved England's position considerably and kept alive the hope of victory in a strategic situation that permitted no other offensive. Although reliable data are hardly available, it seems probable that during the first months of air warfare the British radio exaggerated the actual damage inflicted on German industry. At that time, however, there were many sympathizers with the British cause, who from listening to British declarations carried away the conviction that the actual havoc wrought in these days was telling on German production. It was the incessant repetition of raid descriptions rather than statistical data that gave them that impression.

Another purpose behind the technique of repeating an idea is the creation of mental habits. Neither the question of war guilt, nor of Anglo-French relations during the first phase of this war, nor the practical effects of the war on English society can be easily judged by the average man. He lacks the information, background and training necessary for a considered judgment. It is precisely in those situations to which men lack adequate responses that the psychology of repeated suggestion works best. The propaganda systems of the warring nations compete, among other things, for the judgment of the man on the street. They endeavor to supply him with ready-made decisions and each propaganda system wants him to buy its brand. Instead of letting him come to his own decision about the origin of the war, German propaganda wants Mr. Smith to fall into the mental habit of saying that the war is all due to the intrigues and egoistic designs of England. The more frequently this version is repeated to him, thinks Mr. Goebbels, the more safely will he accept it as his own.

Word Manipulations

Because of the close association in the minds of the general public between a word and the content which it designates, a situation, once it is described in certain terms, begins to take shape in the indicated direction. Tell people that a man is a "liar" and they will not want to have anything to do with him; say to them that he was merely "mistaken" and his chances improve.

Broadcasters have made much of the psychological effect of the word sign. By the skillful choice of words, strategically hopeless situations have been transformed into favorable positions, unfair and base methods of exploitation have been made to sound acceptable, and enemy successes deprived of their effect. Furthermore, by inventing and publicizing certain word labels, propagandists have introduced into the complexity of life the kind of classification and hence the kind of categories which serve their purposes best.

The latter practice forms one of the cornerstones of National Socialist propaganda. German propagandists like their public to think in clear-cut, inflexible categories that guarantee stability, and that, moreover, coincide with National Socialist interests.

As an example of this procedure let us review the formulation applied by German propaganda to economic and class questions in the United States. Before the introduction of the Lease-Lend Bill, German propaganda seemed only mildly concerned with economic and class differences in America. The Lease-Lend Bill, however, although not given as much attention in the German radio as one would have expected, was followed by propaganda designed to create dissent. For this purpose the structure of American society was presented in terms of the tested German categories for which labels were ready at hand. On the one side was "the small clique of inconsiderate business mongers, who desire the continuation of this war so desperately . . . the profiteers and warmongers" and on the other side "the plain citizen, the taxpayer of the United States."

Other divisions, such as those of nations into "haves" and "have-nots," into "young" and "old," into "virile" and "decadent" are too well known to require further documentation from current propaganda material. They serve to illustrate how German propaganda by creating and publicizing certain labels channelized the thinking of the public in the desired direction. The categories created by such labels helped to prevent the establishment of more accurate divisions that would have been less favorable to the German cause.

Another practice, the technique of the euphemism, which is very simple and of long standing, has been practised with equal eagerness by both British and German propagandists. While Nazi propaganda has proved most ingenious in inventing euphemistic labels within the sphere of morality and legality where the German position is weakest, British propaganda has been mainly concerned with creating terms that would give an encouraging turn when the strategic and military situation of Britain was weak.

The terms "glorious retreat," "strategic retreat," "miraculous escape" applied to the British feats in the Norwegian and particularly in the Flanders campaign have received too much attention to invite more comment. After the complete expulsion from the Continent, British propaganda made the best of England's island position. Britain was described as a "stronghold," a "fortress," a "spearhead," a "citadel." Priestley said on July 9, 1940, in a broadcast: "This island is not only a garrison now but it might be called the camp of a vast crusade."

Although the power of words is limited in the face of grim realities, it is also true that by shedding a particular light on a situation words may achieve much. For if the interpretation of a situation appears favorable to potential supporters, help may eventually be forthcoming. When British propaganda described England to the American public as a "citadel of freedom" it conjured up vistas of other citadels that had withstood an attacker successfully in the past. Thus it helped to persuade the American people not to give up England as lost, but rather to rally help for the spearhead of democracy.

Similar British euphemisms in the military field are frequent. One propagandist invited listeners to contemplate the defeat in Greece from a favorable angle because the entire conduct of the war in 1941 was really not designed to be more than a "delaying action." The term "Battle of the Atlantic" also appears skillfully chosen. The indiscriminate sinkings of British ships by German submarines during the first months of 1941 took such a heavy toll of British shipping as to threaten Britain's existence if long maintained. By the mere use of the word "battle" the destruction of British ships was made to appear in the more reassuring light of mutual and planned combat.

German broadcasters on the other hand have made it a habit to refer to the bombardment of the civilian population in London and other British towns as "reprisal actions," or simply as "armed reconnoitering flights." Similarly "euphemistic" is the term with which German propaganda has chosen to describe the Reich's attitude of exploitation and maltreatment of occupied territories. "The work of reconstruction" is the usual expression and in keeping with this formulation Hitler is called "the hero of construction." (July 6, 1940.)

As anyone may anticipate who has followed the declarations of Hitler and other prominent Nazis, the word "peace" appears frequently in Nazi propaganda. Hitler's vague propositions to the British to come to an agreement with Germany on her terms are referred to constantly as "magnanimous peace offers." "Peace" is recurrently described as the ultimate goal of National Socialism. This incorporation of the word peace into the Nazi vocabulary is especially significant in that it links the whole question of misplaced labels to the problem of symbol words, the other prominent technique of word manipulation. Peace in the mouth of a German broadcaster is an empty word, a label for something that does not exist, for the intentions of Nazism are essentially and lastingly militaristic.

In many ways propaganda is like shooting warfare, where the weapons and the defense techniques of one side adjust themselves to those of the enemy's arsenal. If the enemy emphasizes aerial warfare, one's own side is inevitably compelled to arm in the same direction and if possible to surpass him. If the British speak of a lasting world peace in the future, as indeed they do (thus reinforcing one of the strongest political desires of the democratic American public), Germany cannot permit that trump to win the game. She adds the word peace to her own verbal arsenal at no cost, because there is no price on words. The mutual taking over of effective symbols, such as takes place between countries engaged in propaganda campaigns, actually thrives on the deceptiveness of word labels.

Symbol words are actually not separated from ordinary words by any clear-cut line of division. They are for the most part words taken out of the current vocabulary, which fuse several meanings and which are charged with emotional connotation. The need for symbol words grows out of the public's inability to envisage abstract ideas without compact verbalization. Symbol words are key words in which more or less complex concepts have found verbal crystallization. Because of the power of symbol words to channelize thinking effectively and because of their power to arouse emotions, propagandists are alert for new symbol words whenever new situations arise.

International propaganda absorbs many symbols of foreign origin. The idea is to beat the enemy at his own game. Whatever the exact origin of the "new order" symbol, it was the Nazi propaganda machine that brought it to prominence. The British, reluctant to see Germany exploit uncontested the great propagandistic value of this symbol, tried to adopt it. But in British hands it is linked with more traditional symbols of a humanitarian and moral nature. Thus the new order symbol, within the context of British propaganda, has another connotation than the German new order symbol which promises essentially a political regrouping of Europe.

Interestingly enough, while it is the function of some symbol words to render an abstract idea concrete, others seem designed to deflect attention from concrete realities. When German propaganda declares that it is fighting against "the shackles of gold," against "sheer power politics," "the system of international finance," or "class prejudice," it may not be at all sincere, but it narrows down and specifies the targets of evil against which Nazism supposedly aims. On the other hand, statements such as, the Germans want to serve "the laws of God," they are setting up "the incomprehensible, the unseizable, the mystic new" (Hans Fritsche, May 21, 1940), seem designed to lead the public's attention away from specific aims. The tendency here is less to create *specific enemy symbols* and more to set up general and *broadly in-*

terpretable self-symbols. The British, for instance, while they describe their opponents in terms of "gangsters," "liars," "the German outlaws," "the power-crazed Germans," refer to their allies as "decent people everywhere," leaving it open to anybody to read his own standards into the word decent.

Another practice of interest is the establishment of counter-symbols, symbols of evil towards which hate and fear can be directed. One function of the counter-symbol is to set off to advantage the positive self-symbols, the symbols describing one's own aims and values. Compared with "the antiquated methods of diplomatic intrigue," Germany's plans to "unite Europe" (July 8, 1940) seem the more worthy of praise. Through the introduction of counter-symbols, standards of judgment are introduced from which the glorified self-symbols benefit greatly, for contrasted with the wickedness of the enemy-symbols they take on added radiance.

The Technique of Prototypes

German propaganda as a rule describes reality in the high coloring and stylized contours of cheap advertising, working constantly with formalized images of complete perfection or imperfection, but to say merely that German propaganda argues in terms of stereotypes would not describe the situation wholly. For the concepts employed in German propaganda in addition to being rigidly molded are patterned after models, that is, after exemplary prefigurations for which the German language uses the word *Vorbild.* The technique of prototypes is probably most likely to succeed with people given to a markedly stereotyped thinking and to a perfectionist contemplation of life. Probably the prototype technique is in part a result of German cultural traits and in part of the centralization of German propaganda and of its normative attitude. An organization like the German Ministry of Propaganda must in the final outcome provoke a concept and description of life in fixed and prearranged images of things as they *should* be. We shall see from an excerpt of a typical German prototype description how the matrices, by which German thinking and arguing are formed, constitute an attempt to regulate the nonmaterial world as well as the material. A mental goose-stepping, so to speak, is introduced to guide propagandists and people as well. To exclude any doubts as to the significance of events and the value of institutions, everything is described in extreme terms, designed to permit one and only one opinion.

The description which is quoted below is from a speech by Hans Fritsche, the highly dramatic German commentator who used to be a lawyer and has retained some of the pathos of courtroom pleading. He said on May 3, 1941, that is, after the capitulation of Yugoslavia and Greece: "Many people feel at this moment that a new page is being turned in the book of history. . . . Do you know that if everything had run the course which the English and their agents in the various European capitals desired, the history of a country and its people would be closed forever. . . . (Then turns to talk about the boy king, Peter, his evil adviser, Simovitch, and the Greek King George) . . . Having now arrived in places where they can safely cash their checks, they hope that the soldiers whom they abandoned to their fate will continue their resistance. These fine gentlemen think now: *après nous le déluge.* The Greek King George disapproves of the capitulation of the Greek troops he left behind. Winston Churchill, not an inch less aristocratic, puts Greece and Jugoslavia on the list of countries he wants to starve as soon as he gets a possibility. . . . If the fugitive George and Winston Churchill could have had things their way, Greece today would be a desert full of ruins and of people dead from starvation. Yet it is now a country in which an industrious people can work undisturbed, and had it not been for the madness of the British soldiers, the country would not have suffered at all by the war and no damage would have been done. . . . When the German troops arrived, they found Belgrade a town in which rabble of every description had had its way, a town which was happy that the German soldiers came to bring with them order and calm, as so many inhabitants of so many towns have been happy to see the German liberators arrive."

Fritsche fashioned his description after the prototypes: "the bad enemy," "the evil leader," "British diabolism," "the German liberators."

The German prototype "evil leader" implies the characteristics most condemnable in a man of responsibility. "The evil leader" is greedy, egotistical, irresponsible, open to bribery, ambitious in his own petty way, sadistic, stupid and cowardly. Whenever Nazi propaganda refers to enemy leaders, they are envisaged in prototype terms. Obviously enemy leaders, even if judged by the hostile standards of an adversary, do not always fit such a model and thus a process of stretching and exaggerating sets in. The main concern of King George of Greece, King Peter of Yugoslavia and Dusan Simovitch is money; they feel no responsibility whatsoever toward their peoples; Winston Churchill finds diabolical satisfaction in starving out the Balkan states; and King George himself would not mind seeing his country in ruins, his people starved to death.

How bright in comparison with such depravity shines the prototype "German liberators." "The German liberators" are disciplined, just, cheerful and well-intentioned. They carry order and a "higher kind of liberty" into the countries which they have come to free. Nazi propagandists, when describing the march of German troops through other countries, like to apply the "liberator" prototype.

Some of the practical consequences of this prototype technique have already been suggested. They bear on morale, on readiness for action and on the reception which propaganda meets with the public in the long run. Where the propaganda of a democratic state, let us say Britain, will at least intimate the many-sidedness of problems and situations, thus permitting scruples and hesitancy to enter the minds of its own followers, totalitarian propaganda through this use of prototypes simplifies situations and points out only those sides which conform to German interests. Besides, it reduces situations to the *known*, namely to the matrix, about which one need not make up one's own mind, for ready-made opinions, sanctioned by the high authorities, are already at hand. Such a technique obviously has its great weakness. Once a saturation point has been reached, the constant repetition and exaggeration becomes unbearably boring. To those who do not share the Nazi frame of reference, as is the case with the majority of the American public, such presentations of events seem absurd. Even the sympathetic listener, once he begins to doubt the validity of the prototype, may reject the propaganda as completely and absolutely as he once accepted it. The prototype technique breeds an all-or-none acceptance or rejection. More realistic description permits more discriminating reactions.

Pointing at Future Successes. The Frequent Use of the Future Tense

Both German and British short-wave propaganda tried to persuade the American public that the future belonged in the one case to the "new order" and in the other to the democracies. Their techniques included the device of repetition, of analogical argument and of confusion of con-cepts.

To reconcile people with the painfulness of defeat English broad-casters drastically reduced their comments on Britain's military setbacks and deflected attention to the future. In the darkest hours, during the summer and fall months of 1940, British propagandists concentrated on remarks about the future. References to the plight of Britain were fre-quently coupled with remarks regarding better things to come. "The hour is dark," said Wickham Steed on June 17, 1940, "the peril is great. The dawn will come, the danger will be met and surmounted." "We shall never turn from the conflict," ran the pronouncement of a news announcer, "until Britain stands straight and erect in all her grandeur, until the ruined and enslaved states and peoples have been liberated and until civilization is free from the nightmare of Nazidom. That this day will come we are more sure than ever. It may dawn sooner than we now have the right to expect." (June 13, 1940.)

In passages like the one quoted above, the purpose for the sake of which momentary hardships are endured, is stressed. Such remarks are meant to make concrete and desirable the aims for whose accomplish-ment men must suffer. It is hoped that the wish to achieve these goals will become a substantial morale factor in prevailing over obstacles. This, of course, is the function of all war aims.

German broadcasters, too, even when the position of Germany seemed favorable have again and again referred their foreign audiences to the future. This is probably a repetition of the technique used with the German people themselves who on the whole do not like the war and have to be reassured with promises of future peace and prosperity. Speaking of the future, German broadcasters present the defeat of Eng-land not as a hope but as an accomplished fact. A remark by Kaltenbach on September 16, 1940, illustrates this practice and its coupling with descriptions of Germany's peaceful aims. "When the defeat of Great Britain shall have been accomplished," says Kaltenbach, "Germany can well afford to rest on her laurels and turn her thoughts to the great work of reconstruction which lies ahead."

Another statement illustrative of the German *technique of the ac-complished fact* is the following: "Superior man power, superior equip-ment, superior industrial organization and superior political training of two young and virile nations shall (put) Great Britain's claim to world domination to the final test. The result of this test is a foregone conclusion, Great Britain's defeat." (September 1, 1940.)

The speculations of various German historians and philosophers draw on a parallel they believe to exist between the laws of nature and the laws governing social processes. This tradition has not been without effect on German propaganda. German propagandists are wont to compare those institutions and political forces whose decline they desire with decaying and aging organisms. On the other hand, the German body politic and German institutions are conceived of as vital, young and flourishing organic beings. Hence the conclusion is implied or stated explicitly that British democracy is doomed to death while National Socialist Germany in the prime of youth is looking ahead to a thousand years' existence. Such analogies are extended by German propaganda even to the Reich's ally, Japan, which is described as a young nation, notwithstanding the fact that at other times it is praised because of its old and venerable culture.

Furthermore, German propaganda has taken advantage of the existing fears and hopes of an age that is keenly aware of its own insecurity. National Socialism has used for its own purpose deep-rooted expectations of revolutionary changes to come, introducing a new era. The *irresistibility* of a truly revolutionary and progressive cause has been claimed by German propaganda for the Nazi movement. In this connection, one is tempted to think that the fact that the Nazis, led exclusively by utilitarian considerations, have annexed the word "revolution," testifies to its present respectability and even esteem.

In the following quotation the various techniques just discussed are blended according to the prescription that combination and integration work most effectively. "Our age is a revolutionary age. There can be no doubt about that. Nor can there be any doubt that Britain, or more correctly speaking the British ruling clique, the British plutocracy, started this war . . . not in order to bring about a better order which is coming anyway, one way or another, but in order to maintain the status quo. . . . But life is progressive by nature. It cannot be stopped. Attempts to interrupt natural evolution by force lead to explosions. The world is ripe for a new order . . . because historical evolution has reached this point when transition cannot be avoided. And Germany stands among the nations that realize the necessity of this transition." (Okay, December 11, 1940.)

Argumentative Form

As a rule, broadcasters switch back and forth between an argumentative and a dogmatic form of presentation. Passages of reasoning, in which explanations and justifications are given and conclusions drawn from the evidence cited are interchanged with direct assertions. Yet the general effect of feature programs (news bulletins, naturally, do not enter into this discussion) is the impression of their preponderantly reasoned nature. This skillfully achieved effect naturally enhances the credibility of the propaganda material. Even if listeners are unable to subject the premises themselves to scrutiny, the mere process of argumentation reassures them and inspires confidence.

How is it that in spite of the frequently dogmatic manner in which radio propaganda presents its statements the impression prevails that the course of argument was taken? The particular structure of the majority of broadcasts offers one explanation. Many feature programs constitute a *sequence of loosely connected individual passages* rather than an organized discourse on a single topic.

Radio propaganda thus relies more on the cumulative effect of a series of individual points than on the impact of an argument well documented. A talk delivered by Lord Haw-Haw on April 20, 1941, illustrates this technique. In this speech Haw-Haw covered eighteen different ideas which were poorly integrated and connected. Yet the cumulative effect of this presentation was probably to reduce the awareness of the audience to coherence and logical form. So many points are made that the weakness of some of them escapes the attention of the listening public. The listener is helpless before the wealth of material which is presented. The fact that the various points are linked up in one way or another leads the listener to believe that the connections are reasonable and that he has heard one coherent argumentative discourse. There remains only a general and rather vague impression of having followed an argument where reasons and explanations were given. Although the details cannot be remembered, they have not failed to leave their mark.

Among the various forms of reasoning the analogical argument is the most interesting to the propaganda analyst. The argument by analogy affords more color and entertainment than the severe forms of deductive and inductive reasoning. New situations and problems which the individual usually finds difficult to judge are related to familiar experiences and so brought within the existing frame of reference. Hence analogies abound in propaganda statements. The particular function of analogies in short-wave broadcasts to the United States has been to make the European struggle less remote by comparison with situations that lie within the range of the American public's experience. The great logical weakness of analogical argument, of course, lies in the temptation to compare two situations that are not actually alike in their fundamental aspects. Psychologically, however, the analogy is a powerful weapon.

The Germans have cleverly presented analogies in which Germany's actions are compared to those of the United States. On April 7, 1941, immediately after the Reich's declaration of war on Yugoslavia, Fred Kaltenbach tried to convince American listeners that under the given circumstances the only thing the Germans could do was to declare war on Yugoslavia. "Now suppose, Harry," he argued by hypothetical analogy, "that the United States had entered into a pact of friendship with Mexico and that the pact was afterwards interfered with by English secret agents and English intrigues in Mexico City. Suppose that the legitimate government of Mexico was overthrown by a military clique favorable to England . . . would the United States stand by idly? I think not. Do you remember the American punitive expedition to Vera Cruz in 1911 to avenge an insult to the American (navy)? Now why should one expect any less of Germany?"

Analogies like the one quoted above can be effective because they play on the American sense of fairness. The average American may be reluctant to blame another nation for a course of action which he believes to have been taken similarly by his own country.

In the background of the present struggle looms the specter of the first World War. Statesmen, strategists, propagandists and the public naturally have been preoccupied with analogies between the two struggles. British propaganda has drawn parallels between the late German Kaiser and Hitler and on the ground of such analogies predicted the eventual downfall of the Fuehrer. Defeats in the military field have repeatedly been discounted by British propaganda, which argues that Britain would win out in the end in spite of temporary setbacks as in the last war. In the spring of 1941, however, British propagandists began to abandon this line of argumentation in favor of a more realistic view. Frequently British propaganda seeks analogies even further back in the past, and refers to the first great conqueror of Europe, Napoleon. Thomas Woodrooffe, a British spokesman, drew in a broadcast a joint parallel between the Kaiser, Napoleon, and Hitler. "Between Hitler and his dream of world domination," he declared, "stands (the British fleet) as it stood between ... Napoleon and his dreams of empire, between the Kaiser and his German World Reich." (December 12, 1940.)

German propaganda also capitalizes on first World War parallels, although the argument runs in the opposite direction. German propagandists assert that all conditions having changed fundamentally, the outcome of the war must of necessity also be different. "The last war," Weepy stated on April 4, 1941, "proved those people right who had seen in the hunger blockade the best means of bringing about the collapse of Germany, if not at once then in the course of time. In this war there is only greater disappointment in store for those who believe that the long hunger blockade will prove to be once again the most effective means of crushing German (morale). Admittedly the British fleet for the time being is in a position to block the passage of supplies to Germany from overseas. But Germany can do very well without these imports. During this war German agriculture has produced not less but more than in peacetime ... supplementary quantities can now be easily imported from the countries in the East, Southeast and South of Europe."

Besides self-sufficiency other factors cited as improving Germany's present situation, in comparison with World War I, are the "newly won spiritual unity" of the country, the strength of her air arm, and, up to the Russian campaign, the treaty with the Soviet Union.

THE APPEAL TO MOTIVES AND EMOTIONS

The Use of Prestige

The use of prestige is essentially a form of emotional appeal. Through training and experience we endow many symbols with an emotional aura of reverence and unqualified esteem. When confronted with these symbols we bow and accept uncritically what we are told. The association of his message with prestige symbols is thus one of the oldest tools of the propagandist and advertiser. The suggestions of a doctor may be accepted by an irascible patient who would reject the same advice coming from his wife.

The BBC has selected men as speakers who enjoyed prestige on various grounds, so that there was frequently a combined effect of different forms of prestige in one and the same person. In addition, the British have brought before the microphone such a long and colorful procession of broadcasters that a listener could discover among them the type of prestige personality that would affect him in particular. Statesmen, writers, scholars, strategists, people of different nationalities, women and youngsters have all appeared before the microphone with their specific experiences, their eyewitness accounts, and their expert opinions.

British spokesmen are selected either for their broad and general knowledge of human nature or for their particular information in a specific field. The first category includes such men as J. B. Priestley, David Low, St. John Ervin, and Noel Coward.

Wickham Steed, on the other hand, is an expert in the specific field of international affairs. He himself does not hesitate to point at times to his background of political experience. "Speaking personally," he introduced a comment on May 10, 1940, "as an old student of international affairs in general and of pan-Germanism in particular, I. . . ." A little later in the same talk he again draws the attention of his listeners to his experience and also to his impartiality: "I shall speak," he says, ". . . from a strictly nonpartisan standpoint . . . my standpoint is that of a man who lived and worked abroad too long to have been able to identify himself with any political school." Wickham Steed, incidentally, falls in with a habit of J. B. Priestley and many of the other prominent British broadcasters when he constantly stresses the first person singular. Their talks are distinguished by a generous sprinkling of "I's." This highly personalized style is the outgrowth of their existing prestige as well as an additional factor which enhances it. For a person of importance refers with natural self-confidence and assurance to himself in the first person and at the same time invites others to accept his statements on the guarantee of his oral signature.

As a rule, the BBC uses a master of ceremonies who is careful to introduce speakers by their full title and office so that their position is realized from the start. Further references by the speakers themselves coupled with a pronounced Oxford accent tend to reinforce the original impression. Moreover, there is an abundance of *Sirs* and *Lords* in the titles presented.

Many of the British symbols in this war are of a universal nature. British propagandists talk of the "whole world," "the universe" of a "United States of the World," "the whole of human society"; they have referred to the present struggle as "the civil war of mankind," as "not a European struggle" but a "world conflict." "The war," said Wickham Steed on August 2, 1940, "is a world-wide fight for the method of freedom," and on another occasion a British spokesman pointed out that "decent people everywhere" are joining the British cause.

Thus, British propaganda tries to universalize England's prestige through the twofold claim that Britain is fighting the cause of mankind and that the best people in the world are on her side. The British attempt to create a prestige of numbers is based on the correct psychological assumption that individuals are inclined to join a cause that has already been underwritten by others.

"We are keeping things going," said George Wilde on August 1, 1940, "the same as we've done since Shakespeare's time and before." Other broadcasters have implied that a country which can point to a Francis Drake and a Walter Raleigh, etc., can be trusted to hold out and finally overcome the enemy. The prestige of a long and glorious past is fused in such remarks with the prestige of the homeland of great men.

Statements that England is the cradle of democracy, the land of the Magna Charta, have been reiterated by Leslie Howard and J. B. Priestley on various occasions. "Magna Charta," said Priestley on June 15, 1940, ". . . was one of the instruments and examples, the first of them, of the peculiar genius of the Anglo-Saxon people, a genius that, I need hardly remind you, crossed the Atlantic to establish a new and still greater commonwealth of free peoples. . . . The highroad that our people reached at Magna Charta is the highroad that we are all on to this day, all of us."

When prestige is involved in German propaganda broadcasts it is usually of an impersonal kind rather than of the personal brand that we have observed with British radio speakers. German propaganda relies on secret archives and unearthed documents for prestige value. The story of these suddenly discovered documents of "world historic importance" is too well known to need retelling. Outside of such mysterious documents preference is given to statements from internationally renowned sources. Thus, for instance, Sven Hedin, the Swedish explorer, has been quoted on many occasions.

German speakers seek to develop their own personal prestige by such devices as irony and haughtiness. Lord Haw-Haw in particular gave himself an air of superiority in this manner.

While the German radio has not attempted specifically to give its own speakers a prestige build-up, it has definitely tried to tear down the prestige of British broadcasters. David Low, J. B. Priestley, Wickham Steed and Leslie Howard have all been ridiculed by the German radio in direct attacks. "Well," said E. D. Ward, on January 31, 1941, "after years of experience Mr. Howard has acquired a splendid speaking voice. His diction and delivery are pleasing, and many of the things he says are vastly amusing when he least intends them to be so."

In a speech on February 11, 1941, Haw-Haw lashed at both Priestley and the British cartoonist, David Low. Again on February 18 Kaltenbach jeered at Priestley. Such attacks against individual British speakers must be considered as a further aspect of that basic technique, already discussed, of contesting the enemy every inch of ground.

The Appeal to Hatred. The Supplying of Targets

It is commonplace knowledge today that German propaganda is primarily interested in captivating the masses. Hitler himself and many of his assistants have testified to this fact. The preference of German propaganda for mass audiences rather than an elite is directly related to the outstanding trait that the Nazis ascribe to their public, a sense of being underprivileged. Either, so argues the German propagandist, the people with whom I deal are or imagine themselves to be actually underprivileged, or they will accept my suggestion that they are. Hence, a note of frustration is lodged in some form or other in most German utterances. The pre-existing or aroused dissatisfaction is fostered by Nazi propaganda and channelized in a specific direction.

Lord Haw-Haw in his broadcasts to Britain, which made him one of the world's most renowned radio personalities, showed himself master of the art of fanning and directing hatred, a technique which has since been imitated increasingly in broadcasts to the United States. The Nazi assortment of vile names for the British ruling classes and single individuals, especially for Winston Churchill, may well go down as a unique collection in the history of name-calling. Teasing expressions for the British Prime Minister, like "Winnie in Wonderland" and "Roly Poly Windsy Churchill" alternate with spiteful attacks. "The incompetent fraud," "the evil old wretch," "this mean corrupt little man," are merely a few samples of a broad variety. The ruling classes in Britain are referred to by such titles as "the degenerates of Downing Street," "the hired charlatans," "the apostles of Mammon," and "these fat and pompous plutocrats."

In its broadcasts to the United States up to June 1941, German propaganda had not as yet matched the violence of its language to Great Britain nor had the fanning of hatred against the upper classes been so systematic or so intensive. Yet the trend was notably in the same direction. No dividing line is drawn between the various groups that are pictured as the perpetrators of all evil. Jews, Wall Street bankers, New Dealers, pro-British journalists and the wealthy in general are thrown together in hodgepodge fashion. Neat distinctions, such as German propaganda made during the first phase of the campaign against England, are abandoned. What remains is an undiscriminating stream of abuse.

The men who must be blamed for the conditions in America, says a broadcaster, are "those big bankers, those Wall Street gold and money magicians who know the astounding trick of making money without work, those barons and brain trusters and moral contortionists." They are "the Jewish owners of the sweat shops" who want to continue a world that is "a breeding place of hate, of class warfare and human enmity," men with whom the high circles in "Washington and New York are the closest friends." (All quotations from September 1, 1940.)

By contrast, the picture of Hitler's Third Reich where social justice reigns is presented, serving to make the abuses in the democracies appear still blacker and to channelize the rising emotion of anger. There, the indirect suggestion runs, is an example to imitate. You can have the same wonderful equity that we have in Germany if you will only follow the Fuehrer's advice. "Only the foreign profiteers and Jewish minions of the English banks and all the other international auctioneers could afford to build themselves luxurious palaces in the Germany of post-war days," so goes one of these discussions. (February 2, 1941.) But then the broadcaster continues that after Hitler had come to power he saw to it that the poor people in Germany would have decent places in which to live. "A sufficient number of houses are being built so that all the German people can live under the healthiest and most idyllic conditions conceivable."

In fanning hatred against England, German propaganda has relied on atrocity stories, on whatever rankling sentiments still exist in American hearts against the former mother country, and on existing prejudices.

English bombers, German broadcasters assert, are brutally murdering German civilians, attacking national shrines and cemeteries where American World War soldiers lie buried. Americans are reminded of the days of the Civil War when the English supported the Confederacy in their attempt to break up the Union. Listeners are told that the English have always taken it easy and let other people fight their wars and die for them. "It's such a comfortable feeling, isn't it," jibes Kaltenbach, "to be able to sit back on one's haunches and win one's wars at long distance, like the fellow who preferred to fight with snow balls at 300 yards. . . . English statesmen fought their wars until quite recently with hirelings and littered up other people's landscapes and cities with the havoc and destruction of battle. . . . In this war which England's rulers declared against Germany it was again decided to fall back upon old principles and let the sons of other nations do England's fighting for her." (December 9, 1940.)

Self-Interest and Ego Motives

Neither German nor British broadcasts have put as much emphasis on ego motives as one would be inclined to expect. In the review of appeals to hate the activation of ego motives has already been touched upon. Listeners, we said, are reminded of the material deprivations and the loss of security due to the social system under which they live.

That German propaganda tells a different tale to everyone is by now an old story. Thus, while British listeners were assured that their government had bartered away some of the country's most valuable bases for a few barnacled American destroyers, the American public was addressed on the basis of their national self-interest and warned that they were again being thoroughly exploited by the English. German propagandists assumed the air of well-meaning counselors and of farsighted prophets warning a blinded people for their own good. In one broadcast a letter allegedly written by an anonymous American living in Switzerland was read: "We were [note sentence structure] through lying propaganda from British and international banking interests dragged in. It was not our affair then and it certainly is not our affair now. . . . Why should we fight for British Empire interests? Have we ever received anything but suffering, high-handed robbery and arrogant insolence from Britain?" (February 19, 1941.)

While during January, February and March 1941 British listeners were asked by orators like Haw-Haw to watch out for the imperialistic aims of the United States, the American public was exhorted to protect the interests of their nation against the innumerable British propagandists in the United States whose one object was to "inveigle, frighten, weasel or snare the United States into war by any broad chicanery or strategy they may employ." (January 31, 1941.)

Yet apart from the claim that mothers would lose their sons and girls their sweethearts in the case of a shooting war with the Reich, little specific indication was given as to what Americans would risk by entering the European war. Nor was the picture of what they would gain by staying out very precise.

British speakers, on the other hand, appealed more openly to the self-interests of the American public as the war proceeded. However, specifications of the loss of measurable as well as nonmeasurable privileges that a German victory would inevitably involve were advanced rarely. One of the few attempts in this direction came from Thomas Woodrooffe. Combining a description of material losses with a picturization of the spiritual degradation that a Nazi triumph would bring about, he expounded: "Man would have no memory of the past and no outlook for the future. . . . No thoughts or opinions, no ambitions, no will of his own, no appreciation of the finer things of life, the light in a woman's eyes, the sparkle of sunlight on a wave, a chord of Beethoven . . . a crack from the Music Hall or the *New Yorker*, four aces against a flush, a home run, the Navy beating the Army in the last minute with a touchdown, an argument amongst friends. None of these things would a citizen of the new order know because he would be a slave and nothing more. . . . If you go and trade with Hitler on his own terms, where is your overseas trade coming to? Where are your markets?"

Then going into further detail about the situation in Europe, Woodrooffe describes the life of a German citizen. "He is forced to live on a . . . diet of cereal with only a little meat because there is no fodder to feed the cattle. . . . He puts on his best suit; it doesn't fit because it is made of some queer synthetic cloth. The wind blows right through it. . . . His wife is dressed in some drab shapeless creation and she uses no make-up. . . . Now that is one of the *Herrenvolk*, the chosen people.

As for the conquered . . . all they will know is a life of toil and sweat, without hope. They will never see the fruits of their labor, they will be told what to do. . . . The Nazi idea is to make all Europe the same, a deadened, dull apathetic race of . . . slaves . . . no higher education for their children, no idea of what is happening in the outside world. And that is the new order. That is what Hitler intends for Europe, not only for Europe but for the world, for you and me." (December 19, 1940.)

Other speakers have used general terms to describe the stake of the United States in the war in Europe. "To imagine," said Priestley, "that the United States has no direct interest in this world of evil is like pretending in an earthquake that you may only be feeling a trifle giddy." (July 21, 1940.)

And Wickham Steed confesses quite openly: "We do not indeed imagine, disrespectful although the idea may be, that American nature is more disinterested than British human nature. You can feel quite sure that as this war goes on its world-wide repercussions will become so clear in the Western as they are in the Eastern Hemisphere."

The BBC has given some attention to arousing American nationalism. For this purpose speakers were selected who were intimately enough acquainted with the American scene to strike the right keys and who, moreover, because of their familiarity with American life could serve as personal links between the two countries. Leslie Howard has performed both functions with good grace and taste. He has lived in the United States long enough to claim it as his second home. His first short-wave address was indeed centered around that very fact. "No visitor in a strange land," he starts out to say, "ever had a warmer welcome, made more friends or had better luck or fortune than I in your land, my second country." He then spoke of his "first excited glimpse of New York harbor" and referred to New York as "that fabulous place." (July 16, 1940.)

In a speech on January 13, 1941, Leslie Howard appealed to American vanity by talking about "the sudden and tremendous increase in the stature of this great country." Of President Roosevelt he said, "he is a great figure, greater perhaps than most Americans themselves may realize at the present time, as exalted a democrat as Jefferson and far greater a man and statesman."

Often coupled with such expressions of praise and admiration are references to the close ties between the two big English-speaking democracies. Again it is primarily Leslie Howard who has found the most striking formulations. "When we read the words of President Roosevelt to the King of England on the death of our ambassador," he remarks, "then we know that our nations have come so close together that we can drop the frills and talk together like brothers."

The Appeal to Sympathy

As German propaganda on principle prefers emotional appeals to other types, even at the risk of incredibility, it has not abstained from pleading for sympathy for Germany's suffering women and children. The fact that German bombs have hit many civilian homes in Britain is ignored and implicitly denied by the Reichssender. German raids on British territory are invariably and with exacting consistency represented as reprisal acts against British assaults. It is untiringly reaffirmed that the *Luftwaffe* is merely aiming at military objectives.

The inhumanity of the British blockade is ceaselessly pointed out, notwithstanding, of course, other remarks which state that the blockade is a complete failure. Eden and Churchill, a speaker pointed out, "in their love for the small nations and their guarantee for humanity and justice in all the world declared that merely an economic war through a blockade would take place and when the women and children of the Nazis were starved, there would be a pretty little massacre." (December 8, 1940.)

Americans are discouraged from lending their full support to the defense effort by appeals to their sympathy for the innocent and defenseless. "In closing, Harry," Kaltenbach said on December 9, 1940, "I need not tell you that American bombers sold to Great Britain are intended by their sellers and will be used by their purchasers to slay and mangle German men, women and children."

No doubt the German technique of using the "women and children" argument is designed to be effective for more than its heart appeal. It serves to confuse the American listener and to contest one of the greatest trumps of British propaganda. For, a most forceful argument with which the war situation supplied the British, was the *Luftwaffe's* indiscriminate raids and the admirable courage with which the English stood up to the punishment. German propaganda, by seizing on the argument, doubtlessly tries to bewilder the American public as to where the guilt of brutality actually lies. It also capitalizes on the emotional foundations of sympathy laid by British propaganda.

Until long after the passage of the Lease-Lend Bill the Reichssender tried to stir American sympathies for the new system in Germany by recalling the formative years of the United States. Obviously it was hoped that American listeners would harbor friendly feelings for a country whose history supposedly resembled their own. One broadcaster hoped to elicit such sentiments in the following way: "Which American," he asked, "does not long for those pioneer days of his ancestors when laws were not yet written and much less designated with paragraphs and numbers, but when a strong race of sturdy men and women grew up in America to influence the shaping of the whole world? . . . These (days) have again come to light in the new Germany." (February 2, 1941.)

The American people take pride in their country's contribution to human progress and their hearts are easily stirred at the mention of the nation's great statesmen. German propaganda, therefore, harps on these feelings. "It hardly behooves a young and vigorous nation like the United States," a broadcaster admonishes his audience, "to try to stand in the way of progress and to blindly oppose the new order." (February 10, 1941.) One speaker even suggests a parallel between George Washington and Adolf Hitler. "Isn't it the same today," his appeal for sympathy runs, "as it was then when the American people under George Washington rose against the unjustified . . . measures inflicted upon them by (the) British . . . America became a free country only because one wise man, George Washington, recognized as Hitler and Mussolini have recognized today that. . . ." (September 4, 1940.)

The British appeals for sympathy are preponderantly indirect. They are, nevertheless, or perhaps because of this fact, very moving. The magnificent courage of the English people, of old ladies, of women and children on the bombed island is pointed out, the implication being that such a people deserves sympathy and support. Among the abundance of such descriptions space allows the citing of only one. It was given by Major Hastings in a broadcast on December 5, 1940. He talked of an old lady whom he had observed during a raid on a railway station. "There she sat," he said, "peaceful, composed, implacably knitting, a picture of British calm, partly, no doubt, due to her confidence in the RAF . . . partly also because of this miracle of adjustment characteristic of our people in the face of the unusual and the unpleasant. But I felt that the old lady and the splendid boys in the fighter planes above us were worthy of one another."

British broadcasts, in contrast to German presentations, lay the emphasis on the active contribution of women and even children to the British war effort. They talk less of their passive suffering from air raids. The praise of their fortitude, of course, implies the story of their punishment.

The Anti-Fear Campaign

German propaganda is entirely on the defensive as regards the fear motive. It assures the American public that Germany has no aggressive designs against anybody and certainly not against the Western Hemisphere. The mere thought of such a thing makes German broadcasters both shudder and laugh. Although strangely enough British propaganda has not played up the fear theme prominently, the Germans assert that the English alone are responsible for the alarmed state of this country. To explain away any suspicion of Nazi designs to expand in the direction of the Western Hemisphere, broadcasters argue in two directions. They say that the Germans could never muster a fleet big enough to carry a conquering army to the shores of the United States. And they assure their listeners that the Germans have always felt friendly towards America. An American-born pro-Nazi broadcaster declares: "The French were our ancient allies, the Germans have been our modern allies." (December 10, 1940.)

Thus German propaganda tries to combat one of the most powerful forces working on behalf of Britain. Whether the British mobilized the fear motive or not, the logic of events is working for their cause. The Germans know it and their counter-efforts have been strenuous.

The Limitations of Emotional Appeals

The frequent statement that the effect of propaganda increases with the frequency, the directness and the intensity of emotional appeals is valid only if certain very important reservations be made. The situation which confronted British and German radio propaganda after the outbreak of the war contained various factors which made a degree of emotional modesty in broadcasts to the United States advisable. Among the main obstacles that imposed a certain restraint on the BBC as well as on the Reichssender, two are of general significance for all propaganda: the time factor and the composition of the audience.

The Time Factor

Short-wave broadcasts to the United States during the period covered by the Princeton Listening Center testify to an awareness of the importance of timing by the propaganda organizations of both countries. The emotional intensity of all broadcasts, the British as well as the German, increases as the war moves along. During the spring and summer months of 1940, for instance, no German broadcaster addressed to the American public anything like the excited and exciting challenges that echoed through Haw-Haw's speeches to the British people. Nor did British broadcasters in the beginning of the North American campaign strike emotional keys as openly as they did after the United States had committed herself to aid Great Britain.

When we look for the causes of heightened emotional content in propaganda we find that political or military developments in either the broadcasting country or the United States served as an impetus. When the great political shift within England, from the Chamberlain to the Churchill era, occurred overnight, so to speak; when the destroyer deal was closed with the United States; when the successes in Libya turned the course of development for a while at least, British appeals to America moved almost by jumps in the direction of greater emotionality. On the other hand, German propaganda took the introduction of the Lease-Lend Bill as a signal to go ahead. It began to show its claws during the discussion in the House of Representatives. References to Britain's past record increased. England, so Kaltenbach put it, had always faced the world "with a Bible in one hand and a checkbook in the other." (February 10, 1940.) The wrongs that England had done to America were vividly recalled by German broadcasters and hatred was fanned with mounting passion against Jewish, British and American capitalists. "There are a few," says a broadcaster, "who believe that the country should immediately enter upon a new crusade to make the world safe for that form of international capitalism that is doing business under the firm name of 'Western Democracy.'" (February 10, 1941.)

Propagandists are thus apt to launch emotional appeals in coincidence with events which affect their audiences. Events and propaganda work hand in hand. Furthermore, the propagandist himself is without doubt subject to outside influences. Drastic events stimulate him to formulate his most forceful emotional appeals.

The Composition of the Audience

The material recorded by the Listening Center demonstrates that appeals to homogeneous audiences are more emotional than speeches to listeners that are not addressed on a selective basis. When propagandists talk to general audiences, that is to people of various interests, of both sexes, with different backgrounds, they are inclined to exhibit more moderation than when they address stratified groups. Talks to women, for instance, are characterized by a strong note of sentimentality. Words to the laboring classes are usually inflammatory, and whenever German broadcasts are directed in particular to Americans of German descent, they are distinguished by emphasized appeals to emotions.

Most short-wave broadcasts are selective only to a certain degree. Practically speaking they are meant to reach a general audience. They are designed more to impress many people a little than a few people profoundly. This situation makes a certain emotional reserve advisable. Propagandists have to use an emotional language effective with many different people and yet somehow appeal to emotions shared generally by the majority of their listeners. This not only narrows the range of emotions to which the plea is directed, it also detracts from its depth, frequently making the appeal flat and impersonal.

AMERICA'S SHORT-WAVE AUDIENCE

By Harwood L. Childs

The author of this study is Associate Professor of Politics at Princeton University and Editor of *The Public Opinion Quarterly*. He has been a member of the Executive Committee of the Princeton Listening Center since its establishment in 1939, and director of its research activities since 1940. He is the author of numerous books and articles on public opinion and propaganda, including *A Reference Guide to the Study of Public Opinion* and *An Introduction to the Study of Public Opinion*. As a Fellow of the Social Science Research Council in 1931-32, and of the Guggenheim Foundation in 1937, he has spent much time in Germany studying National Socialism and Nazi propaganda.

AMERICA'S SHORT-WAVE AUDIENCE

T HE importance of short-wave broadcasting is not to be measured by its volume, by the power of sending stations, by the sums of money spent, nor by the cleverness of program makers. Its importance can be determined only by ascertaining what effect, if any, short-wave broadcasts have on those who listen. The Princeton Listening Center had been in existence for more than a year before careful attention was given to this problem. Then, early in 1941, a systematic attack was made on it with funds generously supplied by a special grant from the Rockefeller Foundation.

As a result of its studies the Princeton Listening Center concludes that European short-wave broadcasts to this country have had little effect, thus far, upon the attitudes and opinions of the American people. Such broadcasts have not in any sense been a threat to our national morale. Nor will they constitute such a threat *provided* the integrity of our domestic news services is preserved, and *provided further* that governmental agencies in the United States refrain from taking any actions which impair essentially the quality and comprehensiveness of the information supplied by our domestic communication agencies. If, however, during the stress and strain of war the people of the United States lose confidence in their press and radio; if, because of censorship and misleading propaganda, American citizens believe they can no longer rely upon these agencies for an adequate picture of the world outside, then, and then only, will they turn in large numbers to external sources of information such as foreign short-wave broadcasts. All the evidence now available clearly indicates that propaganda by short wave is a potential rather than an actual danger. One of our best defenses against psychological attacks by short wave is the excellence of our own informational services.

The fact of the matter is that the short-wave listening audience in the United States is small. Although some of the Center's studies show that one third of the people in certain sections of the country have listened at least once in their lifetime to a short-wave program from Europe, the number of those who listen seriously and regularly, day by day, is not more than one per cent of the total population.

Moreover, there is no conclusive evidence that the size of this listening audience is increasing to any marked extent. Of those who were listening to foreign short-wave programs during the spring of 1941, a considerable number had begun the practice in 1939 after the outbreak of war in Europe. Some traced their interest in short wave back to the early 'thirties—to the beginnings of international broadcasting by short wave. The declaration of war against the United States by Japan, Germany, and Italy has probably encouraged others to join the listening audience. But additions to the total number of listeners is usually offset by a large number of people who lose interest as soon as the novelty wears off, or as soon as they become convinced that foreign broadcasts, especially news programs, have little to offer which is not supplied by domestic radio stations. The turnover among short-wave listeners is considerable. Listening tends to be sporadic and haphazard. As sets get older, reception poorer, and novelty loses its charm, listening decreases and is soon given up entirely. As one investigator states: "The act of turning a dial and spending a half hour listening to a somewhat fuzzy broadcast from a foreign land assumes only a minute significance in the life of a modern urban dweller who has countless influences bombarding him from more prominent and persistent communication agencies."

In many respects the short-wave listening audience in the United States is a fairly representative cross section of the adult population as a whole, at least so far as its physical, social, and psychological characteristics are concerned. Short-wave listeners do not differ appreciably from nonlisteners in their attitudes and opinions on questions of public policy. There is virtually no evidence that listeners as a group are more or less Axis-minded, more or less opposed to President Roosevelt's foreign policy than the citizens of the country as a whole. Nor is there any evidence that short-wave listening among foreign language groups, Germans and Italians especially, is more prevalent or essentially different in nature from such listening among other groups in the country. If anything, there is proportionately less short-wave listening among foreign-born or foreign language groups than among native Americans.

When short-wave listeners are classified by age, religious affiliation, and political party preference, the resulting distribution corresponds very closely to that for the nation at large. There is, however, a tendency for a disproportionate number of men to listen in comparison to women. The marked differentials, however, are income and education. All studies point to the conclusion that the listening audience is, by and large, unrepresentative of the population generally in that it has a disproportionate number of persons in the higher income brackets and educational levels. It is not surprising, therefore, to find that short-wave listening is relatively extensive among professional, executive, and managerial classes; that listeners are very often opinion-leaders in their communities; that they read more widely, take a greater interest in public and international affairs, and are on the whole more active publicly.

Even before the memorable seventh of December, 1941, English short-wave broadcasts were favored over those from Germany and other European countries. The overwhelming majority of listeners preferred English programs, listened to them more, and, on the whole, considered them the most reliable. However, there was a growing tendency on the part of listeners to be skeptical of short-wave broadcasts, and to label them all as "nothing but propaganda."

Why do people listen to short-wave programs from Europe? The principal reason why people do *not* listen more than they do is simply because they are not interested in such programs, not because they lack facilities for doing so. Nearly every person in the United States has access to a radio. The studies of the Princeton Listening Center show that at least 90 per cent of the people of the country have a radio in their home, and that in some communities the percentage is much higher. At least a third of these sets are equipped to receive short-wave programs from abroad. The possession of a set capable of receiving foreign short-wave broadcasts may have something to do with the extent of listening, but not everything.

Why, then, do people listen? The answer is not a simple one. In many cases the initial impulse is curiosity; a desire to find out what happens when use is made of the short-wave band on a newly acquired receiving set. This initial curiosity may be further whetted by conversations with friends, by newspaper discussions of short-wave broadcasting, or by books and articles dealing with short-wave programs. A few turns of the dial, a few attempts to get specific stations, however, and this curiosity is soon satisfied.

It is more difficult to determine why some of the listeners continue to listen after this first curiosity stage. A few can be accounted for as fans or "hams." For them, consistent listening to short-wave programs, as well as to other types of radio programs, is a reflection of their mechanical, technical, or scientific interest in the instrument itself, rather than interest in the substance of programs. Whenever short-wave listening continues beyond the novelty or "ham" stage it is usually due to a desire, or a hope, that the listener will obtain quicker, more complete, and more reliable news of what is going on abroad than he can from other sources.

The United States has little to fear, therefore, from the influence of foreign short-wave broadcasts upon the minds of the American people. Although short-wave reception is reasonably good in most sections of the country, it cannot compare in quality to that for domestic broadcasts. Nor are the programs themselves superior to those of American stations. What American citizens see or hear in their newspapers, magazines, motion pictures, and domestic radio programs exerts a far greater influence on their opinions than anything which reaches them via short wave. The quality of domestic radio programs in the United States, especially news broadcasts, has been so far superior to anything foreign countries have offered by short wave, that there is little likelihood that any considerable number of people will prefer to listen to the latter instead of the former.

The formal entrance of the United States into the war against Japan, Germany, and Italy does place the situation in a somewhat different light. The President of the United States has indicated that the freedom of public and private agencies to disseminate news and information will be limited to the extent of forbidding disclosures which may be of value to the enemy, and disclosures the validity of which has not been thoroughly authenticated. These censorial precautions, necessary as they are, will most certainly encourage foreign, enemy broadcasters to try to enlarge their American listening audience by purporting to supply the information withheld or delayed by our own government action. To preserve the prestige of our communication agencies and maintain public confidence in their adequacy as sources of information, it will be necessary for public officials in the 'United States to make absolutely certain that information withheld for military reasons is not, in fact, known to the enemy; and, in the second place, that there is never a delay in the publication of facts which listeners to short-wave broadcasts can get promptly.

The best way to defeat the designs of the enemy in their attempts to build up a large American short-wave audience is to convince the American people that they can obtain from their own domestic stations, or in their own newspapers, as prompt and reliable news as they can possibly get by short wave. Words will not suffice. The American radio listener must learn from actual experience that news which he fails to obtain from domestic sources but finds elsewhere is likely to be unreliable, distorted, and in most cases false. American communication agencies have a well-deserved reputation for reliability, comprehensiveness, and promptness in their informational services. This reputation must be preserved. Efforts to discourage or ban short-wave listening will not be as effective in the long run as this more positive, constructive approach to the problem. And these considerations should also be borne in mind as we take the offensive in the psychological struggle for public and world opinion. The best way to build and preserve a large audience for our own short-wave programs is to enhance their reputation for quality in terms of completeness, accuracy, and promptness.

Short-Wave Listening Projects of the Princeton Listening Center

General conclusions regarding the results of the Center's studies of short-wave listening in the United States have been stated. How were these studies conducted? What is the evidence on which the above conclusions are based?

The Center's studies of short-wave listening consisted of three types of projects. In the first place, using the facilities of the American Institute of Public Opinion, an effort was made to obtain an over-all picture of the American listening audience: the number of listeners, their geographical distribution, their personal characteristics, and their listening habits. Two nation-wide surveys were made; one between January 27 and 31, 1941, the other during the last two weeks of December 1941. Because of the cost of such nation-wide surveys the number of questions had to be drastically limited, and attention focused upon the problem of ascertaining as accurately as possible the number and distribution of listeners.

In the second place, projects were launched in a number of local communities for the purpose of studying intensively the listening habits of short-wave listeners, their attitudes and opinions on questions of public policy, and their reasons for listening. In some instances an effort was made to obtain an accurate cross section of the adult population in these communities. In other cases emphasis was placed on compiling as numerous a list of listeners as possible. In one case a complete census was made.

In the third place, several projects were carried out in selected communities in order to study particularly the extent and nature of short-wave listening within German and Italian speaking groups.

1. The American Institute of Public Opinion Surveys.

The nation-wide surveys conducted for the Princeton Listening Center by the American Institute of Public Opinion employed the same technique of sampling used in the Institute's regular weekly polls. In the first survey the sample consisted of 3,125 persons throughout the United States so selected as to give as true a cross section as possible of the adult population, exclusive of Southern Negroes, in terms of such factors as age, sex, economic status, urban-rural, sectional, and political distribution. Three questions were used to identify the potential and actual listening audience, and four to obtain information regarding listening practices. On the same questionnaire used by the Institute's 175 interviewers there were also questions regarding domestic and foreign policy as well as queries regarding various personal characteristics which could be used as the basis for significant correlations.

Careful scrutiny of the replies to this questionnaire showed that in some cases the persons interviewed obviously confused direct short wave and rebroadcasts. There was also some evidence that a few interviewers inadvertently biased the results by selecting persons for questioning because of their known interest in short-wave reception. To check the accuracy of the returns the Institute addressed a personal letter to the alleged listeners in April 1941, only to find that about 50 per cent of those who had previously claimed they listened in January now stated that they had *not* actually listened to a single short-wave program from Europe at any time since the preceding Christmas. This check-up, however, may not be taken at its full face value because (a) less than 50 per cent of those to whom letters were sent actually replied, (b) because of the interval of time between the original survey and the check-up, and (c) because the check-up itself may have influenced the frankness of the answers.

Exceptional care was taken in the second nation-wide survey, conducted in December 1941, to guard against possible errors due to misunderstanding regarding the meaning of the term "short-wave broadcasts." In the first place the Institute sent a preliminary questionnaire to the 1,000 men and women on its panel of interviewers to find out which of them had some familiarity with short-wave broadcasting. Only those with knowledge of the subject were actually used as interviewers in the nation-wide survey, and they were explicitly instructed that "If respondent has difficulty in distinguishing accurately between different types of news broadcasts, please question further concerning station identification, identity of the broadcaster, and other similar points which may assist you in recording answers on the questions accurately."

In the second place, the questions used on this survey were specially designed to emphasize distinctions between different types of broadcasts and give respondents an opportunity to differentiate them clearly in their own minds. The questions used on this survey follow.

During the past week have you listened to any of the following types of broadcasts of war news?

a. Have you listened to any American news broadcasts from American stations?
   ☐ Yes   ☐ No   ☐ Don't know

b. Have you listened to any news broadcasts from correspondents abroad that come over American stations?
   ☐ Yes   ☐ No   ☐ Don't know

c. Have you listened to any short wave news broadcasts from European stations picked up and rebroadcast by American stations?
   ☐ Yes   ☐ No   ☐ Don't know

   INTERVIEWER: If respondent has difficulty in distinguishing accurately between different types of news broadcasts, please question further concerning station identification, identity of the broadcaster, and other similar points which may assist you in recording answers on this question accurately.

d. Have you a radio in your home which has a special short wave band for getting short wave broadcasts direct from European stations (not rebroadcasts over American stations)?
   ☐ Yes   ☐ No   ☐ Don't know

e. During the past week have you listened to short wave news broadcasts *direct* from European stations which can be heard in this country only on the short wave band of a radio?
   ☐ Yes   ☐ No   ☐ Don't know

   INTERVIEWER: If respondent indicates that he or she has listened to a direct short wave broadcast, please ask about the country from which the broadcast came and then establish that the set used has a short wave band on it, in order to satisfy yourself that the listener actually did hear a direct short wave broadcast, not a rebroadcast over any American station.

f. Aside from news broadcasts, have you heard, within the past week, any short wave broadcast of any other type *direct* from Europe on the short wave band of a radio?

   ☐ Yes   ☐ No   ☐ Don't know

   INTERVIEWER: If respondent has heard some other type of short wave broadcast within the past week, please ask for more information about this broadcast also in order to satisfy yourself that it was a direct short wave broadcast from Europe, and not a rebroadcast.

   If "No" or "Don't know" on e and f, ask:

g. Have you ever listened to a short wave radio broadcast coming *direct* from Europe and heard on the short wave band of a radio?

   ☐ Yes   ☐ No   ☐ Don't know

   If "Yes," ask: How long ago did you hear a program of this sort?

Because this second nation-wide survey of the American Institute of Public Opinion is the most recent, and because it supplies the most comprehensive and accurate information available regarding the extent, distribution, and character of America's nation-wide short-wave audience it is desirable to present the results in detail. In this instance the Institute's sample consisted of approximately 2,900 persons, so selected as to give as representative a cross section as possible of the adult, white population in the United States. In the accompanying table, for the sake of simplicity, only the figures and percentages of those giving affirmative answers are presented. The table gives the number and percentages of affirmative answers on each question asked,* for the sample as a whole, and for numerous subdivisions of it. In the discussion which follows, frequent references will be made to these figures.

It is pertinent to note at this point that the Listening Center had available for purposes of comparison two unpublished, nation-wide surveys of short-wave listening conducted by other commercial agen-

---

* Answers to the second part of question "g" are not included in the table because it did not seem important to make detailed breakdowns for them. Of those who answered *Yes* on question "g," 829 persons, the affirmative answers to the second part of the question were classified as follows:

1 week, up to but not including 1 month		19%
1 month, " " " " " 6 months		34
6 months, " " " " " 1 year		14
1 year and over		30
Quite a while ago		3

This table gives percentages of affirmative replies to short-wave questions on nation-wide survey, December 1941, classified by age, sex, color, occupation, economic status, employment status, geographical distribution, urban-rural distribution, political preference, and war work.

	Total sample	Yes on "a"	Total replies to "a"	Yes on "b"	Total replies to "b"	Yes on "c"	Total replies to "c"	Yes on "d"	Total replies to "d"	Yes on "e"	Total replies to "e"	Yes on "f"	Total replies to "f"	Yes on "g"	Total replies to "g"
National Total	(2902)	91%	2899	76%	2881	41%	2889	35%	2889	7%	2880	4.5%	2876	35%	2595
Sec. 1 (New Eng.)	6.3	94	182	78	182	52	182	46	182	18	181	9.4	181	38	146
Sec. 2 (Mid. Atl.)	27.4	92	794	78	790	37	790	36	789	8	791	5.6	787	36	714
Sec. 3 (E. Cent.)	23.2	90	672	72	672	40	671	36	670	6	669	3.3	668	35	608
Sec. 4 (W. Cent.)	14.1	89	407	75	405	36	404	29	406	4	403	3.7	402	34	365
Sec. 5 (South)	12.7	86	369	79	367	46	369	36	369	9	364	4.6	367	37	324
Sec. 6 (Rocky Mts.)	7.0	93	202	85	200	52	200	38	200	3	202	2.0	202	41	194
Sec. 7 (Pacific)	9.4	94	273	77	265	41	273	30	271	7	270	4.4	270	32	244
Sex															
Men	51.8	91	1502	79	1494	43	1498	37	1497	8	1493	5.7	1493	37	1327
Women	47.6	90	1380	75	1370	39	1374	34	1375	6	1370	3.4	1367	34	1252
Rural-Urban															
Farm	16.6	91	481	76	475	48	480	32	478	7	474	4.0	475	31	413
Small Town	17.0	92	493	81	487	46	488	45	493	9	490	6.5	492	36	429
2,500- 10,000	11.6	89	339	82	338	48	336	35	339	8	338	4.4	338	37	299
10,000-100,000	18.0	91	524	77	522	38	523	36	522	8	520	4.2	521	40	466
100,000-500,000	17.6	90	513	75	511	37	512	34	509	7	509	4.1	510	35	463
500,000 and over	19.2	90	549	72	549	33	555	31	553	5	554	4.0	551	37	509
Economic Status															
Wealthy	2.6	*	75	*	75	*	75	*	75	*	74	*	75	*	56
Average+	10.7	95	310	83	306	52	310	55	311	12	310	7.4	311	53	263
Average	33.9	95	984	82	972	48	980	43	982	10	975	6.5	972	41	848
Poor	42.8	87	1242	72	1236	36	1237	25	1234	5	1234	2.5	1233	30	1156
On Relief	5.7	81	163	59	162	26	163	20	163	2	162	0.6	161	21	156
Old Age Asst.	2.6	*	75	*	75	*	74	*	74	*	75	*	75	7	227
Age															
29 and under	21.2	93	614	78	612	37	612	38	612	7	611	5.1	611	39	559
30-49	46.6	92	1349	78	1339	42	1345	37	1346	8	1239	5.5	1332	38	1197
50 and over	30.5	89	885	75	879	43	881	31	881	7	880	2.9	883	28	803
Political Pref.															
Democrat	44.3	91	1285	76	1280	41	1281	31	1281	8	1277	5.3	1276	33	1148
Republican	33.5	93	971	80	962	45	969	43	969	7	964	4.5	964	40	867
Other	.4	*	11	*	11	*	11	*	11	*	11	*	11	*	11
Didn't Vote	15.6	83	451	67	448	33	448	29	449	6	449	2.9	447	31	415
Too Young	4.3	93	124	78	124	40	124	39	123	11	123	4.8	124	50	108
Occupation															
Professional	6.9	97	201	90	200	42	199	53	199	12	199	8.5	200	51	169
Farmers	16.6	92	480	76	474	48	479	33	477	7	473	4.0	474	30	428
Business Men	5.6	96	164	85	163	58	163	58	164	15	162	8.6	163	47	132
Clerks	21.2	93	612	78	612	56	612	34	610	7	612	5.1	608	41	555
Skilled Labor	10.3	90	299	77	295	42	298	37	299	10	299	5.0	299	41	261

Table continued

	Total sample	Yes on "a"	Total replies to "a"	Yes on "b"	Total replies to "b"	Yes on "c"	Total replies to "c"	Yes on "d"	Total replies to "d"	Yes on "e"	Total replies to "e"	Yes on "f"	Total replies to "f"	Yes on "g"	Total replies to "g"
Semiskilled	12.0	91	350	75	348	36	348	30	351	8	349	4.3	349	26	317
Farm Labor	.0	*	8	*	8	*	8	*	8	*	8	*	8	*	8
Unskilled	5.7	83	168	64	168	27	168	22	168	3	167	.6	167	27	162
Servants	3.8	80	111	67	111	33	111	15	110	3	110	3.7	109	21	105
Students	5.7	92	167	83	164	48	168	48	168	9	167	4.2	165	38	148
Color															
White	95.0	91	2754	77	2737	42	2745	36	2747	8	2736	4.6	2733	36	2458
Black	5.0	79	117	*	116	*	116	*	114	*	116	2.6	116	14	112
Employment Status															
Employed, Full Time	38.6	91	1126	80	1123	42	1125	39	1121	9	1121	6.0	1119	42	1108
Full-time Student	1.4	*	49	*	49	*	48	*	49	*	48	*	49	*	40
Housewife	28.2	89	819	74	810	38	815	34	817	6	814	2.8	813	33	749
Emp. Part Time	6.5	90	190	76	189	38	189	23	190	6	188	4.3	188	26	172
Farmers	10.3	93	293	79	290	54	292	34	292	8	289	4.2	288	29	253
Employers	5.5	96	146	85	144	49	147	54	147	8	146	6.8	147	39	128
Retired	2.9	*	84	*	84	*	83	*	82	*	82	*	84	*	79
Unemployed	5.8	86	169	67	169	34	167	20	168	5	169	1.8	167	26	157
Soldier	.2	*	*	*	*	*	*	*	*	*	*	*	7	*	5
War Work															
Yes, Directly	3.0	*	*	*	87	*	88	*	88	*	88	*	88	*	75
Yes, Indirectly	4.8	92	138	78	137	39	137	45	138	14	138	8.8	136	40	115
No	91.0	91	2640	77	2624	41	2631	35	2630	7	2621	4.3	2621	35	2379
Breadwinner	68.6	91	1997	78	1988	42	1991	36	1989	8	1986	5.0	1982	36	1780
Housewife	27.4	89	794	73	786	38	791	35	792	6	788	2.8	787	33	724
Student	1.4	*	39	*	*	*	38	*	39	*	38	*	39	*	30
Filial	.7	*	20	*	*	*	20	*	20	*	20	*	20	*	15
Widow, Parent	1.7	*	48	*	47	*	48	*	48	*	47	*	48	*	45

* Less than 100 cases.

cies. The first, in point of time, was that made by the Columbia Broadcasting System in September 1940, herein referred to as the Gill Survey after the name of the chief investigator. The poll was taken by means of telephone interviews in the following cities: New York, Baltimore, Boston, Chicago, Detroit, Hartford, Kansas City, Louisville, Omaha, Pittsburgh, St. Louis, Columbus, Dallas, Richmond, Atlanta, New Orleans, Minneapolis, Salt Lake City, Portland (Oregon), and Los Angeles. The sample consisted of 2,598 persons selected at random from the telephone directories in these cities.

The second was a survey conducted for *Fortune Magazine* by Elmo Roper, Inc. in April 1941. The sampling technique he employed was in most respects similar to that used by the American Institute of Public Opinion, and followed the standardized procedure of the well-known *Fortune* surveys. In this instance the sample consisted of 7,469 persons, so selected as to give a true cross section of the adult population, exclusive of Southern Negroes, in terms of various personal characteristics. This poll was especially interesting because of its geographical breakdowns on some of the questions.

2. The Census of Princeton, New Jersey.

The first of the local studies of short-wave listening to be completed by the Center was executed under the direction of Paul M. Douglas, a Princeton senior, during the week of February 17, 1941. This was the only attempt made by the Princeton Listening Center investigators to make anything like a complete canvass of short-wave listeners within a defined area. With the assistance of ten telephone operators, Mr. Douglas undertook to reach by telephone every noncommercial and non-institutional telephone subscriber in Princeton, exclusive of a rather large Italian and Negro population. The telephone interview itself was brief, designed merely to ascertain whether the respondent was a potential or actual short-wave listener. All in all more than 2,000 persons were interviewed in this manner. The telephone interview was then supplemented by a personal interview with those who said they did listen to short wave. In this manner a very careful check was made of the accuracy of the initial answers, and it was possible to make a rather detailed study of the personal characteristics, listening habits, and attitudes of those who listened to short wave. Subsequently, Mr. Douglas made a random sampling survey of short-wave listening among Italians and Negroes in Princeton.

This experiment emphasized how difficult it is, even in the case of a well-defined and limited public, and by means of a complete census, to obtain precision in the matter of short-wave listening. Personal interviews indicated that in a number of cases those who reported by phone that they listened, either confused short-wave reception with rebroadcasts, or simply did not understand the questions asked. The follow-up, personal interviews can be regarded as fairly satisfactory, however; and in spite of the fact that Princeton is not a representative community, the data obtained, when placed beside that from other communities, is illuminating.

3. The Erie County Studies.

The Office of Radio Research of Columbia University, under the direction of Dr. Paul F. Lazarsfeld, undertook a series of studies of short-wave listening in Erie County, Ohio, extending over a period of several months during the spring and summer of 1941. The primary reason for selecting this particular population area for study was the fact that the Office of Radio Research had already been using Erie County as an experimental center for numerous public opinion studies, and had consequently collected a large amount of data regarding the personal characteristics of the residents therein, their interests and habits, as well as their opinions on a variety of social, economic, and political subjects.

In making these studies Dr. Lazarsfeld used the panel technique. A carefully selected sample of 511 people in Erie County, a representative cross section of the total population in that area, was used repeatedly to speak for the people of the county as a whole.

In September 1940 the members of this panel had been asked if they could get short-wave broadcasts on their radios, and if so, whether they ever listened to them. The Princeton Listening Center asked Dr. Lazarsfeld to assemble all existing information regarding those who said they had listened to such broadcasts, and to ascertain the respects in which this short-wave listening audience differed from nonlisteners. This preliminary compilation of existing data was followed in March and April 1941 by detailed personal interviews with those comprising this listening audience. The discrepancies between the results of these interviews and the replies in September 1940 were so marked, however, that in April 1941 a supplementary postcard survey was made of all members of the panel who claimed they were nonlisteners in the preceding September.

The Erie County surveys are particularly interesting for several reasons. In the first place, the sampling technique employed had been worked out and applied with exceptional care. Not only was the panel as accurate a cross section of the people of Erie County as it was currently possible to make it, but the Office of Radio Research already knew a great deal regarding the extent to which Erie County reflected in its interests, attitudes, and activities those of the people of the country as a whole. Moreover, because of the previous studies which the Office of Radio Research had made in this area, much more information was available regarding these short-wave listeners than those in other communities. Nor is it without significance that comparisons could be made between the state of listening to short wave in September 1940 and the situation in March and April 1941. The value of the results obtained, however, was lessened somewhat because the same detailed, personal interviews were not made in September as they were later, and because the sample was so small.

4. The Baton Rouge Surveys.

In July 1940, Professor Edgar A. Schuler of Louisiana State University, on his own initiative, made a survey of short-wave listening among telephone subscribers in Baton Rouge, Louisiana. He employed the random sampling technique, using as his sample 556 residential telephone subscribers exclusive of Negroes. The results of this study, published in the June 1941 issue of *The Public Opinion Quarterly*, were based entirely on telephone interviews.

To ascertain what changes, if any, had occurred in the extent and nature of short-wave listening in this area since this initial survey was made, the Princeton Listening Center asked Professor Schuler to make a resurvey of all short-wave listeners located during the course of this earlier study. This he did during March 1941. Supplementing this study, Professor Schuler, with the assistance of Miss Eileen Ratterree, also made a completely new survey of short-wave listening among white telephone subscribers in Baton Rouge during the spring of 1941. This was essentially a repetition of the 1940 study, except that a new method of sampling at random the list of telephone subscribers was employed, and after short-wave listeners were identified, they were subjected to a detailed, personal interview. In this instance there were 283 cases in the sample as compared with 556 in the 1940 survey.

These two studies, although limited in their scope, were valuable in that they enabled the Princeton Listening Center to analyze changes in the nature and extent of short-wave listening over a considerable period of time. The Erie County Studies were the only other projects affording this possibility.

During December 1940 and January 1941 Professor Schuler conducted a third study of short-wave listening in connection with a special sociological study of neighborhoods in Baton Rouge with which he was associated. The sociological study was based on a random sample of 259 households in that area. By adding a few questions on short-wave listening he was able to identify in still another manner a representative sample of short-wave listeners, interview them personally, and make detailed comparisons of the attitudes of this group with another carefully matched group of nonlisteners.

5. The Chicago Studies.

In April, May, and June 1941 Professor Harold F. Gosnell of the University of Chicago, with the assistance of Alfred De Grazia, conducted three types of short-wave listening studies in the Chicago area. In the first place, a printed questionnaire was mailed to a selected list of radio owners compiled from two sales lists supplied by the Hudson-Ross and Scott radio firms. Secondly, a similar questionnaire was submitted to a number of assembled groups—citizenship classes, members of the University of Chicago faculty, the League of Women Voters, the City Club, residents of the Allerton Hotel, and several university classes.

These two surveys yielded a total of 1,003 cases for analysis and study distributed as follows:

University of Chicago Faculty	164
Hudson-Ross Radio Sales List	111
Hyde Park YMCA Citizenship Class	23
Independence Park Citizenship Class	25
Central YMCA Citizenship Class	15
League of Women Voters	35
Residents of Allerton Hotel	36
City Club	22
Library of International Relations	7
Scott Radio Sales List	256
YMCA College and Northwestern University Radio Classes	279
University Classes of the University of Chicago	30
TOTAL	1,003

This sample was in no sense truly representative of the population in the Chicago area. Although a special effort was made to include Italians and Germans, immigrants and foreign nationality groups were far from being adequately represented. Virtually no unskilled workers were included. The income level of the respondents, their occupational distribution, their age distribution, the proportion of foreign-born, distribution according to educational attainments and political affiliation were markedly atypical. Although this sample was definitely unrepresentative of the Chicago population as a whole, it did contain a large number of short-wave listeners (435) and did afford a satisfactory basis for studying listening habits, reasons for listening, and difference in attitude between listeners and nonlisteners. What these two surveys could not do was to give an indication of the extent and distribution of short-wave listening. For this reason a third project was undertaken, in which an effort was made to sample at random the listening of Chicago people generally. This was done by means of brief, street corner, personal interviews. Interviewers were stationed at nine street corners throughout the city, each corner selected because of the ethnic and economic groups residing in the neighborhood. Although this procedure yielded a sample of only 293 cases, Professor Gosnell believes, on the basis of results obtained from previous use of this technique, that the results gave a fairly accurate and typical picture.

6. The Syracuse Survey.

The noteworthy feature of the Syracuse Survey of short-wave listening, so far as procedure is concerned, was the precision taken to obtain a representative sample of the city's population. To secure as accurate a cross section as possible, quotas were prepared for residence by wards, sex, three age groups (15-34, 35-54, and 55 or over), and five levels of economic status, using home rental value as a criterion. No quotas were prepared for political preference, but instead this factor was used to test the representative selectivity of the sample itself. This was done by comparing the way in which members of the sample said they voted in the 1940 presidential election with the way in which the people of the city actually did vote. This comparison revealed a discrepancy of only 3.6 per cent.

The sample as finally constructed consisted of 300 persons, each of whom was interviewed personally in May 1941 for from twenty to thirty minutes by well-trained, professional interviewers. The results probably give as accurate a picture of the short-wave listening audience in Syracuse as the science of social sampling now permits. How representative these results are of the situation throughout the country cannot, of course, be determined. Professor Herman C. Beyle of Syracuse University directed this particular study.

7. Surveys Among Italians and Germans.

For several reasons the Princeton Listening Center thought it would be desirable to supplement the foregoing studies with an investigation of short-wave listening among certain foreign language groups, especially Italians and Germans. Studies of foreign short-wave broadcasts indicated that special efforts were being made by foreign broadcasters to reach these groups. In the minds of some, there existed the suspicion that the influence of such broadcasts might be greater in these particular sectors of the population than in others. At least it was considered worth while to investigate the extent and nature of this short-wave listening audience.

A nation-wide survey of the Italian and German speaking, short-wave listening audience was impractical. Instead, intensive studies were made of selected groups in Boston and New York City. The New York surveys, of which there were two—one German and one Italian—were made under the direction of Edward A. Suchman of the Office of Radio Research, Columbia University. The Boston survey, confined to Italians, was conducted by Dr. Jerome S. Bruner and Miss Jeannette Sayre of Harvard University.

The procedure followed by Mr. Suchman in his study of short-wave listening among German-Americans in New York was as follows. Marking out a definite area in the Yorkville section of the city, populated for the most part by German-speaking people, he devised a formula for selecting at random 561 households in each of which at least one person was interviewed personally. The study was in a sense experimental in that one of the principal purposes of the survey was to determine whether suspicion or anxiety on the part of the respondents made it impractical. Consequently the questionnaire was not as elaborate as some of those in other surveys, and no attempt was made to contact subsequently those who were not at home when the initial visit was made. Using native American interviewers Mr. Suchman found that surveying German-Americans presented no exceptional difficulties.

The New York Italian study was executed with greater care and precision than the preliminary and experimental German study. Four districts in New York City were selected for study because of their general economic status and the density of the Italian population therein. The four districts were (1) Concentrated Upper (Bensonhurst), (2) Concentrated Lower (Little Italy), (3) Scattered Upper (Washington Heights), (4) Scattered Lower (Lower Bronx).

The information was gathered through personal interviews with a completely random sample of Italian residents in these four districts. For the concentrated districts approximately every fiftieth apartment was taken. In the scattered districts, due to the extremely small percentage of Italians, it was necessary to single out at random any Italian family that could be found. Interviews were made with every member of the family above fourteen years of age. In no case was any adult member not interviewed, or any family in the random sample omitted. In the case of families not at home when the first visit was made, every effort was made to reach them by frequent call-backs. This procedure finally yielded a total sample of 413 individual cases in 99 families.

The study of short-wave listening among Italians in Boston was conducted during the first three weeks of June 1941, and was geared to an analysis of both short and long-wave listening. A sample of 600 Italian residents of Boston's North End, all of them over 21 years of age, was obtained as follows. The North End area was divided into subsections, major axes were drawn across the area, and every eighth doorbell was rung. In this manner a geographical cross section was obtained which represented proportionally the distribution of the Italian population throughout the area. Moreover, a special effort was made to obtain the proper proportions of men and women and of different age groups. The personal interviews were conducted by residents of the area, all of whom spoke both English and Italian and were known in the neighborhood. The main purpose of this first project was to ascertain how much and what kind of radio listening, both short and long wave, went on, and to determine superficially what types of people listened to what kinds of programs.

The second project of the Boston Italian study consisted of an intensive examination of the listening habits, attitudes, and preferences of 62 persons in the larger sample of 600 distributed as follows: (1) 21 short-wave listeners; (2) 20 persons listening primarily to local, long-wave Italian programs; and (3) 21 persons listening primarily to local programs in English. The technique of interviewing this selected group of 62 persons may be of some interest. Guided by a specially prepared, elaborate schedule, the interviewers, each of whom had a wide knowledge of the community, subjected the respondents to questioning that often lasted for more than four hours in individual cases. Some of the most valuable data was obtained from information volunteered by the interviewees, supplemented by "family bull-sessions" after the interviews had officially ended.

The third phase of this Italian study was an attempt to check the reliability of the answers to questions on short-wave listening. An interviewer, claiming to be a radio expert from a fictitious "Radio Institute," examined the radio sets of all those who had stated that they listened to short wave, asking various irrelevant questions on reception, but always including one concerning the position on the dial where the respondent claimed to obtain the best short-wave reception.

Further Observations Regarding the Projects as a Whole

Before presenting the results of these seven projects it will be useful to restate certain important considerations. In the first place, it is to be noted that a variety of procedures were followed. In several instances the purely random technique of sampling was employed. In other cases the quota method was used. In one case a complete census of the population of a selected community was made. And in one instance virtually no attention was given to obtaining either a complete census or a representative sample. Excluding from consideration the Gill and Roper Surveys to which reference has been made, but which were not conducted under the direction of the Princeton Listening Center, there were in all 9,611 persons who were questioned regarding their short-wave listening. This group as a whole is not a representative sample of the adult population of the United States, although some segments of it do possess a representative character. However nonrepresentative of the total population, the information obtained from these people probably does give a fairly accurate picture of short-wave listening habits and behavior.

A second important consideration is the time factor. Some of the surveys were made in January, others later in the spring, summer, and fall. These differences in time, in view of the rapidly changing domestic and international scene, make any attempt to draw general conclusions about the *attitudes* and *opinions* of short-wave listeners in comparison with nonlisteners open to serious objections.

In the third place, it is important to note that the number and nature of the questions asked by the different investigators varied, although in general the information sought was quite similar. Moreover, the interviewing procedure varied all the way from brief telephone questioning to extensive and lengthy personal interviews.

Size of the Listening Audience

How should the term "listening audience" be defined? To be included in such an audience is it sufficient that a person shall have listened *once* to a short-wave program, sometime, somewhere? Or must he have listened at least once during the day of the interview, during the preceding week, month, or year? Moreover, should some degree of frequency of listening be required?

The American Institute of Public Opinion in its first nation-wide survey in January 1941, found that 10.8 per cent of the sample claimed actually to have listened to a short-wave program at least once during the month preceding the interview. Resurveying the people of the country eleven months later it found that 7 per cent had listened to short-wave news broadcast direct from European stations *during the preceding week*. Although not strictly comparable it is of interest to note that the results of the Gill Survey of selected cities in 1940 revealed that 17 per cent of a predominantly urban sample were listening as frequently as once a week. The *Fortune* study, made in April 1941, disclosed that 7.8 per cent of the people of the country claimed to have listened at least once since the beginning of the year.

The difficulties of ascertaining precisely the number of short-wave listeners in the United States as a whole are many. There is not only the problem of defining the word "listener," but there is the much more difficult one of making certain that the person interviewed understands clearly what is meant by short wave. Because of the experience acquired prior to the December 1941 nation-wide survey of the American Institute of Public Opinion, and the nature of the questions asked in that study, the Center believes that the figure, 7 per cent, is probably as close an approximation to the extent of weekly short-wave listening at the present time as it is possible to obtain.

The local studies, especially in those cases where a complete census was taken, or where particular care was exercised to obtain a representative sample, are also very valuable in indicating the extent of short-wave listening. Professor Schuler's 1940 survey of telephone subscribers in Baton Rouge revealed, for example, that 15.6 per cent of this group were current or recent listeners, and this figure may be accepted with considerable assurance. In a similar type of survey made during the spring of 1941 he found that 21.9 per cent *had at some time* previously listened to short-wave broadcasts direct from Europe. Douglas, in reporting the results of his 1941 census of telephone subscribers in Princeton stated: "Although 23.3 per cent of the telephone owners interviewed claimed to be short-wave listeners, only 17.1 per cent could be considered to be even likely listeners, and actual investigation proved that only 13.3 per cent of the total practised listening on any noticeable scale." Lazarsfeld found that 36 per cent of a carefully selected cross section of the residents of Erie County, Ohio, owned a short-wave receiver, but that only 10.4 per cent used them to listen to news by short wave.

On the basis of his very carefully prepared sample Professor Beyle concludes that 35 per cent of the residents in Syracuse have heard short-wave programs at least once. This is precisely the finding of the American Institute of Public Opinion in its December 1941 nation-wide survey. (See table, p. 313.) It is not surprising that a large proportion of those who have short-wave bands on their radios have listened at least once to short-wave programs. As Professor Beyle states: "The figures on this point may easily be more a criterion of interest in possession and facility than an indication of interest in the substance afforded by the facility."

If the size of the listening audience is measured in terms of those who have listened at least once to short-wave programs, the number of listeners is large. A more significant measure, however, is the frequency or regularity of listening. All the evidence available points to the inescapable conclusion that the number of frequent or regular listeners is extremely small. Of the 10.8 per cent of the total population which, according to the findings of the American Institute of Public Opinion in its first survey, claimed to have actually listened to a short-wave program at least once during the month preceding the interview, less than 50 per cent indicated that they had listened to English programs as many as three times; 33 per cent, five or more times; 25 per cent, ten or more times; and only 6 per cent, thirty or more times. Of those who had listened at least once to German programs the corresponding percentages were 57, 31, 18, and 4. Apparently only about 0.006 per cent of the adult population listen to England as often as once a day, and the comparable percentage for German programs is 0.002. This suggests that there may be daily audiences of 430,000 and 140,000 for English and German programs respectively.

The surveys of short-wave listening in selected communities further substantiate the conclusion that the number of those who listen regularly and frequently is small. In Syracuse Professor Beyle found that whereas 35 per cent of the total sample had listened at least once to a short-wave program from Europe, only 17.3 per cent had heard them occasionally, and only 4.3 per cent claimed that they had heard them often or regularly. Curiously enough a relatively high proportion of those who claimed to listen to Italian broadcasts asserted that they listened often and regularly.

In Baton Rouge Professor Schuler found that "the most common frequency of listening is daily (24%); next, once a week (21%); then, twice a week (19%); three, four, or five times a week (13%); once or twice a month (5%); and the remainder less than once a month (11%). A few (5%) did not know how often they listened." Translated into percentages of the total population surveyed it would appear that only about five per cent listened as often as once daily.

In Princeton Douglas found that 11 per cent of those who had ever listened did so as often as seven times a week; 12.3 per cent, three times a week; and 19.2 per cent, once a week. In Chicago Professor Gosnell found that 14 per cent of those who had listened at all did so more than six times a week; 15.4 per cent, from three to six times; 29.2 per cent, one to three times; and 20 per cent less than once a week.

Not only is the number of persons who listen to short-wave programs from abroad regularly and frequently very small, but the listening audience tends to be haphazard in its selection of programs. Gill found that approximately 70 per cent of those who claimed to have listened did not try to tune particular programs and stations but just tuned any station that was on. The fact of the matter seems to be that there is only a slight tendency on the part of listeners to confine their attention to the programs of a single country.

Is the size of the short-wave listening audience increasing or decreasing? In Syracuse about one in four of the listeners claimed to be listening more at the time of the survey than when they first began to listen. About a third claimed that there had been no change in the frequency of their listening. But four out of ten said that they were listening less than when they first began.

In Princeton Douglas found that 63 per cent of the listening audience was listening less than when they first began; 16.4 per cent, more; and 17.8 per cent, about the same. In Chicago Professor Gosnell reports the corresponding figures as 36.6, 18.2, and 17.9.

Such evidence as is available seems to indicate that there is a tendency for short-wave listeners to lose interest in such programs as the novelty wears off. This does not necessarily prove that the total listening audience is becoming smaller, for, as Dr. Lazarsfeld in his Erie County Studies points out, newcomers may stabilize or even increase the totals. In his opinion the significant fact is the relatively large turnover among short-wave listeners.

During the early days of international short-wave broadcasting, 1931-1939, there is some evidence that the number of listeners increased rather rapidly. Professor Schuler states, "Listeners report first beginning to listen to short wave in 1933. The number beginning to listen increases in the following years, reaching a maximum in 1939, with fewer for 1940 and 1941. Twice as many began listening in 1939 as in any other year. . . . A full half of the short-wave listeners report a decrease in listening since they first began. About a third report no change, while a fifth report an increase."

Professor Beyle finds that "among those who listened to the short-wave programs there are two distinct modes as respects the period of time over which they have been listening. One out of three have been listening more than two years. This may evidence some prewar political interest, but most likely this mode is chiefly swelled by those who are mere distance fans. One out of four have been listening about one year. Doubtless the war interest is prominent in these cases."

How is the increase or decrease in the amount of short-wave listening to be accounted for? Professor Beyle sought the answer by asking, "Why do you listen more or listen less frequently now than when you first began?" "The free responses to this question were inductively classified. It is perfectly clear that 'war and international affairs' explain practically all of the increased listening. 'Mechanical facilities' were accredited by scarcely anyone; and none spoke of 'general interest' or of some 'other specific interest.' On the other hand, scarcely anyone spoke of 'war and international affairs' as being the occasion or cause of their decline of listening. In the following order they mentioned some 'other specific interest,' 'general interest,' and 'mechanical difficulties.' Only about one in twenty of the 'hearers' mentioned 'mechanical difficulties' as a reason for their decline of listening."

Professor Schuler also found that increased listening, when it occurred, was due to "the desire to get war news." But "almost half of those reporting a decrease give as their chief reason increased difficulties of reception, mainly due to interference. Others say the decrease in listening is because they are too busy now, they find the war tiresome, the novelty has worn off, and they prefer our (i.e. United States) broadcasts."

Physical Characteristics of the Listening Audience

In its studies the Princeton Listening Center devoted a considerable amount of attention to the personal characteristics of the listeners. In what respects—physical, social, and psychological—do they differ as a group from the population of the country as a whole? And to what extent are these differences related to each other? The principal physical characteristics to which attention was given were age, sex, nationality, nativity, and linguistic ability.

When the short-wave listeners in the first American Institute of Public Opinion Survey were classified according to age, little difference was found in the proportion under thirty and those over thirty, except that the proportion of listeners decreased somewhat after fifty. Reference to the table on page 313 shows that the resurvey in December 1941 gave substantially the same picture. In Princeton Douglas found that short-wave listeners were as a rule somewhat younger on the average than nonlisteners. Lazarsfeld failed to detect any significant differences in Erie County, Ohio. In Syracuse Beyle found that "the differentials for the three age groups are only significant in their consistent gradation and extremes, 37.3 per cent for those of the older aged and 29.9 for the younger aged." He also found that "the proportion of the younger group was relatively high among those who listened frequently. Those of middle age were over-represented among those who listened rarely and under-represented among those who listened more frequently. The proportion of those of older years was relatively low among those who listened rarely." Gosnell reports that "there is a tendency for younger people to listen more than older people to short-wave broadcasts. This tendency is not evident in the general group or the faculty, both of which have a high proportion of young people busily engaged in academic work."

All of the short-wave listening studies indicate that listening is less prevalent among women than men. In the first American Institute of Public Opinion Survey the percentage of women listeners was 8 as compared to 12 for men. In the second survey 8 per cent of the men and 6 per cent of the women stated they had listened "during the past week." Douglas found that in Princeton 56.2 per cent of the short-wave listeners were men, and that when the question was asked, "Who listens to short-wave broadcasts on your family radio?" in 43.9 per cent of the cases the answer was the man of the house, whereas only 38.1 per cent indicated the woman of the house. Schuler's Baton Rouge Surveys substantiated these findings. In his 1940 study he found that 66 per cent of the most interested short-wave listeners in each family surveyed were adult men, usually husbands; 16 per cent, adult women, usually wives. In the 1941 survey "of the families who listen to short wave, the members who report listening, in order of frequency, are: man of the house (84%), woman of the house (61%), son (29%), and daughter (11%)." Beyle did not discover any significant differential in this respect, nor did Lazarsfeld.

Short-wave Listening Within Foreign Language Groups

Because of the foreign origin of the short-wave programs a special effort was made to determine whether listening to these programs was more prevalent among foreign language groups in this country than among native Americans. Moreover, special studies were made, as previously indicated, of short-wave listening among Italian-speaking people in Boston and New York, and among German language groups in New York.

There is no evidence to show that listening among aliens is greater than for citizens generally. Whereas the American Institute of Public Opinion found in its first survey that 10.8 per cent of the people of the country as a whole had listened at least once to short-wave programs from Europe in the month preceding the interview, only 8 per cent of the aliens in the sample were found to be in the same category. The situation in individual communities varies, however. In Syracuse Professor Beyle found that "the percentage of persons born in the United States was slightly higher among those who did not listen to the European short-wave broadcasts (88.2 per cent) than among those who had listened (78.1 per cent)." In Princeton Douglas found that substantially the same condition prevailed. In this community 71.2 per cent of the listeners were born in the United States, whereas 90.9 per cent of the nonlisteners were in this same category. Although Gosnell's sample was not truly representative of the population of Chicago it is interesting to note that he found that 85.3 per cent of the listeners and 84.2 per cent of the nonlisteners were native Americans.

Not only are the listeners overwhelmingly Americans by birth but in the majority of instances their parents were also native Americans. This is also true of nonlisteners. The American Institute of Public Opinion found that in 67.4 per cent of the cases the parents of listeners were born in this country. Beyle discovered that for Syracuse the percentage was 57.1 in the case of listeners and 54.4 per cent for nonlisteners. In Princeton the percentages were 60.3 and 68.2 respectively. Professor Gosnell in his Chicago study went even further and ascertained the original country of ancestry, finding that 58 per cent of the listeners and 58.8 per cent of the nonlisteners stemmed from Axis-controlled countries.

On the whole the results of the specialized studies among foreign language groups substantiate the assertion that there is not a disproportionate amount of short-wave listening among these groups. The results of the Suchman study of a representative sample of Italians in New York City showed that only 28 of the 413 people interviewed had ever listened to short-wave programs direct from Europe. Listening among these 28 people was haphazard, and only 13 of them listened regularly to particular short-wave broadcasts from abroad. Most of these listeners confined their listening to newscasts, and devoted about three times as much attention to Italian as compared to English broadcasts. The study also showed that the closer the relationship of the respondent to Italy, the greater the amount of his short-wave listening. Summarizing the situation as he found it in New York City Mr. Suchman states:

"The problem of short-wave listening among Italians in New York City does not appear to be a serious one, at least quantitatively. Very little short-wave listening was found to exist and where it did exist, there was little evidence of any direct political or ideological connotation. The listening, such as it was, was largely determined by the strength of the ties between a listener and his former culture. We find practically no listening among the second generation Italo-Americans, in spite of the existence of Italian ties in their family life. On the other hand, more than half the immigrant short-wave set owners listen to these broadcasts from Italy. In general then, it can be stated that Italian short-wave listening is another reflection of the attempt on the part of the immigrant Italian population to retain its former cultural interests."

The outstanding characteristics of the Italian short-wave listening audience in New York City are these. It is relatively very small. Only 78 people out of a representative sample of 413 owned sets capable of receiving short-wave programs from abroad, and of these only 28 said that they actually listened, of whom only 13 could be said to be regular listeners. Men rather than women were the predominant listeners; old people rather than young people. Most short-wave radio ownership occurred among those with moderate incomes, a group which also listened more than the poor or wealthy. The great majority of short-wave listeners were immigrants, noncitizens, much more at home with the Italian than with the English language. They were, in short, Italians who have maintained closer ties with the home country and things Italian than others. They prefer to speak Italian, listen to domestic Italian radio programs, and read Italian newspapers. There is practically no short-wave listening among second generation Italians. Although Italians who listen to short-wave programs usually have a higher education than nonlisteners, country of birth plays a larger role in listening than education.

The study by Dr. Bruner and Miss Sayre of short-wave listening by Italians in Boston revealed the following significant facts. Of the representative sample of 600 adult Italians in Boston's North End, 27.1 per cent were found to be short-wave listeners. Approximately one third of this group listened at least once a week to foreign broadcasts, either on their own sets or on sets belonging to friends or neighbors.

Of all those capable of receiving such broadcasts on their own sets, 59 per cent actually used them for this purpose.

To what extent was this Italian short-wave listening audience in Boston different from the Italian community as a whole? In age and sex distribution there were no differentials. To some extent the short-wave listener followed the news more carefully than those Italians who listened exclusively to domestic programs, but the difference was not striking. There was no indication that the short-wave Italian audience listened to domestic newscasts in Italian more frequently than the nonshort-wave audience. In fact Italian listeners to domestic programs generally tuned in on Italian programs more often than Italian listeners to short-wave programs. Nor does facility or preference for the Italian language seem to be a factor in determining the extent and amount of listening to short wave. Nor is there any evidence to show that the short-wave listener is more serious in his program interests than others.

Dr. Bruner and Miss Sayre summarize their findings as follows: "Thus far the total effect of our findings on the 600 cases has been negative. The short-wave listener is slightly more interested in news, but not very much so. Other program preferences do not distinguish between the domestic and short-wave listener; nor do linguistic habits, news reading habits, nor the extent to which the listener is an ardent radio fan. One conclusion is clear: the short-wave listener is marked by no simple stigmata which can be unmasked in a necessarily superficial polling study. For the motivations underlying short-wave listening, consequently, the writers deemed it wise to look deeper. To this end a more elaborate case method was employed.

"In this definitely lower-class community, peopled almost exclusively by first and second generation Italians, short-wave listening was found to be a very common habit present in about a quarter of the adult population. Polling community opinion on listening and reading habits yielded no striking correlates of the short-wave habit. Case studies of a group of known short-wave listeners and domestic listeners did, however, reveal several interesting facts about motivations for short-wave listening which, it may be stated tentatively, furnish insight on the problem of why the average listener turns to the short-wave radio and why he believes or doubts what he hears.

"1. A complex attitude, composed of militant identification with

Italy and resentment toward America, which we have termed 'militant Italianism,' appears to give rise in many cases to short-wave listening.

"2. A second factor found to be associated with short-wave listening is scepticism about the truth of news to be obtained from domestic sources. Particularly strong in the militant Italian, such scepticism does not extend to programs from Italy.

"3. A more generalized scepticism was found to be characteristic of other short-wave listeners. These people doubt not only domestic news, but also the news to be heard over the short wave.

"4. In their activistic attitude toward the radio in general, the short-wave listener interviewed stood out, almost without exception, from the domestic listener.

"5. Short-wave listening was found to be a predominantly male pattern both in its initiation and in its maintenance.

"6. Casual short-wave listening has two ascertainable motives at its base. One is the desire for a 'thrill' or 'fun' characteristic of radio fans in the early 1920's and of radio 'hams' at the present time; other occasional listeners seem to derive their satisfaction from scoffing at what they hear over the short wave.

"7. Some short-wave listening appears to be motivated by the need for prestige, the purveying of short-wave news being, in the North End, apparently a mark of superiority.

"8. Rationalizations for believing what is heard over the short-wave radio follow two lines. Among the militant Italians it is simply, 'Italy can do no wrong.' Other cases assert that they believe what they hear because it comes from where the news is happening."

The study of short-wave listening among German-speaking people in Yorkville, New York City, was definitely preliminary in nature, and the results are suggestive rather than conclusive. There were serious doubts at first in the minds of the investigators whether, in view of existing tensions in the international situation, the German language group would cooperate by answering questions readily and frankly. This doubt was quickly dispelled and interviewers encountered no special difficulties. An attempt was made to obtain a truly random sample, but interviewers found at home only one in three of those selected for interview purposes. No effort was made later to interview these not-at-homes, and in this respect the results of the survey are unsatisfactory.

As in the case of New York Italians, so in the case of Germans, the amount and extent of short-wave listening appears to be small. Of the 561 persons interviewed only 52 had sets capable of receiving short-wave programs, and of these only 28 persons stated that they actually listened to them. Curiously enough short-wave listening among the women was slightly more prevalent than among men. The number of listeners under forty years of age was the same as the number over forty. The proportion of listeners in the C income group was slightly greater than the proportion in the B income group. No listeners were found in the A group, and only one in the D group. Of the 28 listeners, 24 spoke with a marked German accent, whereas only 14 of the 24 who could get short-wave programs on their sets but did not do so, had such an accent. There were 14 of the 28 listeners who listened every day, and 7 who listened several times weekly. News programs were the ones most often listened to; music, second. Germany was the country listened to most by 26 of the 28.

Social Characteristics of Listeners

The term "social characteristics" is defined broadly to include such factors as place of residence, economic status, interest in public affairs, political and religious affiliations.

Is short-wave listening more prevalent in one section of the country than in another? Do people in cities listen to a greater extent than those in small towns and rural areas? To answer these questions the American Institute of Public Opinion divided the United States into seven geographical sections and determined the proportion of people in each section in the nation-wide sample listening to short-wave broadcasts. The results are given in the accompanying table.

Section	Percent of sample listening to short-wave broadcasts	
	JANUARY 1941	DECEMBER 1941
1. New England	22%	18%
2. Middle Atlantic	9	8
3. East Central	10	6
4. West Central	8	4
5. South	13	9
6. Rocky Mountain	2	3
7. Pacific	7	7

The most marked deviation from the national average was found in the New England States. Why this is so cannot, with the data available, be answered confidently. In constructing the sample the Institute was careful to have the sectional distribution of those interviewed correspond to the sectional distribution of the adult population generally. The quality of short-wave reception in New England may have had something to do with the deviation, as well as public interest in international affairs, proximity to Europe, the educational attainments of the population, economic conditions, and density of population.

As might be expected, the extent of short-wave listening proved to be greater in urban centers and small towns than in metropolitan centers and rural areas. This may be due in part to the tendency for more families in small towns and medium-sized cities to own radios than for those in villages, rural areas, and large cities.

Economic Status of Listeners

One of the most significant and distinguishing characteristics of short-wave listeners is discovered when they are classified according to economic status. The rule seems to be clear that the higher one goes in the economic scale, the greater the proportion of short-wave listeners. In this respect listening to short wave seems to differ from listening to domestic broadcasts, for numerous studies show that, in the case of the latter, the *lower* one goes in the economic scale the greater the proportion of radio listening. The percentage of people listening to short-wave programs in various economic categories as shown by the American Institute of Public Opinion Surveys follows. It should be noted that the January survey covered listening during the *preceding month*; the December survey, listening during the *preceding week*.

	JANUARY 1941	DECEMBER 1941
Wealthy	23.3%	*
Average plus	15.2	12%
Average	12.1	10
Poor plus	12.1	*
Poor	6.2	5
On relief	7.1	2
Old age assistance	2.2	*

* Not computed—less than 100 cases.

Practically all of the local studies tended to corroborate the Institute's findings. In Syracuse Professor Beyle found that "the proportion of those who had heard the programs (short-wave), at least once, increased markedly with rise of economic level . . . significant differentials were the 60.0 per cent for those in the upper two-fifths of the home-rental-value range, and 27.7 per cent for those in the lowest fifth of the range." Moreover, he found that those of the upper two-fifths of the home-rental-value range were significantly high in their percentage under the classification of "listen often"; and were markedly high in their percentage under the classification of "listen rarely."

According to Professor Gosnell, "When the middle- and low-income groups are compared there are evidences of a tendency for higher income to be associated with listening to short-wave. The poll by the interview method showed that the highest percentage of persons listening to short-wave broadcasts came in the middle-income group, i.e. those persons earning between $1,250 and $2,500 per annum. Though more people in the income brackets above $2,500 possessed radios capable of receiving short-wave broadcasts, a smaller percentage actually used their sets for this purpose. In the Scott group, those people earning below $1,750 listened in smaller proportion than the people in each bracket between $1,750 and $10,000. In the Scott and Hudson-Ross groups the highest proportion of listeners in any one group was found in the $1,750-$2,500 bracket. This group may well contain the highest proportion of listeners in the population. . . . A plausible explanation of this is that persons with very high incomes have so many alternative means of recreation that they spend less time beside their radios, and to them good radios are natural concomitants of a household, nothing to be dwelt on as extraordinary."

In view of the economic characteristics of short-wave listeners it is not surprising to find, as Professor Schuler did in his Baton Rouge Surveys, that "there is a deficiency of short-wave listeners among both skilled and semi-skilled workers. Unskilled workers, who constitute about 9 per cent of the Baton Rouge population, are totally unrepresented among short-wave listeners." The second nation-wide survey of the American Institute of Public Opinion disclosed that business men, professional people, and skilled workers did proportionately the most listening; unskilled workers and servants, the least.

Further light is thrown on the higher economic status of the listeners by the fact that Douglas's Princeton study revealed that 84.3 per cent of the listeners owned cars, whereas only 53.5 per cent of the nonlisteners said that they did. Schuler's results show that the percentage of listeners and nonlisteners owning or purchasing their own homes was 54 and 43 per cent respectively. An even larger differential was found in Baton Rouge in regard to domestic servants. Of the short-wave listeners 66 per cent said they had domestic servants, and only 41 of the nonlisteners were found to be in the same category.

Other Social Characteristics of Listeners

There is very little evidence to indicate that short-wave listeners as a group differ from nonlisteners in their political and religious affiliations. In Syracuse "the 'hearers' divided 62.1 per cent Republican and 37.9 per cent Democrat; and the 'non-hearers' divided 62.3 per cent Republican and 37.7 Democrat. Similarly there was absolutely no difference between 'hearers' and 'non-hearers' of direct European short-wave broadcasting as respects their official vote for Roosevelt and Willkie." In its second nation-wide survey the American Institute of Public Opinion found that substantially the same situation existed nationally. It is worthy of note, however, that among nonvoters the proportion of affirmative replies to *all* short-wave questions was small.

The studies of Dr. Lazarsfeld in Erie County do suggest, however, that one important and distinguishing characteristic of short-wave listeners is their "social activism." He found that listeners were markedly different from nonlisteners with respect to their interest in political affairs, their articulateness, their qualities of opinion leadership, and their participation in community activities. "In every instance," he states, "the short-wave listeners were found to be markedly more interested and active politically than either the non-listening owners of short-wave sets or the non-owners . . . later analysis proved the short-wave listeners to be an exceptional group both from the standpoint of interest in national affairs and exposure to media of communication."

An examination of the social characteristics of short-wave listeners suggests, therefore, that, although politically and religiously the group does not differ essentially from the nonlisteners and the population generally, it is distinctive in certain respects. It seems to comprise a disproportionate share of public spirited, politically active, opinion-leaders in their respective communities, that is to say, agents for disseminating more widely whatever ideas and opinions they acquire from the broadcasts they hear. They are important links in the opinion networks of their communities. This fact suggests further that the significance of short-wave listening is not to be measured solely by the number of listeners. The social characteristics and the influence of listeners must also be taken into account.

Psychological Characteristics of Short-Wave Listeners

To what extent are short-wave listeners as a group different from nonlisteners in their educational attainments, their mental attitudes, their opinions regarding the broadcasts they hear, as well as their opinions on matters of public policy? In all the studies sponsored by the Princeton Listening Center the respondents were asked a number of questions designed to answer these queries. It was obvious at the outset that marked differences in mental characteristics between listeners and nonlisteners would not necessarily show that listening to short-wave broadcasts caused these differences. But such differences would indicate profitable lines of inquiry.

One of the most definite conclusions to which all the projects pointed was the higher educational level of short-wave listeners as a group in comparison with nonlisteners. The American Institute of Public Opinion found in its first survey that, whereas only 8 per cent of those who claimed to have a grade school education indicated that they were short-wave listeners, approximately 17 per cent of those who said they had attended college were found to be in this category. In some communities, as for example in a college community such as Princeton, the influence of the educational factor was even more marked. Professor Schuler found in Baton Rouge that "there is a consistent difference in amount of formal education received, more non-listeners having terminated their schooling at the lower levels, and more short-wave listeners having received some higher education."

There is no doubt that for the great majority of short-wave listeners British broadcasts are preferred. This may be due in large part to the fact that the short-wave listening audience in the United States is primarily an English-speaking audience. The first nation-wide survey of the American Institute of Public Opinion indicated that the great majority of short-wave listeners listened to British broadcasts most, preferred them, and considered them the most reliable. This survey indicated that 93 per cent of the listeners had listened at least once to broadcasts from England, whereas only 55 per cent had listened to those from Germany, 23 per cent to those from France, and 9 per cent to those from some other country. Schuler found that in Baton Rouge "the largest proportion of subjects listen to England (97%), 72% listen to Germany, and fewest (38%) to Italy. The proportion listening to Italy, however, is considerably larger in this cross-sectional sample than in samples secured from telephone subscribers." Professor Beyle also found that "England ranked first with the direct short-wave listeners, slightly over 95 per cent of the 'hearers' having listened to the English programs. Germany ranked second, having attracted about 65 per cent of the 'hearers.' Italy came next in order, claiming the attention of about 42 per cent." In Chicago Professor Gosnell found that "the order of frequency of attention into which foreign broadcasts fall is British, German, South and Central American, and Italian. None of the last three approaches the American audience which Britain possesses. Three-quarters of the Chicago short-wave listeners listen most of the time to broadcasts from England. Practically all of the short-wave listeners hear British broadcasts at one time or another."

What types of programs do short-wave listeners prefer? This question was asked in practically all the surveys. One of the principal reasons for listening to short-wave programs is the desire to obtain news. This is the conclusion reached by all investigators to date. Schuler found that 84 per cent of his listening public claimed that they listened to news most. Douglas discovered that 60 per cent of the short-wave listeners in Princeton listened to news programs primarily, 21 per cent to music, and 15 per cent to talks and other features. Gosnell found that in Chicago "the desire for good or strange music is subsidiary to the desire for news in accounting for listening to foreign short-wave broadcasts. Of the total group 12.2 per cent listen to short-wave primarily for the musical programs, and 37 per cent pay as much attention to music as to any other type of program. The large majority of short-wave listeners are interested chiefly in news, talks, and speeches." In Syracuse "of those who had heard the programs (short-wave) at least once, 73.3 per cent had listened to news, 47.7 had listened to 'talks and other features,' 46.7 per cent had listened to 'music,' while only 4.7 per cent were unable to recall the kind of program they had heard."

Although there is a tendency for short-wave listeners to think that news broadcasts from England are more reliable than those from other European countries, there also exists a considerable amount of skepticism regarding the unbiased nature of short-wave broadcasts generally. At the time the Institute made its survey in January 1941, 51 per cent of the short-wave listeners said they found the news reports coming from England by short wave the most reliable, 6 per cent said they could believe none, and 43 per cent gave no answer. Schuler found that 45 per cent thought England broadcast the most reliable news; 32 per cent expressed no preference or did not reply; 11 per cent said that none of the news reports by short wave were reliable, and only 3 and 1 per cent respectively expressed confidence in the news broadcast from Germany and France. Professor Gosnell states that in Chicago, "in keeping with their political views, the majority of listeners considered the British radio as the most reliable news-source of all foreign radio stations." In his later survey Schuler found that "England is believed to give the most reliable news over its short-wave broadcasts. It is specified by 66 per cent, whereas neither Germany nor Italy is mentioned by even one subject. Ten per cent, however, say that none is reliable, and 24 per cent say that they do not know."

Opinions of Short-Wave Listeners on Questions of Public Policy

The information now available does not answer directly the question of the specific effect of European short-wave broadcasts upon the attitudes and opinions of the American people. To determine this effect controlled experiments would be necessary and the influence of short-wave programs would have to be isolated from the influence of other factors. Significant differences in the opinions of listeners as a group and nonlisteners may indicate either reasons for listening or the effects of listening.

In practically all the short-wave listening studies conducted under the direction of the Princeton Listening Center the respondents were asked a number of questions on public policy, the majority of them relating to issues arising out of the war. Some interesting conclusions may be drawn from the answers to these questions.

The listening audience on the whole proved to be more skeptical than nonlisteners concerning the armed might of the United States and England, although they expressed considerable faith in England's word. Short-wave listeners in comparison with nonlisteners were also more pessimistic about the outcome of the war, a prevailing attitude which may be due in large part to a more realistic view of world conditions rather than to any pro-Axis tendencies. Listeners were more decided in their opinions on questions of public policy than nonlisteners. The percentage of nonlisteners who answered questions on public policy with "Don't Know" was comparatively high. For example, less than one fifth of the listeners in one study said that they did not know the real issue in the present war, whereas over one fourth of the nonlisteners gave the same indecisive reply. It is also interesting to discover that the listeners, in answering questions concerning the issues involved in the war, were inclined to give more theoretical or non-materialistic replies, using such expressions as "freedom," "democracy," "dictatorship," and the like, whereas nonlisteners tended to give more materialistic responses such as "power," "greed," and "imperialism."

Those who listened to short-wave programs were, as a whole, more interventionist in their attitudes than nonlisteners. A higher percentage of nonlisteners than listeners were of the opinion that they would not be personally affected by a German victory. Moreover, a relatively high percentage of nonlisteners insisted that we should stay out of the war even if England should be defeated because of American aloofness. The results of the various studies did show, however, that a comparatively high percentage of listeners were following the discussions of the Lease-Lend Bill and were in favor of it. In fact the opinion prevailed among them that the United States should go even further in its aid to England than the bill called for. On the whole, the foreign policy of President Roosevelt proved to be more popular with listeners than nonlisteners.

Some of the Listening Center studies included questions regarding peace at the end of the war. Interestingly enough a majority of both listeners and nonlisteners were unwilling to express opinions concerning the conditions of a just peace. Of those who did have some convictions, a higher percentage of listeners wished to return the overrun countries to their former governments, whereas the larger percentage of nonlisteners emphasized the necessity of punishing Germany.

Why Do People Listen

None of the nation-wide surveys contained questions that probed directly into the reasons why people listen or do not listen to short-wave

programs, although an analysis of listening practices, program preferences, and the personal characteristics of short-wave listeners does throw
some light on the problem. On the basis of this information and more
detailed information obtained from some of the local surveys it appears
that sympathy for the Allies, quality of reception, desire for news,
curiosity about foreigners, the urge for variety and thrill, as well as
income status and educational attainments, are important factors determining the extent of listening.

Douglas found, for example, that a large proportion of short-wave
listeners were really radio fans—frequent and persistent listeners to
domestic long-wave as well as foreign short-wave broadcasts. Lazarsfeld
discovered that "their short-wave listening does not detract from their
regular radio listening, but is a sign of great interest in the radio in
general." Not only that, but "they also mention newspapers and
magazines as sources of their information in greater numbers than
non-listening groups."

Many of the people interviewed said that it was difficult for them
to obtain information about short-wave programs, with the result
that they had gradually given up the attempt and lost interest in the
programs. Press notices, so they said, were very inadequate. Others
referred to the age and loss of vitality of their receiving sets in explaining why they had given up short-wave listening. Many seemed to
find, after a few experiments, that domestic long-wave broadcasts,
newspapers, and other media proved to be the most satisfactory sources
of information and entertainment; after the novelty of short-wave
reception had worn off, they turned to these other media.

Interesting comments were written on the Chicago questionnaires
which reflect some of the listeners' reactions to the whole field of
short-wave broadcasting. Questions concerning the reliability of foreign news broadcasts frequently elicited a condemnation of foreign
propaganda. Dislike for propaganda was added to a general displeasure
with the type of program broadcast from European stations. Music
was supposed to be only mediocre in quality. The news programs
were not news, but "old stuff" to American listeners. A woman wrote:
"Used to listen to BBC until we found the news was stale." General
agreement would be granted the remark of one listener: "Our newspapers and radio stations give both sides, what the English say and
what the Germans say. So why listen to foreign stations?"

The case histories of many listeners were found to be similar: "We listened when it was a novelty, but have since become tired of the fruitless practice." Opinions on the quality of short-wave reception were varied, even among those with identical receiving sets. One thoroughly disgruntled woman who had moved to Los Angeles and possessed an expensive set complained that short wave was "made to *sell*, not to use. Short wave is a fake . . . it is non-existent." Another woman wrote, "Reception is so poor when I *have* tried, though my radio is of the best, that I haven't taken time to bother with it." These were extreme positions. Several listeners compared the merits of domestic listening with those of foreign stations and preferred the former. "Too much static and fading and too good music on chains." On the whole, there is no general satisfaction with the quality of short-wave reception or the quality of the broadcast contents.

This cannot be considered a typical picture of the attitude toward short wave held by most of the listeners. It is to be expected that the displeased would raise their voices higher in condemnation than the satisfied would in praise. The above picture is probably quite accurate in presenting the reasons why the nonlisteners do not listen, along with the fact that they probably do not know about the foreign programs or cannot get them on their receiving sets.

It is more difficult to discover the opposite picture, that is, why the listeners do tune in on the short-wave programs. The reasons are varied and many, but one of the principal ones is the desire to obtain news. By far the largest percentage of those questioned gave this as their main reason for listening. They hope to obtain more complete and more recent news than they can get in their newspapers. For the great majority of listeners in the United States other types of short-wave programs have little appeal. Music, talks, dramatic skits, and novelty programs of various kinds are, as a rule, not to be compared in quality or interest with similar programs over domestic stations.

But short-wave news, even though the listener recognizes its bias, does have an immediacy, a directness of contact with events abroad, that domestic news broadcasts do not have. It is frequently stated that domestic radio in the United States is primarily an entertainment medium. As such it has attained a measure of excellence above that of most, if not all, other countries. But this is not the case with short-wave broadcasts from abroad. They are primarily informative, at least that is the primary purpose they serve. Hence it is not surprising that such programs are of special interest to those keenly aware of international affairs, who eagerly desire the latest news, and wish to keep as fully abreast of developments as possible. This is probably the basic reason why so many listeners are to be found in the upper income brackets and educational levels.

In other countries where the entertainment quality of domestic radio falls far below the standard set in the United States, non-news programs by short wave may have a decided appeal. Undoubtedly the audience for Nazi programs in Africa and South America may be of an entirely different complexion from that in the United States. But this only goes to show that so long as domestic sources of radio entertainment are kept at a high level the likelihood of extensive short-wave listening for entertainment reasons is small.

That foreign short-wave broadcasters have misunderstood the function that short wave may serve, so far as the United States is concerned, is shown by the fact that they devote so much time to music, dramatic skits, and other features in their programs to this country. There is very little chance that such programs can ever compete successfully with our own domestic programs in this respect. Only in so far as they are able to supply a better brand of news than listeners can obtain elsewhere, will foreign broadcasters be able to increase the size of their listening audience and enlarge the scope of their influence. It is extremely doubtful that they will be able to do this, and the fact that they have not done so probably explains why the amount of serious listening to short-wave programs in this country is so small. A surprisingly large number of listeners have no faith whatever in the reliability of news broadcasts from abroad, and this explains why, after the first pangs of curiosity have been satisfied, so many people give up listening to them.

When the Princeton Listening Center began its studies of propaganda by short wave, interest in the subject in the United States was largely confined to radio technicians, a few listeners, and a small group of academic students of public opinion and international relations. Today the subject is of concern to all who are thinking in terms of the grand strategy which will win the war. The resources of American short-wave stations are now being mobilized by the government so that the United States itself may become an effective combatant in the radio war already waged for several years by the other belligerents, in fact by the

Axis powers long before the actual war broke ut. Plans are in the process of formulation, and to a certain extent have already been put into operation, to carry the fight to enemy countries, there to offset the propaganda being disseminated by the Axis and to undermine enemy morale. American short-wave stations are also active elsewhere, notably in Latin America, winning support for the American cause. These undertakings have been accompanied by the creation of a federal organization for recording, analyzing, and interpreting psychological warfare directed by short wave against us or otherwise calculated to aid the enemy. Finally, students of public opinion and propaganda are constantly on the alert, seeking new methods and techniques to strengthen our defenses and improve our own means of attack. What, if anything, remains to be done?

The studies of America's short-wave listening audience reveal that, for the present at least, this audience is not of such a character or size as to constitute a real danger. There is no evidence that the events of December 7, 1941 and the entrance of the United States into a fighting war has changed the situation appreciably. This is a tribute, in the first instance, to our domestic news agencies, to our newspapers and radio stations and their success in maintaining the confidence of the American people in the integrity of their reports and services. This confidence in the integrity of news and public information must be preserved. To determine whether this is being done, periodic surveys of the American short-wave listening audience should be continued to the end that any evidences of diminishing confidence may be quickly detected and measures taken to deal with the situation.

Studies of short-wave listening in the United States will not be sufficient, however. The major problem of short-wave propaganda today, so far as the United States is concerned, is to transform the existing agencies of dissemination into instruments for broadcasting more convincingly and effectively America's reasons for fighting, and giving to her enemies a clearer picture of what a victory for the United States and her allies will mean. In other words, a coordinated, convincing, and astute program of radio broadcasts must be designed for active service at home, in enemy countries, and throughout the world.

The problem of short-wave propaganda, however, is only one phase of the more general problem of the future role of American propaganda in this war. It is essentially a problem of propaganda content, which is much more important than the problem of technique, or even that of propaganda organization. It is, in the final analysis, a problem of opinion leadership. The realities of this war will certainly pierce, if they have not already done so, so deeply into the minds and souls of men, that the struggle for world opinion will not be won merely by news programs and dramatic skits. The war for men's minds will be won, finally, by those nations whose war aims, whose ideological objectives, whose strategies of argument and persuasion, carry to the peoples of the world hopes and aspirations for something better after the fighting is over. Ideas, not words, are the stuff of which effective propaganda is made.

INDEX

NAME INDEX

Numbers indicate pages. Those in italics refer to footnotes.

SUBJECT INDEX

Numbers indicate pages. Those in italics refer to footnotes.